# 1 MONTH OF
# FREE
# READING

at

## www.ForgottenBooks.com

By purchasing this book you are eligible for one month membership to ForgottenBooks.com, giving you unlimited access to our entire collection of over 700,000 titles via our web site and mobile apps.

To claim your free month visit:
www.forgottenbooks.com/free535373

ISBN 978-0-428-98092-4
PIBN 10535373

# ST. LOUIS
# CATHOLIC HISTORICAL
# REVIEW

Issued Quarterly

EDITOR-IN-CHIEF

REV. CHARLES L. SOUVAY, C. M., D. D.

ASSOCIATE EDITORS

REV. F. G. HOLWECK

REV. GILBERT J. GARRAGHAN, S. J.

REV. JOHN ROTHENSTEINER

EDWARD BROWN

*Volume II*        *JANUARY 1920*        *Number 1*

PUBLISHED BY THE CATHOLIC HISTORICAL SOCIETY OF SAINT LOUIS

209 WALNUT STREET, ST. LOUIS, MO.

# CONTENTS

# Catholic Historical Society of St. Louis

### Established February 7th, 1917

## OFFICERS AND STANDING COMMITTEES
## 1918–1919

*President*—MOST REV. JOHN J. GLENNON, D. D.
*First Vice-President*—RT. REV. MGR. J. A. CONNOLLY, V. G.
*Second Vice-President*—EDWARD BROWN
*Third Vice-President*—LOUISE M. GARESCHE
*Secretary*—REV. JOHN ROTHENSTEINER
*Assistant Secretary*—MARY CONSTANCE SMITH
*Treasurer*—RT. REV. MGR. J. J. TANNRATH, Chancellor

*Librarians*
*and Archivists*
{ REV. F. G. HOLWECK
REV. CHARLES L. SOUVAY, C. M., D. D.
REV. GILBERT J. GARRAGHAN, S. J.

*Executive*
*Committee*
{ RT. REV. MGR. J. A. CONNOLLY, V. G., President
RT. REV. MGR. J. J. TANNRATH, Chancellor
RT. REV. MGR. P. W. TALLON
REV. CHARLES L. SOUVAY, C. M., D. D.
REV. F. G. HOLWECK
REV. MARTIN L. BRENNAN, Sc D.
REV. JOHN ROTHENSTEINER
EDWARD BROWN, Secretary

*Committee*
*on Membership*
{ RT. REV. MGR. P. W. TALLON
RT. REV. MGR. J. J. TANNRATH, Chancellor

*Committee*
*on Library*
*and Publications*
{ REV. CHARLES L. SOUVAY, C. M., D. D.
REV. F. G. HOLWECK
REV. GILBERT J. GARRAGHAN, S. J.
REV. JOHN ROTHENSTEINER
EDWARD BROWN

## COMMUNICATIONS

General Correspondence should be addressed to Rev. John Rothensteiner, Secretary, 1911 N. Taylor Ave., St. Louis, Mo.

Exchange publications and matter submitted for publication in the ST. LOUIS CATHOLIC HISTORICAL REVIEW should be sent to the Editor-in-chief, Rev. Charles L. Souvay, C.M., DD., Kenrick Seminary, Webster Groves, Mo.

Remittances should be made to Rt. Rev. J. J. Tannrath, Treasurer, 209 Walnut St., St. Louis, Mo.

# THE LANGUAGE QUESTION IN
# THE OLD CATHEDRAL
# OF ST. LOUIS

St. Louis was a French settlement. It was founded by French-men and for Frenchmen. During the Spanish regime, the official Spanish language was used only in government documents. French was spoken in the families, in the streets, in the shops, in court, and French, exclusively, was the vernacular of the Church, even in presence of the highest Spanish officials. French remained the language of the Church also after the United States had seized the reins of government in the Territory west of the Mississippi, when eastern Americans, Englishmen and Irishmen passed the open door to St. Louis and to the Western land of hill and prairie. Only on extraordinary occasions, when curiosity led this new element in the population of St. Louis to the Catholic chapel on Second Street, a sermon would be preached also in English. The French Creoles of St. Louis were not ready to plunge headlong into the new order of things. They raised no vigorous protest against the transfer subsequent to the Louisiana Purchase, but when the Spanish and French flags went down and the American flag was hoisted, they shed tears. [1]

It is safe to say, that the French language remained in full and indisputed possession of the Church at St. Louis, during the interregnum from the day of the departure of Father Janin (Nov. 12, 1804)[2], to the day when, sent by Bishop Du Bourg of Louisiana, Father Rosati arrived (Oct. 19, 1817). All these thirteen years no legitimate pastor

---

[1] L. Houck, History of Missouri, II 375.

[2] Father Janin, the sixth Parish priest of St. Louis gave up his charge four days before De Lassus with the Spanish officials and soldiers left the city to descend to New Orleans November 16, 1804. The Irish priest, Father Thomas Flynn, who took charge of the parish December 5, 1806, to January 2, 1808, was no legitimate parish priest; he was "elected" pastor by the people, or rather, without any explicit faculties in the Louisiana Territory, by permission of the forlorn Catholics of St. Louis and perhaps also of the quasi-Vicar General Maxwell of Ste. Genevieve, performed a pastor's functions. Father Maxwell was called "Vicar General," but it would be difficult to say, whose Vicar General he was. The Propaganda, February 21, 1807, expressly states, "cum nullus in eadem dioecesi existat, qui facultates spirituales interim ab apostolica hac S. Sede obtinuerit, donec novus in eadem dioecesi episcopus praeficiatur"; i. e., after the cessation of the jurisdiction of Bp. Peñalver over Louisiana, there was nobody in that diocese who obtained faculties for jurisdiction from the Apostolic See. On September 1, 1808, Bishop Carroll was made Administrator of the diocese of Louisiana; it is quite improbable that before the coming of Father Flynn, Father Maxwell was appointed Vicar General by Bishop Carroll. Father Flynn had come from the East; November 8, 1806, he wrote to Bishop Carroll that he had taken possession of St. Louis. Father Savine, who is said to have been the eighth pastor of St. Louis, resided at Kahokia, Ill., and served St. Louis the third Sunday of every month, from December, 1812, to September, 1817. Other priests who occasionally performed services at St. Louis during the interregnum were Father J. Maxwell of Ste. Genevieve, Father D. Olivier of Prairie du Rocher, Ill., and the Trappists Urbain Guillet, F. M. Bernard, and M. Jos. Dunand of Florissant and the Monks' Mound, Ill. Maxwell and Flynn occasionally may have preached in English.

resided in the little presbytery adjoining the church. The order of instructions in the church of St. Louis continued to follow the beaten tracks and the English speaking Catholics were looked upon as intruders.

Whilst Bishop Du Bourg resided at St. Louis (January 5, 1818 to November 19, 1820) the sermon at High Mass was always preached in French. But because a considerable number of Irish Catholics had come to St. Louis and made the city their home, men who were good Catholics and liberal to the Church like Jeremiah Connor,[3] Bishop Du Bourg made the new rule, that every Sunday, after Vespers, a sermon should be preached in English. This appears from a letter of De Andreis, the saintly Vicar General, (February 20, 1818), to Father Rosati: "At every Sunday at morning, we preach in French, and afternoon at the Vespers in English." (The English is De Andreis'). Again, on March 2, he writes to the same: "I have here scarcely occasion to speak English and I preached English but twice, and very seldom I hear confession in such tongue." (The English is De Andreis'). And again: "My work . . . does not leave me time . . .: to preach twice on Sundays (le feste), in French and (these last three Sundays) in English, because Monsignore is absent." (Original written in Italian).

This indicates that Bishop Du Bourg, either personally or through his Vicar General, preached in English every Sunday. De Andreis, January 1, 1820, wrote to his brother: "I speak and preach in French and in English." Bishop Du Bourg wrote and spoke English well. The English of De Andreis shows that he thought in Italian. Also Father Niel, after the demise of De Andreis (October 15, 1820) pro-rector of the Cathedral and President of St. Louis Academy, was able to preach an English sermon, but he seemed to have discontinued the practice. In 1823, therefore, when he made an attempt at regulating the financial affairs of the congregation, the Irish Catholics "were led to believe that there would be an English sermon every second Sunday at High Mass" (cf. the petition below). But if then any promise had been made by Father Niel, it was never realized. It was difficult for the French clergy of those days to leave the established groove. The expectations of the Irish Catholics were never complied with (cf. the petition).

When, in March 1825, Father Niel[4] left for Europe to raise funds wherewith to pay the debt of the struggling parish of St. Louis, Father

---

[3] Jeremiah Connor, the second sheriff of St. Louis was a bachelor. He had come to St. Louis from Georgetown, D. C. He gave a thousand dollars to put the old presbytery of St. Louis in readiness for Bishop Du Bourg. He gave also to the city the great thoroughfare, called now Washington Avenue, from Third Street to Jefferson Avenue. In 1820 he sold to Bishop Du Bourg the two squares on which the Jesuits, in 1822, erected their college. (W. B. Stevens, St. Louis, I p. 777). On March 17, 1820, St. Patrick Day was celebrated for the first time in St. Louis by the Irish Benevolent Society (organized October 10, 1819, Jeremiah Connor, president). F. L. Billon, Annals of St. Louis II. J. Jeremiah Connor died September 23, 1823.

[4] Father Francis Niel, born at St. Antonin, Languedoc, France, left Bordeaux with Bishop Du Bourg June 17, 1817, came to St. Louis with the Bishop, January 5, 1818, and was ordained priest in the old Spanish chapel of St. Louis, March 19, 1818. He never returned from his trip to France. His last letter to Bishop Rosati is dated from Paris, September 12, 1835. (Archives.)

Edmond Saulnier[5] was appointed pro-rector of the Cathedral. He was notoriously a poor speaker, hardly able to preach in French, still less in English. Nor did he ever learn enough English to preach a fair sermon. As late as July 21, 1847, Saulnier in a sort of Diary, kept by himself, stated that he was made light of by his confreres for reading his sermons from a copy (*cahier*).[6] It was but a matter of course that the Irish became impatient. Even the poor courtesy of an afternoon sermon was denied them, because there was no one to preach it. Besides Bishop Rosati and the Flemish Jesuits at Florissant, there was only one priest in Missouri who could preach a decent sermon in English; this one priest was the Fleming, P. Leo de Neekere, C.M.[7] At St. Mary's of the Barrens, then the only English speaking parish in the new State of Missouri, he had learned English fairly well, being gifted with an extraordinary memory. Saulnier saw that something had to be done to provide for the instruction and spiritual need of those who knew no French. Wherefore, March 1, 1826, he wrote to Bishop Rosati:

> "I shall be pleased to see Mr. De Neckere, but I shall be still more so, if he can stay; he could do a great deal of good by preaching in English every Sunday. No doubt he could even make some converts. It would be a treat for the Protestants to hear him. In regard to his health Mr. De Neckere would be better off here in St. Louis than at the Barrens, because here he would enjoy better accommodations than there. I know that very often his sickness is only imaginary; he is too retired, he needs distraction. . . ."

On April 3, 1826, Bishop Rosati sent Fathers De Neckere and Odin to New Madrid to give a mission. After their return the Bishop gave De Neckere his papers for St. Louis (May 15). On the same day Rosati started for New Orleans. The Bishop assumed that the coming of Father De Neckere would check all friction in the church of St. Louis. We permit Father Saulnier to give an account of what happened after De Neckere's arrival.

> . . . . It had not been my intention to write to You at this time, but the course things have taken forces me to do so. First, I must tell you that last Sunday at eight o'clock, I invited the Irish to assemble before Vespers. Twelve of them came; there may have been a few more, but this does not matter. I told them the reason why I called the meeting, that is, to grant them a favour: that in the future Mr. De Neckere would preach in English every Sunday after Vespers. But they would not listen to my proposition, unless I would grant them the right of having a sermon in English every

---

[5] Edmond Saulnier was born at Bordeaux, March 13, 1798, arrived at the Barrens in Ma, 1819, and was ordained priest at St. Louis, September 22, 1822. From November, 1831, to July, 1832, he was pastor of the missions in Arkansas (v. *St. Louis Hist. Review*, July-October, 1919), was appointed pastor of Vide-Roche (Carondelet) in August, 1832, and pastor of French Village, Ill., in 1842. In 1845 he was curate at the Cathedral of St. Louis and since 1851, chancellor of the Archdiocese. He died March 22, 1864, in the chapel of Calvary Cemetery, the only survivor (with Father St. Cyr) of the French Regime.

[6] The documents used in writing this sketch are in the Archives of the archiepiscopal chancery office, St. Louis, and have mostly been translated from the French.

[7] P. Leo Raymond De Neckere was born June 6, 1800, at Wevelghem, Flanders; he crossed the ocean with Du Bourg in 1817, and was ordained priest in the Cathedral erected by Du Bourg, October 13, 1822. During his stay in the Seminary at the Barrens he joined the Lazarists. He was consecrated Bishop of New Orleans in the Cathedral of that city, June 24, 1830, and died of yellow fever September 5, 1833.

second Sunday at High Mass. I told them that I could not abolish a custom which had always existed in St. Louis, that the French had a sermon in French every Sunday at High Mass, that I could not change this unless a Superior order told m e to do so. How the French would complain if we were to preach to them in English! They would leave the church, as the Irish do when they notice that the sermon is to be in French. Besides, the French enjoy this right since the day when St. Louis was founded, and Msgr. Du Bourg changed nothing in this respect, although four years ago there were three times as many Irishmen in the city as there are now. But this is not all. Some Irishmen held a meeting in the city and made up a lengthy petition, signed, not by the most respectable amongst them, but mostly by men of objectionable conduct. For those , of whom I know that they practice their religion, refused to sign, like Higgins, Walsh, English, etc. Furthermore, I was told by those who would not sign, that the petition shows but little respect to my character. I leave the decision to You, Monseigneur, but for my part I expect more assistance for Mr. De Neckere from non-Catholics than from the others. If the French did not pay better than the Irish, I do not know what would become of my support. I made the arrangement with Mr. De Neckere that I would, pay him ten dollars a month or more, if he wished. All is calm at present. Msgr. Du Bourg has informed You of the rest. . . . . (June 6, 1826).

The petition, it is true, was not signed by all the Irish Catholics of the city. Men like James Timon, father of Father Timon, (later on Bishop of Buffalo) and James Timon Jr., who had signed, had later on their names taken off the list. One of them, Peter Walsh,[8] even wrote a formal protest (in English) against the petition, in the form of a postscript to Father Saulnier's letter:

Rt. Rev. Sir:
Pardon the liberty I take in obtruding myself at this crisis; but I should consider myself in a certain degree a criminal, were I deficient in making You acquainted with what I deem a petit schism in our church of St. Louis and raised only by·a few discontended spirits, and those not of a respectable class. A petition has been framed by them, I understand, in terms not the most elegant, to obtain a certain grant of you; but be assured, Sir, not one respectable Catholic Irishman has signed it. For my part, I have not been at their meeting and do in conjunction with most of my respectable Irish acquaintances protest against and repel said Petition; while·I and my friends naturally desire instruction from the pulpit, yet we deem it our duty as Catholics, to be subject to the will and direction of those superiors which the Church has placed over us, and I do consider the petition ill-timed and proceeding from a source not entitled to attention.
I have the honor to be, Rt. Rev. Sir, your obedient servant
P. WALSH.

On the following day, June 7, Saulnier wrote again:
I have been told that the petition of which I spoke to you in my preceding letter, was sent to you, but it seems that at present grass has grown over it. I have been informed that the man who raised this commotion, is a worthless fellow (*surtout*), who felt insulted when I reprimanded him for talking whilst I performed a marriage ceremony; I know that he resented and still resents having been reproved publicly and to his face. He would be glad to see me far from here. You have, I suppose, seen my reasons; I believe they are just, and if it were otherwise there would be no end of trouble in the parish.
Mr. De Neckere takes great interest in his English sermons, and I hope he will do a great deal of good in the future. There is a rumor that the Americans will raise a collection of 300 dollars for him.

---

[8] Peter Walsh, born in Sligo, Ireland, in 1783, came to New York in 1803, and to St. Louis in 1820; he was a commission merchant and Justice of the Peace; died 1851.

But all was not calm, as Father Saulnier imagined. Te petition was sent to New Orleans and was received by Rosati at the Barrens, August 27, 1826.[9] If its terms are not of the most elegant, it appears to be very tame in comparison to similar eastern documents of the same period. We reprint the entire petition, together with the names attached to it:

Saint Louis, Missouri,
June, 1826.

To the Right Reverend Louis Wm. Du Bourg,
Bishop of the Upper anl Lower Louisianas and Floridas.[9]
Right Reverend Father,

We your petitioners, members of the holy R. Catholick Church and parishioners of the Parish of Saint Louis Mo. humbly sheweth.

That some time in the year of our Lord 1823, at an aggregate meeting of the Roman Catholicks of this Parish, the following resolution was unanimously agreed to; The Reverend F. Niel in the Chair, and the then acting Church Wardens present.

Resolved, that each family will pay for the support of the parish Priest two dollars per annum, to make up the Sum of five hundred dollars per year, provided, the said contribution is not sufficient to make up the said sum of five hundred dollars per annum, the Church Wardens are to make up the deficiency, and pay to the Parish Priest the said sum of five hundred dollars, out of any monies collected in the Church for the sale and rent of Pews, or otherwise. And further that at a subsequent meeting, the Reverend F. Niel P. Priest, did for the further consideration of one hundred and fifty dollars, to be added to the above five hundred dollars, making a total of Six hundred and fifty dollars per annum; did agree to give up his right to certain sums allowed him at Marriages, Buriels, etc. unto the Church, and thereby changed only the receivers right. In showing the foregoing resolution to your Reverence, your petitioners do not Complain.

But your petitioners do complain,. and most humbly and respectfully shew, that at the time the above resolution was passed, the amount then deemed sufficient for the support of our Parish Priest and his Coadjutor, and was granted at their own request. — And further—Your Reverence's petitioners do most humbly and respectfully shew, that at the time the above regulations were passed, your petitioners were led to believe that there would be an english sermon every second Sunday at high Mass. And further that your Reverence's petitioners have truly and faithfully complyed with the above regulations as far as in them lay, although our expectations have never been complyed with.

Your Reverence's Petitioners do most humbly and respectfully shew, that a meeting of the American part of the Catholic Congregation was called on last Sunday by our acting Parish Priest at his room, then and there. told us that the Reverend Wm. Denackary would stay here if we could separately raise a sufficient sum to maintain him. Your Reverence's petitioners did then most respectfully state, that the Sallery of Six hundred and fifty dollars, as above stated, did support two clergymen heretofore, and that they deemed the same amount now sufficient, but your Reverence's petitioners did offer to raise their subscriptions, one dollar each per annum, provided we would get an english Sermon every second Sunday, which was refused by the Reverend Edm. Saulnier.

---

[9] On May 15, 1826, Bishop Rosati started for Louisiana and did not return to the Barrens before July 19. (*Diary* of Bp. Rosati,) When the petition arrived at New Orleans, Rosati was gone; this explains the long delay. The postal service at that time was very imperfect.

[9] It is difficult to say why the petition was addressed to Bishop Du Bourg. Everybody in St. Louis knew that Bishop Du Bourg was on his way to Europe; on his way to New York he had been at St. Louis on Ascension Day and had been received with the highest public honors.

Your petitioners do most humbly and respectfully shew, that so long as the great distinction is kept up between what is termed the French and the American part of this congregation, by giving after Vespers an english, Sermon, and always at high Mass the French Sermons and exertations, a a language that few or none of the Americans understand, and that the said American part can have no satisfaction in attending at high Mass, only the contemplation of being present at the August mistery of our divine religion.

Your Reverence's petitioners do distinctly and most respectfully state that a very large majority of the French population that composes in part this congregation, do understand perfectly the english language, to these your petitioners would beg leave to add, that a great number of respectable Citizens of this place, of other denominations who attend at our Church, and who do not understand the French language, would form not only a very large majority who understand the english language, but would leave very few who do not understand it.

Your Reverence's petitioners, do most humbly and respectfully state, that it is not our intention to dictate to your Reverence any rules or regulations for the Parish which forms a part of the Diocese, which it has pleased God to place you over, far be it from us, we only wish to make known to your Reverence these our grievances which we labor under, trusting therefore to the justness of our Claims, and your Reverence's known liberality, we deem it not necessary to state to Your Reverence, the great advancement it would be of the glory of God and our holy religion, to have a Clergyman who is capable of giving suitable and frequent explanations of that. faith "once delivered to the Saints," in the language of the State and in which all business is here transacted, to so mixed a population as this rapidly growing City is daily pouring in upon us, with their existing prejudices, that Clergyman your petitioners are confident they have now got in the person of the Reverend Wm. Denackary, but the time that he is at liberty to preach to us in the language we understand is at a very unseasonable hour, and indeed an hour that a majority, or a great part of the American Catholics cannot attend, as they reside at some considerable distance. in the country, and is of necesity obliged to return home even before Vesper hour.

Your Reverence's petitioners do humbly and sorrowfully state, that there has of late been a great apathy or total neglect in a number of lukewarm Catholics to the important duty of hearing Mass on Sundays, on this, and no other account, than that of never hearing an English instruction at the time of Mass.

Your Reverence's petitioners do therefore most humbly and respectfully request that your Reverence be pleased to direct, that every second Sermon be prached at the time of high Mass, in the English language, and your petitioners shall ever be Your faithful Children in Christ.

| | | | |
|---|---|---|---|
| PATRICK QUIGLEY | JOHN LAMANDE | AUGUSTE GUELBERTH | P. DOWLING |
| JAMES FORTUNE | HUGH FITZPATRICK | P. ROCHEBLAVE | PATRICX MCDONNOGH |
| ROBT. COONEY | BARNEY DIGNAN | L. T. HONORE | THOS. BANY |
| MATHEW DOUGHERTY | WILLIAM TIFFLE | WILLIAM MCGUIRE | RINGROSE D. WATSON |
| MICHAEL MCLAUGHLIN | JOSEPH WOGAN | D. MONNESTESSE | JOHN WATSON |
| MICHAEL REILLY | THOS. LAUGHLEN | LOUIS GARANDE | PATRICK CLEARY |
| EDWARD HARRINGTON | JAMES BARRY | LOUIS LAMOND | JAMES BELLAY |
| MICHAEL ROURKE | DENNIS MURPHY | FRANCIS FOOSHAY | WILLIAM MCCLUSKEY |
| JOHN MCGOVERN | JAMES HAMMOND | JOHN RODGERS | F. D. BELCOUR |
| WILLIAM TIERNAN | OWEN COLLINS | MATHEW BEHEDGE | C. G. BRUN |
| CORNELIUS CAUGHLIN | PETER WARREN | JOHN HIGGINS | PATRICK MURPHY |
| PATRICK HODNETT | MICHAEL GORMAN | PATRICK HIGGINS | WILLIAM MCKNIGHT |
| TIMOTHY COTTER | JAMES BONNEY | LAWRENCE RYAN | HENRY HEAGERTY |
| JOHN THORNTON | JOHN MULLEN | JEREMIAS HARRINGTON | JAMES ROACHE |
| MATHEW TREANY | JOHN ROCHE | JAMES MURPHY | PATRICK SULLIVAN |
| ARTHUR FLEMMING | JOSEPH BOUJER | DENNIS MURPHY | JOHN SHADE |
| | | ANDREW MURPHY | |

But the Bishop could work no miracles. Fredericktown, Kaskaskias and òther neighboring towns had exhausted his resources; from the Seminary he could not take away any of the professors, etc. (Rosati's letter to Saulnier Sept. 10, 1826). In this sense he sent a communication, not to the signers of the petition, but to the trustees (*marguilliers*) of the church of St. Louis, September 1, 1826:

"As God is no respector of persons, so those of his ministers whom he has appointed the pastors of his flock, make no distinction between the souls entrusted to their care. French and Americans, Creole and Irish are equally dear to us, because we think them equally entitled to the spiritual assistance which is in our power to afford them. But imperious necessity often renders ineffectual our most ardent desires and reduces us to the painful impossibility of doing what we would think our happiness to do. The parish of St. Louis has hitherto had a greater share in the sollicitude of her pastors than any in the diocese, and if those amongst the parishioners who speak the English language have been often deprived of instructions from the pulpit, it has not been the effect of neglect or disregard on our side. We have been more deeply affected than any other by the consideration of the sad effects that are to be expected from this inconvenience. But we cannot give what is out of our power and in such circumstance the only remedy which we can find for our evils is to have recourse to the Lord of the harvest and beseech him to send evangelical workmen into his harvest. In the meantime we think it our duty to exert ourselves in order to raise a national clergy who, knowing the languages spoken in the country, may be able to assist all their countrymen."

The practice of preaching English after Vespers only was continued. But even this arrangement did not last. On July 26, Saulnier, who was never friendly to De Neckere, wrote to Rosati:

"Mr. De Neckere suffers from the heat. But is there anything of which he does not complain? I shall comment upon this more fully when I see you. . . ."

From Father De Neckere's own letters, however, it appears that he was continually ill. To save his life he was compelled to leave St. Louis and return to Flanders. Before Rosati had received the petition of the Irish Catholics, he gave permission to De Neckere to go to Europe (August 12, 1826), to return, if possible; otherwise he was to stay in Rome.

His departure caused great discontent amongst the Catholics of St. Louis. It seems that reports of an ill feeling between Saulnier and De Neckere had leaked out; sharp tongues attacked Saulnier and accused him of having driven away the young Flemish priest by jealousy anud harshness. Father Saulnier was wounded in his feelings. On Sept. 2 he wrote to the Bishop:

"One more word. A Presbyterian church[10] has been built at St. Louis in tasteful style; by its refinement it attracts the curious. Another (Episcopalian) temple is in course of erection, and will have a very fine appearance. Mr. De Neckere who is gone, left his hearers half converted. What

---

[10] The first Presbyterian church at St. Louis was organized by Rev. Salmon Giddings. On January 3, 1818, this Rev. Salmon Giddings had opened a school for young ladies and gentlemen in his house on Fourth and Market Streets. The church of which Saulnier speaks stood on the west side of Fourth Street near Washington Avenue. The first Episcopalian church was built on Third and Chestnut. (Walter B. Stevens, *op. cit.*, p. 708 and 717.)

is to become of the Catholics of poor St. Louis? If you could do without Mr. Timon he could attract crowds to the Church. You can hardly conceive how glad the Protestant ministers are since Mr. De Neckere is gone. Whilst he was here they complained that their church was deserted. I have nothing to say. God will arrange things as He sees fit. But I deplore it very much that I am so devoid of talent as not to be able to preach. The Devil is doing good business at present. I hope the time is not far off when again we can twist his tail.

But see, how 'far malice has gone here, since I am accused in town of having ill-treated Mr. De Neckere, of having been so jealous of him as to demand his removal. Well, God knows better than that, thanks be to Him forever."

"I had the best intentions in obtaining Mr. De Neckere from Msgr. Du Bourg; everybody was so delighted to hear him; and now I am accused of having been jealous of him, to have ill treated him and that for this reason De Neckere left. . . . all the Flemings who ever came to St. Louis, have caused trouble." (Letter, Sept. 12.)

In November and December of the same year, the Irish Catholics of St. Louis had a pleasant surprise; Father Timon, C.M., the son of one of their citizens, preached the jubilee in English. But after that, for eighteen months, Father Saulnier had to supply the English ser-' mons. He even went beyond the episcopal instructions, and to satisfy both parties gave two short sermons in French and English at every High Mass. On July 7, 1827, he wrote to the Bishop on this subject:

"If it could be done, there ought to be at St. Louis a larger number of ecclesiastics for the divine services and somebody who could preach contro-versial sermons in English. I believe that there would be much more fruit produced than there is now. From my part I do all I can: every Sunday I preach at High Mass in French and in English. I am well contended. There are several people who approached the ' Sacraments after having neglected them for eight, nine, ten, nineteen and twenty years. . . ."

On February 28, 1828, he wrote:

"If the inhabitants of St. Louis would have you among them and if you had a priest for the American Catholics who could preach to them in English, things would turn out better in the Church in regard to religion as well as to those continual financial troubles."

In June 1828, a new star arose in St. Louis to realize the hopes of the English speaking Catholics. Regis Loisel[11] was ordained priest in the Cathedral, June 29, 1828. He was born in St. Louis, but considered French his mother tongue. He spoke English well, although like all the Creoles of that period, with a strong French accent. On July 5, he received his faculties and his appointment as curate at the Cathedral, together with a pastoral instruction to Father Saulnier. To this very explicit pastoral letter Saulnier answered July 29, 1828:

In your letter which I received through the kindness of Mr. Loisel, I have with pleasure read of various plans which I would very much like to

---

[11] John Timon was born of Irish parents at the old Jesuit mission of Conewago, Pa., February 12, 1797. His Father opened a dry goods store in St. Louis in 1819. John joined the Lazarists at the Barrens, in 1823, and was ordained priest in 1825. In 1835, he was appointed the first Visitor of the Lazarists in America; in 1838, superior of the missions in Texas. In 1839 he was nominated Coadjutor to Bishop Rosati, but refused to accept the burden. On October 17, 1847, he was consecrated Bishop of Buffalo, at New York. Died April 16, 1867.

[12] v. St. Louis Catholic Historical Review, Vol. I, No. 2, p. 103.

carry into effect; but permit me to submit my objections before I commence to obey you. You desire that the English sermon be preached at nine o'clock; that after benediction there should be catechism for the children, then for the negroes; that Mr. Dussaussoy[13] should give popular instructions before and after Vespers; that Mr. Loisel and Mr. Dussaussey should from time to time go to Edwardsville, to Kahos, to Vide Poche; this is a pretty mess; pardon, Monseigneur, but I see great difficulties in all this; before we commence this order of things we must know if we can keep it up; if we cannot carry it out, it is better not to start at all.

First: nine o'clock is too early for the English sermon, not only for the people in the country, but also for the Americans in St. Louis. I cannot see that any other hour would be more proper than after Vespers or after High Mass, or rather during High Mass, having alternately a sermon in English and on another Sunday a sermon in French. This arrangement would satisfy everybody, after the demands which have been made. However, there are still some drawbacks in having the English sermon preached every other Sunday during High Mass: there would be a considerable crowd of Americans (as last Sunday after Vespers), so that the church could not hold them and there would not be room for all; these great numbers serve to show how necessary it is to have another, more spacious church. The French would leave the church when they hear that the sermon is to be in English and the English would go when the sermon is in French. Then the irreverent behavior of the Americans during the Holy Sacrifice is very distressing. If you would issue some regulation on this point, it might do some good and keep them in due respect. As soon as you give a decision, I shall not delay action.

Father Saulnier writes again August 2, 1828:

"You instruct me, Monseigneur, that Mr. Loisel should preach at nine o'clock. For the Americans, especially for those from the country, the hour seems to be inconvenient; there is no other hour possible but after Vespers, or every other Sunday during High Mass, or every Sunday after High Mass. It is true, the country people could not derive any benefit from an English sermon preached after Vespers, but there are so few of them that this would form no real obstacle. You saw the great number of hearers he had on the Sunday, when you assisted at the English sermon of Mr. Elet; well, in a little while there will be the same numbers for Mr. Loisel, and I would like to see, where all these people find room during the morning services.

Furthermore you want catechism for the children after Vespers, other catechetical instructions for the negroes, popular conferences before and after Vespers by Mr. Dussaussoy; then you wish that these gentlemen go to Kahokias, to Vide Poche and to Edwardsville and also to the Convent. This is expecting rather much; we would have to have more priests and additional hours. Pardon, Monseigneur, for taking the liberty to speak to you in such a shocking manner; it is I who do not understand, because I am too stupid. Please excuse me, the good God has created me just as I am. . . ."

But the Bishop did not yield. He would not permit Father Saulnier to preach in English during High Mass; on August 17, 1828, he instructed him: "Preach in English at Vespers or even after High Mass."

Father Loisel, without a fault of his own, was a failure. He was a saintly man, but no great speaker; besides he was subject to fevers and rheumatism to such a degree that several times he was compelled to

---

[13] Father Dussaussoy was a nephew of the Blessed Sophie Barat. He had been stationed at St. Michael's, La., and arrived in St. Louis during Passion week 1828; he was appointed curate to Father Saulnier at the Cathedral, but, molested by various bodily complaints, he left St. Louis, April 11, 1829, and returned to France.

spend weeks in the house of his mother, Mrs. Lebeau. Consequently
again, for months, there would be no sermon in English at the Cathedral, for the simple reason that there was no one to preach it (letter
of June 30, 1829) "except for Saulnier's little English" (letter, Sept.
19, 1831). And thus things remained until Father Lutz[14] had given up
the idea of evangelizing the Indians and, in December 1831, returned
to St. Louis to stay. Because, towards the end of November 1831,
Saulnier had resigned his position at the Cathedral, and had been sent
to the Post of Arkansas. Lutz was appointed to take his place. Father
Lutz knew English fairly well, although he was only five years in this
country. In his missionary trips to Kansas, Illinois, and the Northwest Territory he had been thrown together with Indian agents and
other English speaking men and had acquired some facility in using
the English idiom. Saulnier, in one of his letters, written in the spring
of 1832 from Arkansas, proposed Father Lutz for the purely English
speaking mission of Little Rock.

Shortly after the arrival of Father Lutz, after a retreat (February
26 to March 3, 1832) made by Bishop Rosati in the Bishop's house,
with Fathers Rondot, Lutz, Condamine, and Roux, on Quinquagesima
Sunday, March 4, 1832, a new rule was made regarding the sermons,
and, on March 7, a rule regarding catechetical instructions.

English sermons[15] were to be preached at High Mass on the first
and third Sunday of every month; on all other Sundays in French.
After Vespers the sermon was to be preached in English, when the
morning sermon had been in French and vice versa. The Jesuits were
to preach the English sermons in the morning. Catechism begins at
2:30 P. M. in French by Roux, in English by Lutz, as long as Lent
lasts. Every evening, on week days and Sundays, there would be a
sermon. [16] At the Lenten devotions Father Lutz sometimes preached
in English.

On Monday, April 2, 1832, at the Lenten devotions, prayers, for
the first time, were said in English at the Cathedral. So the contest
for recognition of the English speaking part of the parish at High
Mass, a contest which had lasted six years, was won to the satisfaction
of the Irish Catholics. To keep up the concession, however, the Fathers from the Jesuit College, Verhaegen, Elet, Van de Velde, Van
Lommel and others had to preach the sermons at morning services.

---

[14] Joseph Anthony Lutz was born in Germany, at Odenheim, Baden, in 1801. Ordained
priest at Paris he was sent to St. Louis by Father Niel, with the clerics Surault and
Chiaveroti, and arrived November 5, 1826. He was appointed pastor of Kahokia and Vide-
Poche, but resided at St. Louis. After hving spent some time in the Indian missions, he was
appointed pro-rector of the Cathedral. On Septuagesima Sunday, January 24, 1834, Father
Lutz preached the first sermon in German in St. Mary's chapel and taught catechism in
German; this henceforth was to be done every Sunday. St. Mary's chapel had been dedicated
on the second Sunday after Easter, May 6, 1832, by P. Verhaegen, S.J., assisted by Fathers
Roux, Jeanjean and Bouillier. P. Verhaegen preached, Father Lutz said the Mass, at 8:30
A. M. In 1842 to 1845 he built St. Patrick's church at St. Louis, was appointed Vicar General
for the Germans in 1846, but left the diocese April 15, 1847, and died at New York February
6, 1861.
[15] Five Minutes' sermons were unknown in those days. The sermons at the forenoon
and afternoon services were great and long oratorical efforts in the style of Bossuet and
Fenelon, answering to all the requirements of rhetoric.
[16] The day before, March 6, the Bishop had written in his *Diary*: † Crux † heu, quam
gravis † ("Alas, how heavy is the Cross!")

According to Bishop Rosati's *Diary*, the afternoon sermon was sometimes preached in St. Mary's chapel in the former St. Louis Academy.

In fall of 1836, a priest from the diocese of Boston, Father Jamison, came to St. Louis to the great delight of everybody concerned. He had arrived whilst Bishop Rosati was on the confirmation trip in Ste. Genevieve, St. Francis and Perry Counties. The Bishop found Jamison at the episcopal residence, when he returned to St. Louis, October 27, 1832, and incorporated him at once into the diocese for the English speaking members of the parish. As soon as Father Verhaegen, then President of St. Louis University, heard of this arrangement, he wrote to Bishop Rosati (November 14):

"Rev. Mr. Lutz has told me, Monseigneur, of the arrangement which you have made with Rev. Mr. Jamison. We are very glad to hear that this worthy priest has decided to stay at St. Louis and we anticipate abundant fruit from his labors. I must, however, make an observation, Monseigneur and, I believe, you will agree with me on this subject. Our Fathers told me that under present circumstances they would feel mortified to appear in pulpit before a congregation which must contribute to Dr. Jamison's support and would not see him at his post They, therefore wish that Mr. Jamison should preach in the morning and they will gladly assist him in the great work of preaching as often as their services are required. You will, therefore permit us, Monseigneur, to retire from the exercise of this function. Rest assured, that when circumstances later on shall demand that we take up our former post again, we shall do so with all our heart."

But Father Jamison did not stay long. Conditions in the West did not suit his taste and he returned to the East (first to Cincinnati). The Jesuit Fathers again took the charge of preaching in English at the morning services, much against their wish, as appears from a letter, which P. Verhaegen wrote to Bishop Rosati on August 4, 1839:

"Our Fathers complain much of the burden which is put upon them by having to preach at the Cathedral. I understand this and you, Monseigneur, will also easily understand, if you consider the fatigues which are inseparable from teaching. They are few in number, they have daily four to five hours to teach, most of them are feeble and those who are capable of preaching at the Cathedral, as ill luck would have it, have a weak constitution. Besides, I think, Monseigneur, that the English sermon is impaired in its usefulness and that it is very expedient, not to say *very necessary*, for the prosperity of our religion in St. Louis, that there be at the Cathedral an *American* priest, who could give there regular instructions. This gentleman might double his usefulness by taking charge of the spiritual direction of the *academy* (*pensionnat*) of the Ladies of the Sacred Heart, which still more than any other exterior ministry weighs heavily upon our shoulders. Please, Monseigneur, reflect on the remarks which I have submitted to you and arrange things so that those at our house who are already overburdened may have no reason to complain because exterior ministrations are heaped upon them. . . ."

On April 25, Bishop Rosati with Fathers Lutz and Lefevre started east to assist at the Fourth Council of Baltimore. Before he left, Bishop Rosati appointed P. Verhaegen his Vicar General and Administrator. Verhaegen[17] resided at the Cathedral. On June 1,

---

[17] Father Verhaegen was dignior on the *Terna*, proposed by Bishop Rosati for the Coadjutorship of St. Louis Diocese (Timon, Verhaegen, Pise), mentioned in Bishop Dubois' letter to Rosati, of July 7, 1835. (*Archives*). On the Terna which Bishop Rosati sent to Rome April 23, 1840, P. Peter Verhaegen was dignissimus (Verhaegen, Timon, Odin).

Bishops Rosati, Portier and Miles and Fathers Lutz and Lefevre sailed for Europe on the Steamer *British Queen*.

P. Verhaegen saw, what he had seen before, that in the matter of preaching things could not go on at the Cathedral of St. Louis as they had done so far. Still, although he saw that the French sermons had lost a great deal of their importance, he kept up the old rule of preaching in English during High Mass only on the first and third Sunday of the month, but of his own free will he added other instructions in English as appears from his letters to Bishop Rosati.

"The French sermons are *poorly attended* and in consequence religion suffers. If Monseigneur would bring along a good French speaker for the Cathedral, you would fill a great void. Regarding the English sermons, I cannot complain of the attendance, but I also cannot suppress my conviction that, as soon as I leave the bishop's house, religion will fall to a low ebb, unless a clever American or Irish priest will replace me. The unhappy Prud'homme always preaches in St. Louis and makes proselytes. His success he owes to his well rounded periods. An excellent speaker at the Cathedral would produce a favorable reaction. You, Monseigneur, know as well as I do, the personnel which surrounds me, and I am convinced that you know as well as I, that in point of talent, it presents very feeble attractions to the public."[18] (Letter, July 8, 1840.)

"It seems that God deigns to bless our labors. The Cathedral, I believe, is better attended than ever these last three years. Everybody seems to be satisfied. My *lectures* after the first Mass have helped, with the grace of God, to spread knowledge amongst Catholics and Protestants, and, if I can continue them, I expect happy results. We have just celebrated the feast of the glorious Assumption of the Blessed Virgin Mary and we had, at the Cathedral alone, nearly 300 communions." (Letter, August 18, 1840.)

"You ask me, Monseigneur, to suggest some means to make your journey most profitable to your diocese. You know that I take great interest in everything that might contribute to its prosperity. I believe that you should procure a good French preacher for the Cathedral and two good speakers for the Americans. 2. Bring few priests along, because you could not place them to the advantage of religion unless they know English. 3. Buy only what is absolutely necessary. Believe me, the money will be worth more to you than religious articles, no matter how beautiful and useful and convenient they may be. They will be very expensive when delivered here. *Expertus loquor.* 4. Banish all sense of shame in the good cause in which you are engaged—demand, beg, knock everywhere *et aperietur vobis.*" (Letter, December 16, 1840.)

"Thanks be to God, my health is excellent and I have been strong enough to give a popular instruction every morning and three lectures a week for Protestants principally, in the evening. I had 2,000 to 3,000 hearers. These lectures, they say, have done an immense deal of good. They brought about several conversions and inspired a great number with the desire and determination to take instructions. The city papers spoke of them in the most flattering terms. The Protestants found our Lent too short, to me it appeared longer than usual. God be praised; to Him be all the glory of the efforts I am making to fight against error and to vindicate truth. I can

---

[18] These priests were Father P. J. Fischer, a native of Lorraine and later on Pastor of St. Mary's Church, and the two Frenchmen: Jacob Fontbonne, superior of the Sisters of St. Joseph and, since 1842, pastor of Carondelet, and Jos. Renaud. who, in 1847, and again in 1853, returned to France. Father Lutz, in 1841, was in Europe, with Bishop Rosati. The latter never returned to St. Louis. On November 30, 1841, he consecrated at Philadelphia his Coadjutor, Peter Richard Kenrick, and having spent some time in Hayti on an occasional mission, he deid at Rome, September 25, 1843.

say that piety gains daily, and I see clearer than ever that St. Louis offers a fertile field to missionaries who are pious, zealous and *well trained.* The underlined words remind you, Monseigneur, of what I remarked in another letter." (Letter, April 19, 1841.)

When in December, 1841, Bishop Peter Richard Kenrick, Coadjutor of Bishop Rosati, arrived in St. Louis, he saw that the church on "French sermon days was practically deserted." Shortly before starting east, Bishop Rosati, on April 8, 1840, had blessed the cornerstone of the new Jesuit church of St. Francis Xavier. Since the vernacular in this new church was exclusively English, there was great danger that the English speaking population would attach themselves to St. Francis Xavier to the detriment of the Cathedral. (Letter of Bishop Kenrick to Bishop Rosati, written February 20, 1842).[19] Therefore Bishop Kenrick abolished French at the morning services altogether. The French sermons were to be preached after Vespers. Then he called Father George Hamilton from Alton to the Cathedral and replaced him by Father Donnelly. Before the coming of Father Hamilton, there was no priest at the Cathedral who, according to Bishop Kenrick's judgment, spoke English well.

The French sermons on Sunday afternoons were soon given up. The young generation of Creoles had been Americanized and preferred English to French. At present in the City of St. Louis the Gospel is being preached in nearly every language of the European Continent, except in French.

F. G. Holweck.

---

[19] When, in 1829, F. Van Quickenborne who was Vicar General of the diocese of St. Louis, built the Jesuit College, Saulnier suspecting that some day an English speaking church would be connected with the establishement, in a letter of May 9, 1829, most earnestly warned Bishop Rosati: "These gentlemen are going to have a church; in town rumours circulate, that the English now soon would have an English priest who would preach to them every Sunday: *Principiis obsta, sero medicina paratur* [Resist in the beginning, medicine comes too late]. What can a simple priest do against a Vicar General?" Since at the Cathedral the Irish received but little encouragement, a chapel, in connection with the Jesuit college, with regular instructions in English, was a menace to the Bishop's church. The Flemings at Florissant learned English much faster than the French of the diocesan clergy. *Hinc illae lacrimae!* This is the reason, why Father Saulnier wrote to Bishop Rosati, that "all the Flemings who ever came to St. Louis have caused trouble."

# DU BOURG

# AND THE BIBLICAL SOCIETY

(New Orleans, 1813)

Under the caption, *A Bible Distribution among the Catholics of Louisiana,* the late Martin I. J. Griffin recounted, in his *American Catholic Historical Researches* (July 1903, pp. 123–125), the attempt made in 1813 by agents of the Connecticut and Massachusetts Missionary Societies to foist upon the unsuspecting creoles of New Orleans French and Spanish translations of the New Testament published by the recently created British and Foreign Bible Society. New Orleans was an ungrateful soil for the Society to thrive in; for the Creoles, as a whole, though rather lukewarm in their Catholicity, were ever impervious to protestant proselytism. The incident, therefore, might well be let pass unnoticed by the historian, were not the names of Father Anthony de Sedella and Louis William Du Bourg interwoven in the story; the conduct of both men in this occurrence adds a welcome indication towards the estimate to be formed of their characters.

Martin Griffin's article was based solely upon the account of the event published by Samuel I. Mills, one of the Society's agents; indeed it was scarcely more than a reprint of that part of Mill's *Journal* relating to the incident, and although the editor wisely abstained from drawing any conclusions, yet the story made the reader somewhat uneasy. *Audiatur et altera pars.* This is now possible, for we are in possession of Du Bourg's side of the question. Having the independent testimony of the two principals, we are able to sketch more completely and fairly this curious and little known episode of Du Bourg's administratorship of the New Orleans Diocese.

The Rev. Samuel I. Mills was a Presbyterian minister, sent by the Connecticut and Massachusetts Missionary Societies to the South-western part of the United States to get information about its religious condition and establish Bible Societies. At the outset, the "Standing Committee on Missions," formed in 1805, had conceived no thought, it seems, of proselytizing among those "outside the pale;" the purpose of the assembly being rather to provide for the many Presbyterians scattered through the newly-acquired territory, and destitute of ministerial help. For this reason, the Synod had welcomed the establishment, at Philadelphia, of an American branch of the British and Foreign Bible Society, and set eagerly to the work of distributing the Scriptures. By its agency large shipments of copies of the Bible, especially of the New Testament, were disposed of "among the hungry people famishing for the 'bread of life.' " [1] But it was to be expected that the zeal of the missionaries would soon extend beyond the pale of presbyterianism and thirst for conquest. Bible distribution was for this zeal a natural outlet. A glib tongue, a certain gift of ingratiating himself with the well disposed and religiously inclined people, the display of deep concern in the spiritual welfare and enlightenment of the simple folk, an unctuous speech and tone of voice served the cause powerfully; in a short while the preacher offered his books; and, as he gave them gratis — supreme token of his disinterestedness — even those of his hearers who, at first, had listened to him only grudgingly, could not be so rude as to refuse the present. As the success of his ministry was measured according to the number of copies which he distributed, glowing reports soon reached headquarters, where every heart did exult in the glorious prospect "that the righteousness of Zion shall go forth as brightness, and the salvation of Jerusalem as the lamp that burneth." [2]

Our Rev. Samuel I. Mills, together with one Rev. Mr. Smith, leaving Natchez, Miss., on March 12, 1813, arrived in New Orleans on the 19th. At once two glaring facts, which the preachers' peculiar logic could not help linking together as cause and effect, stood out prominently before their bewildering gaze: the benighted Creoles were woefully ignorant of religion—at least of that type of religion known to the New Englanders—; and no wonder, for not one single Bible could be found anywhere in the whole city. Here was a virgin soil, full of promise. Without delay the two missionaries bent all their efforts to exploit it. We must hear the tale from Mills' own lips, as he recounted it in his *Journal*. [3]

> The greater part of the inhabitants are French Catholics, ignorant of almost everything except what relates to the increase of their property, destitute of Schools, Bibles and religious instruction.
> In attempting to learn the religious state of these people, we were frequently told that they had no Bibles and that the priests did not allow of their distribution among them. [4] An American, who has resided for two or

---

[1] I. Daniel Rupp. *An original History of the Religious Denominations at present existing in the United States.* Philadelphia, 1844. Presbyterian Church, p. 582.

[2] *Op. cit.,* p. 601.

[3] We cite this *Journal* as quoted by Martin I. Griffin in the above mentioned article.

[4] It is scarcely necessary to point out the gross misstatement lurking under this materially correct affirmation. Let us remember that Mills is speaking of the French Creoles, whose priests were likewise French. It is materially exact that the French clergy did not allow of the distribution of the Bibles among their flocks; the reason for the prohibition was that the Bibles offered for distribution were usually the publications either of De Barneville's "Société biblique catholique," founded about 1719 (De Barneville was a notorious Jansenist), or of the "Société biblique française de Loudres," founded in 1792, that is, translations without notes, and with an heretical taint. That the Church, even the French clergy did not frown upon the reading of the Scriptures in the vernacular, is sufficiently evidenced by the large number of editions of the Bibles of Carrières and of Vence. The Church's position, on this question of modern translations of the Scriptures for the use of the Catholic people, had been, not many years before the events narrated, authoritatively stated in a letter of Pius VI to Archbishop Martini, who was publishing an Italian translation of the Bible: "At a time that a vast number of bad books are circulated, to the great destruction of souls, you judge exceedingly well, that the faithful should be excited to the reading of the Holy Scriptures; for these are most abundant sources, which ought to be left open to every one, to draw from them purity of life and doctrine; to eradicate the errors which are widely disseminated in these corrupt times. This you have seasonably effected, by publishing the sacred writings in the language of your country, so as to place them in the reach of all" (April 1778).

three years at a flourishing settlement and which had a .Catholic Church, informed me that he had not seen a Bible during his stay. He had heard that a woman from New York had lately brought one into the place.

 Upon our arrival at New Orleans we were soon made acquainted with a few religious people. . . . We found that, in order to have the Bible circulated freely, especially among the Catholics, the consent of those high in office must be obtained. We were frequently told that the Catholic priests would by no means favor the project. We were referred to the Father Antonio,[5] as he is called, who has greater influence among those of his order than even the Bishop, who has lately arrived from Baltimore.[6] If the consent of the former could be obtained, it was allowed by those with whom we conversed, that much might be done towards distributing the Scriptures among the French Catholics. We took a convenient opportunity to call upon the reverend Father. The subject was mentioned to him. He said he should be pleased to have the Bible circulated among those of his order; and that he would approve of the translation distributed by the British and Foreign Bible Society. In addition to this he said he would aid in the circulation of the Scriptures should an opportunity present. We inquired of him whether the priests in the different parishes would likewise favor the good work. At this inquiry he seemed surprised, and answered, "How can you doubt it? It is for their interest to circulate the Scriptures." Upon this point our sentiments were hardly in unison. However we felt no disposition to contradict him.

We have since called upon the Bishop. He also gave his consent and said he would contribute in favor of the infant institution. This disposition of the Catholic priests to circulate the Scriptures has very much surprised all with whom we have conversed on the subject in this city. The priests acknowledge the nakedness of the land. Father Antonio gave it as his opinion, that we should rarely find a Bible in any of the French or Spanish Catholic families in any of the parishes. And the Bishop remarked, that he did not believe there were ten Bibles in the possession of all the Catholic families of the State. When we came to this place we found a number of French Bibles and Testaments had been sent here for distributing gratis, and had been on hand for some time. They are now all disposed of and repeated inquiries are made for those books by the Catholics. I happened to be in Mr. Stackhouse's store a short time since. During my stay, which was short, five or six persons came in inquiring for the Bible in the French language. Mr. Stackhouse informed me that if he had 50 Bibles he could dispose of them at once to the Catholics.

Such, in part, was the report sent East by Mills. No stress needs be laid upon the superficial nature of the information given by the missionaries' advisers in New Orleans as to the exact position of the Very Rev. Louis W. Du Bourg in the Diocese. No Catholic, be he even of the party which strenuously fought against the Administrator, would ever style him Bishop. No Catholic either, be he ever so poorly instructed, could state that the priests did not allow of the distribution of the Bible among the faithful. This is simply the old and trite accusation, ever refuted, but persistently repeated of protestantism against the wise cautions of the Church in this matter. Well might our two Biblical Society agents express genuine surprise that both Father Anthony and "Bishop" Du Bourg did not show themselves averse in principle to the distribution of bibles among the Catholics; this surprise only shows how completely their minds were possessed by the old prejudice; and that the prejudice was ineradicable, Mills manifests

---

[5] Father Anthony de Sedella, O.M.C., Père Antoine, as he was called, the Rector of the Cathedral.

[6] The Very Rev. L. W. Du Bourg, Administrator of the Diocese.

by his disbelief of Father Anthony's assurance that the other priests of the Diocese were, in this matter, sharing his opinion.

But whatever the tenor of their conversation with the famous Capuchin, and whether or no, the question of principle laid aside, he was not, as to the appreciation of the edition presently to be distributed, hoodwinked by the two preachers, the interview with Du Bourg, while courteous and, on the whole, satisfactory to the two preachers, was not altogether, however, the touching unison which Mills reports. We even understand that there was throughout on the part of the New Englanders a disingenuousness which succeeded in imposing upon unsuspecting Du Bourg, as when they acknowledged the propriety of the Administrator's approving only the distribution of such translations as had received the Catholic Church's sanction, and explicitly declared that their purpose was "not to make proselytes to any denomination of Christians, but to afford to each of them the means of reading the Divine Word in a manner consistent with their own religious principles." How insincere these protestations, when Mills and his partner must be cognizant that the French translation they were endeavoring to circulate was Calvin's rendition, one justly abhorred by the Catholic Church authorities!

The two preachers lost no time in sending to their patrons of the Missionary Society *their* report of the wonderful success obtained both with the Catholic priests in charge of the Church in New Orleans, and in the matter of Bible distribution; nor was the Missionary Society slow in giving wide and loud publicity to this report. With what painful astonishment it was received by the Catholic Clergy in the Eastern States, who were fully conversant with the nature, policy and methods of the Biblical Society, and cognizant of what kinds of versions the Society was endeavoring to poison Catholic minds with, may easily be surmised. Du Bourg's friends in Maryland at once warned him of the abuse made of his name; and to the friendly warning thus sent by Father Simon Bruté we owe the letter of explanation written by the Administrator. Usually Du Bourg used the French language in corresponding with his dear friend of Mount St. Mary's; but this time he wrote in English, so that Bruté might give, if needs be, proper circulation to his letter.

> Pointe Coupée, Lower Louisiana, September 13, 1814.[7]
>
> Rev. Simon Bruté —
>
> Your esteemed favour of the 10th. of July last, my very dear Friend, reached me only yesterday at this place, in the course of my visit thro' a part of the Diocese, having been detained and even opened somewhere on its way. The circumstance mentioned in it, had already been communicated to me from another quarter. But not conceiving it to be of a nature capable of creating any serious alarm, I had bestowed upon it but transient attention. The degree of importance which you appear to attach to it, induces me now to give you, as far as my recollection will afford, a detail of the transaction which may have given rise to the publication by which your attention has been so forcefully engaged —
>
> Early in the year 1813, two Baptist[8] Missionaries, whose names at present escape my memory, on a visit to the city of New Orleans, were intro-

---

[7] The original of this letter is in the *Catholic Archives of America*, University of Notre Dame, Ind., in the Box labelled Bishops and Archbishops of New Orleans, No. 8 of the Letters of Bishop Du Bourg.

duced to me by a common friend, requesting my countenance on their project for circulating thro' the extent of my Spiritual jurisdiction, French and Spanish translations of the Holy Scriptures. — My answer to them was, in the first place, that a *promiscuous* reading of *all* the books of Scripture was uniformly viewed by the Catholic Church as more likely to prove injurious than beneficial, particularly to the uninformed part of Christians, and more especially to such as were wholly left to their own sense of them. They did not express any marked difference of opinion from me in this respect. I then proceeded to manifest my earnest wish that copies of the New Testament might be circulated among the laity of this Diocese: but observed that no translation of the same would ever receive my countenance, that had not the approbation of the Church, to whom alone it was our belief that the interpretation of Scriptures essentially appertained. The Gentlemen appeared to be sensible of the propriety of this *proviso* from a man in my station. Their views, apparently, and even professedly, were not to make proselytes to any denomination of Christians, but to afford to each of them the means of reading DIVINE WORD, in a manner consistent with their own religious principles. — I did not therefore suspect that, undertaking to print French and Spanish translations of the Sacred Books, for the avowed purpose of disseminating them thro' countries entirely catholic, they could harbour an idea of departing from those fair and honourable principles, by choosing any, that, far from having received the sanction of their church, had on the contrary been inured with her stigmas. It was under that impression I cursorily examined a copy of a French New Testament, with which they presented me. The circumstance of its being professedly reprinted from a Paris edition, connected with my implicit confidence in the gentlemen, and the short time allowed for that examination, prevented it from being as minute as it should have been. I compared it however in many of the most important places with the original text, and finding them to accord, I was induced to believe the translation to be a Catholic one. *I freely acknowledge I was too precipitate in that judgment.* — I did not however, as you assert, probably on the report of the Gentlemen, subscribe for or verbally engage any number of copies, and it was not till the Missionaries had left the place, which happened a very few days after our second interview, that on a closer investigation, I discovered it to be *Calvin's Genevan* translation. I am sorry the Gentlemen have thus exposed themselves; and I authorize you to publish, if you deem it at all necessary for my vindication and that of our doctrines, that, whatever inclination I may have manifested to them of being friendly to their design, was founded upon my entire conviction that they would act conformably to the principles I had laid down, and from which I will never depart —

As to the compliment they pay to my *liberality,* for condescending *to receive the Bible from Protestant hands,* if it means anything else than a disposition in me to support any measure calculated to promote general good, without infringing upon any of those rules, which as a Member and Pastor of the Cath. Church I am bound to enforce, by whomsoever such a measure may be proposed, it certainly cannot entitle the Gentlemen to my acknowledgments. It is well known, that, for fifteen centuries previous to the birth of the first Protestant, the Bible was the exclusive treasure of the Roman Cath. Church. From her hands unquestionably have Protestants received it; upon her authority alone can they themselves be certain that it is the *pure and unadulterated* word of God,—and that authority, of which *the Reformation* cannot have divested her, at least in our eyes, is still, and ever will be, the *sole* and *unshaken* foundation of our profound veneration for the sacred volume — I am cordially, my Dear Sir,

Your invariable friend

WM. DU BOURG, Adminis.

Apostolic of Louisiana.

---

* The Administrator's memory is here at fault, unless he had been from the beginning under a misapprehension in regard to the protestant denomination of Mills and his companion. This slight misstatement does not render the present account less trustworthy than that of Mills calling Du Bourg "Bishop."

A few lines in French follow this long letter; they are devoted to personal news. Then the Administrator, reverting to the subject of the above communication, adds:

> I need only tell you to make of the above whatever use you may deem fit, avoiding, however, *as much as possible,* a paper war, which, owing to the difficulties inherent in my situation in this city, cannot be but most undesirable.

No one will deny that this letter of Du Bourg to Bruté, though written with an apologetic view, is worthy of at least as much credence as the report of Mills, written with a view to extol his missionary achievements.

We grant that the Administrator of the Louisiana Diocese, as he humbly acknowledges, was too hasty in the judgment which he passed, after a too summary examination, upon the edition of the New Testament spread by the Biblical Society. This New Testament from Du Bourg's description, was Olivetan's French rendering, revised and approved by the "Venerable Company" of the pastors and Professors of Geneva: Bertram, Beza, de la Faye, Jacquemot, Rotan and Simon Goulart. "The circumstance of its being professedly reprinted from a Paris edition," would not have misled a more wary critic, for there were several Paris editions of the Genevan Bible. But Dr. Du Bourg's unsophisticated heart, incapable of suspecting deceit in others, because he himself was incapable of deceit, or, as he puts it, his "implicit confidence in the gentlemen," was mainly responsible for the mistake.

But of mistakes there was none regarding the principles. Not a jot would the Administrator waver on the point that any version of the Scriptures to be put in the hands of Catholics should have the Church's sanction and approval. In vain did Mills try to construe his language as meaning "he would contribute in favor of the infant institution"; he had never expressed any more than "a disposition to support any measure calculated to promote general good, . . . by whomsoever such a measure may be proposed," provided that such a measure should in no way "infringe upon any of the rules, which as a Member and Pastor of the Catholic Church he was bound to enforce." How genuinely, therefore, did "the gentlemen" appear "to be sensible of this *proviso* from a man in his station," we must leave undecided; but their peddling among Catholics a French version of the Scriptures distinctly and justly hateful to Catholic Church authorities brands as insincere their pretension "to afford to each of them" (the Christians) "the means of reading the Divine Word, *in a manner consistent with their own religious principles."* And in view of this to asseverate, as they did, that their purpose was not "to make proselytes to any denomination of Christians," may well be qualified as a capital piece of double-dealing: they might not, indeed, care to make proselytes to any protestant sect, provided they succeeded in de-Catholicizing Catholics.

Two years later, Mills was again in New Orleans on behalf of the Bible Society. This second visit was made some two weeks after the

solemn *Te Deum* celebrated at the St. Louis Cathedral in honor of Gen.
Jackson's victory of New Orleans (January 23), "the gentlemen"
arriving in the city on February 10. They now had a liberal supply of
bibles, and at once began the distribution among the wounded American and English soldiers, the prisoners, and the people. Once more
we turn to Mills' report, describing the aid readily given to the work
by Father Anthony, and the attitude of the Administrator.

> Some more than two years ago, the Reverend Father[9] engaged to assist
> in the distribution of French Bibles and Testaments. Soon after I arrived
> in the city I called upon him in company with Mr. Hennan. We informed
> him that the Testaments had been received from the Managers of the Phila-
> delphia Bible Society and presented him with a number of copies. He ex-
> pressed his great satisfaction and repeatedly invoked the blessing of God
> on the donors. He observed, that God would certainly bless the generous,
> pious men, who had exerted themselves to give to the destitute His holy
> word. He expressed his desire to obtain an additional number of copies,
> and engaged that he would make the most judicious distribution of them
> in his power. He remarked that he would give them to those persons who
> would be sure to read them through.
> After our visit to Antonio, his attendant[10] called for two or three copies
> of the Testament. The man who attends at the Cathedral[11] was anxious to
> receive one. His choir of singers likewise requested a supply.
> Soon after the distribution of the Testaments commenced, Mr. Hennan
> called upon Mr. Dubourg, the administrator of the Bishopric, and informed
> him that the Testaments, printed by the Managers of the Philadelphia Bible
> Society, had been received and that some copies had been given to the
> people. The Bishop observed that he had been made acquainted with the
> circumstances by some of his people, who had called upon him to ascertain,
> whether he would advise them to receive the Testaments. He added, that
> as they were not of the version authorized by the Catholic Church, he could
> not aid in the distribution of them. When the distribution of the Testa-
> ments in the convent was suggested, the Bishop remarked, that the parents
> of the children who received instruction at the place were at liberty to
> furnish them if they thought best.
> I had myself an interview with the Bishop; during his conversation
> he expressed to me his regret that the Roman Catholic version of the Tes-
> tament printed at Boston in 1810 had not been followed, rather than the
> version printed by the British and Foreign Bible Society. He observed,
> however, that he should prefer to have the present version of the Testament
> in the possession of the people, rather than have them remain entirely igno-
> rant of the Sacred Scriptures.

In the light of the clear and uncompromising statement of principles contained in the letter of Du Bourg to Bruté, we cannot hesitate
to believe that Mills' report of Hennan's interview with the Administrator has emasculated the latter's declaration. To say that "he could
not aid in the distribution of the Testaments." is perhaps very cleverly,
but probably not very exactly describing the attitude of the prelate.
We may understand, too, what kind of "regret" he must have expressed to Mills himself that "the Roman Catholic version of the Testament printed at Boston in 1810 had not been followed" by the Philadelphia publishers; and it is an easy enough task to reduce to its

---

[9] Father Anthony.
[10] Father Kuana.
[11] Possibly the sacristan, or beadle.

genuine proportions the statement that "he should prefer to have the present version of the Testament in the possession of the people, rather than have them remain entirely ignorant of the Sacred Scriptures."

At all events, it will not be amiss to note here the difference between the procedure adopted by Mills and his associate in 1815, and their conduct in 1813. At the time of their first visit, they had begun by asking the Administrator's consent to distribute the Scriptures amongst Catholics; in 1815, they first distribute their wares, and then go to see the Administrator. It can scarcely be alleged they, this time, proceeded to the distribution by virtue of the consent given two years before, as that consent was qualified by the proviso that the version be one approved by the Church. It must be concluded, therefore, that the agents of the Biblical Society, who undoubtedly knew the unreceivableness of the version, had not a clear conscience, and thought it wiser to put the Administrator face to face with the *fait accompli*. One cannot fail to appreciate the finely pointed reply of the prelate — the almost imperceptible irony of which both missionaries seem to have failed to catch—, on being advised that the Bible distribution had been commenced. Most curious and illuminating it would certainly be to know whether the bible-peddler was told of the answer made by Du Bourg to those who inquired "whether he would advise them to receive the Testament"; and if, as we are inclined to believe, Du Bourg made known his answer, why, we are wondering, was it not entered into the report of the interview?

To close this sketch of the episode, just one word on the conduct of Father Anthony de Sedella in this affair: it stands in striking contrast to that of the Very Rev. William L. Du Bourg. Much as we may discount Mills' account, and even if we credit to the naturally high-keyed tone of thought and expression of Spanish mind the repeated invocation of the blessing of God upon the generous, pious men who had exerted themselves to give to the destitute His holy Word; still there will and must remain the fact that the Capuchin Rector of the Cathedral of New Orleans gave his unreserved approval to the missionaries of the Bible Society and to their work. If he, a Spaniard by birth, was ignorant of the heretical origin and bias of the Genevan French Bible, he at least should have known the value of the Spanish translations of Cassiodore de Reina and Cyprian de Valera. Not only did he make no inquiries as to what versions were used in the Philadelphia editions, but he laid down no such conditions for his support of the Bible agents, he stated no such reservations of principles as Du Bourg was careful to emphasize. This, on the part of a Doctor of Divinity—for such Père Antoine is said to have been[12]—, is a lack of theological acumen most regrettable in one who should be the intellectual leader of the flock and the watchful guardian of their faith.

CHARLES L. SOUVAY, C.M.

---

[12] C. M. Chambon, *In and Around the Old St. Louis Cathedral of New Orleans*, p. 48.

# AN APPEAL

## HISTORICAL MATTER DESIRED

## by the Catholic Historical Society of St. Louis

✠

Books and pamphlets on American History and Biography, particularly those relating to Church institutions, ecclesiastical persons and Catholic lay people within the limits of the Louisiana Purchase;

Old newspapers; Catholic modern papers; Parish papers, whether old or recent:

*We will highly appreciate the courtesy of the Reverend Pastors who send us regularly their Parish publications;*

Manuscripts; narratives of early Catholic settlers or relating to early Catholic settlements; letters:

*In the case of family papers which the actual owners wish to keep in their possession, we shall be grateful for the privilege of taking copies of these papers;*

Engravings, portraits, Medals. etc;

In a word, every object whatsoever which, by the most liberal construction, may be regarded as an aid to, or illustration of the history of the Catholic Church in the Middle West.

Contributions will be credited to the donors and preserved in the Library or Archives of the Society, for the use and benefit of the members and other duly authorized persons.

Communications may be addressed either to the Secretary, or to the Librarians of the

*Catholic Historical Society of St. Louis,*

209 Walnut Street, St. Louis, Mo.

# NOTES

✠

## HISTORICAL

Our appreciated contributor, the Rev. Lawrence J. Kenny, S.J., of St. Louis University, last June roused to an uncommon degree the interest of the College Department of the Catholic Educational Association by his paper entitled "Preserve the Records." It had been to us a great disappointment when we did not find this paper in the voluminous *Report of the Proceedings* of the meeting. Our disappointment, however, lasted but a short time; and we have just experienced a keen pleasure, which we are sure was shared in by many, on reading in the February *Bulletin* of the Association (pp. 7-18) the twelve well-digested, illuminating and genial pages of Father Kenny. *Multum in parvo* seems to be his motto; and as he has mastered the secret of stripping science of the cumbersome trappings of so-called technicalities, and is an expert in treating grave subjects in a most attractive way, we cherish the hope that his plea, voicing so well the earnest appeal of History's devoted students, will find an echo in the minds of the many who can so easily, with a mite of good will aid the cause of preserving and making known the documentary relics of a past worth preserving and knowing. And let them not forget that to-day's present will to-morrow have lapsed into the past.

---

Speaking of the "fuller Catholic co-operation" for which "not a few historical societies in the large cities and State capitals are eager to-day," Father Kenny justly emphasizes how pleased such societies would be "if the churches that have made service flags and service lists would deposit these with them." Repeatedly did we ourselves sound in the pages of the REVIEW a like appeal on behalf of our own *Catholic Historical Society of St. Louis*. We are happy to record that our trumpet call was heard. Now, thanks to the exertions of the Right Rev. Chancellor of the Archdiocese, Msgr. John J. Tannrath, and the co-operation of the Reverend Clergy, we are in possession of a bulky volume containing the list of the *Catholic men from the Archdiocese of St. Louis in the service of the United States during the war with Germany and Austria*, 1917-1919. This is very well. Historians, however, are ever insatiable: they presently suggest that the good work should not stop here. As their desire is neither beyond the limits of reasonableness nor impossible of attainment, we may be permitted to express aloud what they say in a timid whisper. Upon almost every parish service flag golden stars were glimmering; among the Catholic men in the service, not a few were gassed or wounded; many distinguished themselves and have reiceved public acknowledgment of their bravery from our or from foreign governments. Side by side, therefore, with the roll of honor of the young men who responded to the country's call does it not seem meet that we should keep a special memory of those brave among the brave? A note in the list, paper clippings containing the mention of noble deeds, copies of public testimonials may thus become a precious and most welcome supplement to the volume above mentioned.

---

A brave among the brave, "a knight without fear and without reproach, a born soldier, a born leader, with a definite trenchant decision in his manner and in his talk that inspired confidence and cast out fear," such was the Right Rev. Msgr. Patrick W. Tallon, who departed this life on January 15. Others have ably pictured and will yet picture the sterling qualities of the man and of the priest, faithful always, and in all and to all; they have recalled and will yet recall the staunchness of character of that man of strong sympathies who came forth "with the word duty seared into his soul." Suffice to us here to record the memory of his relation to the *Catholic Historical Society of St. Louis.*

He never made pretence to be an historian, not even a lover of history. He disliked self-display; yet how easily he could assimilate the facts and spirit of times long since gone by, he unwittingly manifested on occasions as, for instance, in his masterful sermon preached at the new Cathedral on the 6th of January, 1918, at the centennial of Bishop Du Bourg's coming to St. Louis. We cite this instance because, being the most recent and his last public appearance in the pulpit at a solemn function, it is still in the memory of all. But how often before had he not evinced, in more or less solemn occasions, that facility to marshal the facts of history and make them subserve the moral aims of the teacher of Christian truth? No one who is not a steady and loving worshipper at history's shrine can thus freely draw from its treasures. We know, indeed, that the best hours which Father Tallon spent in his library were the many devoted to tête-à-tête with the writers of history; a mere glance at their tomes on the library shelves revealed to the onlooker a habitual and thorough perusal of these volumes. Nor were Father Tallon's historical tastes confined to the far-away past of far-away lands and nations. As neither his physical appearance nor his mind bore any of the wrinkles which we usually associate with the Biblical threescore and ten years of age, his tenacious memory, stocked with a wealth of interesting reminiscences, could span back many years. He had known at first hand men and conditions now reputed to belong to another age, and he could revert to this past age, without ever falling into the unamiable mood of the *laudator temporis acti.* He had been in sympathy with those men and conditions, but was as much in sympathy with the men and condition of this our time, with, however, a legitimate and most praiseworthy desire that the good accomplished at other times should survive, and that the men and conditions of those times, so fraught with precious lessons for ours, should pass truly into the realm of history and not be buried into the sepulchre of oblivion.

Shall we wonder, then, that the very first word breathed anent the organization of a Catholic Historical Society should have touched a responsive chord in Msgr. Tallon's soul and at once should find in him a zealous apostle? Not only did he second with his habitual enthusiasm the motion which resulted in the foundation of the *Catholic Historical Society of St. Louis,* and become one of the charter members of the new-born society, but he evinced his unflagging interest in its work by every means at his command, especially in his capacity as Chairman of the Committee on Membership; and so long as his health permitted no one was ever more faithful in attending its meetings.

It was but meet and just, therefore, that the Executive Committee should, at its first meeting after his death, voice the wish that a formal tribute be paid by the society to his memory. We herewith subjoin the resolutions drawn up in pursuance of this wish, and approved unanimously at the following (March) meeting of the Historical Society:

WHEREAS, The Catholic Historical Society of St .Louis has been deprived by the decease of the Right Reverend Monsignor Patrick W. Tallon, of a charter member and an ardent promoter of the Society; and,

WHEREAS, The members of the Society, individually have lost by his death a genial companion and friend; therefore, be it

RESOLVED, That the Society at its meeting this day, the Feast of St. Patrick, give this formal expression of its regret and the deep sorrow of its members for one who was in every way so worthy of their love and respect; one whose upright and noble life was a standard of emulation to all.

RESOLVED, That a copy of these resolutions be inscribed on the records of the Society and published in the next issue of the St. Louis Catholic Historical Review.

Rt. Reverend J. J. TANNRATH,
EDWARD BROWN,
Committee.

Another loss occurred since the writing of the Notes for our last issue must also be recorded here—we mean to speak of the disappearance of the *St. Louis Republic,* which passed out of existence on December 4, 1919, after a career of one hundred and twelve years. To remark that newspapers have rapidly won to themselves a place of prominence among history's richest sources of information, is in itself a trite enough statement; however, when a newspaper has for one hundred and twelve years been identified with a great American city like St. Louis, and recorded day by day the pulse of its life and varying moods and wonderful development, what a unique treasure to history must the files of such a newspaper be! We cannot do better than quote here in this connection some lines from the Editorial announcing to the surprised public of St. Louis the passing of the city's veteran newspaper:

One hundred and twelve years ago *the Republic* was born. There was a fringe of well-settled country along the Atlantic Coast. Villages were springing up in the wilderness that was to be the Middle West. the Louisiana Purchase had been negotiated five years before, while the West and Southwest were foreign soil.

The country was still finding itself, still learning how to make the Constitution work, still an experiment. The War of 1812 was yet to be fought, the
Mexican War was not dreamed of, and while the seeds that made Civil War
were sown, no premonition of the great event troubled the people.

Through those stirring times *The Republic,* under one name or another,
chronicled the events that make the history of the United States, and continued
to do so through the wonderful period of national growth that brought the
United States up to the Great War the most powerful nation in the world.

And while *The Republic* consciously and purposefully recorded the story of
the years, its very character and make-up unconsciously reflected the revolutionary processes which transformed the land from a country of agricultural pioneers
to a complex organization bound together with railroads, steamships, telegraph
and telephone lines. The isolated village of 1808 waited months and months for
news that comes now in an hour. The horizon of the people who dwell in the
Mississippi Valley was broadened in that time from the confines of the scattered
communities where pioneering Americans lived until the great events of the
whole world were carried to the homes of the people every day in *The Republic*
and were matters of daily comment. To keep up with the widening field, the
business of journalism itself was transformed. Dailies succeeded weeklies, the
patient hand compositor laid down his "stick" and learned the typesetting ma-
chine, the little hand press became a roaring monster of steel driven by steam.

In view of such a long career, pity 'tis that nowhere, that we know
of, is to be found a complete collection of the paper. All students of
the past of St. Louis will long join in lamenting on this account the late
birth of historical societies, and the fact that none of the city's early
citizens had the foresight to anticipate the advent of these societies, and
garner up for the benefit of unborn generations the daily records bought
at the newspaper stand.

------------

If the clergy of the Cathedral of St. Louis in early times did not
think of preserving for us the paper which they read over their frugal
cup of coffee in the morning, after their Mass and thanksgiving—were
they, after all, as eager for the morning paper as we have become? We
doubt it—, nevertheless, they were on the alert to let no record of the
past, no matter what its apparent insignificance, go to the waste basket.
As was remarked in the early pages of the REVIEW, Bishop Rosati, for
one, had a genuine taste for history. He, it seems, succeeded in im-
parting the same taste to those who lived with him at the Cathedral
residence. Here is an evidence of it. It is a copy of an old scrap of
paper found in the Chancery Archives, which relates to the foundation
of Carondelet, and gives a somewhat new version of the origin of the
nickname, Vide-Poche, by which the village was often designated
among the inhabitants of St. Louis. The handwriting is unknown; but
on the back of the paper are, besides a note concerning which more
anon, a few words by Bishop Rosati's own hand making it clear he
preserved this seemingly worthless document, because it dealt with the
"Memoirs of the Diocese."

Carondelet, Mo., êtabli 1767 par Mr. Deterchet Delor; cet endroit portoit
d'abord le nom de la Prairie à Catalan, nom d'un chasseur, qui s'y étoit placê
avec une pètite cabanne pour la chasse; ensuite quelqu'un, en passant par cet
endroit, avoit demandê quelque chose à manger, et n'ayant rien trouvé, l'appella
du nom de Vuide poche, quel nom lui a resté, en depit du nom de Carondelet,
d'apres le nom du gouverneur de la N. Orleans. Dans l'année, que l'ancienne Egl. .

de S. Louis avoit été detruite, on a batie l'Eglise de Vuide poche, 1819[1], et les bancs, l'autel de l'ancienne Eglise de St. Louis out été transportès á Carondelet pour y être placé pour l'usage des habitants en 1820.

As may easily be seen, this document is far from being a model of correct French style, and bears unmistakable marks of foreign idiom and spelling. Here is a rendering in unpretentious English:

Carondelet, Mo., established in 1767 by Mr. Deterchet Delor[2]; the place at first bóre the name of Prairie à' Catalan, from a huntsman who had settled there in a little cabin for hunting; later on someone, passing through the place, asked for something to eat, and, finding nothing, called the spot Vide-Poche [Empty Pocket], which nickname has stuck to it, despite the name of Carondelet, from the Governor of New Orleans. In the year that the old church of St. Louis was torn down, the church of Vide-Poche was erected (1819), and the pews and the altar of the old church of St. Louis were carried to Carondelet, to be devoted to the use of the inhabitants, in 1820.

We mentioned above a note written in the same handwriting on the back of the paper. We submit it with pleasure to Father Lawrence J. Kenny, S.J., as supplementary evidence in favor of his able plea for "Missouri's Earliest Settlement," being at the mouth of the River des Pères (Vol. I, pp. 151-156):

1740. Il y a eu un établ. des Pr. Jes. tout prêt de Vuide poche, à la Rivière des Pères.

That is:

1740. There was an establishment of the Jesuit Fathers in the immediate vicinity of Vide-Poche, at the River des Pères.

Whatever may be the authority on which our unknown writer assigns the date 1740—he does not necessarily mean this to be the date of the inception of the establishment, and may refer to a time when it was still in existence—certain it is, at all events, that early in the last century the memory of the existence of this establishment was still preserved, and this undoubtedly by means of some documentary evidence.

---

In the same collection of papers relating to early times of Missouri's settlements, is a copy made by Father Edmund Saulnier, in 1836, of some old records bearing on these settlements. Whilst some of the statements contained in these (undated) records may not pass unchallenged and their chronology is often at fault, we intend to publish them at an early date.

---

We may be pardoned to give here, *ne pereat*, a little etymological note relating to the early river trade between St. Louis and New Orleans. Judge Wilson Primm, in his famous article on the "History of St. Louis," reprinted in the *Missouri Historical Society Collections*, Vol. IV, No. 2, mentions, among the dangers attending a trip from St. Louis to *the City* (New Orleans), or vice versa, about the time of the War of Independence, the circumstance that a numerous band of robbers, under the guidance of two men, named Culbert and Magilbray, had located themselves at a place called Cottonwood Creek, "La rivière

---

[1] What follows was added by Father Saulnier and is clearly borrowed from some older document, the original of which the aboVe is probably a transcript.

[2] Comp. Houck, *History of Missouri*, ii, 63.

aux Liards." From this haunt they sallied forth on the passing crafts, usually well laden with merchandise. The spot was, in after years, long known to the river men under the puzzling name of Dardanelle. Whence did this name derive? Not certainly from any old-world reminiscence, of which the Mississippi boatmen must have been quite innocent; still less from any real or fancied resemblance between the Mississippi River and the famous straits. But it was a spot where the river folks must be carefully on the lookout. *"Dors d'un oeil,"* that is, literally: "sleep only with one eye," or, more colloquially: "keep your eyes open," was the watchword. Passing from French lips to ears untrained to French sounds, "Dors d'un œil" was naturally enough transmuted into the higher sounding and more classical "Dardanelle."

We owe this interesting view of the origin of the name to Mr. Louis Fusz, who had it sometime in the fifties from the lips of his first employer in St. Louis, Pierre Chouteau Jr.; the tradition which, no doubt, Pierre Chouteau gathered from old river men in the family's employ, is quite trustworthy, and the explanation most likely to be true.

---

On the mission of Bishop Rosati to Haiti we need not reckon upon mere *on-dits* and oral tradition; written sources are neither hard nor far to seek. It was, therefore, with eager curiosity that we had, some time ago, taken up the long article on "The Church in the Island of San Domingo" (second installment), contributed by Mr. Peter Condon, A. M., for the *Historical Records and Studies* (Vol. XIII, May, 1919). Shall we say we experienced something like a mild shock when we learned that in January, 1842, Bishop Rosati went to Haiti on his way from Rome *to his newly erected diocese* of St. Louis (p. 49; italics ours)? Those who are aware that the diocese had then been more than fifteen years in existence will understand our surprise. True, the statement occurs in an incident clause of very secondary importance, and, on the score of this unhappy phrase, it were unjust to discredit the author's treatment of his special subject. Withal to us, of St. Louis, the one short paragraph devoted to this Dominican mission is insufficient to satisfy our legitimate curiosity about the work, even outside the Diocese, of our first Bishop. With the aid of a few letters of his to or from Haiti, the instructions which he received for this diplomatic mission and his report to the Holy See at his return, we shall, at some future date not far distant, endeavor to give in the REVIEW that page— almost the last—of the life of Bishop Rosati.

---

We must regard as a red-letter day December 30, 1919, which saw the birth of the *American Catholic Historical Association* at Cleveland, Ohio. For months, we should rather say for years, had Dr. Peter Guilday of the Catholic University of America, strenuously labored to bring about this happy consummation. Complete success has crowned his efforts. From far and near students of Catholic Church History had given their hearty adhesion to the movement, and many gathered for the inaugural meeting. As a result, the *American Catholic Historical Association* is now a living organization, with body and soul, and no prophet nor prophet's son is needed to forecast that it has a long and bright and active future before it. Of this the names and qualifications of many of its members are a sure omen, and the assurance is still increased, if possible, when we look at the list of officers for this year: President, Dr. Laurence Flick, of Philadelphia; Vice Presidents, Rev. Richard Tierney, S.J., of New York City, editor of *America,* and Rev. Victor O'Daniel, O.P., S.T.M., associate editor of the *Catholic Historical Review,* Washington, D. C.; Secretary, Dr. Carlton J. H. Hayes, of Columbia University, New York City; Treasurer, Rt. Rev. Msgr. Thomas C. O'Reilly, D.D., L.L.D., Vicar General of Cleveland, O.; Archivist, Rev. Peter Guilday, Ph.D., of the Catholic University, Washington, D. C. The Executive Council of the Association is made up of the aforementioned officers, to whom are added Rev. Gilbert P. Jennings, L.L.D., pastor of St. Agnes' Church, Cleveland, O.; Rt. Rev. Msgr. Joseph F. Mooney, Vicar General of the Archdiocese of New York; Rev. C. L. Souvay, C.M., S.S.D., of Kenrick Seminary, St. Louis, Mo.; Rev. William Busch, of St. Paul Seminary, St Paul, Minn., and Rev. Zephyrin Engelhardt, O.F.M., of Santa Barbara, Cal. At a conference held in Philadelphia on January 10-11, in preparation for the meeting of the Executive Council to be convened in New York City on February 28, it was thought advisable to make the Catholic University of America the permanent headquarters of the association.

How encouraging the prospects are may well be gauged from the fact that, at the time of that February meeting of the Executive Council, the founders of the association numbered eighty-five. There is no reason to doubt that the association *vires acquiret eundo,* and before the next general meeting, to be held at Washington, D. C., probably December 28-30, it will count its members by the hundreds. The plan is to arrange, in connection with that first annual meeting, three conferences: 1. Ancient Church History (Bishop Shahan, chairman); 2. Mediæval Church History (Rev. Paschal Robinson, O.F.M., chairman), and 3. Modern Church History, including American Church History (Dr. Thomas F. Meehan, chairman).

The importance of this new organization, to which must be added due appreciation for the honor conferred upon one of the members of our editing staff, dictates that we should keep our readers informed of the activities of the association. We are all the more prompted to do so, because of the problem, bound to arise sooner or later—rather sooner, if we read the signs of the times aright—of the relations of the new body with local Catholic Historical Societies such as ours.

---

To refer at any length in these pages to the epoch-making meeting of the American Hierarchy at Washington, D. C., last September were truly *Iliadem post Homerum scribere.* Neither is there any need of our reverting presently to the momentous Pastoral Letter of the Archbishops and Bishops of the United States in conference assembled to their clergy and faithful people. Both the meeting and the Pastoral

Letter undoubtedly constitute events of great magnitude in the history of the Church in America, and are destined to exert an immeasurable influence upon the shaping of our Catholic lives and activities hereafter. Still, at the same time they affect us only as an individual unit of no official character in the Church; they, therefore, considerably go beyond the bounds of our activity as a local historical Society. The Pastoral Letter itself, whilst containing an authoritative retrospect of the progress accomplished by the Church in this country, is not, and could not be, and indeed does not claim to be an historical paper, any more than the Conference of the Hierarchy was an Historical Society meeting. Obviously, their value and importance lie elsewhere. We are not, however, for all that, debarred from seeking in the masterful pages of the Pastoral light and guidance for the furtherance of our own aims; and availing ourselves of this freedom, we shall be pardoned to quote here a few lines which may well be considered a welcome confirmation of our own spirit and our own program.

". . . In the spiritual order there has been a steady advance. The issue between truth and error with regard to all that religion implies is now quite clearly drawn. As human devices, intended to replace the Gospel, have gradually broken down, Christianity, by contrast, appears distinct and firm in its true position. The Church indeed has suffered because it would not sanction the vagaries of thought and policy which were leading the world to disaster. And yet the very opposition which it encountered, an opposition which would have destroyed the work of man, has given the Church occasion for new manifestations of life. With larger freedom from external interference, it has developed more fully the power from on high with which the Holy Spirit endued it. Far from being weakened by the failure of outward support, its activity is seen as the expression of its inner vitality. Its vigor is shown by its ready adaptation to the varying conditions of the world, an adaptation which means no supine yielding and no surrender of principle, but rather the exertion of power in supplying as they arise, the needs of humanity. Because it maintains inviolate the deposit of Christian faith and the law of Christian morality, the Church can profit by every item of truth and every means for the betterment of man which genuine progress affords. It thrives wherever freedom really lives, and it furnishes the only basis on which freedom can be secure.

"The inner vitality of the Church has been shown and enhanced by the action of the Holy See in giving fresh impetus to the minds and hearts of the faithful; in stimulating philosophical, historical and biblical studies... At the same time the Sovereign Pontiffs have promoted the welfare of all mankind by insisting on the principles which should govern our social, industrial and political relations; by deepening respect for civil authority; by enjoining upon Catholics everywhere the duty of allegiance to the State and the discharge of patriotic obligation. They have condemned the errors which planned to betray humanity and to undermine our civilization . . ." (*Progress of the Church*, p. 7).

Again:

"The growth of the Church in America was fittingly brought to view at the celebration, in 1889, of the first centenary of the Hierarchy. Within a hundred years the number of dioceses had risen from one to seventy-five. During the last three decades the same ratio of progress has been maintained, with the result that at present one-sixth of the citizens of the United States are members of the Catholic Church, in a hundred flourishing dioceses.

But what we regard as far more important is the growth and manifestation of an active religious spirit in every diocese and parish . . ." (*Ibid.*, p. 8).

". . . It is the Church not of one race or one nation, but of all those who truly believe in His name. The more you dwell upon its teaching, its practice and its history, the stronger will be' your sense of unity with the multitude of believers throughout the world. You will clearly understand that the true interest of each part, of each diocese and parish, are the interests of the Church Universal" (*Ibid.*, p. 9).

It will, no doubt, be of interest to our readers that the National Catholic Welfare Council has issued an edition of this Pastoral Letter in pamphlet form (80 pages), which is for sale at ten cents a copy ($8.00 per hundred; and in case 500 or more copies are desired, $7.00 per hundred).

---

## BIBLIOGRAPHICAL

*The Library of the Catholic Historical Society of St. Louis.*

In the fall of 1918 the librarians of the Catholic Historical Society of St. Louis made the first attempt to collect a library. The following circular was sent out:

St. Louis, December 4, 1918.

The undersigned, Librarians of the Catholic Historical Society of St. Louis, make the following appeal on behalf of the Library of said Society:
The special object of this Library is to assemble, preserve and render accessible to members of the Society and other duly authorized persons, all available historical material, whether in manuscript or in print, bearing on the origin, development and present status of Catholic life, both in its lay and ecclesiastical aspects, in the region known as the Louisiana Purchase. With a view to build up as large a collection as possible of the material named, as also of such collateral material as may illustrate the special field of interest of the Catholic Historical Society of St. Louis, the Librarians earnestly solicit from the Catholic clergy and laity, as also from the'general public, contributions under the following heads:

1—Books and pamphlets on American history and biography, especially those bearing on Catholic institutions and persons, clerical and lay, within the limits of the Louisiana Purchase.

2—Files or single copies of old newspapers; files or single copies, whether back or current issues, of Catholic journals and weeklies; parish bulletins, calendars and other papers, (e. g., programs, circulars, etc.), whether of old or recent date. In this connection it is respectfuly urged upon the Reverend Pastors that they send 'regularly to the Catholic Historical Society of St. Louis copies of their respective parish bulletins and other publications.

3—Letters, narratives, documents and other manuscript material regarding early Catholic settlers and settlements. In the case of family papers which the owners wish to retain in their possession, the privilege of being permitted to take copies of the same will be appreciated by the Librarians.

4—Engravings, portraits, medals, curios, and in fine, any object whatever, which, by the most liberal construction, may be regarded as illustrating the history of the Catholic Church in the territory comprised in the Louisiana Purchase.

All gifts and contributions will be credited to the donors and preserved in the Library or Archives of the Society for the use and benefit of the members and other duly authorized persons. Contributions to the Library and all correspondence relating thereto should be addressed to Reverend F. G. Holweck, 2653 Ohio Ave., St. Louis, Mo.

The Librarians of the St. Louis Catholic Historical Society take this occasion to bespeak the generous patronage of clergy and laity alike on behalf of the Society's official publication, which under the title "St. Louis Catholic Historical Review," made its initial appearance in October, 1918. The annual subscription for the Review, to be issued quarterly, is Two Dollars. Subscriptions will be gratefully received by any of the officers of the Society.

Rev. F. G. HOLWECK,
Rev. CHARLES L. SOUVAY, C.M., D.D.,
Rev. GILBERT J. GARRAGHAN, S.J.,
Librarians.

Since the Historical Society has no quarters of its own, the Pastor of St. Francis de Sales Church offered a room in his parochial residence where the library could be kept until better housing can be procured for it. The Rosati letters and other documents which are archdiocesan property, are kept at the chancery office, 207 Walnut Street, but the books, files, pamphlets, etc., which have been acquired since December, 1918, are preserved at 2653 Ohio Avenue. Since much of the material had been collected before the library was started, it is impossible to give the names of all the donors. We give them where it is possible. Our list is not complete; it will be finished and continued in later issues of this REVIEW. Many thanks to those who have so liberally responded to our appeal. We hope that within a short time our modest library will be not without value to historians.

### HISTORICAL AND BIOGRAPHICAL WORKS.

P. M. Abbelen, Mutter Maria Karolina Friess. St. Louis, 1892. (Gift of the author).

H. Alerding, History of the Catholic Church in the Diocese of Vincennes. Indianapolis, 1883. (Donated by Rev. Charles Bilger of Madison, Ind.).

Cl. W. Alvord and C. E. Carter, The Critical Period, 1763-1765. (Collection of the Illinois State Historical Library, vol. X. Springfield, 1915.

Cl. W. Alvord and C. E. Carter, The New Regime, 1765-1767. (Collection of the Illinois State Historical Library, vol. XI.). Springfield, 1916.

Cl. W. Alvord, Kaskaskia Records, 1778-1790. (Collection of the Illinois State Historical Library, vol. V.) Springfield, 1909. (These three valuable volumes were given by Rev. J. Rothensteiner).

Baltimore, History of the Third Plenary Council of B. Baltimore, 1885

Baunard Abbé, Histoire de Madame Duchesne. Paris, 1878. (Formerly property of Rev. A. Huettler, Holy Ghost Church, St. Louis).

W. H. Bennet, Catholic Footsteps in Old New York. New York, 1909.

Beuckmann, F., History of the Diocese of Belleville. Belleville, 1914. (Gift of Rev. Berckenbrock, St. Libory, Ill.).

Beuckmann, F., History of the Diocese of Belleville, St. John's Orphanage Edition. Belleville, 1919. (Donated by the author).

L. Blankemeier, Katholiken von St. Louis als Geschäftsleute (62. Gen. Versammlung des Centralvereins, Souvenir). St. Louis, 1917.

H. E. Bolton, Athanase de Mezières and the Louisiana-Texas Border, 1766-1780. Two vol. Cleveland, 1914. (Donated by Rev. F. G. Holweck).

H. E. Bolton, Kino's Historical Memoir of Pimeria Alta. Two vol. Cleveland, 1919. (Donated by Rev. F. G. Holweck).

Brunner, P. Franz Sales, Leben und Wirken. Carthagena, 1882. (Donated by the Fathers of the Precious Blood of Carthagena).

Arthur W. Calhoun, Ph.D., A Social History of the American Family. Two vols. Cleveland, O., 1917. (Gift of Rev. F. G. Holweck).

Capuchin Order, St. Joseph's Province in the U. S. Rise and Progress. New York, 1907. (Donated by Mr. Jos. Frey, deceased, of New York).

Benediktiner in Conception, Mo., und ihre Missionstatigkeit. Conception, 1885. (Donated by Rt. Abbot Frowin).

G. P. Curtis, The American Catholic Who Is Who. St. Louis, 1911.

DeAndreis, Felix, Life of. St. Louis, 1900.

J. H. Deiler, Geschichte der Deutschen Kirchengemeinden in Staate Louisiana. New Orleans, 1894. (With other works of Mr. Deiler, donated by his wife, New Orleans, La.).

J. H. Deiler. Louisiana ein Heim fur Deutsche Ansiedler. New Orleans, 1895.

J. H. Deiler, Die Europæische Einwanderung nach den Ver. Staaten. New Orleans, 1897.

J. H. Deiler, Zur Geschichte der Deutschen am Unteren Mississippi. New Orleans, 1901.

J. H. Deiler, Geschichte der New Orleanser Presse. New Orleans, 1901.

J. H. Deiler, The Settlement of the German Coast of Louisiana. Philadelphia, 1909.

Das Deutschtum der Katholiken von St. Louis in seinen zwanzig Gemeinden. St. Louis (Amerika) 1896.

J. H. Dubourg, Life of the Cardinal de Cheverus, Archbishop of Bordeaux, Philadelphia, 1839. (Donated by Rev. P. Crane, St. Louis).

Edwards, R., The Great West and her Commercial Metropolis, and a Complete History of St. Louis, 1861. (Donated by Rev. P. Crane).

Engelhardt, P. Zephyrin, O.F.M., The Holy Man of Santa Clara (Fr. Magin Catala). San Francisco, 1909.

Engelhardt, P. Zephyrin, O.F.M., The Missions and Missionaries in California. Five vols San Francisco, Cal.

W. H. English, Northwest of the River Ohio, 1778-1783. Life of Gen. Geo. Rogers Clark. One vol. Indianapolis, 1897.

J. N. Enzlberger, Schematismus der Kath. Geistlichkeit in den Ver. Staaten. Milwaukee, 1892. (Gift of Rev. F. G. Holweck).

Franziskaner Provinz vom Hl. Herzen Jesu, 1858-1908. St. Louis, 1908.

Franziskanerschwestern von der Provinz zur hl. Klara in Nord Amerika. St. Louis, 1915.

Gmeiner, John, The Church and Foreignism. St. Paul, 1891.

J. A. Gough, A Reminiscence of the Eucharistic Congress of Montreal. Belleville. 1910.

Habenicht, J., Dejiny Czech uv Americkych. St. Louis, 1904, and a number of other Bohemian Books (printed at St. Louis, Hlas, and donated to the Historical Society by Rev. Chas. Bleha).

P. B. Hammer, Eduard Dominik Fenwick, der Apostel von Ohio. Freiburg, 1890.

J. J. Hogan, Bishop of Kansas City, On the Mission in Missouri. Kansas City, 1892.

F. G. Holweck, Kirchengeschichte von St. Louis (Souvenir der 62. General Versammlung des R. K. Centralvereins). St. Louis, 1917.

F. G. Holweck, Nach Fünfzig Jahren. St. Louis, 1916. (Gift of the author).

F. G. Holweck, Der Freundeskreis des Pastoralblattes. St. Louis, 1917. (Gift of the author).

F. G. Holweck, History of St. Francis de Sales Parish. St. Louis, Mo., 1917. (Gift of the author).

G. F. Houck, A History of Catholicity in Northern Ohio. Two vols. Cleveland, 1903. (Donated by J. Molitor, D.D., Columbus, O.).

Louis Houck, The Spanish Regime in Missouri. Two vols. Chicago, 1909. (Gift of Rev. F. G. Holweck).

Louis Houck, A History of Missouri. Three vols. Chicago, 1908. (Gift of Rev. F. G. Holweck).

W. J. Howlett, Life of Rev. Chas. Nerinckx. Techny, Ill., 1915. (Gift of Rev. Ch. VanTourenhout, Ste. Genevieve, Mo.).

Hundt, Ferd., Die Deutschen Katholiken in Amerika. Chicago, 6 Sept., 1887.

P. R. Kenrick, Erzbischof von St. Louis, in seinem Leben und Wirken. St. Louis, 1891.

Klein, Fel., The Land of the Strenuous Life. Chicago, 1905. (Given by F. G. Holweck).

Kostbaren Blut, Hundertjährige Gedächtnissfeier der Gründung der Genossenschaft der Missionspriester. Collegeville, Ind, 1915.

Kostbaren Blut, Schwestern in O'Fallon, Mo. O'Fallon, 1898.

Krueger, Rud., Geschichte des Centralvereins. St. Louis, 1917.

F. von Lama, P. Wilhelm Judge, S.J. Freiburg, i. B. 1912.

J. McCaffrey, History of the Cath. Church in the 19th Century. Two vols. St. Louis, 1909.

Anna Minogue, Loretto, Annals of the Century. New York, 1912.

Missionary Society of the Most Precious Blood. Centenary Celebration. Collegeville, Ind., 1915. (Gift of Rev. C. Vogelmann, C.P.P.S. St. Louis, Mo.

Missions in America. Chicago, 1891.

New Orleans, Two Hundredth Anniversary of the Foundation of the City. *Morning Star*, 6 April, 1918.

O'Hanlon, Canon, Life and Scenery in Missouri. Dublin, 1890. (Given by Rev. A. Happe).

Opelousas History of the Cath. Church in Opelousas. (Gift of Rev. A. B. Colliard, Opelousas, La.).

F. Palou-J. Adam, Life of Ven. Padre Junipero Serra. San Francisco, 1884.

Paulist Fathers, The Light of the Cross in the 20th Century. Three vols. New York, 1910. (Donated by Mrs. L. Ganahl, St. Louis).

Peoria, Geschichte der Deutschen Kath. Gemeinden. (Souvenir 45. Gen. Vers. des Centr. Vereins). Peoria, 1900.

Rainer, Jos., Dr. Salzmann's Leben und Wirken. St. Louis, 1876.

Redemptorist Foundation in New Orleans, 1847-1897. (Donated by Very Rev. A. J. Gunedling, C.S.S.R., New Orleans, La.).

Corn. Roach, Official Manual of the State of Missouri. Jefferson City, 1916. (Gift of the author).

Rothensteiner, J., The Catholic Church and Civil Liberty. St. Louis, 1915. (Gift of the author).

Rothensteiner, J., Chronicles of an Old Mission Parish. St. Louis, 1917.

Rothensteiner, J., Der erste Deutsch-amerikanische Priester des Westens. St. Louis, 1916.

Rothensteiner, J., The Missionary Priest a Hundred Years Ago. St. Louis, 1918. (Gift of the author, like the preceding essays).

Rothensteiner, J., Bishop Wm. L. Dubourg and what His Coming Meant to St. Louis. St. Louis, 1918.

J. Th. Scharf, History of St. Louis City and County. Philadelphia, 1883. (Gift of Rev. J. Rothensteiner).

J. Schubert, Kirchendeutsche und Vereinsdeutsche.

John Gilmary Shea, The Catholic Church in Colonial Days, 1521-1763. New York, 1886. (Donated by Rev. F. G. Holweck).

J. G. Shea, Life and Times of the Most Rev. John Carroll, 1763-1815. New York, 1888.

J. G. Shea, History of the Catholic. Church in the U. S. Two vols. New York, 1892.

W. B. Stevens, Missouri's Centennial. Columbia, Mo., 1917.

W. B. Stevens, St. Louis, the Fourth City, 1764-1909. St. Louis, 1909. (Donated by Rev. F. G. Holweck).

J. T. Sullivan. Sacerdotal Jubilee of Rt. Rev. J. J. Kain, second Bishop of Wheeling. Wheeling, 1891. (Gift of Chas. Van Tourenhout).

T. J. Sullivan, The Catholic Church in Wisconsin. Milwaukee, 1895-1898. (Formerly property of Rev. F. Pommer, St. Louis, Mo.).

W. S. Thomas, History of St. Louis County, Mo. Two vols. St. Louis, 1911. (Donated by Rev. Aug. Happe, Denver, Col.).

Ursuline Convent and Academy, St. Louis, Mo. St. Louis, 1899.

Verwyst P. Chrys. O.S.F., Missionary Labors of Father Marquette, Menard and Allouez in the Lake Superior Region.

Vieracker, P. Corbinian O.M. Cap., Geschichte von Mt. Calvary. Mt. Calvary, 1907. (Gift of the Capuchin Fathers of Mt. Calvary, Wis.).

Waibl. Eug., Die Katholischen Missionen im Nordöstlichen Arkansas. (Gift of the author).

Walsh, Wm., Life of the Most Rev. Peter Richard Kenrick. St. Louis, 1891.

O. Werner, S.J., Orbis Terrarum Catholicus. Friburgi Brisgoviæ, 1890. (Gift of Rev. F. G. Holweck).

White, Father Andrew, the Apostle of Maryland.

Who is Who in America, vols. VIII, IX and X. Chicago, 1914-1919. (Gift of Msgr. J. J. Tannrath).

Zardetti O., Westlich, oder Durch den Fernen Westen Nord⁀Amerikas. Mainz, 1897. (Gift of Rev. F. G. Holweck).

Zeller, J., Conversion of Two Lutheran Ministers, a. 1863. New York, 1918.

Zurbonsen, A., Clerical Bead Roll of the Diocese of Alton. Quincy, 1918. (Gift of the author).

## PARISH SOUVENIRS.

Albers, B. Francis, O.F.M., St. Antonius Gemeinde, St. Louis, Mo., 1894.

Alexianer-Brueder, Jubelfeier in Chicago, Ill., 9-11 Mai, 1916. (Gift of the Ven. Brothers).

Alexian Brothers, Chicago, Ill., Golden Jubilee. Chicago, 1916.

Alexian Brothers' Hospital, St. Louis, Mo., Golden Jubilee, 1919. (Gift of Rev. P. Const. Vogelmann, C.PP.S.

St. Alphonsus Church, New Orleans, La., Golden Jubilee, 1908. (Gift of Very Rev. T. Guendling, C.S.S.R.).

St. Augustinuskirche, Cincinnati, O., Goldenes Jubilæum. 1908.

P. Berchmans O.M. Cap., Church of Our Lady of Sorrows, Golden Jubilee. New York, 1917. (Gift of Mr. Jos. Frey, New York).

Karl F. Bilger, Geschichte der Gemeinde in Celestine. Evansville, Ind. (Gift of the author).

St. Bonifatiusgemeinde, Chicago, Ill. Festausgabe des "Pfarrbote," Juni, 1904.

St. Bonifatiusgemeinde, St. Louis, Mo., Goldenes Jubilæum. 1910.

H. F. M. Brand, 25th Anniversary of his Ordination. St. Louis, 1810.

Brand, F., Jubilee Book of the DeSoto Dramatic Club. St. Louis, 1919. (Gift of the author).

P. J. Byrne, Centennial of the Catholic Settlement of Ruma, Ill. Belleville, 1918. (Gift of the author).

St. Fidelis Church, Victoria, Kansas, 1911. (Gift of the Capuchin Fathers, Victoria, Kans.

St. Francis Seminary, Goldenes Jubiläum. Milwaukee, 1906.

Chr. Goeltz, History of St. Philip's Parish. East St. Louis, 1917. (Gift of the author).

P. Al. Hoffmann, St. John's University. Collegeville, 1907.

St. Johannesgemeinde in Joliet, Ill., Goldenes Jubilæum. Joliet, 1902. (Gift of the Franciscan Fathers at Joliet).

St. John's German Catholic Church, Vincennes, Ind. July, 1902. ( Gift of Rev. M. Fleischmann).

St. John the Baptist Parish of Schuykill Co., Pottsville, Pa., 1917.

St. Joseph's Maennersodalitaet, Silbernes Jubilæum, St. Louis, 9 Juni, 1907.

P. Ild. Kalt, O.S.B., Das Kloster der Benediktinerinne St. Scholastika, Silberes Jubilxum, Little Rock, 25 Juli, 1904.

Kenrick Seminary, Historical Sketch. 1916.

P. Francis Koerdt, O.S.B., Windhorst, Tex., Silbernes Jubilæum, 1917.

F. X. Lasance, 35 Years a Priest, 24 May, 1918. New York.

Leo Haus, New York, Silberness Jubilæum. 1914.

St. Liboriusgemeinde, St. Louis, Mo., Goldenes Jubilæum, 13 Oct., 1907.

St. Marien Schulverein, St. Louis, Goldenes Jubilæum, 2 Juli, 1905.

St. Mary's Church, Cape Girardeau, Mo., Goldenes Jubilæum, 1918. (Gift of Rev. E. Pruente).

St. Mary's Parish, Madison, Ind. (Rev. Ch. Bilger). 1915.

St. Mary's Church, Alton, Ill., Goldenes Jubilæum. 1908.

Maxville, Mo., Immaculate Conception Church, Diamond Jubilee, 1917. (Gift of Rev. Ch. Sohlefers).

Rev. J. Meckel, M.R., Souvenir of Golden Sacerdotal Jubilee, 8 May, 1919.

St. Michael's Verein, St. Antonius Gemeinde. Milwaukee, 1911.

New York, Souvenir of Greater New York. 1916.

St. Peter's Gemeinde, St. Charles, Mo., 1 Jan., 1900. St. Louis, 1900. (Gift of Rev. F. Willmes).

J. H. Schlarmann, D.D., Cathedral Fire, Belleville, Ill., 4 Jan., 1912.

H. Schrage, St. Agatha Gemeinde, St. Louis, Mo., 1899.

Starved Rock Pageant, Starved Rock State Park, Ill., Centennial, 4-6 July, 1918.

Church of the Most Holy Trinity, Diamond Jubilee, Brooklyn, 1916.

J. E. Waibl, St. Roman's Catholic Church, Jonesboro, Ark., 1905. (Gift of the author).

A. Zurbonsen, Golden Jubilee of St. Mary's Congregation, Quincy, Ill., 1917. (Gift of the author).

## PAMPHLETS AND DOCUMENTS.

P. M. Abbelen, Relatio de Quaestione Germanica in Statibus Foederatis, 1886.

Alexianer Hospital, Urteile der Presse. Chicago, Ill., 1916.

Along the Mississippi, Streckfuss Steamboat Co., St. Louis, Mo.

Andachten, Katholische, Geschrieben von Georg Dellring, Marktstetten, 1836. (Manuscript).

Bernard, Edgar, S.J.A., Miracle on American Soil. Grand Coteau, La.

The Borromean, Commencement, 1918. Grand Coteau, La.

Calvary Cemetery Association, Charter, By-Laws and Rules St. Louis, 1898.

Catechisme imprime par l'ordre de Msgr. Jos. Rosati, Evêque de St. Louis. Lyon, 1841. (This Catechism was the property of Térèse Aubuchon).

A Catholic Daily Newspaper, printed, not published.

The Catholic Almanacs and Directories; a full set (1822-1919), is in the Chancery Office. The Historical Library possesses the Directories of 1864, 1868, v870, 1871, 1886-1893, 1894. 1907, 1909, and 1912. (Gift of Rt. Rev. J. J. Tannrath).

Charter and By-Laws of the United States Catholic Historical Society. New York, 1899.

Constitution and By-Laws of the American Catholic Historical Society of Philadelphia.

Deiler, Hanno J., Volapük. New Orleans, 1888.

Encyclopædia Day at Dunwoodie, Feb. 4, 1918.

Gould's Blue Book for the City of St. Louis, 1915. (Gift of Rt. Rev. J. J. Tannrath).

Gury, Compendium Theopogiæ Moralis. Lyon-Paris, 1852. This book (two small volumes), was the property of Father St. Cyr.

F. C. Kelley, Archbishop Quigley; A. Tribute.

P. F. Larbes, O.F.M., Gedenkblatt dem hw. Msgr. J. Rainer zum Goldenen Priesterjubilæum, Cincinnati, O., 1917.

Ch. Maignen, S.T.D., Father Hecker, Is He a Saint? London, 1898. (Donated by Rev. F. G. Holweck).

The Metropolitan Catholic Almanac and Laity's Directory for the year of our Lord 1854. (Gift of Rev. John Sesnon).

N. Nilles, S.J., Tolerari Potest. Oeniponte, 1893.

Ordo Divini Officii. Baltimore, 1818. St. Louis, 1821, 1824, 1827, 1829, 1832, 1869. New Orleans, 1838, 1839, 1840, 1845, 1847, 1848, 1850, 1852, 1853, 1855, 1857, 1859, 1860. (Gift of Rt. Rev. J. J. Tannrath).

B. O'Reilly, L.D., Life of Pope Pius IX. New York, 1878.

Pastoral Letter of the Archbishops and Bishops of the United States assembled in conference at the Catholic University of America, September, 1919. Official copy in 4°; and popular (pamphlet, in 12°) edition.

Pastoral Letter of Most Rev. J. J. Kain, Archbishop of St. Louis, 1896.

E. Preuss, Zum Lobe des Unbefleckten Empfängniss. Freiburg, 1879. (Gift of Mr. R. Krueger).

Standard Guide to Cuba. New York, 1906.

W. B. Stevens, A Reporter's Lincoln. St. Louis (Missouri Historical Society), 1916.

Course of Studies for the Parish Schools of the Archdiocese of St. Louis. Revised, 1918.

Tolerari Potest. Buffalo, 1893.

Tornado, Pictorial Story of St. Louis Tornado. St. Louis, 1896.

The United States Catholic Almanac, or Laity's Directory, for the year 1836. (Gift of Rev. Thomas J. Walsh).

St. Vincent de Paul Society, Manual. St. Louis, 1861. (Gift of Rev. M. Brennan).

C. C. Woods, Robert McCulloch. St. Louis, 1915. (Missouri Hist. Soc.).

Zurbonsen F., Prophezeiungen zum Weltkrieg. Koeln, 1915.

Catholic Charities and Social Activities of the City of St. Louis. St. Louis, 1812.

St. Louis Public Library, Annual Report, 1914-1915.

Fleur de Lis, Centennial Number, St. Louis University, November, 1919.

St. Vinzenz Waisenverein, St. Louis, Mo., Goldenes Jubilæum, June 13, 1900.

Newsboys' Home of Father Dunne. Historical Number.

## PERIODICALS AND REPORTS.

Acta et Dicta, St. Paul, Minn., Vol. I, No. 1; Vol. III, No. 2; Vol. IV, No. 2; Vol. V, No. 2.

Historical Records and Studies of the United States Catholic Historical Society, New York. Full set. (Gift of Rev. F. G. Holweck).

The Catholic Historical Review of Washington, D. C. Full set.

llinois Catholic Historical Review, Chicago, Ill. Full set.

Louisiana Historical Review of the Louisiana Historical Society, New Orleans, La. Full set.

Abbey Student of St. Benedict's College, Atchison, Kans. (Founded in December, 1891). Full set. (Donated by the Benedictine Fathers of Atchison).

Records of the American Catholic Historical Society of Philadelphia; a large amount of stray numbers. (Gift of Rev. F. G. Holweck).

The American Catholic Historical Researches of Martin Griffin, Philadelphia; a good number of stray copies.

The Guardian, Little Rock, Ark. St. Vincent's Infirmary Number, September 14, 1918.

Stray numbers of the following Historical Periodicals:

The Mississippi Valley Historical Review of the Mississippi Valley Historical Society, Cedar Rapids, Io.

Journal of the Illinois State Historical Society, Springfield, Ill.

St. Louis Historical Collections of St. Louis, Mo.

Catholic University Bulletin. Washington, D. C.

German American Annals, Philadelphia, Pa. (Gift of Rt. Rev. J. J. Tannrath).

The Missouri Historical Review of the State Historical Society of Missouri, Columbia, Mo.

Minnesota Historical Bulletin of the Minnesota Historical Society, St. Paul, Minn.

Catholic Cabinet, a Monthly Periodical, I and II. St. Louis, 1844 and 1845. (Donated by Rev. Rothensteiner).

Herold des Glaubens, St. Louis, Mo. Full file since 1889. (Gift of Rev. F. G. Holweck).

The historical numbers of "Centralblatt and Social Justice." St. Louis, Mo. (F. Kenkel).

The Western Watchman, St. Louis, Mo. Centennial Number, October 25, 1918.

G. L. Osborne, List of Genealogical Works in the Illinois State Historical Library. Springfield, 1919.

G. Fowke, Prehistoric Objects. Classified and Described. (Missouri Historical Society, Department of Archeology). St. Louis, Mo., 1913.

A large number of Official Reports of the "General Versammlungen des D. R. K. Central Vereins" of the "Catholic Union of Missouri" and the "St. Vincent's Orphan Society," St. Louis. (Donated by Mr. R. Krueger).

Stray Reports of the Association of the Holy Childhood. Pittsburg, Pa.

Maryknoll, N. Y.; St. Louis Preparatory Seminary, Kenrick Seminary, St.

Reports from the following Colleges and Institutes:
Louis; Provincial Seminary of St. Francis, Wis.; Catholic Normal School and Pio Nono College, St. Francis, Wis.; St. Francis Solanus College, Quincy, Ill.; St. Louis University, St. Louis, Mo.; Fleur-de-Lis, St. Louis University; St. John's University, Collegeville, Minn.; Conception College, Conception, Mo.; New Subiaco College, Ark.; Military Academy of St. Charles, Grand Coteau, La.; Ste. Geneveive College, Asheville, N. C.; Bulletin of Army and Navy Courses, Washington, D. C.

A large collection of War Literature, pamphlets and books, prepared by one of the librarians (catalogue may follow later on).

A large collection of articles, historical and political, taken from various newspapers and periodicals, prepared by one of the librarians.

# DOCUMENTS FROM OUR ARCHIVES

## Correspondence of Bishop Du Bourg with Propaganda

### XVII.

### BISHOP DU BOURG TO CARDINAL FONTANA,

*Prefect of Propaganda*[1].

Eminentissime Praefecte,

Ex literis Sacrae huius Congregationis ad me datis Junii 29 proxime elapsi, disco P. Augustinum Ercolani, nuper Evangelii prae-conem in Wallachia et Byzantii, ad hanc dioecesim, Sacra approbante Congregatione transire. Miror tamen literas has per alium latorem mihi transmissas fuisse, et nec adventasse dictum Patrem, nec quidquam mihi de se scriptis significasse; quanquam, si me non fallunt quae de eo collegi testimonia, vix admirationi sit locus; audio enim a viris omni fide dignis, quibus notissimus Romae fuit, eum inconstantiori animo esse, aeque facilem in dimittendo proposito, ac ardentem in amplectendo; quod si ita sit, nihil profecto erit quod de eius amissione lugeam; vix siquidem alius est in toto christiano orbe terrarum tractus, ubi maiori prudentia animique firmitate sacerdotibus opus sit, quam ista vineae pars pusillitati meae commissa. Hinc est quod pro meipso primum dein pro collabora toribus meis quotidie sapientiam a Deo efflagitem, ut nobiscum sit et nobiscum laboret, rogans ut, sicut licentioris vitae homines, ita et inconstantes et praecipites a dioecesis meae finibus arceat.

Ea occasione significavit mihi Eminentia Vestra Sacram Congregationem id in votis habere, ut, quandoquidem Patris huius adventu novum operarium acquisiturus eram, eius loco alium ex nostris missionariis, qui anglicam linguam didicerunt, Neo Eboracum mitterem, cuius episcopus propter inopiam sacerdotum, laborum mole obruitur. Quocirca advertere velim Eminentiam Vestram 1°. plurimos adhuc dioecesi meae deesse ut urgenti non paucarum partium necessitati fiat satis; 2°. paucissimos ex iis in anglica lingua jam satis profecisse ut Neo Eboraci accepti esse possint; 3°. penes me non esse quaemquam ex meis fratribus in alienam dioecesim mittere, nisi forte aliquis id expetat; 4°. Etsi potestas adesset, certe expectari non posse me velle, post tot susceptos labores, tot sumptus erogatos ad colligendam copiam fidelium co-

[1] Archives of Propaganda. *Scritture Referite nei Congressi.* America Centrale. Dal Canada all'Istmo di Panama. Codice No. 4, Dal 1818 a tto il 1820. Docum. No. 141.

adjutorum, ullum ex talibus ablegare. His adiicere possim, quod ita distractus sit Ecclesiae Neo Eboracensis status, adeo labefactata episcopalis auctoritas, ut vigentibus actualibus circumstantiis, nulli sacerdoti auctor esse velim ut ad eam se conferat.

Paucos infra menses animus mihi est unum e presbyteris meis Romam mittere, qui Eminentiam Vestram et Sacram Congregationem de statu meae dioeceseos oretenus docebit. At differre diutius non possum Eminentiam Vestram rogare ut duo matrimonia invalide contracta propter impedimentum affinitatis in primo gradu . . . curet in radice sanari . . .

S. Ludovici, in agro Missouriano, die Febr., 2, 1820.
Humillimus
    Lud. Guil. Episc. Neo-Aurel.
Emin. mo. Card. Fontana, Praefecto S.C. de Propg. Fide—Romam.

## TRANSLATION.

Your Eminence:—

A letter of Propaganda, in date of June 29 last[2], advises me that Father Augustine Ercolani[3], erstwhile employed in the missions of

---

[2] This Letter is apparently lost.

[3] Augustine Mary Ercolani was an Augustinian monk, and had been a missionary in Bulgaria and Valachia, with headquarters, it appears, at Constantinople Whether he had not been employed in another missionary field before is not altogether clear. At any rate, for reasons unrecorded, he left the Order and the Eastern Missions and came back to Rome. Arrived in the Holy City, he reported to the Vicar General of the Augustinians, begging readmittance. Shortly afterwards, however, he seemed to be undecided whether he should remain in the Order, and asked to go to Monte Citorio. As the question of the American missions was almost constantly agitated in the Lazarist house, Father Ercolani conceived the project of turning towards the Western world; he was directed to Cardinal Quarantotti, who introduced him to the Secretary of Propaganda by the following letter (Archives of Prop., *Scritture Referite*, Codice 4, Docum. No. 107):

"February 25, 1819.

"Msgr. Pedicini, Secretary of Propaganda:
"Right Reverend Sir:—
"The bearer is Father Augustine Mary Ercolani, who comes from Constantinople. For reasons which he disclosed to me and which he will explain also to you orally, he wishes to be transferred from the Mission of Bulgaria and Valachia to that of America. For this purpose he will be introduced to His Eminence. Card. Fontana, Prefect, by the Vicar General of the Lazarists at Monte Citorio, who will join in asking to have him sent to aid his missionaries in America. I beg you, therefore, most earnestly to inform said Cardinal and interpose your good offices to the end that the intentions of this gentleman may be realized . . .

"John Bapt. Card. Quarantotti."

How Ercolani impressed the Secretary and the Prefect of Propaganda we do not know. At any rate, as he had been an Augustinian monk, it was most natural that further information should be sought for from the Superior of the Order. Here is the answer of the Augustinian Vicar General to the letter of enquiry of Msgr. Pedicini (*Ibid.*, Docum, 106):
"Right Reverend Monsignor:—
"When Father Augustine Ercolani reported to me to present his obedience he did not tell me that he had left the Missions of the Orient to pass over to that of America; but that he wanted to resume the habit of the Order and come

Valachia and Constantipole, is, with the approval of the S. Congregation, to come to this Diocese. I wonder, though, why the aforementioned letter came to me through another bearer, and why Father Ercolani has not come, and has not even written a line to me. However, if I am not misled by the information which I have received about him there is scarcely room for wonder. For I have been told by men absolutely trustworthy, who knew him well in Rome, that he is rather inconstant and as quick in relinquishing a project as he was in adopting it. If this be true, I have nothing to regret if I lose him; for I must say that there is scarcely any country in all Christendom where priests need

---

back to the Community; and I replied that I was glad to admit him again. It is true that I could not give him room in this convent of St. Augustine . . .; and he showed himself satisfied of this arrangement. On his return from Gennazzano, where he went to make a pilgrimage to Our Lady of Good Counsel, he intimated that he was still in doubt as to coming back to the Order, and begged leave to go to the house of the Mission at Monte Citorio, to communicate certain messages which had been entrusted to him, and to be permitted to go to confession outside the Order. That is the last conversation which I had with him. He is a man of good morals, but hot-headed and very changeable in his resolutions, as is evidenced by his having in so short a space of time left successively two Missions. Besides, I doubt if he has the amount of prudence and knowledge that is required. . .

"St. Augustine's Monastery, March 12, 1819.
"Fr. Settimio Rotelli,
"Vic. Gen. of the Augustinians."

Unflattering as was this testimonial, Propaganda decided nevertheless to send Ercolani to Louisiana; and from a letter of Father Colucci, C.M., in date of July 23, 1819 (*Ibid.*, Docum. 104), we learn that the project was still standing, and that, together with the ex-Augustinian monk, Propaganda was to send D. Francis Jacobelli, Canon of the collegiate church of Vico in the Diocese of Alatri. The testimonial given about this priest is quite in contrast with that sent concerning Ercolani. Thus wrote Father Colucci to the Secretary of Propaganda:

"In compliance with the request wherewith His Eminence, the Cardinal Prefect, and Your Lordship have honored me, touching the gentleman whom it is question to send to America in company with Father Ercolani, it seems to me that I may say that D. Francis Jacobelli, Canon of the collegiate church of Vico, in the Diocese of Alatri, whilst he did us the favor of helping us to hear confessions in various missions we were giving in that Diocese, and lived with us, proved himself to be an ecclesiastic endowed with a fair modicum of knowledge, with solid judgment, with active, yet prudent and discreet zeal, with great courage in the face of obstacles, indefectible patience and great docility to the direction of others; we noticed, moreover, that the people esteem and appreciate his merit; and for this reason it is to be feared that his Bishop might make opposition to his departure. He is about forty years of age, and quite healthy and strong. When he first expressed his desire of embracing the career of the foreign missions, I wished, before proposing his name to our Superior, to consult on this subject my companions, who were more able than I to observe his conduct; all unanimously answered that he would prove a complete success. . .

"Colucci, C.M."

From Bishop Du Bourg's letter, we understand he was in possession of very much the same information in regard to Ercolani, as we have gleaned from the above-quoted documents, and we may with him conclude that the ex-Augustinian's failure to go to America was small loss to the Louisiana mission. That Jacobelli did not come seems to be regrettable; of the reasons which detained him in Europe, we have no other inkling but that which may be gathered from Colucci's letter.

more prudence and steadiness of mind than in this portion of the Lord's vineyard entrusted to the care of your humble servant. Hence, every day I pray God earnestly to grant, in the first place, to myself and also to my colaborers, the gift of wisdom, that He may abide and labor with us; beseeching Him to keep away from my Dioese not only persons of questionable morals, but also those that are inconstant and precipitate.

Your Eminence informed me, by the same occasion, that it was the wish of the S. Congregation that, as I was to get, by the coming of Father Ercolani, a new worker, I should, in exchange, send one of our English-speaking missionaries to New York, as the Bishop of that place is overburdened with work, owing to the paucity of priests. In this regard permit me to submit to Your Eminence the following considerations: 1. Many more priests are still needed in my Diocese in order to satisfy the wants of quite a number of places; 2. Very few are those who have become proficient enough in English to be suitable for New York; 3. I have no authority to mission to another Diocese any one of my brother-priests, unless he asks to be transferred; 4. Even if I *had* this authority, I could scarcely be expected to be willing, after all the labors undertaken, all the money expended in recruiting a number of faithful colaborers, to give away any of them. I might well add, too, that so distracted is the Church of New York, so weakened the authority of its Bishop that, in the present circumstances, I should never approve of any priest going there.

It is my intention to despatch to Rome within a few months one of my priests[4], who will make a verbal report of the state of my Diocese to Your Eminence and to the S. Congregation. However, I cannot wait any longer before asking Your Eminence to obtain the *Sanatio in radice* ... of two marriages invalid on account of an impediment of affinity in the first degree ...

St. Louis, Missouri, February 2, 1820.

✠ Louis, Wm., Bp. of New Orl.

To His Eminence, Cardinal Fontana, Prefect of the S. Congregation of Propaganda, Rome.

## XVIII.

### BISHOP DU BOURG TO CARDINAL FONTANA[1].

Eminentissime Praefecte:

Litterae Vestrae humanitatis plenae, quae nuper accepi, docent

[4] The priest in question was to be the notorious *Count* Angelo Inglesi, who since his arrival in St. Louis in September, 1819, had, by his suave manners, absolutely fascinated everybody, and Bishop Du Bourg more than everyone else. The Bishop intended to ordain him, as indeed he did, on March 20. We intend to publish in the near future a summary of what is known of this curious and enigmatic *Roman Count*. Cf. *Pastoral Blatt*, Febuary, 1918: Ein dunkles Blatt aus Du Bourg's Episkopat. A sketch of Rev. Angelo Inglesi, a Clerical Fraud; by Rev. F. G. Holweck; also *Records of the American Catholic Historical Society of Philadelphia*, March, 1916, pp. 74-87.

[1] Archives of Propaganda. *Scritture Referite nei Congressi.* America Centrale. Dal Canada all'Istmo di Panama. *Codice* 4. Dal 1818 a tto il 1820. Docum. No. 144.

Sacrae isti Congregationi non arrisisse quas ipsi direxeram preces de assignando mihi in Coadjutorem Revdo. Patre Antonio a Sedella, benigniusque me invitant ut alium Sacerdotem ad tantum opus proponam, qui, si fieri potest, meipso senior non sit.

Fateor hac clausula me valde coarctari, Tres enim dumtaxat habeo quos hujusmodi ministerio aptos judicaverim. Primus est Rev. D.nus Ludovicus Sibourd, Vicarius meus Generalis, qui in summa rerum angustia per sex et amplius annos, Novae Aureliae prudenter ita administravit, ut omnium in se, etiam hostium, animos conciliaverit. Sed is sex circiter annos meipso provectior est, licet adhuc veges et me multo robustior.—Alter est Rev. D.nus Bertrandus Martial, Burdigalensis sacerdos, duobus abhinc annis in istam Dioecesim advectus, morum comitate, ingenii solertia, sinceraque pietate, mihi imprimis plebique carissimus, cui potissimum debetur Novae Aureliae ad meliorem frugem reditus. Hic novem annis, ut puto, me minor existit.—Tertius est Rev. D. Josephus Rosati, Neapolitanus, Cong.is Miss.is sacerdos, triginta ad summum annos natus, vir modis pene omnibus absolutus. Cum vero Rev. D. Martial nuper ad Collegii, pro Christiana et literaria liberorum institutione in Inferiori Louisiana; Rev. autem D. Rosati ad ecclesiastici Seminarii, in hac Superiori parte, fundationem, me auctore, manum admoverint, opera profecto ne dicam utilissima, sed inter omnia maxime necessaria, quae ipsis discedentibus, ad terram prosterni necesse est, unum tantummodo superest, qui sine gravissimo incommodo mihi in Coadjutorem adjungi queat, nempe praefatus Rev. D.nus Ludovicus Sibourd. Nec vero obstare videtur quod paucis annis me antecellat; tum quia, quantum aetate, tantum viribus et virtute praestat; tum praesertim quia, cum praecipua Coadjutoris eligendi ratio sit, ut paulatim incolarum in inferiori Louisiana mentes episcopali gubernationi assuescant, plurimum refert, ut ipse eligatur, cui jam quadam consuetudine devincti sunt.

Generalem Dioecesis meae status rationem in decursu labentis anni per unum e Sacerdotibus meis ad Sacram istam Cong.em transmittere cogitans, hoc unum, utpote urgentissimum negotium, impraesentiarum ipsi submitto, rogans ut, si bene videbitur, quamprimum Rev.di D.ni Lud.ci Sibourd Episcopalis institutio, sub titulo in partibus, cum jure ad hanc Dioccesim consecrari valeat, ad me dirigatur per manus Rev. mi D.ni Archiepiscopi Burdigalensis, Interim D.O.M. pro sospitate . .
me profiteor . . .                                    ✠ L. Guil., Ep. Neo-Aurel.
  S.ti Ludovici (Missouri)
  die 4a. Martii 1820.


## TRANSLATION.

Your Eminence:—

Your so amiably condescending letter, which I received some time ago[2], advises me that the S.-Congregation of Propaganda did not con-

---

[2] This cannot be the letter of December 11, 1819, which we published in our last issue (Vol. I, p. 310), as no mention is made there of Father de Sedella. A number of the Letters of Propaganda to Bishop Du Bourg have not been found so far.

sider favorably the request which I had addressed to it to appoint for
my Coadjutor the Rev. Father Anthony de Sedella, and most kindly in-
vites me to propose for this office some other priest, not older than I, if
possible.

I must confess that this latter qualification restricts considerably
my choice. For I have only three priests whom I should consider fit
for this office. The first is the Rev. Louis Sibourd, my Vicar General,
who, amidst very difficult circumstances, for six years and more has
administered the Church of New Orleans with so much prudence that
he has won the sympathy of all, even the refractory. But he is six
years or so older than myself, although he is still quite robust and more
vigorous than I. The second is the Rev. Bertrand Martial, a priest
from Bordeaux, who came to this Diocese two years ago; his suavity
of manners, his remarkable mind and his genuine piety have endeared
him at once both to the people and to myself; to his exertions is due
the return of New Orleans to better sentiments. He is, I think, nine
years my junior. The third is the Rev. Joseph Rosati, from Naples[3],
priest of the Congregation of the Mission, thirty years of age at most[4],
but a man accomplished in every way. Now as the Rev. B. Martial and
the Rev. J. Rosati have undertaken under my auspices, the one the
foundation of a college for the religious and literary education of boys
in Lower Louisiana, and the other that of an Ecclesiastical Seminary in
Upper Louisiana, these works which are, I shall not say very useful,
but really necessary above all others, will fatally crumble down if these
two gentlemen are taken away. There remains, therefore, but one candidate to whom the Coadjutorship may be given without grave inconvenience, namely, the Rev. Louis Sibourd. The fact that he is a few
years my senior does not seem really to be in the way: first, because his
vigor and his virtue are in proportion to his years; secondly and mainly,
because, as the principal reason for giving me a Coadjutor is that the
minds in Lower Louisiana may gradually grow reconciled with the
government of the Bishop, it is of the utmost importance to select a
man with whom they are already quite accustomed.

As I am thinking of sending, through one of my priests[5], the general report of my Diocese for the past year to the S. Congregation,
I submit to it presently but this one affair, which indeed is the most
pressing; and beg that the same Congregation, if it so please, forward
me without delay, in care of the Most Rev. Archbishop of Bordeaux,
the appointment of the Rev. Louis Sibourd to a Bishopric *in partibus,*
and with right of succession to this Diocese, adding the proper dispensation, so that he may be consecrated by only one Bishop. Meanwhile
I pray God to preserve in good health . . . and subscribe myself . . .

✠ L. Wm., Bp. of N. O.

St. Louis, Mo., March 4, 1820.

---

[3] Not from the city, but the kingdom of Naples.

[4] Joseph Rosati was born on January 13, 1789; he was then thirty-one years
old.
[5] See above, Note 3, on Letter XVII.

## XIX.

## BISHOP DU BOURG TO CARDINAL LITTA[1].

St. Louis le 5 Avril 1820.

Eminence:

Recevez mes très humbles et très affectueux remerciemens pour l'intérêt que vous avez daigné pendre au cruel embarras où je m'étois mis dans l'affaire de mon Coadjuteur . . .

J'ai réitéré ma demande en faveur de Mr. L. Sibourd dont l'âge ne m'est pas bien connu, mais que je suppose être d'environ soixante ans; celui de l'autre que j'avais proposé est de 72. Si cette circonstance formoit une difficulté, j'avoue que je ne saurois comment la lever; je n'ai dans mon Diocèse que lui qui convienne aujourd 'hui à cette place; les autres Prêtres sont ou plus vieux ou très jeunes à l'exception de MM. Andreis, Rosati et Martial. Les deux premiers sont trop nécessaires à l'établissement de leur Compagnie, et le dernier à la formation d'un Collège important qu'il vient de commencer daus la basse Louisiane, pour en être détachés . . .

La division du Diocèse est encore, dans mon oipnion, et dans celle de plusieurs de mes plus sages coopérateurs une mesure prématurée; 1° Tant qu'un certain homme existera, la situation d'un Ev. titulaire à la Nouvelle Orléans seroit extrêmement désagréable. 2° La haute et la basse Louisiane  sont et seront encore pendant quelques années très nécessaires l'une à l'autre , , , 3° L'Etat du Missouri est encore si nouveau, qu'il offriroit très peu de chose à faire à un Evêque; n'ayant que 7 on 8 postes qui puissent faire subsister modiquement un Prêtre. Dans un pareil état de choses, il me semble, Eminence, qu'il vaut mieux laisser le Diocèse dans son intégrité, en donnant à l'Evêque un Coadjuteur avec lequel il puisse partager ses secours et ses travaux.

. . . . . .
        . . . Mr. Rossetti et sa petite compagnie  sont occupés à accélérer les travaux de mon Séminaire. . . .

✠ Lud. Guil. Ev. de la Louis.ne.


## TRANSLATION.

St. Louis, April 5, 1820.

My Lord Cardinal:

Deign Your Eminence accept the most humble and affectionate thanks for the interest which you have so kindly taken in the painful embarrassment wherein I was intricated in the matter of the Coadjutorship. . .

I . . . have reiterated my petition in favor of the Rev. L. Sibourd, whose age I do not know exactly, but suppose to be about sixty; the other man I had ventured to propose[2] is seventy-two years old. If this circumstance were to be considered an obstacle, I confess

---

[1] Archives of Propaganda. *Scritture Referite nei Congressi.* America Centrale. Dal Canada all'Istmo di Panama. *Codice 7.* Dal 1821 a tto il 1822.
[2] Father Anthony de Sedella, O.M.C.

my inability to find a way out; for I have no one else in the Diocese who would do, the other priests being either older or very young, except the Revs. De Andreis, Rosati and Martial. The first two are so indispensable for the establishment of their community, and the other to the foundation of an important College, which he has just started in Lower Louisiana, that they cannot be taken away. . . .

According to my opinion and the opinion of several of my wisest colaborers, the division of the Diocese appears as yet premature: 1. As long as a certain man[3] is living, the situation of a titulary Bishop in New Orleans is to be extremely unpleasant; 2. Upper and Lower Louisiana are, and will for yet some years to come be very necessary to each other. . . 3. The State of Missouri is still so young that it would afford very little work for a Bishop to do, as there are only seven or eight places which can afford to maintain—and that poorly enough—a priest. Owing to these conditions, it seems to me, Your Eminence, that it is better to leave the Diocese as it is, giving, however, to the Bishop a Coadjutor with whom he may share his income and his work. . . .

. . . Father Rossetti and his little band[4] are working to help hastening the building of my Seminary. . .

✚ L. Wm., Bp. of Louisiana.

---

[3] No doubt, Father de Sedella.

[4] Father John Mary Rossetti was a Milanese priest, who had gathered around him a little band of clerics and pious young laymen to whom he was a kind of Superior. At the time of Bishop Du Bourg's journey through Milan, in the early months of 1816, Father Rossetti was so deeply touched by the prelate's description of the sorrowful plight of the Church of Louisiana, so moved by his earnest appeal for laborers to work in that forsaken portion of the Lord's vineyard, that he forthwith proffered his services and those of the sodality under his direction. On further consideration, however, it was arranged by common consent that the Bishop would take immediately along only one of the young clerics, Joseph Tichitoli, and that Father Rossetti would hold the rest in reserve to start later, promising to keep always on hand in the meantime the funds necessary for the journey. They had to wait, until, early in 1818, preparations were made at Monte Citorio for another expedition, made up of Father Francis Cellini, Messrs. Philip Borgna and Joseph Potini, clerics, and Brother Bettelani, of the Congregation of the Mission. The two bands met at Genoa. Father Rossetti had with him two priests. Fathers Charles Mariani and Marcellus Borella; a cleric, Mr. John Rosti, and five young laymen: John Bosoni, Peter Vergani, Angelo Mascaroni, Joseph Pifferi and Vincent Turatti. They all sailed from Leghorn on July 4, 1818, and landed at Philadelphia October 1st. The Lazarists of the band set out at once on their westward journey, and arrived at the Barrens on the 5th of January, 1819. Rossetti and his companions remained in Philadelphia awaiting orders. They reached the Barrens January 4, 1820, almost a year to the day after the arrival of their former travelling companions.

## XX.
## PROPAGANDA TO BISHOP DU BOURG[1].

N. 14[2].

Illme ac Rme Dne.

Licet Amplitudo Tua florente adhuc aetate, ac valetudine utatur, perspectis tamen rationum momentis, quae adducta sunt, Sacra Congregatio Coadjutorem tibi assignare non recusabit, qui in amplissima ista Dioecesi, praesertim vero in inferiore illius parte, tibi praesidio sit, ac adjumento. Verum D. Sibourd, quem novissime ad hujusmodi munus proposuiti, nimis aetate provectus videtur; aliunde vero qua ille prudentia, quo studio, quaque doctrina sit praeditus plane ignoramus. Quare cupio, ut de illius meritis, et qualitatibus plene nos doceas, antequam de ipsius deputatione ratio habeatur. P. Augustinus Ercolani, qui isthuc sese conferre decreverat, a suscepto consilio recessit. Presbyterum, quem Roman mittere statuisti, ut Nos de istius Ecclesiae statu, ac necessitatibus instruat, libenter expectabimus, quidque ad ejusdem Ecelesiae utilitatem S. Congregatio conferre poterit studiose praestabit. Interim tibi petitas duas dispensationes adjicio, Deumque precor, ut A. T. diutissime servet ac sospitet. Amplitudinis Tuae,

Romae ex Aedibus S. Congnis. de Prop.da Fide
    die 26. Augusti 1820.
            Uti Frater Studiossissimus,
  ✝ Julius M. Card.lis de Somalia Pro-Praefectus.
                C. M. Pedicini, Sec.ius.
Rmo. D. Lud. Guill. Du Bourg,
    Epo. Neo Aurelianensi in America (S. Ludovicum).

## TRANSLATION[3].

Right Reverend Sir:

Although Your Lordship is still young in years[4] and enjoying good health, in view of the importance of the reasons which you advance, the S. Congregation will not refuse to give you a Coadjutor to assist and aid you in the administration of your vast Diocese, particularly the southern part of it. However, the Rev. Sibourd, whom you lately proposed for this office[5], appears to be too old[6]; moreover, what are his prudence, his

---

[1] Original in Archives of the St. Louis Chancery.

[2] With the exception of the Propaganda Letter No. 10, published in our last issue (Vol. I, p. 310), the earlier letters of Propaganda to Bishop Du Bourg seem to be lost.

[3] This letter, as is evident from its contents, is an answer to Bishop Du Bourg's own letter of February 2 (cf. above, XVII.).

[4] Bishop Du Bourg was then in his fifty-fifth year, being born on February 13, 1766.

[5] See Letters XIV, of June 25, 1819 (Vol. I, pp. 303 and foll.); XV, of the same date (Ibid., pp. 308 and foll.); XVI, of December 11, 1819 (Ibid., pp. 310-311), XVIII, of March 4, and XIX, of April 5, 1820 (in this issue).

[6] It will be remembered that in the letter XVIII (above), Bishop Du Bourg stated that Father Sibourd was "six years or so" older than himself; and to Cardinal Litta (Letter XIX), he declared "not to know exactly Father Sibourd's age, which he supposed to be about sixty."

zeal, and his knowledge, we are completely ignorant of. Hence, I wish you to give us full information touching his merit and qualifications, before we can consider the question of his appointment.

Father Augustine Ercolani[7], who had determined to pass over to America has now changed his mind.

We will gladly await the coming of the priest whom you intend to send to Rome to make known to us the condition of your church and its needs[8]; and whatever help it is in the power of this S. Congregation to afford for the good of that Diocese will certainly be extended. Meanwhile you will find herewith enclosed the two dispensations which you asked for; and I pray God to keep Your Lordship yet many years and in good health.

Your Lordship's Most Devoted Brother,

✛ Julius M. Card. de Somalia, Pro-Prefect.

C. M. Pedicini, Secretary.

Rome, Palace of the S. Congregation of Propaganda, August 26, 1820.

To the Right Rev. Louis Wm. Du Bourg, Bishop of New Orleans in America. St. Louis.

---

[7] See above Letter XVII, Note 3.

[8] See above Letter XVII, Note 4.

# ST. LOUIS
# CATHOLIC HISTORICAL
# REVIEW

---

Issued Quarterly

---

EDITOR-IN-CHIEF

REV. CHARLES L. SOUVAY, C. M., D. D.

ASSOCIATE EDITORS

REV. F. G. HOLWECK

REV. GILBERT J. GARRAGHAN, S. J.

REV. JOHN ROTHENSTEINER

EDWARD BROWN

---

*Volume II*     *APRIL—JULY 1920*     *Number 2—3*

---

PUBLISHED BY THE CATHOLIC HISTORICAL SOCIETY OF SAINT LOUIS

209 WALNUT STREET, ST. LOUIS, MO.

# CONTENTS.

(55)

# Catholic Historical Society of St. Louis
## Established February 7th, 1917

## OFFICERS AND STANDING COMMITTEES
### 1920-1921

*President*—MOST REV. JOHN J. GLENNON, D. D.
*First Vice-President*—RT. REV. MGR. J. A. CONNOLLY, V. G.
*Second Vice-President and Treasurer*—EDWARD BROWN
*Third Vice-President*—LOUISE M. GARESCHE
*Secretary*—REV. EDWARD H. AMSINGER

*Librarians and Archivists*
{
REV. F. G. HOLWECK
REV. CHARLES L. SOUVAY, C. M., D. D.
REV. GILBERT J. GARRAGHAN, S. J.
}

*Executive Committee*
{
RT. REV. MGR. J. A. CONNOLLY, V. G., President
RT. REV. MGR. J. J. TANNRATH, Chancellor
REV. CHARLES L. SOUVAY, C. M., D. D.
REV. F. G. HOLWECK
REV. MARTIN L. BRENNAN, Sc D.
REV. JOHN ROTHENSTEINER
REV. EDWARD H. AMSINGER
EDWARD BROWN, Secretary
}

*Committee on Library and Publications*
{
REV. CHARLES L. SOUVAY, C. M., D. D.
REV. F. G. HOLWECK
REV. GILBERT J. GARRAGHAN, S. J.
REV. JOHN ROTHENSTEINER
EDWARD BROWN
}

## COMMUNICATIONS

General Correspondence should be addressed to Rev. Edward H. Amsinger, Secretary, 744 S. Third St., St. Louis, Mo.

Exchange publications and matter submitted for publication in the ST. LOUIS CATHOLIC HISTORICAL REVIEW should be sent to the Editor-in-chief, Rev. Charles L. Souvay, C.M., DD., Kenrick Seminary, Webster Groves, Mo.

Remittances should be made to Edward Brown, Treasurer, 511 Locust St., St. Louis, Mo.

# EARLY MISSIONARY EFFORTS
# AMONG THE INDIANS
## IN THE DIOCESE OF ST. LOUIS

The missionary spirit has always and everywhere been a distinctive mark of the Catholic Church. The injunction of her Divine Founder and Master, "Go and teach all nations," never ceased ringing in the ears of her ministers and ever found a ready response in the hearts of her people. The history of the development of the Church is largely the history of her missionary labors. It was, therefore, to be expected that the planting and the growth of the Church in the Mississippi Valley should be closely identified with many generous efforts to gain for the religion of Christ the various savage tribes called Indians, then inhabiting the vast tracts of land bordering on the mighty Mississippi, and its tributary rivers and streams. And, indeed, here as elsewhere the Catholic missionary followed in the wake of the explorer, or, rather, the first explorer was also the first missionary, the intrepid Father Pierre Marquette of the Society of Jesus. After the pathfinder came band on band of zealous messengers of the Gospel, whose chief concern it was to win the poor savages to the religion of the cross. The Jesuits, whilst there were Jesuits, were most prominent in this religious movement, and their establishments dotted the land from far away Canada, along the shores of the great lakes, down the course of the Illinois River, and on the banks of the River of the Immaculate Conception, as Father Marquette called the Mississippi, down as far as the Gulf of Mexico. Noteworthy above others were the original Kaskaskia's Mission on Lake Pimeteoui, then Fort St. Louis,[1] the home of Father Allouez and Gravier on the Illinois River, and lastly the new Kaskaskia Mission, of which the Jesuit Relations give us such glowing pictures of Christian faith and piety, together with its dependencies, Fort Chartres, Prairie du Rocher and Ste. Genevieve. The Fathers of the Foreign Mission from Montreal had established their center at Cahokia with the Commission to evangelize the immense tract watered by the Missouri and its tributary streams, "the most beautiful region in the world," as Father Vivier calls it in 1750. Further down the Mississippi there were a number of stations conducted by Jesuits or Capuchins. Of course, these missionary centers were not always of the same relative importance, increasing or de-

---

[1] It would appear that Fort St. Louis and Starved Rock are the same place. The mission called St. Louis took its name from the Fort St. Louis, and was probably at the great village, which village was just below Starved Rock. Starved Rock is the place where the Illinois made their last stand against the Pottawotomies.

creasing frequently in accordance with the frequent shifting of the
Indian population. An approximately correct idea can be gained for
the years 1722-1728 from a Memoir[2] concerning the Church of Louisiana, dated November 21, 1728, found in the archives of the Ministry
of Marine of France. We will give the leading parts of this lengthy
document in a literal translation of the French original, connecting
them by a resumé of the less important matters. "By ordinance of the
Commissioners of the Council of May 16, 1722, and with the consent
of the Bishop of Quebec, the Province of Louisiana was divided into
three religious jurisdictions," apportioned to three missionary orders,
each to have at its head a Grand Vicar of the Bishop of Quebec.

The first included all the country which is found in ascending the river St.
Louis (Mississippi) from the sea (the Gulf of Mexico) to the height of the
entry of the river Ouabache (Ohio) into the river St. Louis; and all that part to
the west of this river in the said extent of country. The churches and missions
in this jurisdiction were to be filled by the Capuchins and their Superior was to
be always Grand Vicar of the Bishop of Quebec, in the department, and to reside
in New Orleans.
The second jurisdiction was to extend over all the country which is found
in the upper part of the province above the river Ouabache, and was to be in
control of the Jesuits, whose Superior residing at the Illinois, was to be always
Grand Vicar to the Bishop of Quebec in this part.
The third jurisdiction was to comprise all the country east of the river
(Mississippi) from the Gulf to the Ohio, and was to be given to the Carmelites,
whose Superior was likewise Grand Vicar, and ordinarily established at Mobile.[2]

The Capuchins at once took possession of their district; the
Jesuits had been established in theirs for upwards of fifty years; the
Carmelites were, indeed, at Mobile, but as the Bishop of Quebec
seemed dissatisfied with their management, their jurisdiction was by
episcopal order united to that of the Capuchins. Whereupon the Carmelites withdrew to France. Now there were but two jurisdictions:
the old Illinois country under the Jesuits, and the remainder of Upper
Louisiana, together with the entire extent of Lower Louisiana under
the care of the Capuchins.

In the month of December, 1723, continues our memoir, the company (of the
Indies), judging that the Capuchins would not be able to furnish enough clergymen to supply all the cures and missions in a region so vast . . . fixed the
boundary of their jurisdiction at Natchez, leaving them all the country below
this post, both to the east and to the west, and giving the remainder to the
Jesuits, who, in this department had for fellow-laborers two priests of the Foreign Missions.

This arrangement alarmed the Capuchins; they demanded a guarantee that no further encroachments would be made on their sphere of
activity. The guarantee was given by the Council and confirmed by
Royal Patent on July 15, 1725.

---

[2] Memoir concerning the Church of Louisiana (1722-1728), dated November 21, 1728.
Cf. Martin T. J. Griffin. *The American Catholic Historical Researches.* XXII. No. 2.

But the Capuchins, as the Memoir continues, had more zeal than ability to furnish men. The Province of Champagne, from which those of Louisiana came, is small and unfruitful of subjects. The company then seeing that they were not providing as many clergymen as were needed to fill the ecclesiastical posts of this district, and knowing, moreover, that they were little fitted for missions among savages, decided on a new partition which, being accommodated to the character and the particular talents of the two orders, should fix unalterably their relations from this time forward. They decided to establish the Capuchins in all the French posts, and to charge the Jesuits with the spiritual management of the savages, under the will and pleasure of the Bishop of Quebec, who had warmly approved this arrangement.

In consequence the Council made an agreement on February 20, 1726, with the Jesuit Fathers by which they engaged to furnish missionaries not only in all places of their district, but also at the homes of the savage nations . . . in the territory conceded to the Capuchins.

The Superior of the Jesuits was to reside in New Orleans, on condition, however, that there should not be any ecclesiastical functions in New Orleans without the consent of the Capuchins. "In the month of December, 1726, there departed from France the number of Jesuits necessary to supply the missions which they had agreed to establish, and they were immediately assigned to their stations. The presence in one city of two Grand Vicars with divided authority was to bring on a serious disturbance of ecclesiastical peace; yet the work of the Indian Mission entered upon a new era of prosperity.for at least thirty-six years. The names of all the missionaries then laboring in Louisiana, both Capuchins and Jesuits, were given at the end of the Memoir.

Capuchins: Pere Raphael, V. G. of the Bishop of Quebec, and Curé of the City of New Orleans; P. Hyacinthe, Vicar, and Pere Cecile, both at New Orleans. P. Theodore with the Chapitoulas; P. Philippe at Village Allemand, in the German Village; P. Gaspard at Balize; P. Mathias at Mobile; P. Maximin with the Natchitaches; P. Philibert with the Natchez; P. Victorin, Recollect, joined to the Capuchins with the Apalaches.

Jesuits: Pere Petit, Superior at New Orleans; P. Poisson and P. D'Outreleau, both with the Arkansas; P. Tartarin and P. Boulenger, both with the Kaskaskias; P. Guimereau with the Metchigamias; P. Souel with the Yasous; P. Baudouin with the Chicasaws; P. Guenne with the Alabamas.

Pere Petit, adds the Memoir, had been with the Choctaws. There will be a new missionary to the Castonitas. Messrs. Thaumur and Mercier, priests of the Foreign Missions, are with the Jesuits serving the Cahokias and Tamarois.

The golden age of the Illinois Missions, however, was then already on the decline, chiefly on account of the Indians' indulgence in strong drink and the consequent licentiousness. This decline was to assume alarming proportions about 1750, when Father Vivier, S.J., could write of Kaskaskia:

This station contains more than six hundred Illinois, all baptized, with the exception of five or six; but the "fire water" which is sold them by the French, and especially by the soldiers, in spite of the reiterated prohibition on the part of the King, and that which is sometimes distributed to them, under pretext of maintaining them in our interest, has ruined the mission and caused the greater part of the converts to abandon our holy religion. The Indians, and particularly the Illinois, who at other times, are the gentlest and most tractable of men, become, when intoxicated, frantic and brutally ferocious. Then they attack each other with knives, inflicting terrible wounds. The greatest good we do among them is the administration of baptism to children who are at the point of death.[3]

It was a sad state of affairs, so different than that described by Penicaut in 1711,[4] not to mention the detailed accounts of the Jesuit Relations. But the end was to come in a manner no one could have expected, by the suppression of the Order, which had been the life of these missions. At one fell swoop in 1764 all the Jesuit missioners were recalled by the Council of the Indies, and, with one exception, deported to France. The Society of Jesus was dissolved, as far as France was concerned; but Providence watched over an Order that was to take up again the work of Christianizing and civilizing the Indians of the Mississippi Valley and to carry it beyond the Mississippi, yes, beyond the plains and the valleys' natural bulwarks, the Rocky Mountains.

## I. THE FIRST MOVING OF THE SPIRIT.

It is my purpose to sketch the missionary efforts among the Indians in the Old Diocese of St. Louis. Now the Diocese of St. Louis is first mentioned as a probable or desirable foundation in the letter of Bishop Flaget, dated June 26, 1816. Writing to Archbishop Neale of Baltimore, the Bishop of Bardstown says, among other things:

According to your request, I candidly pass my opinion about the erection of a new See at St. Louis: I firmly believe that the place is of the utmost importance for the good of religion, not only on account of the many Catholics that live there now, of those that will immediately emigrate thither as soon as they hear that there is a Catholic bishop, but much more so on account of the many nations of Indians that have never heard of the Christian faith. The bishop that is to be sent thither must be accompanied by a good number of priests, and zealous ones, because the country is almost destitute of them. . . If the Holy Father was to send a Jesuit as a bishop and give him five or six companions, I do not entertain the least doubt but in less than twenty years St. Louis would be the most flourishing diocese of all those that are in the United States.[5]

[3] Cf. Letter of Father Vivier, S.J., to a Father of Society of Jesus, dated at Illinois, the 17th of November, 1750. *American Catholic Historical Researches*, vol. XI, No. 4.

[4] Cf. *American Catholic Historical Researches*, vol. VII, No. 2, for a brief extract from Penicants Journal of the Kaskaskias'. Mission, to conditions obtaining then: We can give but one remark concerning the spiritual condition of the mission in 1711: "By far the greater number of the Illinois are Catholic Christians. . . . The church (a very large one", is kept very clean inside. There are three chapels, the large one for the choir and two side chapels. There is also a tower, and in it is a bell. The people attend very regularly at High Mass and Vespers. The Jesuit Fathers have translated for them the Psalms and hymns from the Latin into their own language.
The Illinois, both at Mass and at Vespers, sing a couplet alternately with the French, who keep to the original language. For example, the Illinois sing a couplet of a Psalm or hymn in their own tongue, and the French sing the succeeding couplet in Latin, and so on; and all in the same tone in which it is sung in Europe by Catholic Christians."

[5] Bishop Benedict Joseph Flaget's Letter to Archbishop Neale, June 26, 1816. From the Archives, Baltimore. Cf. Printed in *American Catholic Historical Researches*, vol. XIX, No. 3.

This was written in 1816, on June 26. About three and a half months previous to this Bishop Flaget had written about this matter in a somewhat veiled manner, probably acting for Bishop Du Bourg of New Orleans, then in the first flush of apostolical zeal, seeking laborers and soliciting means in Rome, the Italian States, France and Belgium, for his boundless diocese of Louisiana. There was a gentle hint on this communication addressed to the clergy and laity of the Missouri Missions, that Ste. Genevieve might be chosen as the episcopal seat instead of St. Louis, especially as St. Louis now boasted of having a theater, probably the first theater on the west side of the Mississippi. The good bishop expressed the hope "that the citizens of St. Louis would come to their senses, and that they would not cast aside, out of love for vanity and falsehood, the incalculable benefits which will infallibly result from the presence of a bishop in their city."[6] By a strange chain of circumstances Bishop Du Bourg himself was led, we may say, forced, to come for the first years of his episcopacy to St Louis instead of New Orleans, and to found here those institutions which he had originally intended for the South. It is also noteworthy, though in a much lower degree, that Bishop Flaget, who had opposed the choice of St. Louis on account of its theater, had as companion on the steamer Piqua that carried him and Bishop Du Bourg down the Ohio and up the Mississippi to St. Louis, a band of strolling players. But the reception extended to the new Bishop was a most hearty one in the French style. A great parade of the inhabitants was held. Two carriages brought the prelates from the landing to the church, four of the most prominent men of the town, Messrs. Didier, Pratte, Sarpy and Belcour, carried the canopy under which the Bishops walked to the altar: St.. Louis was a diocese in fact, though not in name, and now began the work of christianizing the Indians in dead earnest.[7]

---

[6] Bishop Flaget Circular Letter to the Priests of Upper Louisiana, March 3, 1816, in *American Catho ic Historical Researches*, vol. XXI, No. 4.
Also in Dr. Charles Souvay's article "Rosati's Election to the Coadjutorship of New Orleans," in *Catholic Historical Review* (Washington), vol. III, pp. 5 and 6.

[7] Of this important historical event we catch a passing glance in an intimate letter of Mrs. Anne Lucas Hunt, written on the very days of the occurrences to her father, J. B. C. Lucas, at Washington, D. C., dated St. Louis, January 4th and 5th, 1818: "The steamboat arrived here yesterday and brought a company of players who will perform in the old theater this winter.
The Bishops (Du Bourg and Plaget) are to be here at 12 o'clock to-day and will be received with great parade in the church by the inhabitants of this place. Mr. Hunt found Messrs. Didier, Belcour, Sarpy (who gave him this information) in grand council at the church door; the whole town is in an uproar about it, and one-half on the river shore in anxious expectation. . . . Ann L. Hunt." On the following day Mrs. Hunt wrote a postscript which, as usual is the best part of her letter: "As my letter is not yet sealed I will give you a description of the installation of Bishop Du Bourg. Two carriages took them both from the landing to the presbytery; four priests attended them thence to the church, besides twelve little boys, who walked in procession before the two Bishops, who were under the dais (canopy), which was supported by Messrs. Didier, Pratte, Sarpy and Belcour. Our old church was handsomely decorated and a crimson throne erected, to which Bishop Flaget led our Bishop and, having seated him, left him and returned to the altar, from whence he addressed our Bishop very handsomely. But I thought the answer was the best of the two. Bishop Du Bourg is certainly more eloquent than the other; at all events, he speaks more handsomely. The church was never so crowded since I have been here, nor will those four walls ever see such another day as this. All the people appear to be much pleased with their new acquisition. May it continue so, is the wish of your affectionate daughter, Ann L. Hunt."

The Indians of the Western plains were not altogether unknown
at the time. French traders and trappers had visited the tribes in all
directions. And Indian delegaticns had frequently been seen in the
streets of St. Louis. As early as 1750 Father Vivier wrote:

> Among the tribes in Missouri there are some who seem most favorably dis-
> posed for the reception of the Gospel; for example, the Panismahas. One of.
> our priests wrote one day to a Frenchman who was trading with these Indians,
> and begged him in his letter to baptize those of their children whom he found to
> be at the point of death. The chief of the village, seeing the letter, asked: what
> is the news? "None," answered the Frenchman. "What!" said the Indian, "be-
> cause we are red men may we not learn the news?" "It is from the Black Chief,"
> replied the Frenchman. "He has written advising me to baptize the children who
> are dying, so that they may go to the Great Spirit." The Indian chief, perfectly
> satisfied, said to him: "Do not put yourself to any trouble in this matter. I
> will take upon myself the task of giving you notice whenever there shall be a
> child in danger." On assembling his people, he said "What do you think of
> this Black Chief? We have never seen him; we have never done him any service;
> he dwells far from us towards the rising sun, and yet he thinks of our village.
> He wishes to do us good, and when our children come to die, he wishes to send
> them to the Great Spirit. The Black Chief must be very good.[8]

Such and similar occurrences, breathing forth the true charity of
Christ that must warm every true heart, carried the fame of the Black
Chiefs, or Black Robes, as the missionaries were called by the Indians,
from tribe to tribe, from nation to nation, and awakened in their hearts
the desire of having one of their kind among them. In the course of
our sketch we shall learn of many an Indian delegation coming to St.
Louis to obtain, if possible, a missionary for their people who still
preserved the memory of some Black Gown now long in his grave,
but who had done a kindness to their fathers long ago, or who had
instructed them in their childhood, and perhaps baptized them in some
mission chapel that afterwards fell in ruins. A few days after his arrival in St. Louis Bishop Du Bourg wrote to a friend in France who
had expressed a fear that the bishop's supporters might injure the
interests of France by working for distant lands: "The good which
they do here will return to them a hundredfold" and then continues:

> "Turn your eyes on hundreds of Indian tribes that seem but to wait for in-
> struction in order to embrace the faith. How touched you would be if you
> could be witness of the frequent deputations which I receive from them the re-
> ligious respect which they testify to me, and the urgent prayers which they ad-
> dress to me, to be their father, to visit them, and to give them men of God."[9]

Among the numerous companions of Bishop Du Bourg, the saintly
Father Felix De Andreis of the Congregation of the Missions, was the
first one to conceive the idea of a missionary life among the Indians.

---

[8] Jesuit Mission to the Illinois, 1750, in *American Catholic Historical Researches*,
XI, 4.

[9] *Annales de l'Association de la Propagation de la Foi.* I, 1. In quoting the Annales
we have found great help in the excellent translation made of many letters by Naina dos
Santos, and published in *Records of the American Catholic Historical Society of Philadelphia*, vol. XIV No. 2, pp. 140-216.

Even before he set foot upon the land to be hallowed by his labors, whilst preparing himself for his life-work under the roof of St. Thomas' Seminary at Bardstown, he gave strong expression to his desires and hopes. Writing to the Vicar General of the Congregation of the Missions at Rome, under date of January 5, 1817, Father De Andreis says:

"I feel strongly impelled to devote myself, in a particular manner, to the conversion of the Indian tribes who live beyond the Mississippi. Here (in Kentucky) no trace of them remains, while, on the contrary, the Mississippi, which serves as a boundary to the United States, and separates them from the immense widerness, which extends even to the Pacific Coast, flows by St. Louis, and makes of it the central point of all these savage nations. Among these, so far, the light of the gospel has never penetrated, though they seem well disposed to receive it. Therefore, I intend, when our seminary is well established, to leave Father Rosati at its head, and to wend my way, in *Nomine Domini*, along the banks of the Mississippi and Missouri, preaching the gospel to these poor people. Before I leave St. Louis I will have the Catechism translated into their language. This I can do with the assistance of some Indians who come from time to time to St. Louis, and persons of the place who are pretty well aequainted with their language. I have received from men of experience much information, both with regard to the difficulties to be encountered and the manner of overcoming them, and, with the help of God, the undertaking seems as easy as if I already witnessed its execution. I shall have much to suffer, but of this I do not think, nor will I allow my mind to rest on it one moment. Too much already have I thought about myself, and I am ashamed to have done so; but in future, nothing but God and the interests of His glory shall occupy my attention. I see clearly that He is very merciful in my regard, for I should be an infidel did I not trust in Him and follow solely the impulse of His spirit.

"To tell the truth, the Indians are uncivilized, ferocious, inconstant and haughty. They habitually lead a very austere life, and sometimes spend several days without taking any nourishment; but then, if they chance to kill a buffalo or a deer in their hunt, they will eat it all at once, almost raw. They wear very little clothes, and torment their bodies to please the 'Great Spirit.' The old people, with the women and children, remain in the wigwams, but the others are nearly always away hunting beasts, whose skins they prepare very skillfully, and exchange them with the Americans for provisions and strong liquors. They are exceedingly fond of liquor, so much so that this propensity constitutes one of the principal obstacles with which the missionary has to contend, in the work of their conversion." [10]

One year later, about forty days after his arrival in St. Louis, February 24, 1818, Father De Andreis writes, among other details concerning the new mission, the following account of the unfolding of his plans in regard to the Indians. The letter is addressed to Father Sicardi in Rome:

"Let us now proceed to the numerous Indian tribes. There are among them fifty different nations; they acknowledge one only God. whom, in their language, they call Chissemenetu, which means 'Father of Life'; to him they address their prayers and offer the first fumes of their pipe. To please this god, they treat themselves most cruelly. Indeed, their whole religion consists in these practices, some of which are too horrible to relate. They live like the very animals of which they are constantly in pursuit. Their chase provides them with food and scanty clothing (for they go almost naked), and enables

---

[10] Rosati's *Life of Felix De Andreis*, pp. 157 and 158.

them to trade with the white people, who, in exchange for furs and venison, give them powder, spirits, paint to decorate their bodies and silver rings for their ears and nostrils.   Their aspect 'is frightful, and one feels inclined to doubt if their reasoning powers be fully developed.   I have seen several, and have conversed wtih them by means of an interpreter.   In general, they regard priests with great respect, calling them Mecate-o-coriatte, which means Black Gown.   They also call them "Fathers of Prayer."   Some few among them are Catholics, and, in spite of the efforts made by Protestant missionaries to imbue them with false doctine, they constantly refuse to adopt it, objecting that the true "Fathers' of Prayer" have no wives and children like the Protestant ministers, but that they devote themselves wholly to God and the salvation of souls.   Notwithstanding the difficulties attending the work of their conversion, I am convinced that, when the first obstacles are overcome, it will be almost easy.   The chief impediment is the language, which is not the same among the various tribes, though the dialects are very much alike, and the Indians of different nations understand one another.   With the assistance of an interpreter, I have made some attempts to arrange their principal language according to grammatical rule.   It is a difficult undertaking, as my interpreter, knowing nothing of such laws, cannot translate word for word, nor supply me with equivalent expressions for every idea.   However, I have begun a small dictionary ,and made some translations.   Their . scarcity of ideas renders their language poor in words.   They are constantly obliged to express themselves with the aid of circuumlocution, especially on the subject of religion."

In December, 1818, Father De Andreis returns to the subject in a letter to Father Baccari, the Vicar General of the Congregation in Rome:

"As to the savages, it is rather a more difficult task.   These poor creatures seem incapable of forming any idea of spiritual and divine things.   They know that there is a God, and they begin all their employments by an act of worship (a fact which should make many Christians blush with shame!)   When they come to trade with the white people, they begin to smoke, and directing the first cloud on high, they say: 'Anaregare kill chakanda,' which means: 'May this ascend to the Divinity.'   But these notions only concern the present life.   They believe that God has given them a religion different from ours, and if they are told of a future life they understand nothing about it.   With patience and time, however, something will be made of them."[12]

Always hopeful amid a thousand discouragements, and consumed with the zeal for the Kingdom of God, Father De Andreis seemed to be on the point of attaining his purpose.   In 1820 Bishop Du Bourg was preparing to visit "those immense forests," and Father De Andreis was invited to accompany him.

"Alleluia! Deo Gratias!" he wrote from the Barrens.   "At length we are to commence a mission among the savages.   I am to have the happiness of accompanying the Bishop to visit these unfortunate people!"

But these wishes were, as Father Rosati wrote, the last sparks of that flame of charity which burned within his heart, for he was soon to depart for heaven, for which he constantly sighed, that he might be united forever with his God.   Like St. Vincent, who was not able

[11] Rosati's *Life of Felix De Andreis*, pp. 179 and 180.

[12] Rosati's *Life of Felix De Andreis*, p. 193.     .

before his death to behold the establishment of his missionaries in the Island of Madagascar, for which he so ardently longed, and had made so many sacrifices; like St. Francis Xavier, who had to stop on the threshold of China without entering the kingdom, because God called him to Himself; so was Father De Andreis to see the Indian tribes, and to approach them, without having it in his power to liberate them from the hands of their ignorance. God destined others, after his death, to undertake this work.

## II. THE FIRST ATTEMPTS.

But what the saintly Dr. Andreis had dreamed of and longed and prayed for was soon to be attempted. On October 21, 1822, John M. Odin, then only in deacon's order, wrote from the Barrens to a friend, Mr. C., in regard to the earliest effort made from St. Louis for the conversion of the Indian tribes of the West:

We have the consolation of seeing a mission opened, or at least, begun, among the savages. Father Lacroix, chaplain to the Ladies of the Sacred Heart of Florissant, near St. Louis, has made two journeys to the great Osages. He was cordially received, and conceived great hopes of seeing the faith prosper among this tribe. Forty persons, children and old people, received the waters of baptism.

The second visit was short. He preached, however, before the entire tribe and the chiefs, answering, said that they were happy to hear the word of the Great Spirit. He pushed on further, also, along the banks of the Missouri, a hundred leagues beyond the nation of the Osages, among a great number of other savages. The fever, from which he suffered almost constantly, during this second mission, prevented him from prolonging his sojourn, and obliged him also to abandon his intention of building a church in this part of the country. The poor savages exist in great numbers.[14]

How this missionary undertaking came about is well explained by Father Michaud, who wrote the following account to the Vicar General of Chambéry in 1823:

In 1820 a number of chiefs of the Osage nation came to St. Louis by the order of the Indian agent. Sans-Nerf (principal chief of this nation) was at their head. They all visited our Bishop, whom they call the 'Chief of the Black Robes.' As they have a high opinion of him, and as respect for priests seems natural to them, since they know by tradition that 'Black Robes' visited their forefathers, they came in full dress. Their copper-colored bodies were coated with grease, their faces and arms were striped in different colors, white lead, vermillion, verdigris and other colors formed a great variety of furrows, all starting at the nose. Their hair was arranged in tufts. Bracelets, ear-rings, rings in their noses and lips completed their head-dress. Their shoes are made of buckskin which they ornament with different designs in feathers of various colors; hanging from their robes are little pieces of tin, shaped like small pipes. These are to them the most beautiful ornaments. Their great object is to make a noise when they walk or dance. Their heads are ornamented with a sort of crown in which are mixed up birds' heads, bears' claws and little stag horns. A woolen robe hung over the shoulders covers nearly all the rest of the body; and

13 Rosati's *Life of Felix De Andreis*, p. 205.

14 *Annales de l'Association de la Propagation de la Foi*, I, 2.

again, to this robe are fastened the tails of different animals, etc. Such is the attire in which the chiefs of the Osages paid their respects to the Bishop of Louisiana. He has in his room a handsome ivory crucifix, a small picture of St. Thomas and a few other paintings. The sight of the crucifix struck them with astonishment. They gazed at it, their expression wondering and softened. The Bishop profited by this occasion to announce to them Jesus Christ. 'Behold' (said he to them through the interpreter who accompanied them), 'behold the Son of the Master of Life, who came down from heaven to earth, who died for us, as much for the redskins as for the white skins. It was to gain our happiness that He suffered so much and that He shed all His blood. It is He,' added the Bishop, 'who has sent me here to make known to you His will.'

It is impossible, the Bishop said, to describe the attention that all these poor savages paid to him, and the emotion which they experienced when the interpreter repeated to them th words of the Bishop. They raised their eyes and their hands to heaven and then to the crucifix. All the spectators were moved by the scene. Before taking leave of the Bishop. Sans-Nerf said to him, through the interpreter, that if he wished to come and visit them in their homes he would be well received. that he could do a great deal of good, and that he could pour waters on many heads. The Bishop promised to do so, and presented each one with a little crucifix and also a medal which he hung around their necks by a ribbon, admonishing them to guard them carefully. They promised him to do so, and have kept their word.[15]

From a letter of John Odin, deacon, we add to Father Michaud's account the following anecdote:

Some time ago a great number of savages were in St. Louis. One of them was taken on some errand to a house where the Bishop happened to be. The moment he perceived the Bishop, he ran to him, seized his hand and kissed it with every demonstration of friendship. Having departed without remembering to go through the same ceremony, he recalled his mistake, only when already at some distance from the house. He turned back immediately, running all the way, and uttering loud cries, kissed the Bishop's hand and departed once more.[16]

Bishop Du Bourg, enthusiastic as he was, and of a romantic turn of mind, at once decided to assist the Osages himself, and De Andreis was to accompany him. But De Andreis died, and Bishop Du Bourg had so many calls on his time and talent, and cherished as many grand dreams that he soon decided to entrust the Osage Mission to one of his most excellent priests, Father Charles de La Croix,[17] as we have already stated in the words of the deacon, Odin. But the beginnings of a great undertaking, be they ever so humble, deserve to be remembered in all their details. We will, therefore, give entire the second part of Father Michaud's letter, which treats more fully of the events that transpired in the first Osage Mission:

In 1821 Father Lacroix set out to open the mission to the savages. On the occasion of his first visit, as they were about to depart on a hunting expedition, he could only see one village. He was very well received and baptized a great many children. As he had promised to visit all the villages of that nation of Indians, he was obliged to return last summer. He left Florissant, which is

---

[15] *Annales de l'Association de la Propagation de la Foi*, I, 5.

[16] *Annales de l'Association de la Propagation de la Foi*, I, 2.

[17] An excellent Sketch of the Life and Labors of Father Charles de la Croix from the pen of our of our indefatigable colaborer, Father F. G. Holweck may be found in the *St. Louis Pastoral Blatt*, vol. 53, No. 7 (July, 1919).

situated five leagues from St. Louis, on the 22d of July. After traveling twelve days on horseback across prairies, broken by forests and streams, he reached the first village which he had already visited in the spring. They were delighted to see him again. He was accompanied by several persons who intended to trade with the savages. All the warriors came to meet them.

"They were conducted, with great honor, to the head chief and invited to feasts, prepared by the savages, and so were kept going until evening, from cabin to cabin. At these repasts they were presented with a wooden dish, filled with boiled maize or buffalo meat (boeuf sauvage), but each dish had to be duly tasted.

The head chief and six of his principal warriors offered to accompany the missionary in his visit to the other villages. Ten days were passed thus, and the missionary was received everywhere with the same eagerness. At one of these villages more than a hundred warriors, covered from head to foot with their handsomest ornaments, came quite a distance to meet him. They rode finely trained horses. The occupations of the men are war and hunting. The women are very hard working. They it is who build the cabins, and who carry loads of firewood on their backs. The quantity they take at one time is astonishing. The whole nation is clothed, decently at least. Everyone is covered with a robe.

Polygamy is practiced among them, for it is the custom that when a savage demands a girl in marriage and is accepted, not only she, but all her sisters also belong to him and are looked upon as his wives. They pride themselves greatly upon having several wives. Another great obstacle to their civilization lies in their strong distaste for the cultivation of the soil and for all kinds of work. They care for nothing but war and hunting.

One day the missionary celebrated the Holy Sacrifice. All the chiefs were present and also as many savages as the place would hold. He has told me that he was greatly moved by the respectful attention which they showed, and the exactitude with which they rose and knelt, raising their arms and eyes to heaven. After Mass he distributed to all the chiefs a number of crosses, fastened to ribbons, which he threw around their necks. He also baptized several children.

For several years Protestant missionaries, sent out and well paid by the American government, had been settled among these savages, and had built up establishments where they cared for the children of this nation for a certain time. Buy they were not successful, and nearly a year ago the Indians took away all their children, saying that they had realized that they were not Black Robes, as they had thought they were at first.

The soil of this portion of Missouri is very fertile, and there are prairies six or seven leagues in extent. In summer the heat is excessive. It was during this journey that the missionary was attacked by burning fever, which forced him to leave the Osages. He was obliged to travel twelve days on horseback, sleeping at night in the woods, not coming across a single miserable cabin. This is how they go about arranging their camp. Having chosen the most suitable place, they unload and unharness the horses, which they let run loose in the woods that they may pasture during the night. They build a hut with the branches of trees, and having gathered wood they light a big fire. Over this they boil a piece of young buck placed on a stick planted before the fire, the meat being turned from time to time. This fire serves also to drive away bears and other wild beasts. After their repast, they roll themselves up in a buffalo skin and fatigue renders this poor bed very comfortable."[18]

### III. Help From Unexpected Quarters.

Father Michaud makes mention of several Protestant missionaries, sent out and well paid by the American Government, as settled among the savage Osage Indians. This fact brings before us the policy obtaining under the Presidency of James Monroe in regard to measures to be used for civilizing the savages. It was "the era of good

---

[18] Annales de l'Association de la Propagation de la Foi, I, 5.

feeling," and even the Indians were to share in its blessings. An assured appropriation of $10,000.00 had been made by Congress for the education of the government's wards. As Father Gabriel Richard,[19] member of Congress from Michigan, wrote to Bishop Edward Fenwick of Cincinnati in 1823:

> The President and Mr. Calhoun, the Secretary of the War Department, have expressed their willingness to aid in a particular manner those who will undertake the difficult task of civilizing and christianizing the Indians. I have enclosed to you two circular letters, which Mr. Calhoun gave me, expressly to send to you. The laws allow the President to spend yearly $10.000.00 for the purpose of aiding the schools that are or may be established for the instruction of young Indians. You will see that the whole is not to be done by the Government, a beginning must be made by the benevolence of some charitable persons. You will find by the enclosed papers that the Government is disposed to pay two-thirds of the expense of the necessary buildings. . . . In addition to this, Mr. Calhoun, the Secretary of War, told me yesterday that the Government, besides paying two-thirds of the expense for the buildings, will give $20 for every Indian child instructed, and for the number of thirty children $300.00."[20]

Of course, Bishop Du Bourg was at once made aware of this government offer and acted upon it, although we did not find anything more than an allusion to it in his own writings. We copy the letters from Bishop Fenwick's account of the "Progress of the Catholic Religion in the Western States of North America." The first circular of the War Department reads as follows:

DEPARTMENT OF WAR, *Sept.* 3, 1819.

Sir—In order to render the sum of ten thousand dollars annually appropriated at the last session of Congress for the civilization of the Indians, as extensively beneficial as possible, the President is of opinion that it ought to be applied in co-operation with the exertions of benevolent associations and individuals who may choose to devote their time and means to effect the object contemplated by the act of Congress. But it will be indispensable, in order to apply any portion of the sum appropriated in the manner proposed that the plan of education, in addition to reading, writing and arithmetic, should, in the instruction of the boys, extend to the practical knowledge of the mode of agriculture, and of such of the mechanic arts as are suited to the condition of the Indians; and in that of the girls, to spinning. weaving, and sewing. It is also indispensable that the establishment should be fixed within the limits of those Indian nations who border on our settlements. Such associations or individuals who are already actually engaged in educating the Indians, and who may desire the co-operation of the government, will report to the Department of War, to be laid before the President, the location of the institutions under their superintendence; their funds; the number and kind of teachers; the number of youths of both sexes; the objects which are actually embraced in their plan of education; and the extent of the aid which they require; and such institutions as are

---

[19] Father Gabriel Richard, one of the most versatile and energetic priests of the times. Besides his labors and hardships in the immediate service of Christ as a faithful priest, Father Richard was a prime mover in a number of important undertakings in the cause of civilization. He was one of the founders and first professors of the University of Michigan; then the publisher and editor of the first paper ever published in that State; and he enjoys the distinction, some think not a very enviable one, of being the only Catholic priest who was sent to Congress. Father Gabriel Richards' congressional laurels very probably prevented his receiving the mitre.

[20] The whole correspondence may be read in *American Catholic Historical Researches,* vol. X, No. 4, pp. 154-159, under the caption: An Account of the Progress of the Catholic Religion in the Western States of North America, London 1824. Ohio Mission.

formed, but have not gone into actual operation will report the extent of their funds; the places at which they intend to make their establishments; the whole number of youths of both sexes which they intend to educate; the number and kind of teachers to be employed; the plan of education to be adopted; and the extent of the aid required.

This information will be necessary to enable the President to determine whether the appropriation of Congress ought to be applied in co-operation with the institutions which may request it, and to make a just distribution of the appropriation.[21]

Additional regulations were issued by Secretary Calhoun on February 29, 1820, from which we will transcribe the main points of interest:

The position selected for this establishment (of schools for the education of Indian children), with an estimate of the costs, is to be submitted to the Secretary of War, to be laid before the President:

Government will. if it has the means, and approves the arrangement, pay two-thirds of the expense of erecting the necessary buildings. The President of the United States will contribute out of the annual appropriation to each institution which may be approved by him, a sum proportionate to the number of pupils belonging to each, regard being had to the necessary expense of the establishment and the degree of success which has attended it.

A report will be annually made for each establishment on the 1st of October. . . . It is considered to be the duty of all persons who may be employed or attached to any institution, not only to set a good example of sobriety, industry and honesty, but, as far as practicable, to impress on the minds of the Indians the friendly and benevolent views of the government towards them, and the advantage to them in yielding to the policy of the government and of co-operating with it in such measures as it may deem necessary for their civilization and happiness. A contrary course of conduct cannot fail to incur the displeasure of the government, as it is impossible that the object which it has in view, can be effected, and peace be habitually preserved, if the distrust of the Indians, as to its benevolent views should be excited.

(Signed) J. C. CALHOUN,[22]

Department of War, February 29, 1820.

Bishop Du Bourg was not slow in making use of this offer: In fact, he obtained more than was here promised. We again quote our deacon, John M. Odin, who from his position at the Barrens was well informed on what was transpiring in ecclesiastical circles. The letter is addressed to Director of the Seminary at Lyons, March 20, 1822:

"Bishop Du Bourg, en route for Baltimore, stopped at Washington to confer with the President of the United States, concerning the mission to the savages which he is planning to establish. The question was carried to the Senate, and although nearly all the members were Protestants, they resolved to grant a sum of money for the furtherance of this project. They promised, moreover, to pay a small pension to the missionaries, and to furnish them with the necessary agricultural implements. The savages themselves show the most favorable dispositions."[23]

From this it appears that a special appropriation was made for the specially difficult Western missions.

---

[21] Cf. Note 20.
[22] Ibidem.
[23] Annales de l'Association de la Propagation de la Foi, I, 5.

Bishop Du Bourg himself writes on this subject to his brother in Bordeaux March 17, 1823:

Providence deigns to grant a success to this negotion, far in excess of my hopes. The government bestows upon me two hundred dollars a year for each missionary and that for four or five men, and it promises to increase the number gradually, and I am sure that it will do so. For an enterprise such as this, it was essential that I should have men especially called to this work, and I had almost renounced the hope of ever obtaining such, when God, in His infinite goodness, has brought about one of these incidents which He alone can foresee and direct the results.[24]

The question of means was now settled, at least sufficiently to warrant further steps. But where shall the men be found best fitted for the arduous undertaking? Naturally, his thoughts often dwelt on the former glories of Jesuits in the neighboring Illinois. If he could obtain some members of the re-established Order, all would be well. But the prospects of such a piece of good fortune seemed very remote indeed. Lazarists he had in his diocese, but they were needed for the seminary and for the old parishes and missions. Secular priests, though willing, were not specially adapted for the work.

In a letter to his brother, dated January 30, 1826, Bishop Du Bourg sums up the results of his anxious meditations on this subject:

I had long been convinced that nothing could be accomplished here without the religious orders. A man living isolated from his kind grows weary of the apparent uselessness of his efforts. The intense heat exhausts his strength and checks his ardor. Too often he loses his life, or in the fear of losing it he abandons his post. He is fortunate indeed, if he does not prove the truth of those words of the Holy Ghost: "Woe to him who is alone!" and from a being, full of vigor and activity he becomes a good-for-nothing, and the scorn of his fellowmen. There is not the same danger for the religious community. Union makes strength of all kinds. Their members are constantly renewed and increased, hence they are able to provide for their own losses.

It is to this end that I have worked from the very beginning, to secure the help of the Order of Saint Vincent de Paul, and that I have made every effort to induce the Jesuits to come here, the former Order for the seminary, the latter for the Missouri missions, and more especially, for work among the Indians. The expense of all this has been great, but I am far from regretting it.[25]

As early as February 24, 1921, Bishop Du Bourg wrote to the Prefect of the Propaganda, Cardinal Fontana, asking His assistance in gaining the Jesuits for the work of converting the Indians, who, as he states, are very numerous in the upper part of his diocese. He was greatly aided by the Holy Father, who wrote to the Superior General with a view to endorse his wishes. But up to that date all efforts had proved unsuccessful.

"However," concludes Bishop Du Bourg, "I understand that the Superiors of the Society are now showing more willingness to undertake the work. I have accordingly recommended to Father Inglesi to make use of every resource his intelligence and zeal could muster, in order to bring this project to maturity. I beg

[24] *Annales de l'Association de la Propation de la Foi*, I, 5.

[25] *Annales de l'Association de la Propaganda de la Foi*, II, p. 394.

likewise Your Eminence to second his efforts. There is particularly one of the Fathers of the Society, *De Barat* by name, now in the Little Seminary of Bordeau, whom I know to be most anxious to come here; his piety, knowledge and zeal are beyond par. I beg most earnestly the Vicar General to give him to me, and beseech to this end the aid of Your Eminence's most powerful influence. With him some of the younger French Jesuits will be glad to come, and also others, of riper years, from among those who came lately from Russia to France. Five, or six at most, would be sufficient, if to them were added two or thrre from Maryland—a thing most desirable, on account of their knowledge of English, and also because, as they are well provided financially, they could supply the want of their brothers. With this help, the Gospel cannot fail to make headway among the numberless nations on both sides of the Mississippi and the Missouri.

Bishop Du Bourg's efforts in this regard were soon to be crowned with perfect success. There was at White Marsh, near Baltimore, a Novitiate of Jesuits; the Master of novices was Father Charles Van Quickenborne, a native of Ghent. The novices were Jodocus Van Ashe, Peter J. Verhaegen, John Elet, Smedts, Peter J. De Smet, Felix L. Verreyt and De Maillet. These young Belgians had been induced by the untiring zeal of Father Charles Nerinkx to go to America with him and to join the Society of Jesus.[26] They were accepted at Georgetown by the Provincial Father Anthony Kohlman, and began their novitiate on the 6th of October, 1821. In September, 1823, Bishop Du Bourg came to Georgetown to request from the Provincial a colony of Jesuits for the Indian Missions. Father Van Quickenborne and Father Timmermans, with the novices Van Asshe, De Smet, Verhaegen, Verreyt, Smeds, Elet and Brothers Peter De Meyer and Henry Rychmans, offered themselves for the enterprise. They left White Marsh about the middle of April, 1823, procured wagons for their luggage, crossed the Alleghany Mountains, reaching Wheeling after a journey of two weeks. Here the travellers procured two flatboats,, which they lashed together, and floated down the river to Louisville, where they met their beloved Father Nerinkx; thence they went down the Ohio as far as Shawneetown, and journeyed across the broad expanse of Illinois to St. Louis, which they reached May 30, 1823. That same evening Father Van Quickenborne rode on horseback to Florissant, accompanied by Father De La Croix. Here the Novitiate of St. Stanislaus[27] was founded by the advent of the pilgrims from White Marsh in Maryland. A letter written by Bishop Du Bourg to his brother at Bourdeaux, March 17, 1823, throws an interesting sidelight on this providential occurrence:

The Jesuts of whom I speak (says he) had their institution in Maryland, and finding themselves excessively embarrassed for lack of accommodation,

---

[26] Maes, *Life of Rev. Charles Nerinckx*, pp. 332-347. Howlett, *Life of Rev. Charles Nerinckx*, pp. 356-359.

[27] Florissant, or St. Ferdinand, is one of the very lodest religious centers in the State of Missouri. Originally settled by the French under the Spanish Regime about 1790, it became a dependency of the Canonical Parish of St. Louis under P. Bernard de Limpach; later on it had pastors of its own. From 1809-1810 it was the home of the Trappists under Abbot Urban Guillet, and for the next ten years remained in charge of the Father Prior, Maria Joseph Dunand. The farm on which the Jesuit establishment of St. Stanislaus was erected, was originally called the Bishop's Farm, now the Priest's Farm. The building put up by Father Dunand before 1820 is still in use.

were on the point of disbanding their novitiate, when I obtained this pecuniary encouragement from the government. They have seized this opportunity and have offered to transport the whole novitiate, master and novices, into Upper Louisiana and form there a preparatory school for Indian missionaries. If I had had my choice, I could not have desired anything better. Seven young men, all Flemings, full of talent and of the spirit of Saint Francis Xavier, advanced in their studies, about twenty-two to twenty-seven years of age, with their two excellent masters and some brothers; this is what Providence at last grants to my prayers.

Near the spot where the Missouri empties into the Mississippi, outside the village of Florissant, already so happy as to possess the principal institution of the Ladies of the Sacred Heart, I have a good yielding farm, excellent soil, which, if well cultivated (which it is not at present), could easily provide sustenance for twenty persons at least, so far as the important question of nourishment is concerned. True, there is only a small house on the place, but in this country a big cabin of rough wood, such as will be suitable for the apostles of the savages, is quickly built. It is there that I will locate this novitiate, which will be, for all time, a seminary especially intended to form missionaries for the Indians, and for the civilized and ever-growing population of Missouri. As soon as the actual subjects are ready, we will commence the mission in good earnest. In the meantime, I propose to receive in the seminary a half-dozen Indian children from the different tribes, in order to familiarize my young missionaries with their habits and language, and to prepare the Indians to serve as guides, interpreters and aides to the missionaries when they are sent to the scattered tribes [28]

On August 6th, 1823, Bishop Du Bourg resumes the subject so dear to his heart:

. . . . The acquisition which I have made of Jesuits for Missouri causes me to feel singularly peaceful about these distant parts. These good fathers are in possession of my farm at Florissant. To reach it they walked more than four hundred miles, of which two hundred miles were through inundated country, where the water was often up to their waists; and far from murmuring, they blessed God for granting them such an Apostolic beginning. They were very agreeably surprised, not expecting to find such a pretty place; for it is my policy to speak only of the drawbacks to those whom I invite to share my labors. The superintendent of Indian affairs, upon whom depends much of the success of our missions to the savages, received them with an interest both kind and active, and shows himself in an especial way, their protector. Moreover, the Fathers, including their novices, are well calculated to inspire confidence. An unlimited devotedness, which is proof against the greatest dangers and privations, is associated in them with rare goodness and talents of a high order. They complain of nothing, they are satisfied with everything. Living in the closest quarters in a little house, sleeping on skins for want of mattresses, living on corn and pork, they are happier than the rich on their down beds, surrounded by luxury, because they know happiness far more exquisite, and are not hampered by self-indulgence. It is my duty, however, to try to procure for them, at least the necessaries of life, and also the means of exercising their zeal and extending their field of labor. It is in this that I hope to be seconded by the Association for the Propagation of the Faith.[29]

Once more Bishop Du Bourg pours out the joy and gratitude of his heart in a letter from New Orleans, dated August 20, 1823:

In the midst of these trying cares (the seminary, the Cathedral, the religious houses and schools, and the demands of New Orleans), my thoughts were

---

[28] *Annales de l'Association de la Propagation de la Foi*, I, 5.
[29] *Annales de l'Association de la Propagation de la Foi*, I, 5.

ceaselessly and irresistibly drawn towards the totally abandoned missions of the natives. I needed for their re-establishment a band of apostolic men, men fearless of all sorts of privations and suffering. God has deigned· to give me men such as these, in· that society, as famous for its brilliant success as for its overwhelming reverses to which He grants a new birth, in these days, for the consolation of religion. A detachment of the Society of Jesus, animated by the spirit of Xavier and Regis, arrived some months ago in the state of Missouri. In order to draw them to me I could not refrain from buying a small cultivated domain, which might furnish them at least with the most pressing necessities· of life. This establishment which has cost me about thirty thousand francs, is intended· for a preparatory school for missionaries to the savages and also to the civilized peoples along the great Missouri River, the numbers of which are increasing with marvelous rapidity. It includes at the present two Fathers, seven fervent scholastics, all of whom are old enough to be ordained; three Brothers, and a few negro farm hands. The American government has promised me some small help, but it will be quite insufficient for their needs. To those ·chief institutions, already established, may be added a Cathedral, a farm and a bishop's mansion, at St. Louis, several new churches in the state of Missouri, two houses of the Ladies of the Sacred Heart already in running order, a third one in process of construction, and one of the Sisters of the Cross for the education of girls, and finally, two colleges for boys, for which I have had to make advances, or sacrifices, more or less great, without, in the meantime, having any sources of revenue other than the funds of divine Providence, and the hope of the yearly help which the Association for the Propagation of the Faith promises me.[30]

Good results came in due time. The Bishop writes on June 24, 1824:

. . . The Jesuits of Missouri have at last opened their college for the little Indians. They have only six or eight for whom the government allows them eight hundred dollars. They will take the college of St. Louis; in this way they will insure its stability. The poor Fathers are in great need."

And again January 31, 1826:

You can see by the letters of Father Van Quickenborne the progress made by the Jesuits in a very short time ,and with very small means. I have been unable to assist them as substantially as I would have liked, having still something to pay on the establishment which I have given them. As soon as this debt is discharged, if our brothers in Europe continue to help us as liberally as heretofore, I intend to spend a quarter, perhaps a third of these donations to aid the Fathers in their important work. They will also need more subjects, for the field which I have assigned to them is immense, but I believe that all will come in good time.[31]

Father Van Quickenborne now drew up, at the suggestion of the government, his plan for the improvement of the Indians. It was as follows:

1. Our little Indian seminary should continue to support the present number of boys from eight to twelve years of age, while the Ladies of the Sacred Heart in our neighborhood should bring up about as many girls of the same tribe. They should be taken young, from eight to twelve, to habitate them more easily to the customs and industry of civil life, and impress more deeply on their hearts the principles of religion.

---

[30] *Annales de l'Association de la Propagation de la Foi,* I, 5.
[31] *Annales de l'Association de la Propagation de la Foi,* I, 5 and II, p. 394.

2. After five or six years' education, it would be good that each youth should choose a wife among the pupils of the Sacred Heart before returning to his tribe.

3. Within two or three years two missionaries should go to reside in that 'nation to gain their confidence and esteem, and gradually persuade a number to settle together on a tract to be set apart by government. Agricultural implements and other necessary tools for the new establishment to be furnished.

4. As soon as his new town was formed some of the couples formed in our establishments should be sent there with one of the said missionaries, who should be immediately replaced, so that two should always be left with the body of the tribe till it was gradually absorbed in the civilized colony.

5. Our missionaries should then pass to another tribe and proceed successively with each in the same manner as the first.

6. As the number of missionaries and our resources increases, the civilization of two or more tribes might be undertaken at once.

The expense of carrying out this plan might be estimated thus:
Support of 16 to 24 children in the two establishments.........$1900
Three missionaries ............................................. 600

Total ...............................................\$2500[32]

"Such was the great scheme projected by the Jesuits of the West, never indeed to be realized, but, as their history shows, one which would have approached, if it did not obtain, complete success."

### IV. Missionary Efforts Under Bishop Rosati.

But whilst the Jesuit Fathers were slowly maturing their great missionary plans, the Lazarists, and even the secular clergy were called upon to take part in actual work of Christianizing the Indians. Joseph Rosati, the Superior of the Vincentians in America, was, on March 25, 1824, consecrated Bishop of Tenagra, and entrusted with the care of the Church in Upper Louisiana, that is Missouri, Arkansas, the Northwestern Territory, the vast Indian Territory, and the best part of Illinois. One of the new bishop's first acts (August 24, 1824), was to send Father John M. Odin, a newly ordained member of his Order, together with the deacon, John Timon,[33] on a missionary trip through Arkansas and Texas. It was on the 8th day of September, 1824, that the youthful messengers of God's Kingdom started out from the Barrens on horseback. From New Madrid, where they made their first stop, they penetrated through swamps and sparsely settled regions to the Arkansas River, near Little Rock. From there they rode down to Pine Bluff, and reached at last the ancient settlement so often

---

[32] Document in the Archives of the Catholic Historical Society of St. Louis.

[33] John M. Odin, C.M., born at Ambierle, in France, February 25, 1801, became a member of the Vincentian Order, was raised to the priesthood in 1824; after Rosati's elevation to the episcopate Odin became President of the Barrens; made Bishop of Claudiopolis and Vicar Apostolic of Texas in 1841; promoted to Archipiscopal See of New Orleans February 15, 1861. Died Ascension Day, May 25, 1870, in his native city. John Timon, C.M., born in Conewago, Pennsylvania, of Irish parentage, on February 12, 1797. Came to St. Louis and entered the Seminary of St. Mary's in April, 1823; ordained in 1825. Was a noted controversialist. Was appointed Visitor of the Lazarists in 1835, and Bishop of Buffalo, on September 5, 1847. He died on April 16, 1867.

mentioned in our early annals, the Post of Arkansas[34] at the confluence of the Arkansas River and the Mississippi. Here they visited the village of the Quapaw Indians. Father Odin celebrated the divine sacrifice on an altar erected at the entrance to the wigwam of the Chief Sarrasin

Now will I die happy, exclaimed the aged chief, who had seen the days of the early Jesuit missionaries at Arkansas Post, "now will I die happy, as I have seen my father, the Black Gown of France.[35]

Though all were pagans, they yet preserved an affectionate remembrance of the religion that had been preached to their fathers and then destroyed by evil-minded men. Owing to sickness and impassable roads the missionaries returned to the Barrens.

As early as 1823 a missionary center for the Indians of the North was planned at Prairie du Chien, at the mouth of the Wisconsin River. But the lack of priests, and later on, the widespread disturbances among the Indians, precluded the possibility of success.[36]

The Jesuits, as a matter of course, did not content themselves with their Indian schools at Florissant, but bravely launched out upon the deep to save what could be saved by individual endeavor. "To carry out his plans," says Shea, Van Quickenborne, in August, 1827, visited the old Osage Village, near Harmony, and in the house of the Presbyterian missionary, baptized ten, heard confession and said Mass, for many of the tribe were Catholics (since Father De La Croix's days). He then visited the villages on the Neosho, where, to the joy of the Indians, he spent two weeks and baptized seven of the tribe."[37] But a number of other important works awaited the zealous Father's care and labor, among them the formation of the great Western Institution of Learning, the St. Louis University, in 1828. The Church at St. Charles as well as the convent of the Ladies of the Sacred Heart at St. Charles were built by him. Yet the Indian missions were always present in his mind.

Another effort to bring the Indian nation into the pale of the Church was to be made by one of the secular clergy, the Reverend Anthony Lutz. It was early in May, 1827, that a delegation of the heathen Kanzas[38] Indians with their chief, White Plume, came to Gov-

---

[34] The Poste of Arkansas is one of the earliest settlements in the entire Mississippi Valley. Its religious history, however, was not always an edifying one, as Father F. G. Holweck has shown in his highly interesting sketch in the St. Louis Pastoral-Blatt,
Even in the earlier days of the old Jesuit missions the Poste bore a bad name for irreligion of the inhabitants. The last Jesuit priest withdrew from the place about 1760, "until they were disposed to respect religion there." Cf. Illinois Historical Collection, vol. I, p. 84.

[35] J. G. Shea, History of the Catholic Missions among the Indian Tribes, p. 454.

[36] Cf. Illinois Catholic Historical Review, vol. II, p. 190, s. s.

[37] Shea l. c. p. 457.

[38] The first mention of the Kansas or Kanzas tribe of Indians is that in Don Juan de Oñate's Account of his Expedition to the Great Plains in search of the elusive city of Quiviras, in 1601:
"Proceeding on the day of the glorious levite and martyr, San Lorenzo," Oñate's narrative states, "God was pleased that we should begin to see those monstrous cattle

ernor William Clark,[39] the Superintendent of Indian Affairs for the West, residing at St. Louis, for the purpose of obtaining Catholic missionaries. A Protestant preacher, who offered his services, was quickly rejected by the savages. General Clark sent the delegation to the Cathedral. Here Father Lutz heard of their wishes, and immediately decided to undertake the mission, if Bishop Rosati would consent. The Bishop was absent from St. Louis at the time, but when he returned, about September, Father Lutz gave him no rest, begging, opportune, importune, that the Kanzas mission be assigned to him. General Clark seconded the petition of Father Lutz, and as he was the most influential personage at the time in St. Louis, Bishop Rosati gave his consent, though somewhat reluctantly, partly on account of the youth and inexperience of the missionary, partly on account of the dearth of priests necessary for the care of the ever-growing Catholic population. The appointment was dated from the Barrens, July 23, 1828.

As you have manifested to us from the very first day of your coming to St. Louis your ardent desire of devoting yourself to the salvation of the indigenous tribes that wander through the forests of this vast diocese; and as Divine Providence seems now to open a way to the conversion of the nation called the Kansas, we, in accordance with your fervent wish, and knowing you well qualified as to the science, prudence and doctrine necessary for this undertaking, send you as messenger of the Gospel to the aforementioned people and appoint you as missionary of that and of the neighboring tribes, giving you the necessary faculties, *arbitrio nostro valituras*. In the meantime, we humbly pray the Supreme Pastor of Souls that He maydeign to accompany you on your journey with His all-powerful grace, sustain you in your undertaking and give abundant fruit to your labors.[40]

Father Lutz was only 26 years old when he set out for the land of the Kansas. Father Saulnier in his letter to Bishop Rosati expressed grave doubts as to the young man's qualifications. Not very robust physically, of a lively disposition, impatient of contradiction, and lacking in perseverance, Father Lutz, indeed, was not the man to make an ideal missionary among savages; yet, though his zeal outran his discretion, he certainly deserves credit for his good will and for the results obtained. On July 30, 1828, the young and enthusiastic

---

called *cibola* (buffalo). Although they were fleet of foot, on this day four or five of the bulls were killed, which caused great rejoicing. On the following day, we saw great droves of bulls and cows, and from there on the multitude which we saw was so great that it might be considered a falsehood by one who had not seen them . . .; and they were so tame that nearly always, unless they were frightened or chased, they remained quiet and did not flee."

Marching onward, the Spaniards came to the temporary villages of the roving Escanjaques (Escansaques) or Kansas Indians. "They were not a people that sowed or reaped, but lived solely on cattle (buffalo) meat," Oñate reports. "They were ruled by chiefs, and like communities that are freed from subjection to any lord, they obeyed their chiefs but little. They had large quantities of hides which, wrapped about their bodies, served as clothing; but the weather being hot, all the men went about nearly naked, the women being clothed from the waist down. Men and women alike used bows and arrows, with which they were very dexterous."

Cf. Fr. Zephyrin Engelhardt, O.F.M., in *Franciscan Herald*, March, 1920.

[39] Governor William Clark, the companion of Meriwether Lewis on the celebrated Journey of Exploration to the Rocky Mountains, 1804-1816. Brother of George Rogers Clarke, of Kaskaskia fame, and Superintendent of Indian Affairs until his death, which occurred in St. Louis September 1, 1838.

[40] Archives of Catholic Historical Society of St. Louis.

apostle of the Kanzas started, in company of the Indian Agent, Baronet Vasquez, and several others, for his destination near the mouth of the Kansas River. Baronet Vasquez was a Catholic. The great influence of this gentleman with the Indians seemed to insure the success of Father Lutz's mission. But before the end of the journey, early in August, Baronet Vasquez died and the good Father had to convey the sad news to the family of the departed. The Chouteaus had a great trading establishment on the Kansas River.[41] They, too, were Catholics and most of their employes also. Father Lutz speaks of the morals of these frontiersmen in rather harsh terms.[42] Of the savages his opinion was even worse, so much so that he declined for the present to confer baptism on any adult among them, saying "that they must first be made human beings, the members of Christ's body." As far as we know, Father Lutz sent three letters from the Kansas mission to Bishop Rosati. The first of these seems to be lost. It contained an account of the death of the Indian Agent, Baronet Vasquez. The opening sentence of the second letter, dated September 28, 1828, alludes to this unfortunate circumstance. Father Lutz's Latin letters are rather verbose, probably owing to the fact that elegant Latinity seemed most desirable in communications addressed to such an elegant Latinist as the Bishop of St. Louis certainly was. We would prefer the rugged English of a Lefevere. Yet this letter is of utmost importance and interest, and has never, as far as we are aware, been published except in the *Annals of the Propagation of the Faith,* Vol. II, September 18, 1829, in a somewhat abbreviated French translation. Our readers, we hope, will be pleased to have "the earliest record extant of the exercise of the Catholic ministry along the Kansas River," as Father Garraghan calls it, in a completed form: Absolute completeness even this version cannot claim; but the omissions we made are only of trivial matters or of more complimentary phrases, and are everywhere indicated by three dots.

*Territory of the Kansas Indians, on the river of the same name, Sept. 28, 1828.*
Right Reverend Father, Most Illustrious Prelate:

In my first letter, sent to Your Paternity at the end of August, I gave you the news of our agent's, Mr. Vasquez' death, and at the same time I explained to you the singular condition in which Divine Providence has placed me, happily or unhappily, I cannot decide; you may judge for yourself. This one thing, however, seems certain, that I have earned many things to the advantage of my soul, which, if Mr. Vasquez had lived, I should have experienced not at all or very late. The name of the Lord be blessed. Through the death of this one man my affairs had assumed such a hopeless aspect that it became necessary for me to cast myself entirely into the arms of the all-controlling Father, just as a child casts itself upon the bosom of its mother; a course exactly befitting one

---

[41] "The Chouteaus," as Father Garraghan states in his beautiful booklet, 'Catholic Beginnings of Kansas City,' "were the most prominent of the early Indian traders in the region around the mouth of the Kaw," p. 47, giving as references in regard to the various Chouteau trading houses an article in *Kansas Historical Collection,* No. 9, pp. 573-574.

[42] The letters of Father Lutz from the country of the Kansas contain a few scathing denunciations of treacherous, lying and stealing white trash he met on his excursions. Of the Chouteaus themselves he speaks in the highest terms of respect.

who has accepted the Lord as his inheritance and the chalice of salvation, and now realizes that he has come to that part of his grand office to be the messenger of Christ the Lord, sent out by Him into the wide world, without scrip or staff. But these usual accompaniments of the lives of Christ's missionaries, have been sufficiently dwelt upon in my first letter; if perhaps more than proper, I would ask your pardon for the beginner, who at that time had not learned to bear the glorious cross of Christ in silence, without the noise of many words, but is now learning, through the grace of God, to think little of all these things, however burdensome they be, as long as Christ is preached to the poor. May the Lord preserve this good will and greatly strengthen it. Now I will briefly explain what has been done so far, what must yet be done, and why I have not sent a letter ere this, all which matters I know you wish to know.

You Grace must realize that, owing to the great distance between the setlements here, it is very difficult to send letters from this country. The agent's house, where I fixed my residence. is on the banks of the Kansas River sixty-five miles from the former home of the late Mr. Vasquez.[43] The little towns, however, which supply mailing facilities, are more than fifteen miles away. Therefore, when we wish this thing to be done, we have either to take our letters there ourselves or send them by a trusted mssenger. One of these towns is named Liberty, the other Independence. The latter town is situated on our side of the Missouri River, the former on the opposite side. . . The town of Liberty I was not as yet able to visit, but in a little while I can and must do so, as I am resolved to see the entire surrounding region. Independence I have visited but once, and at times I have sent messengers there for my mail, if there was any. Camp Leavenworth, which is 35 miles from our home, has no service of public conveyances, so that its inhabitants are forced to send their mail to Liberty. a distance of 36 miles. Considering these facts, you will certainly not blame me if you should fail to receive a letter from me. . . In regard to this preliminary visit to the country of the Indians, it must be confessed that it was altogether necessary. I myself feel deeply its various advantages. I will relate them briefly: It is there I began to learn the very alphabet of apostolical life, to accustom the body to its hardships, and to put a correct estimate on the greatness as well as the excellence of my office; then to know the Indian ways of living, their mode of feeling and their superstitions, the various conditions of these regions and the distance between places; to understand the characters of the various persons with whom I certainly or probably may have to live, to decide what persons should be consulted, what persons avoided by me, who of them are of good will, who of evil disposition. I also learned the pecularities of the Kansas dialect, wherein it seemed different from our idioms, and what special difficulties it offered; lastly, I was helped to decide where the missioners' residence should be established, what provisions could be made for their sustenance, and what matters we should lay before the civil authoritis. I hope and wish that an occasion may be offered when I can speak to you about these matters. Now permit me to recount in detail how my time in these parts was passed. I departed from St. Louis on July 30th; on August 12th I arrived at the former home of Mr. Vasquez, the Indian agent, where I remained five days before starting for the Kansas River; on August 19th I reached the house erected by the government on the banks of the Kansas River. On August 20 I had the first interview with the chief of the Kansas nation; on August 24, I, together with an interpreter, visited the family of the chief and other families, sixteen in number, living only about two miles from our stopping place; and this I did several times. On September 17th I obtained my fervent wish of organizing a meeting with the barbarians. On September 18th, I set out for Camp Leavenworth, where I remained six days, certaainly longer than I had intended. On October 1st I will return to the home of Mrs. Vasquez, as I find no means of subsistence here, and the Kansas tribe, with the exception of three families, has already gone on its hunting excursion. These things, here mentioned in a general way. you may be pleased to read at greater length. The house of the agent, Vasquez, on the

---

[43] Barunet Vasquez, son of Benito Vasquez, of St. Louis, was of Spanish extraction.

banks of the Missouri River, was heretofore considered the meeting place of the Indians, but now, after his death, the visits of the Indians are becoming less frequent, the house of the new agent having been established elsewhere, I believe on the Kansas River. The widow Vasquez still resides at the old house. She is a matron of great piety. She has a small family, but a well-educated one; she takes good care of me, almost as if I were one of the children of the household, providing me with the necessaries of life on my journey; she shines forth with good example in frequenting the sacraments and practicing devotion; and she edifies her family with her virtues. Not so the other Catholics, alas! that live in the neighborhood. They are "slothful bellies," not much different from the Cretans, addicted to drink and much talking, ignorant, to pass over in silence the rest of their vices. I except two or three persons from this charge. Some of them live with Indian concubines, refusing the grace which is offered to them by my ministry. Only two could I prevail upon to dismiss their concubines and contract in legitimate marriages. The third one tried to deceive me, but in vain. . .

I leave this corner of the earth with no small regret, but I feel a stronger impulse towards the Barbarians, and I desire to arrive among them as early as possible, as it is to be feared that, through a longer delay I might find the chief of the nation (Nombe-ware,[44] i. e., the Furious, or Moushouska, White Plume), no longer among the living. Having been ailing for a long time he began to carry things to extremes, and that is a two-fold manner. Indignant at the evils that had befallen him, White Plume, armed with a pistol, rushed forth and threatening death to God, directed a shot towards heaven, exclaiming, "Oh, would that I had destroyed thee this time for having sent so many evils to my family and to my whole nation!" (During the past year about 180 of the Kansas tribe, together with the chief's principal wife, two sons and many other members of his family, were taken by death). As White Plume's illness became worse, he repented of his word and deed and earnestly asked forgivenesss from Heaven. But God delayed hearing the prayer of the sick man and willed that the barbarian should begin to improve in health only two days before my advent. White Plume was hardly notified of my coming when he gathered all his strength and had himself placed on a horse, in order to welcome the Taborco[45] (the name by which he always addressed me). I was greatly surprised at seeing him enter my room, especially as rumors were current that he had died. I ran to meet him, and as he seemed to stagger, I supported him with my hand, offered him a chair and pressed his proffered hand. He that was wont to speak with stentorian voice now gave forth such a gentle whisper that the meaning of his words could hardly be gathered by the interpreters: "O, my Father, you are welcome. At last you are here whom I have so long desired. I am happy; but I would rejoice still more if I could celebrate your coming in perfect health. May the Great Healer (Washkanta) ,I pray, restore my health. It is my intention to assist you in all things that you wish to do among the Kansas. My only son (the others had all died), I will send to be educated by you as soon as you have a home. In the same way all the chiefs of our nation in my obedience shall act towards you. How long will you stay with us? When will you have a house? Remember this: Do not have your house too far away from mine. The nearer it is the more it will please me, so that I may consult with you in the government of the

---

[44] White Plume, or the Furious, it will be remembered, had been in St. Louis early in May, 1827, to ask for a missionary for his people. In St. Louis he met a number of the clergy, probably also Father de la Croix, the future missionary to the Osages. Washington Irving, in his "Adventures of Captain Bonnville, U. S. A., in the Rocky Mountains and the Far West," gives a pleasant account of the old chief in 1832; when White Plume gave proofs of having acquired some of the lights of civilization from his proximity to the whites, as was evinced in his knowledge of driving a bargain. He required hard cash in return for some corn with which he supplied the worthy captain, and left the latter at a loss which most do admire, his native chivalry as a brave, or his acquired adroitness as a trader." Irving, Captain Bonnville, ch. II. From the same account it appears that the Kansas had begun to raise corn, but had not left off their hunting excursions. White Plume was still inhabiting the great stone house on the Kansas River, "a palace without a wigwam within," as Irving says. The Kansas were still at war with the Pawnees.

[45] The Tabosco is the Kansas word for Black Gown, or Black Robe, meaning the Catholic priest. "Washkanta," also Wakonda, is the Great Spirit.

Kansas. I am not able to talk with you very long to-day, my voice having become so weakened; but I am expecting our hunters, who will bring me buffalo meat, with which I can regain strength." Knowing full well what authority this great chief wielded among his people and how necessary it was for the prosperous course of my undertaking, I determined to leave no stone unmoved in order to restore his health. I wanted to give him medicine, to keep him in my house and to take watchful care of the sick man, but prudence objected to all those things; if he should die using my medicines this whole wild and superstitious nation would blame me. The two interpreters, who stood by, seemed to hint at the same time. I, therefore, superseded the medicine with a goblet of rich wine, after drinking which the chief said that it had warmed his stomach, and begged earnestly that after a few days I should send him another specimen of the same medicine. This I readily promised to do.

Returning home he sent ten messengers, men and women, in various directions, to meet the hunters and to announce the coming of Tabosco. They smoked in honor of Tabosco on the whole journey, they sang and shouted for joy. At last the inhabitants of the four villages arrived from their long journey and brought heaps of buffalo meat. White Plume overflows with vigor, enjoying as perfect health as he did when he was most robust. Two chiefs brought me a very large portion of buffalo meat, and they stood wondering at me eating of it, although it was not cooked. "Behold," one said, "Tabosco has no aversion to us. He is not squeamish and delicate, as the Fathers of the Osages," meaning thereby the Protestant missionaries). "Do you not see in his eyes how he loves us, how affable he is," said one to another in a low voice. They desired to spend the night in my bedroom, and I readily obliged them. Like two satellites they enclosed me, lying on the floor in the middle of my room, one on my right side, the other on my left. With great big eyes they looked at me performing my morning prayers. They hardly dared to breathe. Having returned home the next day, White Plume visited me once more. But he now spoke in loud tones, talking much of his joy and that of the entire tribe and asking many questions. He enquired attentively of Tabosco, what is the purpose of his mission, what are the causes which led him to stay with them four months of this year, what education he would give the children, and what obedience would be required. At last I suggested that I desired very much he should, as opportunity offered, convoke the other Kansas, to whom I could then explain the things I had at heart. He answered that this could hardly be done before the middle of September, because not all would be back from their hunting excursion before that time. It would seem more satisfactory, he said, to select the time when they would come together for the government's annual distribution of gifts. I acquiesced and dismissed the man. I then began to cut the timbers and to adorn the chapel. When I had finished this work I took care to examine the country and to consider what I must build if I should happen to come to reside here. White Plume now visited me for the third time: "Write," he said, "to Red Hair (General W. Clark),[46] that as Vasquez is dead, he should send us another agent who will properly attend to our affairs. We do not want an American. We ask for a Frenchman, certainly none other than Cyprian or Francis Chouteau. The five other chiefs of the Kansas are likewise in favor of these two. Sign my name and the names of these, and urge at the same time your own undertaking, so that you can more easily and more quickly come to stay with us. I have great hopes that our nation will, by your help, be shortly changed for the better."

I wrote immediately commending their request and my own to the governor and, impatient of delay, I expected the new agent from day to day. And, behold, there arrived Mr. Dunnay McNair,[41] a youth of about twenty years sent by

---

[46] In 1832 a brother of the General Clark of Columbia River fame was Indian Agent among the Kansas, as successor to Vasquez and Dunnay McNair. Cf. *Bonneville's Adventures,* ch. II.

[47] Dunning McNair, son of the first Governor of Missouri, Alexander McNair, was a Catholic, although his father probably never became affiliated with the church. Cf. Edward Brown's Sketch of the Life of Alexander McNair, in *St. Louis Catholic Historical Review,* vol. I, p. 231 s. s.

Governor Clark, who has no little confidence in the young man. He is to take the place of the agent with the Kansas. Governor Clark, having been advised by me of the death of Mr. Vasquez, had immediately appointed him, not having as yet received my first letter. The young man is a Catholic of good morals, and endowed with sufficient knowledge, sincere and prudent, a friend and defender of religion, most attentitve to his work, and friendly to me. We do not yet know whether he will be agent with full power or not. He helps me very much by his authority and his kindness. He frequently says that nothing is to be despaired of (*nil desperandum*), under the auspices of Governor Clark, who really takes great interest in the success of the mission, and he assures me that the sale of thirty-six sections of land will certainly be held in the month of October or November, and then our work could be begun. The vice-agent requested White Plume to call an assembly of the Indians, telling them that he wished to explain some matters to them in council. The messengers go out and call together the warriors of four of the villages. The third day after the call had gone out about two hundred and forty Indians from the surrounding country come there and listen to what the vice-agent might proclaim. For the whole day the Kansas remain in session. The medals are distributed and the laws and the treaties are explained, the thieves are whipped, and the cultivation of the land is urgently recommended, and the permanent location in one village is demanded. The Tabosco is presented to them. The annual distribution is promised when the Kansas shall assemble at Fort Leavenworth, and many other things are approved. The barbarians agreed with almost everything except the plan of permanently locating in one village, and abandoning their hunting life. Rumors, clamors and complaints arose, but in vain. With all my strength I urged the necessity of the matter contained in the first point (uniting the tribe in one village), and I argued against the foolish and destructive plan adopted by them, to remove their home a hundred and fifty miles from our house. (This, a large party among them had decided on, against the wishes of White Plume, at the very time that they returned from their hunting grounds, and had seen for the first time the elegant place offering such various conveniences). They now understand how proper and useful it would be to unite in one village, where all their tents should be fixed. The place selected at a distance of about one day's journey, was approved by all with the exception of a few stiff-necked people, who, however, have to follow the crowd. After having visited, as I hope to do, the four villages, I will examine the proposed location and describe it in my next letter. The agent now having finished what he wished to propose, I arose and demanded in a loud voice that all should remain the next day also, as I had some things to announce to them. The next day at 8 o'clock all were gathered in the chapel, which is as large as the study hall in St. Louis College. They all assembled at the ringing of the bell. Those present were the new agent, two interpreters, three other Catholics; a large altar, beautifully ornamented, the picture of the Blessed Virgin Mary in the middle of the altar, on the right side a large crucifix, on the left a picture of the sorrowful Virgin of the same size. The Tabosco, clad in his sacred vestments, gravely walked from his chamber and entered the chapel. All genuflect, the *Veni Creator* with the oration is intoned. High Mass is sung. At the consecration all are commanded to bend the knee, there is deep silence. After the Mass all sit down. Tabosco stands at the epistle side and preaches. After every sentence the barbarians exclaim "How!" That is, "Good!" It would take too long to repeat word for word what I said; let it suffice that I preached on the purpose of my coming and mission, on the desire of my heart to procure the salvation of all the Kansas, on the One God and His attributes, making no mention, for the present, of the Trinity, on God the Creator and Giver of all good, on the human soul being immortal, on God the Judge and Rewarder, on the eternal fire, and the joys of Heaven, on sin and the sins in particular, to which the Kansas are specially addicted, or the necessity of hearing Tabosco's preaching, on the obedience due to him, on Christ the Lord crucified, on the gratitude to God, who is now offering to them his grace in abundance; lastly, on the education of their children, to be undertaken by us, on the raising of the Holy Cross among them, and on the visits to be made to the four villages, and the children to be baptized. These are in brief the things which I had explained to them in our first meeting. The ceremony concluded with the canticle *'Benedictus Dominus Deus Israel'* and the 'Our Father' and the 'Hail Mary.' The Canticle pleased them very much. Their tears flowed in the presence of the Crucified Lord. They repeated to one another what they had heard, one the things concerning heaven, the other the things concerning hell. another the. sufferings of Christ. "Ah," exclaimed White Plume, "how I was enlightened to-day!" "Wazzeche, wazzeche," that is, how good to have a Tabosco! others exclaimed. But I sigh; give me souls, O Jesus; may thy kingdom come. As regards the baptism of the infants, it is very much desired by the Kansas. This reason, besides others, moved me to promise then in public not to return to St. Louis before I had baptized all the little ones; especially as so many of them have died since the time I came here. Indeed, an old man, when dying, asked day and night, to see the Tabosco, in order to receive baptism. He was deprived of baptism by a sad circumstance and died, leaving to his relatives his anxieties about their future state and the punishments to be undergone by them unless they were willing to receive the salutary waters. Certainly, a firm faith in this sacrament, forcing others also to believe in it. At the time when this Indian called me I was detained at Fort Leavenworth. After the death of the old man the family asked me what I thought concerning his doom. Having given the proper answer I sent the greatly relieved inquirers home.

Perhaps Your Paternity will ask, why I have not already made my home in the country of the barbarians. This I had certainly wished to do and already fixed the day on which I should undertake the journey with an interpreter, but the contrary seemed to be more advisable on account of the celebration of certain feasts, which occupy the barbarians for the space of two weeks, and which are the occasion of great tumult, drunkenness and strife. I preferred to postpone the visit rather than expose my dignity to insult. I take great care to preserve the authority of my person, never tolerating even the least thing contrary to the respect due to me. In the beginning some loose women of the barbarians began to uncover their bodies immodestly in my presence, to whom I said indignantly that they should cover themselves or go away. On another occasion, when I happened to see some immodest women lying on the floor of our house, surpassing the former ones in looseness, I took to flight and requested the interpreter to report the matter to White Plume, which. having been done, I never had another similar experience.

Two warriors have been assigned to me, to be at my service, but only when I am exercising my religious functions. It is their office to preserve order and silence whilst I say Mass or preach, to accompany me and to close the door, and call the people to church by ringing the bell. This is considered a great honor and much desired by many. Having explained to them their duties, I promised to give each one a little cross when I should return from St. Louis. The name of the one is "Tatsche Sagai" (Wild Wind); of the other, "Nikananseware" (Exterminator of Men). Let me add a few words on the location of the buildings erected by the government on the banks of the Kansas River. Fancy a valley, half a league wide and long, with five large houses, of which one is for the agent of the nation, the second for the interpreter, the third for the blacksmith, the fourth for the farming expert, the fifth, built of stone, is for White Plume. The first four follow one another in a straight line. the fifth is two miles farther on. As to the mission house, I intend to build it where the air is purer, if this be agreeable to the Governor and to the other members of the mission. The soil is most fertile; there are many forest patches all around, but not too many; but the salubrity of the air is not the same everywhere. Every newcomer is forced to pay tribute to the bilious fevers and chills obtaining here. In all these parts around the Missouri and Kansas Rivers there is nothing more usual than that the new settler is attacked by fevers, headaches and pains of the stomach. I for myself had the bilious fever five days; after that I felt well and had an insatiable appetite. The air at Camp Leavenworth is even worse.

Just now there are at least one hundred persons there on the sick list. I went there with the vice-agent (McNair), the interpreter, and 108 of the Indians, to attend the annual distribution of gifts to the tribesmen. At first I felt very well; on the third day I myself and Mr. McNair had to fight against an attack of chills and fever for the space of four days. Here I heard the confessions of two soldiers, one an Irishman and the other a Frenchman; I baptized six infants and comforted the sick. I will go there once more in the beginning of November, to baptize a number of the infants of the officers and to perform the other religious functions. I was received with the highest honors by the officers, who invited me to their mess, and in the evening entertained me with military music. I have distributed various books, of which I have a great number, treating of the Truth of the Catholic Faith. There is a murderer in the prison, soon to suffer the death penalty. I will try to convert the doomed man and to prepare him for death. I have baptized at other places and at different times 28 infants, and shall baptize many more.

Of the other Indian nations I have visited only the Shawneons, who seem to be more intent on acquiring temporal goods than those that will last forever. Their time seems not yet come. Nevertheless, I will try again and see if an opening can be made there. It would, indeed, be gratifying if I could win to Christ this tribe, living along our way in elegant houses. An invitation to visit the Iowa tribe, about 60 miles from our house, was extended to me by their agent, General Us, who also promised to do what he could to provide shelter and food for me, if I should decide to take up my abode with his nation. The next neighbors of the Iowas are the Ottawas, who use about the same language. This journey cannot possibly be made, that is, at present, because the agent is now absent from home, to return to those tribes only about the middle of November. The gifts you intended for White Plume I have delivered and thereby given great pleasure to the chief. The barbarity and superstition of the Kansas tribe is too great to find ready belief. Therefore, I am in no hurry to admit any adult to holy baptism. They must first be made human beings, then members of Christ's body. . . .

To-morrow I will go to the home of Mrs. Baronette Vasquez to prepare her several daughters for First Holy Communion and instruct the faithful in the duties of Christian life. . . .

I kiss your paternal hand, the hand of our Common Father. Your most obedient son, JOSÉPH ANTHONY LUTZ,
Missionary Priest with the Kanzas.

This letter held out great hopes for the imminent conversion of the Kansas Indians; yet the work seemed beyond the power and endurance of our man. Father Lutz, White Plume's Tabosco, never returned to the promising field. On November 12, 1828, he wrote his last letter *Ex Agro Kanzas Rivi* to his beloved bishop. It contains only a few points of minor interest. The reasons for his premature return to St. Louis are an early and probably very severe winter, and the hopelessness of achieving any good in the unknown and pathless country. The Kanzas had promised to return home by the end of October, and had even now, November 12, given no sign of fulfilling their promise," thus making it doubtful whether the Tabosco could administer baptism to all their children before his departure for St. Louis." It seemed they were purposely delaying their home-coming. It would, therefore, be their own fault if their children should not receive the sacrament of regeneration. As to the mission-cross, I will in any case, erect and bless it, if not solemnly, then privately, in the presence of some of the Kansas.

The last month he had spent at the home of Mrs. Vasquez, teaching, preaching, baptizing, hearing confessions and saying Mass. "Visiting the town of Liberty, he found but one Catholic in the whole place, the wife of Dr. Curtiss, a native of St. Louis." His attempts to visit Fort Leavenworth once more was frustrated by his guide, who left him, *media in via,* so that he had to return home. Messrs. Francis, Cyprian and Frederick Chouteau were putting up a grand building on the Kansas River, which would serve as the Emporium, or trading post, for all the Shawneons and Kansas. "Francis Chouteau treats me very kindly and promises me his continued support," Father Lutz concludes his last letter from the Kansas River. His missionary attempt was but a faint promise of the greater things to come.[48]

### V. JESUIT MISSIONS IN THE INDIAN TERRITORY.

The ancient glories of the Jesuit Missions of the Illinois were to be renewed in a measure beyond the great river, far to the west; but the rise and progress of this new effort is intimately connected with certain dishonorable dealings of our government, State and national, in regard to the nations that once possessed the land from ocean to ocean. Treaty upon treaty was made and broken with disastrous consequences, until the Indian has almost vanished from the face of the earth. "A Century of Dishonor" is the title of the book that treats of our broken faith with the Indians. It is a sad story, but well worth our attention. As we proceed in our sketch we will meet with a few examples of our burning shame.

"The government of the United States," says an elegant writer, probably Father O'Hanlon, in the November number, 1843, of the *Catholic Cabinet* of St. Louis., "having deemed it good policy to concentrate the aborigines of the country, commonly called Indians, assigned for this purpose a territory, beyond which, within a distance of 1500 miles, no suitable habitation for white men can be made. This Indian territory is bounded by the States of Missouri and Arkansas towards the east, by the so-called American desert on the west; by Texas on the south, and by the Missouri and Platte rivers to the north. It has been assigned as the permanent abode of the various Indian tribes scattered throughout the Union. The Pawnees, Omahas, Kanzas, Osages and Missourians roamed at large over the lands of this territory, before this plan was adopted by our government, which as a necessary consequence of the new appropriation, was obliged to confine them within certain limits; and to persuade them to cede part of their lands to their red brethren east of the Mississippi. In consequence of this arrangement the Choctaws, Chickasaws, Cherokees. Creeks, Seminoles, Senecas, Pottowatomies, Ottawas, Chippewas, Otoes, Miamis, Shawanees, Delawares, Kickapoos, Iowas, and Foxes, emigrated—some by force, others by persuasion, but all most unwillingly from the various States of the Union to the respective portions of the territory assigned to them by the U. S. Government. The original inhabitants of this territory are called the indigenous tribes. and are savage and wretched to the extreme; the emigrant tribes are more or less civilized, according to the different relations they have had with the settlers of the States. The whole number of the Indians of this territory amounts to about 80,000 souls. With regard to their numbers, it may be observed that they appear gradually to decrease, owing to their inordinate mode of living, their vicious habits, the unsuitableness of the soil, the change of air by emigration, etc. So that they may be said, in the language of the Prophet Osee, "to disappear as early dew that passeth away—as the dust that is driven with a whirlwind out of the floor—and as the smoke out of the chimney (c. 13, v. 3).

[48] Archives of the Catholic Historical Society of St. Louis.

It is true that the emigrant tribes have some civilization; but, generally speaking, with all the vices of the white men, they have brought few or none of their virtues over to the Indian wilds.

Many efforts at converting these unhappy children of the wilderness had been made, as we have seen, and were being made by the representatives of various Christian denominations; but these divisions and consequent dissensions proved the chief stumbling block to their success. Our author continues:

The state of our Holy Religion is truly deplorable among these unhappy people. Almost all the tribes are in favor of Catholic missioners, and feel a kind of natural aversion to Protestant preachers. And yet, in the absence of the former the latter are almost everywhere to be found; and the whole territory has about 30 Protestant missionary establishments. But every plantation not made by the hand of the Father shall be rooted out. Vain are the efforts of these unsent apostles to make proselytes among the Indians. They may, indeed, scatter hundreds of Bibles among the savages; but these are neither prized nor understood. The principle that faith is to be conceived by the Bible—and by the Bible alone—proves quite incomprehensible to the illiterate and savage mind; and the consequence is that all the Protestant congregations of the Indian territory do not amount to 500 souls.

While a few of the Indians, whose devotion is bought and paid for, like any other marketable commodity, are nominal adherents to Protestantism; while thousands daily worship their Manitos and indulge in all the execesses of unbridled licentiousness; the voice of the Catholic Church is almost unheard, except on the banks of Sugar Creek, tributary stream of the north fork of the Osage River. We would, however, willingly indulge the hope that within a few years a line of Catholic Missions may be established from the Missouri River down to Texas—a plan by no means difficult of execution, and one which would be of incalculable advantage to religion. The field is large and the harvest promising, but the laborers are by far too few.[50]

These fond hopes, held out in 1843, were not realized, owing to the rapid changes in the political and social conditions of these regions, as well as to the vices and weaknesses of the Indians themselves. Yet great efforts were made by the Church and untold good was accomplished in behalf of the Indians, as our author shows:

Twenty years ago the zealous Bishop of Upper and Lower Louisiana, Louis William Valentine Du Bourg, directed the views of his ever active zeal towards the unfortunate Indians, especially the Osages. With the co-operation of the Rev. Charles Van Quickenborne, then Superior of the Jesuits of Missouri, two schools were opened for Indian youths in the township of Florissant, near St. Louis; the Indian boys were placed under the charge of the Jesuits, and the girls under that of the Ladies of the Sacred Heart. To enable them to succeed in this undertaking, the reverend gentlemen under whose care the schools were placed, applied to the government for a moderate annual income from the sum annually appropriated for the civilization of the Indians. This request was readily complied with, but the greatest obstacle to success was found to consist in the unwillingness of the Indian youth to quit their parents' home, their sports and their games, and to go to a distant place for the purpose of acquiring the learning which they so little valued. It was soon discovered that to establish missionary stations among the Indians in their own country would be a more successful and less difficult enterprise. In consequence, this having been deter-

[49] *Catholic Cabinet*, St. Louis, vol. I, p. 406.
[50] *Catholic Cabinet*, vol. I, p. 407.

mined on, the Rev. Charles de la Croix, then missioner in the State of Missouri, now a Canon Regular in Ghent, set out on a visit to the Osages—one of the most savage of the Indian tribes. His efforts were blessed with success, and records now before us prove that the number of children baptized by him on that occasion was very large and the number of marriages he blessed not inconsiderable. Shortly after he was followed by the Rev. C. Van Quickenborne, who also visited the Osage nation, and who was particularly successful in inducing the chiefs and headmen of the tribe to send their sons and daughters to St. Louis County. The schools, composed of Osage, Iowa and Iroquois youths, flourished for a few years, but were finally broken up, in consequence of the complaints of their parents, on seeing their children separated from them by such a distance, as also of the disinclination of the young Indians to bend under the yoke of discipline.[51]

The first idea of Father Van Quickenborne to convert the tribes by separating the children from the parents during the most pliant years of their lives and instructing them in the practice of the true religion and in the ways of civilized life, having proved impracticable, at least on a larger scale, the old Jesuit plan of establishing missionary centers among the Indians, with churches, schools, and a kind of paternal authority, even in civil matters, was taken up and carried forward with gratifying results. We will quote the final chapter of the account as contained in the *Catholic Cabinet*:

In 1835 the Rev. Father Van Quickenborne paid a missionary visit to the Miamis, on the north fork of the Osage River. They are the small remnants of four once powerful nations, the Kaskaskias, the Peorias, the Weas and the Piankeshaws. He was received by them with great joy; and many of them, having been baptized in their infancy by the priests who attended the old French villages in Illinois, showed unfeigned readiness to enroll themselves anew under the standard of the cross. They seemed to be indifferently pleased with the Methodist station, established among them, and willingly promised to return to the faith of their fathers, among whom the Jesuit missionaries had so successfully labored during the early part of the last century. An old woman, whose gray hair and bent-up form showed that she had belonged to by-gone times, crawled up to the missionary, grasped his hand with a strong expression of exultation, and pronounced him to be a true black gown, sent to instruct her hapless and neglected nation. She had lived at least a score of winters longer than any other of her tribe, but yet she distinctly remembered to have been prepared for her first communion by one of the Jesuits who attended the flourishing mission of Kaskaskias. His name she could not bring to mind, but described his dress and features in a manner to show what a deep impression this recollection of her early youth continued to make on her mind. She also gave a description of the old church of Kaskaskia; recited her prayers and sang a Canticle in the language of the tribe. She told the missioner that her constant prayer had been that her tribe, now exiled and almost extinct, might have the happiness to see a true black gown among them. She congratulated those around her on the occasion and cried out, like Simeon, that her eyes had seen him now, and that she was ready to mix her bones with those of her fathers. Her death, which took place a few days after, was a great loss to the missioner. As she was the only person who knew the prayers in the Indian language, and the only one who appeared to have kept herself untainted by the general depravity of those by whom she was surrounded.

The few remaining Miamis have never had any permanent Catholic mission in their situation; yet they continue to be visited at time. Among them, however, in their original residence, near Chicago, Father Marquette, the first explorer of the Mississippi, labored as early as 1675. In 1836 the first Catholic

---

[51] *Catholic Cabinet*, vol. I, 407 and 408.

Missionary settlement was made among the Indians of this territory. The Rev. C. Van Quickenborne, of the Society of Jesus, with Father Hoeken and two lay brothers, opened a mission among the Kickapoos. Suitable buildings were erected, a neat chapel built, and the zeal of the missionaries was displayed in almost incessant labors by day and by night; but the soil proved for the time ungrateful [52]

Of these beginnings of Father Van Quickenborne's missionary labors among the Indians of Missouri and the Indian Territory, we will place before our readers the account given in 1840 by the Rev. P. J. Verhagen, S.J., Provincial of Missouri, to the Most Reverend Archbishop and Rt. Rev. Bishop in Provincial Council assembled:

The Indian missions having been entrusted to the care of this western portion of the Society of Jesus, by the prelates of the United States, we deem it a duty to lay before them some particulars respecting their establishment, progress and future prospects. No sooner was this wide field opened to our labors than the Rev. Father Van Quickenborne, of happy memory, with his characteristic zeal began to make preparations to open a mission among the nearest tribes. For this purpose, he visited several of the Atlantic cities, in order to procure the necessary funds. He succeeded, after great exertions, in collecting about fifteen hundred dollars. On the 20th day of May, 1836, he set out, in company with another Father and two lay brothers for the Indian country, and arrived at his destination among the Kickapoos, on the 1st of June of the same year. The agent of these Indians, not being, at first, favorably disposed, refused the requisite permission for building a house and when at length he consented, the season was so far advanced that all the funds at the disposal of the missioners were expended in raising a frame building 24x20 feet, and several months passed before it was ready for their accommodation. In the meantime they availed themselves of the kindness of a trader, who offered them his log cabin. When the new building was completed it served as a chapel, school and dwelling. About twenty children frequented the school—the chapel was well attended on Sundays —some few received into the church and many infants baptized. This first establishment has continued to progress, slowly indeed, but steadily, and affords a better prospect every year. The latest letters of the missioner give an account of twenty adult baptisms. If the success has not corresponded to the labors and expense, it is owing, first, to the presence and opposition of a Methodist minister who lives among them, to the vicinity of the whites, to the difficulties which was always attend the commencement of such establishments, for instance, the absence of all facilities for the acquirement of the language, etc.[53]

More explicit data as to the progress of the Kickapoo station, including the Kansas Mission near Chouteau's trading house, then the settlements of Plattsburg and Liberty, the mission among the Wyandotts, and lastly Fort Leavenworth, are given in Father Hoeken's Report for 1837. The mission among the Kickapos, to use the original spelling, was begun in the month of June, 1836. The church was blessed on Passion Sunday, and Father Van Quickenborne had hardly left the mission (July 20, 1837), when he died and was succeeded by Father Felix Verreidt. The mission among the Kansas, after the brief visit of Father Lutz, was founded about the same time as that among the Kickapoo. Plattsburg and Liberty date from November, 1837; the Wyandotte mission, as well as Fort Leavenworth from about the same time.

---

[52] *Catholic Cabinet*, vol. I, 408 and 409.
[53] Original in Archives of Catholic Historical Society of St. Louis.

This account finds an interesting supplement in the report of Father H. G. Aelen, S.J., dated September 25, 1839:

On the 25th of September, 1839, he, as superior of the missions, writes from Sugar Creek concerning the Kickapoo station:

The church, which is under the invocation of St. Francis Xavier, is regularly attended three times a month, the number of the faithful is about 20. There is an English school attached to this mission. The resident clergyman is Father A. Eisvogels, S.J., *Fort Leavenworth*. This station is regularly attended by the Rev. A. Eisvogels, S.J., once a month. The congregation is very flourishing, and a great deal of fruit has been reaped, especially of late, both among the soldiers and the workmen. The Rev. Eisvogels, S.J., visits also occasionally Liberty in Clay County and Plattsburg in Clinton County, Missouri.

After a brief account of the Pottawattomie Mission, which we shall quote later on, the Report of Father Aelen continues:

*Ottawas Station.* A band of about 300 of this nation resides on the left bank of the "mer des cygnes," otherwise the Osage River. It is regularly visited every second month by the Rev. H. G. Aelen, S.J. (from the Pottawatomie Mission). The congregation, counting about 20 adults, is zealous, and the prospects for proselytes is very fair. Their language is mostly like that of the Pottawatomies.

*Miamis Station,* comprising the four combined nations, Peorias, Kaskaskias, Weas and Piankeshaws. This station on the left bank of the "Mer des Cygnes," in the Peorias village, has been formed in July last, i. e. 1838, and is attended every second month by the Rev. H. G. Aelen, S.J., who also attends three times a year the church at Westport and the missionary station of Independence, in Jackson County, Missouri.

Concerning the Miami Station, composed, as it was, of the Weas and Piankshaws, the Kaskaskias and Peorias, Shea says on the authority of the *Annales,* that originally Catholics of the Illinois Missions, many of them had become Protestants. The Wea and the Kaskaskia chiefs had, however, remained Catholic. When Father Quickenborne asked the assembled people whether they had become Protestants, all were silent, till a woman, with tears, acknowledged it, "believing it better to be something than to have no worship."[54] This visit of Father Van Quickenborne was his last work among the Indians. The great missionary retired to Portage des Sioux at the confluence of the Missouri and Mississippi Rivers, where he died August 17, 1837. The founder was now dead, but his good work of reclaiming and keeping the Indians for Christ went on without interruption, and with remarkable success.

It is the celebrated Pottawotomie Mission of whose origin and progress I must now give a brief account. The Pottawotomie Indians were a branch of the great Algonquin family, and, at the opening of our western history were in possession of the southern confines of Lake Michigan from Chicago on the west to South Bend on the east. Having come in contact with the Jesuit missionaries at an early date, many Catholics, sometimes entire bands, were numbered among them. Their mission of St. Joseph, near what is now South Bend, in Indiana, became famous as a center of religious influence. But the rapid spread of the

---

[54] Report in Diocesan Chancery, St. Louis.

white population tolled the parting knell of this Indian mission, as well as of the great nation itself. The remnants only reached their new home in what was then called the Indian Territory, that is, all the Louisiana Purchase, with the exception of the States of Missouri, Arkansas and Louisiana. All Iowa, Nebraska, Kansas and the present Indian Territory, with Oklahoma, were considered unfit for white settlers, and therefore, given over to the Indians forever. Before 1838 two great bands of the Pottawotomies had been removed beyond the Mississippi and assigned new homes along the boundary of the State of Missouri, and here, as Father Verhaegen, S.J., the Provincial of the Jesuits informs the Fathers of the Provincial Council assembled at Baltimore, May 3, 1840:

> A second mission (after the Kickapoo station) was established in 1838 among the Pottawotomies on the Missouri River, near Council Bluffs, about five hundred miles west of the Kickapoo station. Two Fathers and two lay brothers commenced this establishment on the 31st of May of the same year. On their arrival they received from the chief four log cabins for a school, dwelling and other purposes, and from the United States officer a block house (24 feet square), which serves as a chapel. One of the Fathers devotes four hours every day to the instruction of the children in the Christian doctrine; the other makes frequent excursions among the neighboring tribes, and according to his report, has baptized many children—nearly two hundred adults have been admitted to the holy communion—the practice of bigamy has been in a great measure removed, etc. The accounts from this station are of the most cheering character and describe in glowing terms the happy disposition of thousands of these poor children of the forest, particularly of the women and children.[55]

The "two Fathers" were the celebrated Peter De Smet and his companion, Felix Verreidt, one of the brothers was Andrew Mazelli, the other George Miles. These Prairie "Pottawotomies" were a mixture of various tribal remnants, the Pottawotomies predominating and giving their name to the entire people. One of their leaders was the celebrated half-breed chief, Billy Caldwell, from Chicago, who had helped to found the first church in that city under Father St. Cyr. The block house given to the missionaries by Colonel Kearney was originally built as a fort, but as the troops had departed there was no need of a fort. and so it was converted into a church, the only church in Council Bluffs for a number of years. It was still in existence in 1855. The mission was placed under the protection of the Blessed Virgin and St. Joseph. Yet, though promising good results, the Pottawotomie mission at Council Bluffs was not without its scandals:

> From time to time the medicine men would excite greatest trouble. Polygamy, too. presented its fearful obstacle, requiring as it did, a restraint on the passions, to which these children of the wilderness were not accustomed; while intoxication, the deadly bane of the red man, at times converted their towns into images of hell.[56]

---

[55] Archives of Catholic Historical Society of St. Louis.

[56] J. G. Shea, *American Catholic Missions.* p. 463. Cf. Francis Cassilly, S.J. Oldest Jesuit Mission in Council Bluffs. Reprint from the *Creighton Chronicle*, February, 1917.

The very year of the foundation of the Pottawotomie Mission near
Council Bluffs was to witness the third great immigration of Pottawotomies, mostly Catholics, coming from the neighborhood of St. Joseph's, on the southern shore of Lake Michigan.  Let us hear what
Father Verhaegen has to say about this matter:

> In the same year (1838), six hundred Catholic Pottawotomies from Indiana,
> who were accompanied, in their removal, by the late Rev. Fr. Petit, on reaching
> their destination, were transferred by him to the care of one of our Fathers.
> Their location is on the banks of Sugar Creek, about seventy miles southwest of
> the Kickapoos station.  This is the most flourishing of all the Indian missions
> and realizes the accounts which we read of the missions of Paraguay.  A letter
> of the missioner, received in January last, states that on Christmas one hundred
> and fifty approached the sacred table and all who could be spared from domestic
> duties assisted with great devotion at the three solemn Masses, the first at
> midnight, the second at daybreak and the third at 10:30.  There is but one
> Father at present at the station, and as his presence is almost always required
> among his six hundred Catholics, he cannot make frequent excursions to the
> neighboring tribes.  His catechists, however, perform this duty for him, and
> often return with several adults ready to receive baptism.  The details of this
> mission would form a lengthy and interesting article, we cannot properly find
> place in a mere report.

What Father Verhaegen at the time failed to give we will endeavor
to supply from the reports of his colaborers and other trustworthy
documents, and, first of all, I shall quote the words of Fathers Charles
Hoeken and H. Aelen, the founders of the mission.  In his report from
the Pottawotomies village, near the Osage River, dated May 14, 1839,
Father Aelen writes.  "If it please Your Grace, I would call this mis--
sion "Conceptio Beatae Mariae Virginis."  On the 2nd day of October,
1838, the Reverend Father Hoeken came to the Osage River and was
about to gather some bountiful fruit, when the Reverend Father Petit,
of blessed memory, on the second day of November of the same year,
arrived there with a large number of Catholic Indians.  A temporary
chapel was raised near the banks of the river, called Pottawotomie
Creek.  After the departure of Father Petit, Father Hoeken remained
with these Indians for a time alone, until the Rev. Father P. Aelen
joined him as his assistant, April 26th, 1839.  On March 10th the entire
multitude of the faithful removed to the river commonly called Sugar
Creek, but renamed by us St. Mary's Creek, there to have their permanent home.  A new church was erected in this place under the title
"Conceptio Beatae Mariae Virginis."  Father Hoeken adds a note to
this report as follows:

> The Indians under my care are of good disposition and fervent, some of
> them were confirmed by Bishop Brutê before their western migration.  But as
> they come from Indiana they were never under the decrees of the Sacred Synod
> of Trent (i. e., the *ne Temere* decree), concerning marriages, consequently they
> are not subject to the proclamation of the banns.  Besides, the Indian mode of
> contracting marriage is altogether different from that of other nations; and
> lastly they do not like to have their names proclaimed in church, because they
> are very much inclined to bashfulness, so much so that at times they can scarcely
> speak, so shamefaced they are.[57]

---

[57] Diocesan Archives of St. Louis.

But these Indians were not converts of recent date. Many of them had received baptism in the far-away mission of St. Joseph's, on Lake Michigan. They had been expelled from their native haunts by an act of governmental tyranny, and the account of their long and weary march from Indiana to the borders of Kansas is a little epic full of pathos and deep human interest. Father Benjamin-Maria Petit was the spiritual leader of these exiled people, their teacher, protector and comforter, and it was he that left us in his letters a beautiful record of their sad journey to the country beyond the Mississippi River. Father Petit was born at Rennes in France, April 8, 1811, attended the college of his native city for the study of law, and had already attained the position of advocate when, in 1835, Bishop Simon Bruté, of Vincennes, arrived at Renes and confirmed the hopeful young man in his determination to become a missionary in America. Arriving at Vincennes in 1836, the youthful Petit was raised to the priesthood in October, 1837. His first and only appointment was to the Indian mission in the region around South Bend, Indiana, where he remained until September, 1838. Hence, Father Petit accompanied the Pottawotomies on their exile to the Far West, and died on his homeward journey in St. Louis, February 10, 1839, not quite twenty-eight years old, but full of merit.

As the Pottowatomie mission of Sugar Creek, Indian Territory,[58] forms one of the glories of the diocese of St. Louis, and as Father Petit is not as well known among us as his heroic life deserves, I will translate the beautiful letters he wrote to Bishop Bruté concerning his stay with the Indians and their departure for the West. Speaking of his Christians at Chichipe-Outipe, near South Bend,[59] Father Petit writes:

Our common mode of life was as follows: The first bell rang at sunrise. Then you should have seen the Indians hurrying along the foot-path along the woods and from the shores of the lakes to our chapel on the hill. Then the second bell warned the belated ones to make speed. When they were all assembled, the catechist recounted the points of the previous instruction: Morning prayer, followed and holy Mass, during which hymns were sung by the congregation. My sermon was translated into the Pottawotomie dialect. After this

---

[58] At the time of which we are writing the Indian Territory was much more extensive than what was commonly given as Indian Territory in our school days. "The Act of Congress of June 30, 1834, regulating trade and intercourse with the Indians, declares that 'all that part of the United States west of the Mississippi and not within the States of Missouri and Louisiana or the territory of Arkansas shall for the purposes of that Act be considered the Indian country." This vast region thus defined, formed part of the Louisiana Purchase from France in 1803. The mission of Sugar Creek (Kansas) as well as the mission at Council Bluffs (Iowa) was in the Indian Territory.

[59] St. Joseph's Mission at South Bend (Indiana), was founded by Father Claude Allouez, S.J., before 1711, for at that period Father John Chardon, S.J., became his successor. The nation of the Pottawotomies is noteworthy in our literary history as having given to Longfellow the matter of his Hiawatha. Their traditions were first recorded by Father De Smet in his Oregon Missions. The "Pontonaomies," as spelled by French writers, were mentioned from 1639. In 1641 they were at Sault Ste. Mary's, fleeing before the Sioux; in 1668 they were all on the Pottawotomie Islands in Green Bay. In 1721 the bulk of the nation was still on their islands; one band was at Detroit, another on the St. Joseph's River (South Bend Indiana). These latter are the people led to the West by Father Petit. Cf. Wisconsin Historical Collection, vol. III, p. 136. The letters of Father Benjamin Marie Petit to Bishop Bruté were published in volume VII, of The Annales de l'Association de la Propagation de la Foi for August. They were translated into German for Father Theodore Bruener's Kirchen-Geschichte Quincy's, 1887. The English translation was made for this article.

I heard confessions until evening. At sundown the whole congregation assembled for catechetical instruction and night prayer. Many of them had the practice of frequent communion, but since the death of Father Deseilles until my coming they had to be content with spiritual communion. I have already baptized eighteen converts and solemnized seven marriages. Their zeal for religion is most beautiful to witness. They will leave their homes to visit and instruct anyone, no matter how far away, of whom they have learned that he had desire to become a Christian. And with what affection they clung to me. "We were orphans," they said, "and we were lost in the night when you came among us, and now we live in light. You are a Father to us, and without your advice we will undertake nothing." I am very happy here, but there is one thing that disturbs my peace of mind. This mission is threatened with dissolution. The government intends to transport my Indians beyond the Mississippi. I am agitated between fear and hope. But my fears and hopes I lay in the hand of Providence.

On July 9th, 1838, Father Petit expresses his joy at finding himself able to understand and speak the language of his people; and at the end of his letter expresses a desire to be permitted to accompany them to their new destination. Since Easter, 1838, he had baptized one hundred and two Indian converts. At length the sad day of parting arrived. On September 14, 1838, Father Petit writes:

I have read my last Mass at Chicsipe-Ontipe. After Mass my dear little chapel was stripped of all its ornaments, and I gathered my children around me for the hour of departure. I shed tears, my Indians cried aloud; it was heart-rending. We, a dying mission, prayed for the prosperity of the other missions and sang:

"In thy protection do we trust.
O Virgin, meek and mild."

The leader's voice was broken with sobbing; but few could carry the song to its end. I had to leave. It is very sad for a missionary to witness the death of what he had loved. A few days later I learned that the Indians, in spite of their peaceful disposition, had been attacked and made prisoners of war. Under pretence of a council they had been brought together, when suddenly they were surrounded by the military, 800 in number, and put under restraint. The government at the same time extended an invitation to me to accompany them to their destination, as the separation from their priest was one of the reasons of their unwillingness to depart. I answered that I could do nothing without consent of my bishop, and that he had refused permission, in order to remove all suspicion, that the church authorities had consented to the harsh measures adopted by the government. But the dispensation of Providence is wonderful. Bishop Bruté was expected at Logansport on September 7th to dedicate the new church; and on the same day my Indian children were to camp near Logansport on their way to the Mississippi. On the morning of September 5th, the Bishop entered my room at South Bend and asked me to accompany him to Logansport. I was quiet as a man who does not move under an oppressive weight. We departed together. On the way we learned that the Indians, who were urged on to quicker movement at the point of the bayonet, had a number of sick people with them; several of them on the wagons having already died of heat and thirst. These reports were like a dagger piercing my heart. The Bishop now gave his consent that I join the Indians on their sad exodus: on condition, however, that I return as soon as another priest could be provided. I feared at first that I would not be permitted to enter the camp without special permission. All the Indians, however, came out to receive my blessing. The Americans were surprised at this. "This man," said the General "has greater influence here than I." I had free entrance everywhere. On the afternoon of September 9th Bishop Bruté came to the camp and confirmed twenty of my people. It was a beautiful day of triumph for the Catholic Faith. On the following day I brought my luggage from South Bend, and am now on the march to found a new mission for my barbarians 400 miles to the west.

W'iy the military acted so harshly in carrying out the sufficiently . harsh measures of the government is not clear, except on the supposition that some of them were far more barbarous than the barbarians themselves, these gentle children of the one-time wilderness. But these Indians were Catholics and, therefore, their sufferings passed unnoticed by the great world. On November 13, 1837, Father Petit continues his report to Bishop Bruté. His letter is dated from

*Osage River, Indiana County (Kansas)* : "On September 12 I returned to Logansport, having to catch up with the emigrants at Lafayette, but the march was accelerated so much that I did not see them, even from afar, until I came to Danville. They were marching along the right bank of the river, whilst the wagon train followed on the left bank. It was Sunday, September 16th. I had just arrived, when a Colonel rode up for the purpose of selecting the location for a camp. Shortly afterward I saw my Christians approaching through the heat· of midday, amid a cloud of dust and surrounded by the soldiery, urging them on to renewed effort. Then came the wagon train with the numreous sick and the children and women heaped pellmell on the carts. The camp was about half an hour's walk from the city, and in a little more than that time I was with them. It was a heart-breaking spectacle. Sick and dying people everywhere; almost all the children were in a state of utter exhaustion and· unconsciousness. The General expressed his pleasure at seeing .me, and gallantly offered me a chair, the only one he had. This was the first night spent under a tent. Early next morning the Indians were placed in the wagons; all the others mounting their horses. Just before starting, Judge Polk, the commander-in-chief, came up and offered me a saddle horse which the government had hired from an Indian, but the Indian approached and said: "My Father, I give you the horse, saddled and bridled as it is." We then started for a new camp, when a longer rest was promised us. At my request the authorities set at liberty the six Indian chiefs, who had until now been treated as prisoners of war. The order of march was now as follows: The U. S. flag was carried at the head of the column by a dragoon, followed by some of the chief officers; then came the wagon train of the General Staff; then the wagons used by the Indian chiefs. After that came 250 to 300 horses, with men, women and children riding in single file after the manner of the Indians, under guard of dragoons and volunteers, who continually urged on the cavalcade with bitter words and taunts. Now came about 40 wagons with the luggage of the Indians, and the sick Indians crowded on top of the luggage. Here the poor creatures lay, continually shaken up, under a canvas cover that was intended to shelter them against the heat of the sun, but served only to deprive them of fresh air; literaly buried aive under the burning cover. A few of them died under the torment. We encamped about six miles from Danville. Then I had the happiness for two successive days to say holy Mass surrounded by my children. I administered the holy sacrament to several in preparation for death, and baptized a few infants, and when we left this camp after our two days' rest, we left behind six graves with crosses at their head. At Danville the General gave furlough to his little army, and departed. He had promised to do so immediately after my advent. Soon we found ourselves on the vast prairies of Illinois, moving from one camp to another under a broiling sun, against which there was no shelter; they are immeasurable like the ocean, and the eye wearies itself to discover a tree in its immensity. No drop of water is to be found there. The journey was a real torment for the poor sick, some of whom died almost every day from exhaustion and fatigue. But all this misery did not prevent us from reciting our night prayers in common, and the Americans, who were led by curiosity to visit us, were astonished to find so much piety among so many trials. It frequently happened that some fifteen to twenty Indians sat around a fire before a tent that was illumined by a single wax candle, singing hymns and reciting the rosary all night; it meant that one of their friends had died and his corpse lay now in the tent. ·Thus they showed him their love and honor. On the following morning a grave was dug, the sorrowing family, without a tear in their eyes, however, remained at the place after the others had departed; the priest blessed the grave and cast the first shovelful of clay on the poor coffin; then a mound was raised over the dead and a little cross placed upon it. On some Sundays, when the lack of drinking water forced us to march on, a time of grace of two hours was granted to me, during which I might perform my religious duties. The Indians attended holy Mass, during which they sang their hymns so sweetly that all visitors were filled with wonderment. To my taste some of their songs had a very beautiful melody. I then preached a sermon on the Gospel, requested all to recite the Rosary on the way and gathered my belongings. The tents were struck, the horses were mounted, and on we marched to the next encampment. As a rule there was no marching on Sundays. The morning prayers and an instruction preceded the Mass. Vespers were chanted in the Indian tongue. Then came the Rosary and a brief sermon; the latter I sometimes preached in Indian without an interpreter. The respect shown me by Catholics along the way is above praise. . . .

I was again attacked by fever, about two or three days' journey this side of the Illinois River. Here an old Frenchman came to the camp and made me promise, with many importunities, to take a few days' rest at his home. The next morning he came with a wagon to convey me away, but I had to decline the invitation for fear I might not be able to catch up with my emigrants if I remained behind. When we arrived at Naples, where we crossed the Illinois River, a Protestant gentlemen who had been married to a Catholic French-woman at Vincennes, and who had heard that there was a sick priest among the Indians, came to offer me his home for the time of my stay. I accepted this invitation ,and through the great care lavished upon me I got rid of the fever. At Naples I took the stage coach and hurried on to Quincy. There I found a German priest, Father Brickwedde,[60] and a German congregation, who all received me with indescribable affection. The same friendly treatment was accorded to me by some Catholic Americans and by a few of the most prominent Protestants of the city. When the Indians arrived at Quincy the inhabitants, who had seen other emigrating tribes pass through their city, could not contain their admiration of the modesty, the quiet and good behavior of our Christians. A Catholic lady, accompanied by a Protestant friend, made the sign of the cross. Immediately the Indian women ran up to her and grasped her hand and shook it most heartily. The Protestant lady tried also to make the sign of the cross, but made a poor showing at it. One of the Indian women approached her, saying, "You, nothing." And she was right. . . .

At Quincy the Indians crossed the Mississippi and wandered from camp to camp through Northern Missouri ever westward across the Missouri boundary to the headquarters of the Osage River, in the present State of Kansas, then but a part of the vast Indian Territory. Father Petit's letter comes to a conclusion:

One day's journey from the Osage River I was met by Father Hoeken, S.J. He speaks both the Pottawotomie and the Kickapoo languages. He told me of his purpose to leave the land of the Kickapoo and to take up his abode among my Christians. Thus Your Grace will see that your purpose as well as mine is attained. Your Grace sought nothing but the honor of God and the salvation of these poor Christians; I sought nothing else. Having departed on September 4th, we arrived November 4th. The number of our Indians at their departure amounted to 800; some have deserted and many died. I do not think there were, at our arrival, more than 650 souls.

---

[60] A very sympathetic account of Father Florentin Augustin Brickwedde, the first pastor of Quincy, Ill., is to be found in Pastoral-Blatt of St. Louis, vol. 51, No. 7. Father Hilary Tucker in a letter dated Quincy, September 27, 1840, gives a brief account of another Pottawotomie migration to the Far West, passing through Quincy. There were 400 Indians, 300 of them Catholics, under the spiritual leadership of Father Bernier.

. Father Petit fell sick once more; the effects of the fever and the terrible privations and hardships were partly counteracted by the tender care of Father Hoeken. On January 2, 1839, Father Petit started for Vincennes, but was again taken ill on the way, and died at St. Louis, a martyr to duty, as Bishop Bruté called him, cheered and comforted by the pious care of the Jesuit Fathers and the visits of Bishops Rosati and Loras. His death occurred on February 11, 1839.

As this long digression has at last brought us back to the place from which we started, that is, the Osage River or Sugar Creek, Mission, we will give a brief account of the success the Jesuit Fathers attained. The Kickapoo mission was, indeed, merged in the Pottowatomie Mission of St. Mary's, on Sugar Creek, directed at first by Father Hoecke, S.J. "Before long the mission, as Shea[61] informs us, contained more than 1200 Catholic Indians; and two schools in a flourishing condition gave every hope of the rising generation. The Fathers were aided in this mission by the Ladies of the Sacred Heart, who began a school at Sugar Creek about the same time." The report from Sugar Creek for 1839 was made by Father H. S. Aelen, S.J. On the distribution of the Catholic Indians he has the following information to give:

The Pottawotomie Mission south of the Mer des Cygnes (Lake of the Swans) sometimes called Osage River. This mission extends itself to all the various bands of that nation, scattered all over their lands. Some of the faithful live on the right bank of the Mer des Cygnes; a considerable number on both banks of the so-called Pottawotomie Creek, and about 400 in a southward direction on the banks of the so-called Sugar Creek. Here is the residence of the attending clergyman, the Rev. H. G. Aelen, S.J., and a church under the invocation of the Bl. V. M. This mission is very flourishing, and no less than 60 adults have been baptized during the last eight months, or from the time that the nation has begun to settle on heir lands.[62]

From this flourishing center the Ottawas and Miamis were regularly visited by Father Aelen; the Kickapoo Station was for a time the residence of Father A. Eysvogels, S.J., who also visited Fort Leavenworth, and came, at times, to Liberty and Plattsburg. We regret very much that we cannot here give a full account of the Jesuit labors among the Indians of the old Indian Territory until its erection into a Vicariate under Bishop John B. Miege, S.J., in 1851, who, by the way, took up his residence at the Pottawotomie Mission.

The question may arise why these Indian missions were not as successful as similar efforts in South and Central America and in California. One reason is to be found in the frequent wanderings of these tribes; and their gradual extirpation through the greed of their white neighbors. Had the Jesuit missionaries of the West been allowed to pursue their plans without let or hindrance, or, better still, had they received the undivided support of the government in the work of Christianization, these numerous and once powerful tribes would now form

---

[61] J. G. She *History of the Catholic Mission,* among the Indian Tribes, p. 464.
[62] Archives of St. Louis and Diocesan Chancery.

large and prosperous communities on our Western prairies. But Catholic efforts were not supported as they should have been, nay, were often antagonized by government under some specious plea or another. Our Catholic people, too, were not as earnest in this great work as might have been expected of them. Other interests seemed to be more urgent. Father Verhaegen, in his appeal to the Council, complains of this lack of means:

The prospect of these different missions with respect to the salvation of souls is such as to animate the missioner with the greatest' courage in the midst of privation and labor. But we cannot conceal fro mthe prelates of the Council, who have placed these missions under our care, that their successful continuance depends upon other encouragement or support than the sweat of the laborers. These missions have hitherto been kept up by remittances from Europe, namely, from the Association of France and from friends in Belgium and Holland, and also by a small annual allowance made by the government— the last, however, is not extended to the establishment at Council Bluffs. These resources are precarious, it may indeed be said, that they nearly failed during the last year. It then becomes a most important question, what shall be done for the continuance of the Indian missions? We leave to the wisdom of the Council to devise the means for the promotion of this great object. In conclusion we submit a statement of the expenses of one mission, that of Council Bluffs, since its commencement.[63]

Yet, in spite of all these difficulties, great good has been attained, especially at the mission on Sugar Creek, and then among the Indians of the Rocky Mountains, made famous to that heroic soul, Father Peter De Smet, S.J., of St. Louis, the founder of the Oregon Missions beyond the Rocky Mountains.

JOHN ROTHENSTEINER.

---

[63] Verhaegen, l. c.

# NOTES ON
# SISTER MARY THEONELLA HITE
## AND HER FAMILY[1]

There are but few old Virginia families which for romantic interest surpass that of the Hites, the founder of which was Baron Hans Joist Heydt (as the name was originally spelled), an Alsatian noble who, to escape religious persecution, early in the eighteenth century fled to Holland, and there married Anna Maria Du Bois, daughter of a Huguenot refugee.

Baron Hans, having heard of the wonderful possibilities of the New World, fitted out two vessels, "The Swift" and "The Friendship," and with his own family and about forty other colonists set sail from Strassburg. He arrived in New York in 1710, and purchasing a large tract of land on the Schuylkill in Pennsylvania, there remained the patriarch of his little colony until in 1734, he acquired the original Van Mater tract of 40,000 acres in the Shenandoah Valley, Virginia, whither he removed. By an additional purchase of 100,000 acres, he became one of the largest landowners in all Virginia, second indeed only to the Fairfaxes, with whom, by the way, he was destined to be engaged in a long and costly litigation. He died about the year 1760, leaving a numerous progeny.

Of his sons, the eldest, Captain Jacob Hite, of New Hopewell, near Leetown, High Sheriff, Justice of Berkeley County and officer of County Militia, was engaged for some years in securing settlers in Europe for the lands owned by his father. For this purpose he made frequent trips to Ireland in his own vessel, and on one of these trips met and married in Dublin, Miss Catherine O'Bannon.

By this marriage he became the father of Colonel Thomas Hite (1750-1779); of John, whose daughter, Catherine, married Theodoric

---

[1] St. Louis readers will find interest in these *Notes* when they remember that Sister Theonella was a relative of Mrs. Mary Ann Malvina (Hite) Boisliniere (1826-1902) wife of Dr. Louis Chêrot Boisliniere (1816-1896) of St. Louis, the parents of Marie Xavier Charlotte, wife of Laurence Vincent Cartan. Other convert relatives of this family well known to St. Louisans were: Mrs. Eleanora Nelson (Guest) Semmes (1820-1875) wife of Samuel Middleton Semmes (1811-1867), and daughter of Jonathan Guest and Mary Stoughton Hite Gantt, daughter of John Hite, and granddaughter of Captain Jacob Hite and Catherine O'Bannon, mentioned in the article. Mrs. Semmes was the sister of Commodore John Guest (1821-1879) of the U. S. Navy, who also entered the Church.

Lee, son of "Light Horse Harry" Lee; of Jacob O'Bannon, slain by
the Indians in 1776; of Elizabeth, wife of Colonel Tavener Beale, Jr.,
(son by a previous marriage of Jacob Hite's second wife, Fanny
(Madison Beale Hite, aunt of President Madison); and of Mary who
married clergymen. On the death of his Irish-born wife, Captain
Jacob Hite married Fanny (Madison) Beale (1726-1776) widow of
Colonel Tavener Beale, Sr., aunt of President Madison.

Due to some disagreement with his family, Captain Jacob Hite
early in the year 1776, leaving his son George at William and Mary
College to finish his education, removed to South Carolina, where in
July following, he with his wife and several children was slain by the
Indians, they having being instigated to this atrocious act by British
agents who resented his espousal of the cause of the Revolutionists.
Two of his daughters, Frances Madison[2] and Eleanor, were taken
captive by the Indians and carried to Florida. Frances Madison, in
attempting to make her escape was tomahawked; her sister, Eleanor,
was later ransomed by Captain Johnson of the British Army, but she
lived only long enough to reach the settlement at Pensacola, where she
died and lies buried.

George Hite (died 1817) who, as we have seen, was at the time of
the massacre of his family a student at William and Mary College,
after finishing his education, served as a Captain in the Revolution,
and was afterward first clerk of Jefferson County. He married, in
1780, Deborah, daugtner of Colonel Robert Rutherford[3] (1728-1803)
and Mary (Dobbin) Howe Rutherford[4] of "Flowing Spring," on the
James River.

To Captain George and Deborah (Rutherford) Hite was born on
February 17, 1793, a daughter whom they named Margaret. She was
one of six children, one son and five daughters. Little is definitely
known concerning her early life beyond the statement in the Gorge-
town Convent Annals to the effect that "her parents took great pains to

---

[2] She is often confused with her mother, notably by the author of "The
Fate of Frances Madison," who there states that the wife of Jacob Hite was
not slain by the Indians but taken captive and later ransomed. The confusion
is due to the fact that the daughter bore the given names of her mother. Colonel
Isaac Hite (her brother-in-law) distinctly states in his diary that Frances
Madison Beale Hite was slain by the Indians along with her husband and several children in July, 1776.

[3] Colonel Robert Rutherford was a native of Scotland who settled on an
estate which he namd "Flowing Spring," on the James River, Jefferson County.
Virginia. He was a member of the House of Burgesses as early as 1758, and of
the Continental Congress. He was an intimate friend of General Washington,
who was wont to address him in letters as "My dear Robin."

[4] Widow of Viscount George Augustus Howe (1724-1758) who came to this
country in command of a British regiment. was promoted to the rank of
Brigadier-General and in 1758 served under Abercrombie at Ticonderoga where
he met his death. He was the brother of Rt. Hon. Richard Earl Howe (1725-
1799), Rear-Admiral and Commander-in-Chief of the British Naval Forces, and
of Sir William Howe (1729-1814), successor to Gage as commander-in-chief of
British military forces in America and who, in 1777, defeated Washington at the
Battle of Brandywine.

bring up their children in the fear of God and to instill into their hearts upright principles; and the children seconded their parents' pious exertions."

In 1825, Margaret accompanied her brother, Robert, to Washington, where she made the acquaintance of a devout Catholic family (whose name has not come down to us), through whose exemplary life she at length became attracted to their religion. After much prayer and study she at last was given the great grace of conversion. Following her baptism in 1827, she entered the Visitation Convent at Georgetown. She pronounced her vows on the Feast of S. Jane Frances de Chantal, August 21, 1828, receiving the name of Sister Mary Theonella.

The Georgetown Annals speak of her characteristic virtues as having been "purity of intention and willing obedience," in her long and arduous service as Infirmarian, Dispensor and teacher of various classes. She yielded up her pure soul to God on December 27, 1845, after eighteen years in religion. The night before she died she said to those around her bedside, "Since I have known God, I have served Him in the best manner I know."

It is extremely interesting to trace the relationship existing between Sister Theonella and six of the Presidents of the United States. Her paternal grandmother, Frances (Madison) Beale Hite, was the daughter of Colonel Ambrose and Frances (Taylor) Madison, the grandparents of President James Madison. Now Frances (Taylor) Madison was in turn the daughter of Colonel James and Martha (Thompson) Taylor, the common ancestors of Presidents Madison, Taylor, Tyler, the two Harrisons, and of Mrs. Jefferson Davis. Again, Frances (Taylor) Madison was the sister of President Zachary Taylor's grandfather. To still further connect her with the Presidents, we have only to recall that Sister Theonella's half-brother, Colonel Thomas Hite, married Frances Madison Beale, daughter by a previous marriage of his stepmother, Frances Madison Beale Hite (President Madison's aunt); that her grand-uncle, Major Isaac Hite (1758-1836) married as his first wife, Eleanor Conway Madison (1783-1802) sister of President James Madison; that her grand-aunt, Elizabeth (Madison) Willis, (another aunt of President Madison,) married Richard Beale, brother of Colonel Travener Beale, Sr.; that her half-niece, Frances Hite (daughter of her half-brother, Colonel Thomas Hite) married Thomas Carver Willis, who were the grandparents of Nathaniel Willis who married Jennie, daughter of John Augustine Washington of Mount Vernon, and of Emma, wife of Bushrod Washington of Clamont Court, nephews of General George Washington.

Sister Theonella's only brother, Major Robert Hite, married Courtney Ann Briscoe, of a family closely allied to that of the two Presidents Harrison. Finally, she was the aunt of George Flagg (son of her sister, Susan, and of John R. Flagg) husband of Elizabeth, daughter of Richard and Christine (Washington) Washington, granddaughter of Samuel Washington of Harewood, and the niece of General George Washington.

Still another Catholic relative of Sister Theonella must be mentioned: Mrs. Sarah Pearce Vick, who bore a papal title. She was the wife of Henry William Vick, of Vicksburg, Miss., and the daughter of James Pearce and Anne Clark. Her grandparents were General Jonathan Clark (1750-1811) of the Continental Army, and Sarah Hite. Jonathan Clark was the brother of General George Rogers Clark (1752-1818) and of General William Clark (1770-1838), Governor of Missouri. Sarah Hite Clark was the daughter of Colonel Isaac Hite (1723-1795) of "Long Meadows," the son of Baron Hans Joist Hite, founder of the family in Virginia. Her brother, Major Isaac Hite (1758-1836) married as his first wife, Eleanor Conway Madison (1783-1802) sister of President James Madison. Mrs. Jonathan Clark's uncle, Captain Jacob Hite, was the grandfather of Sister Mary Theonella Hite.

Authorities: "Hite Family," in *"Colonial Families of the United States,"* by Mackenzie, Vol. I (1896), pp. 185-203; Va. Hist. Mag. Vol. LV., (1896); *"The Fate of Frances Madison,"* Va. Hist. Mag. Vol. IV, pp. 463-'4; *"Diary of Colonel Isaac Hite,"* William and Mary Quart., Vol. VIII., p. 123; *"Madison Family Record,"* William and Mary Quart., Vol. IX (1901), p. 39; *"Memorandum from Note-Book of Major Isaac Hite, Jr."* William and Mary Quart., Vo. X., (1902), pp. 120-'1; County Histories of Virginia and Kentucky; History of Jefferson County, Va., (1886); data from Georgetown Convent Annals through courtesy of Sister Superior.

SCANNELL O'NEILL.

# DIARY OF THE JOURNEY OF THE
# SISTERS OF ST. JOSEPH
## TO TUCSON, ARIZ. (1870)

Early in the year 1870 Right Reverend J. B. Salpointe applied for the Sisters of St. Joseph for the missions in Arizona. Reverend Mother Saint-John Facemaz, then Superior General of the Congregation of Carondelet, hesitated some time before accepting the offer. She placed before the Sisters the dangers of the long journey, and finally, from among the many who volunteered she selected seven. During the spring of 1870 every preparation was made for the perilous undertaking, and the Sisters left Carondelet in the middle of April (1870), reaching Tucson May 26.

*Reverend Mother and Dear Sisters:*

Before leaving Carondelet I promised to write a *Journal* of our trip to Arizona. It seems to me that the fulfillment of this promise is almost out of date. You know we had scarcely time to brush the dust off our habits before opening school; consequently, I was obliged to defer writing the events of our trip until vacation, and I would not have the courage even now to commence it, were it not that Sister Euphrasia is reminding me continually. I have time now, it is true, but not capacity for such a task. Nevertheless, I shall do the best I can, relying on the kind indulgence of our good Sisters.

*April* 20, 1870. After bidding adieu to our good Sisters in Carondelet, we started on our long and perilous journey to Arizona. Our first two stations were St. Joseph's and St. Bridget's Asylums, St. Louis, Missouri, where we were cordially greeted by our good Sisters. We wished them good-bye, repaired to the Pacific Railroad depot, and took the train at 6 P. M. direct to Kansas City. Puff! puff! went the locomotive, and we were off really on our way to Arizona. As the Sisters travel this portion of our journey, I shall not describe it; but it is certainly true that none of them ever went over it with the sadness of heart which we experienced on that ever memorable night. We were going, but not to return in vacation to make the retreat with our dear Sisters. Mother Julia will not call on us when visiting her Province. It is quite probable that we may never again meet here below; and it is only when this thought occurs to me that I know how deeply I love them. Oh! the incomprehensible beauty of our holy Faith! How con-

¹ We are indebted for this *Journal* to Sister M. Lucida, Annalist of the Sisters of St. Joseph. The fiftieth anniversary of the events which it recounts, is, together with its intrinsic interest, sufficient reason for offering it to our readers; they will, no doubt, join with us in expressing cordial thanks to Sister Lucida for the privilege. (THE ED.TOR).

soling to know with an infallible certainty that we are accompishing the will of God, with an assured hope of being reunited in our Heavenly Country to those beloved ones whom we have left here below for the love of Jesus and the salvation of souls. With these and similar reflections we passed the first night until we reached Kansas City.

*Thursday, April* 21, 1870. We were kindly welcomed by our good Sisters, and had the pleasure of meeting there Mother Agatha, who had been sick, but was now better. We spent the day quite pleasantly. It soon became once more our duty to say good-bye; but we were much encouraged on hearing that Reverend Mother Saint John had concluded to accompany us as far as Omaha, Nebraska. We took the train at 7 P. M., and as the cars were new and clean and but moderately filled, we were comfortably seated. We changed during the night—and it was indeed a change in every respect, as the cars were filled with emigrants, crying children, etc. In this crowd we spent the remainder of our second night.

*April* 22, 1870. In the morning we refreshed ourselves with a nice cup of coffee, then proceeded on our journey. The weather was cool and pleasant. An Indian boy played the violin for the entertainment of the passengers. Reverend Mother treated us to apples and maple sugar, and presented us with little statues of our Blessed Mother as souvenirs; but in spite of all, there was a sad cloud hanging over us. It was not surprising, for we were to part from Reverend Mother in a few hours, and that, perhaps, forever in this world. As in similar difficulties, we had recourse to our good Father, St. Joseph. We were detained about two hours after time. We feared that the San Francisco train would wait for us, as we wished it to be gone; for then we could remain one day more with Reverend Mother. As we approached Omaha some of us were crying and others praying; but all were looking eagerly to see if the train was there. We did not wait long, as a messenger came with the welcome news that the train had just left. "Thanks be to God," escaped from each one's lips, and was in every heart. We then went to the Convent of the Sisters of Mercy, where we received a most cordial welcome from those good Sisters. We remained there until the next morning.

*Saturday, April* 23, 1870. After we had the consolation of hearing Mass and receiving the Bishop's blessing we went to the depot. Reverend Mother and Sister Lucina accompanied us. Reverend Mother procured our tickets, refreshments and other conveniences for the journey. The dreaded moment of parting had almost arrived. That moment we shall never forget! We were all seated in the cars when she came in with her little purchases, and at the same time to say "good-bye." We lost all self-control, and after she left us, wept bitterly, our eyes following her until she entered the carriage and drove out of sight. The Arizona missionaries had made their first great sacrifice in leaving their dear

Mother. The same day we passed through the beautiful valley of the La Platte, took supper at Clarks, 121 miles from Omaha. Sister Ambrosia and I went out to purchase some tea. We received it as an alms, and with it several mortifications. The cars were so crowded that night we were unable to sleep.

*Sunday, April* 24, 1870. We breakfasted at Sydney, 414 miles from Omaha. From this place onward the scenery was very interesting, and the conversation of our fellow-travellers amusing. In our car were four Protestant ministers with their ladies, on their way to China to convert those benighted idolators. There were almost as many religious denominations represented as were persons in the car. Whether owing to our presence or not, religion was the principal topic of conversation throughout the entire journey. Everyone maintained his own opinion, and proved it from the Bible, agreeing in one point that "Catholicity is abominable." When the controversy reached its highest point, an elderly respectable-looking gentleman came over to us and handed one of the Sisters a five-dollar bill, proffering his services to us as far as San Francisco. He stated that he was not a Catholic, but had great respect for the Sisters, as he knew them to be "angels of mercy," and that he regarded it a great privilege to serve them when it was in his power. One of the Sisters gave him a small medal of the Blessed Virgin. He hung it on his watch chain, and said that he would keep it as long as he lived. This afternoon we entered the Rocky range, passed through Sherman at an elevation of 8242 feet, the highest point on the line; also the highest point crossed by the railroad. It is a frightful and desolate region, nothing to be seen but snow-clad mountains of rock, whose summits appear to touch the clouds. The cars pass over frightful chasms. The rails are laid on logs resting on pillars whose only support are the craggy rocks beneath. Some of these chasms seem to be about the length of three city blocks. When we were going over these places everyone appeared to hold his breath, and it was only when we were safe on firm ground that conversation was resumed and comments made on the terrors and perils of the place. I chanced to be sleeping when crossing one of these places. Sister Martha woke me, telling me to "wake up and take note of this beautiful scenery." When I saw where we were, sleep forsook me immediately. I was really terrified. The Sisters enjoyed the scenery very much. This night, like the preceding one, we passed with little sleep.

*Monday, April* 25, 1870. We took breakfast at Green River, 845 miles from Omaha. At Byrne we met Sister Andrew's brother, Mr. Byrne, and delivered the little messages of his sister. At 5 o'clock we passed the "thousand-mile tree," so called from its being just 1000 miles from Omaha. It stands at the entrance to the "Devil's Gate," a very appropriately named place, with lofty mountains rising on each side of the track. The railroad winds through a narrow pass in the mountain, at the base of which the Weber River, an angry-looking stream, dashes along with frightful impetuosity. We crossed it eight times within the space of a quarter of an hour. It is probably from this difficulty in crossing that it has received its name. We changed cars at Ogden, a Mormon town of about 6000 inhabitants. It lies between the Weber and Ogden Rivers, thirty-one miles north of Salt Lake City, 1032 miles from Omaha. Many of the Mormon houses are built like the tenement houses of the States; others are in groups of small houses in the yard. The Mormons are a degraded-looking set of people. Perhaps it is prejudice that makes me think so. Here we had the pleasure of meeting with kind friends in the persons of Mr. Doebeck and lady of San Francisco, who did everything they could to make us comfortable. About sunset we passed Salt Lake. The railroad runs along its margin. The city is a beautiful place. On the left are flower gardens, shade and fruit trees covered with dense foliage, which relieve the scene on the right—barren mountains and bleak rocks, presenting in all a lonely prospect.

*Tuesday, April 26, 1870.* Breakfast at Elco, 1307 miles from Omaha. The morning was warm and pleasant. There were a great many Indians at the depot. We threw them candy, and it was really amusing to see these poor old creatures grabbing for it in the dust. Mr. Doebeck occasionally sent us apples, oranges and candy. At noon we stopped at Battle Mountain, where we met Reverend Father Kelly, pastor of Austin, Nevada. He invited us to dinner, which, indeed, we needed badly; but Mother was afraid to leave the carpet bags, etc., so he had her dinner sent in. At supper Sister Martha was rather indisposed, and the good priest brought her supper to the car. He was extremely kind. When we retired at night the heat was as oppressive as that of a St. Louis July; the morning was as cold as a Canadian March. In several places the railroad is protected by sheds to prevent the snow from blocking the track.

*Wednesday, April 27, 1870.* About 6 o'clock we passed a place called Cape Horn. It is an ugly, dreary place. The railroad track runs alongside of a mountain that rises on the right and left. About five or six feet from the track there is a precipice said to be 300 feet deep, which extends about a mile along the railroad. On the opposite side of this precipice are mountains from whose sides issue several streams flowing into the chasm beneath, where, uniting, they rush along with awe-inspiring impetuosity. At 8 o'clock we reached the California gold diggings. They are subterranean, consequently we did not see them. We dined at Colfax with Reverend Father Kelly, who now took a fatherly care of us. We here parted from him, and in bidding us farewell, he presented us with a five-dollar gold piece, with strict injunctions to telegraph to him in case we needed any funds, as he would not fail to supply them. He gave us an introductory letter to Reverend Hugh Gallagher, San Francisco, who rendered us important services while we were there. Father Kelly said that he would apply for a colony of our Sisters for Salt Lake City, were it not that he purposed leaving the mission to enter the Congregation of the Lazarists. He is the first pastor of the mission, and has been there fifteen years. At 7 o'clock P. M. we reached San Francisco. Mr. Doebeck saw us to the bus, and attended to our baggage, but, owing to some mistake in the address, we did not reach the hospital until 9 o'clock P. M. We presented a beautiful sight after our week's journey without arranging our toilet—the distance from Omaha to San Francisco being 1914 miles. We were received most cordially by the good Sisters of Mercy, who did all in their power to make us comfortable. We were sadly in need of rest, as we were completely dizzy from the motion of the cars.

*April* 28, 1870. Reverend Mother Gabriel took us to visit the Magdalen Asylum in the country. Mother was rather indisposed and did not accompany us. Sister Martha remained with her. The Sisters at the asylum were extremely kind to us. They wished to load us with provisions for our journey; but as we were inexperienced in these matters, we did not think we would need them, and accepted only a few knickknacks just to please tnem. We were heartily sorry when hungry in the desert that we had not accepted their offering. We shall ever feel grateful to those good Sisters who proved to us "friends in need," and lavished so much kindness on us.

*Saturday, April* 30, 1870. The good Sisters sent us to the boat in their carriage. We took passage on the steamer *Arizola.*. Captain Johnson, with his officers, treated us with every mark of respect and kindness. Mother was quite seasick and scarcely able to sit up until Monday. In the afternoon Sisters Euphrasia and Martha were seasick, but were well the next day.

*Sunday, May* 8, 1870. With the exception of these little occurrences we had a pleasant trip to San Diego, where we arrived on Tuesday morning, May 3. We stopped at a boarding house until Saturday, May 7, when we left in a private conveyance for Fort Yuma. The carriage was too small for all to ride inside, so one was obliged to ride outside with the driver. Sister Ambrosia volunteered to make the great act of mortification and humility. It is beyond description what we suffered in riding 200 miles in a country like this, without protection from the rays of a tropical sun. Yet, poor Sister did this! About 10 o'clock we passed a white post that marks the southwest boundary of the United States. We dropped a few tears at sight of it, then entered Lower California. At noon we halted and took lunch in a stable 12 miles from San Diego. Sister Maxima and I went in search of gold. Seeing quantities of it we proposed getting a sack and filling it. Just think a *sack* of gold! But we soon learned from experience that "all is not gold that glitters." We camped about sunset at the foot of a mountain, made some tea, and took our supper off a rock. All were cheerful. We wished Reverend Mother could see us at supper. After offering thanks to the Giver of all good, we retired to rest; Mother,

Sisters Euphrasia and Martha under the wagon, others in the wagon, where there was room for only two to lie down. Sister Euphrasia and I sat in a corner and tried to sleep. We had scarcely closed our eyes when the wolves began to howl around us. We were terribly frightened and recommended ourselves to the safekeeping of Him who guides the weary traveller on his way. We feared that they would consume our little store of provisions and thus let us perish in the wilderness; but the driver told us not to fear. During the night Sister Euphrasia was startled from her sleep by one of the horses licking her face. She screamed fearfully and we concluded that she. was a prey to wolves. Next morning (May 9), Feast of the Patronage of our Holy Father, St. Joseph, we were determined to celebrate it in the best way we could. After offering up our prayers, we formed a procession, going in advance of the wagon, Mother walking in front with a Spanish lily in her hand. We followed in solemn order, imagining ourselves in Egypt with St. Joseph as leader. At noon we came to a cool, shady place, in which we rested. The ranchman (a person who keeps refreshments, stable-feed, etc., on the Western plains), invited us to dinner. He offered us a good meal of all we could desire. There were several ranchmen there from the neighboring stations, but no women. There are few women in this country. After dinner they became sociable. We retired to the stable, where our driver and only protector was, and they followed. Some of them proposed marriage to us, saying we would do better by accepting the offer than by going to Tucson, for we would be all massacred by the Indians. The simplicity and earnestness with which they spoke, put indignation out of the question, as it was evident that they meant no insult, but our good. They were all native Americans. For that afternoon we had amusement enough. We resumed our journey. That evening we camped in a very damp place, made some tea, the only beverage we had. We then offered up our evening prayers and retired to rest. Mother, Sister Ambrosia, Sister Maxima and I mounted a rock; the other three went to the wagon. The night was very cold. I believe there was frost. We had only one blanket between seven of us. Sister Martha and I had only light summer shawls. The others were fortunate enough to have brought their winter ones. along. Yet, we all kept up good spirits, being convinced that we were doing the Divine will.

*Monday, May* 9, 1870. We spent the day climbing up and down hills. In the evening we reached the ever-memorable place, "Mountain Springs," the entrance to the American Desert. For several miles the road is up and down mountains. We were obliged to travel it on foot. At the highest point it is said to be 4000 feet above the level of the sea. We were compelled to stop here to breathe. Some of the Sisters laid down on the roadside, being unable to proceed farther. Besides this terrible fatigue, we suffered still more from thirst. Before proceeding further, I shall give you a brief description of the place. We were going south; before us lay the American Desert, forty miles long, 800 feet below the level of the sea. It is said to have once formed a portion of the ocean. It has every appearance of having been covered with water. On the right lies a great salt lake, supposed to have been a part of the ocean, which, being hemmed in by mountains, could not recede with the other water. On the left arise ugly mountains of volcanic rock and red sand. I wished Sister Euphrasia to make a sketch of it, but she said it was not necessary to do it then, as she would never forget its appearance. After a few moments' rest we commenced to descend. We were so much fatigued that it seemed as if our limbs were dislocated. We had yet two miles to descend on foot, the greater part being very steep. We joined hands, two by two, and ran as well as we could. It was certainly a novel sight to see the Sisters alone crossing that lonely mountain in the wilderness. The sides of the road were covered with teams of horses, oxen and cattle that had dropped dead trying to ascend. In one place we counted fourteen oxen which had apparently died at the same time. When Mother saw so many dead animals she wept, fearing we might share their fate. We reassembled at the foot of the mountain and paused to breathe. Everyone had something to remark about the place we had just passed. Sister Maxima said it was "the abomination of desolation." The carriage overtook us there, but we continued on foot, as it was yet too dangerous to ride, though we had quite a distance to go before we could take the conveyance. We travelled as fast as we could, in order to reach a ranch.

Before nightfall the travellers reached a ranch. where they were accommodated for the night. though with much discomfort to all.

*May* 10, 1870. We started this morning at 5 o'clock and entered the desert. It is a vast bed of sand. Travel over it is rendered dangerous on account of the sandstorms. We were told that about a month previous to our crossing there was found a government wagon loaded with firearms which had been forwarded several months before, and a stage coach with seven passengers all buried in the sand. The sand is a good conductor, consequently the heat is extreme. When the sun is at meridian height, the sand is hot enough to blister. In one place we passed a drove of horned cattle said to contain a thousand head. Everyone died of heat the same day. Another place we passed the remains of 1500 sheep, smothered in a sandstorm. In several places the sand is so deep that we were obliged to walk. We could get water only in one place, and when we did get it it was not only hot but so full of mineral that we suffered more after taking it than before. We travelled till noon, then rested until 4 P. M. Recommending our journey to our Heavenly Father, we travelled until midnight. It was then cool and pleasant; the sun shone brightly; we rode and walked alternately. We sang hymns all the time and imagined St. Joseph in our company, protecting us as he did the Infant Jesus and His Blessed Mother through the Egyptian Desert. Thus we felt no fear.

At midnight they reached a ranch where they were kindly received and accommodated until the following evening. They travelled during the night, and at 3 o'clock on the morning of May 12. reached another ranch. The proprietor offered them the use of the barroom, which they declined, preferring a large barn near by. There were 40 Indian men at this ranch, who treated the Sisters with great kindness and respect. Everything was done to make them comfortable until evening, when they resumed their journey.

*Friday, May* 13, 1870.   About 7 o'clock A. M. we left Lower California and entered Arizona.   We crossed the Colorado River about 9 o'clock on what they term here a towboat, which, however, is nothing but a raft.   We were obliged to go over in a carriage, as they did not wish to cross over a second time.   There were four spirited horses. Two men held them by the bridle; and as there was nothing on the opposite side to which the raft could be fastened, two men stood on the opposite bank, holding it with ropes.   As the horses sprang forward, the raft floated back.   At this, one of the horses fell on the raft, which is the only thing that saved us from a watery grave.   The weight of the horse prevented the carriage from rolling into the river.   There stood the carriage with the Sisters hanging over a depth of 17 feet of water.   I saw the danger before it happened and jumped from the carriage.   We barely escaped being drowned and ending our mission and finishing our crown before reaching Arizon.   But our Lord did not wish it.   We must labor longer and assist in cultivating this barren portion of His vineyard.   At 10 o'clock we reached Arizona City, or Fort Yuma, where we received a most cordial welcome from good Father Francisco, V. G. of Tucson.   We remained here three days, and had the inexpressible consolation of assisting at the Holy Sacrifice and receiving our dear Lord in Holy Communion, which imbued us with new strength and courage for the remainder of our journey.   We had the pleasure of hearing a Spanish sermon for the first time.   We were lodged with a good Mexican family.   As some of our Sisters may be going here at some future day, a brief description of the place may not prove uninteresting.   It is located at the junction of the Colorado and Gila Rivers, being much more conveniently situated than Tucson.   It is said to be the hottest place in the United States, but has the advantage of having plenty of fresh water.   Sandstorms are of frequent occurrence.   The population, consisting of Mexicans and Americans, numbers about 4000, the latter having the majority.   No schools have yet been established.   They offered $200 per month if two of the Sisters would remain for a year, but were told by Father Francisco to first build a convent.   The majority of the buildings are of adobe (sundried brick).   Lumber is very scarce and difficult to procure.   There is but one Catholic Church.   The first pastor, who was one of the priests that accompanied the Bishop to Carondelet, was appointed last May. The soil is fertile, but, owing to continual drought, agriculture is confined to those parts where irrigation is practicable.   There is an almost inexhaustible supply of firewood.   The Indians in the vicinity are peaceable.

*Tuesday, May* 17, 1870. We left this place at sunrise and travelled till noon. The remainder of the journey was quite pleasant, as we had a comfortable, covered carriage, good Father Francisco to guard us, a plentiful supply of provisions, etc., and a cook to prepare our meals. From this time forward we had our regular meals—good ones, too—far better than we had expected in such a wilderness. We had a tent to sleep under, but as it was rather warm some of us slept in the wagon on the seats. We travelled until 10 o'clock P. M.

*Wednesday, May* 18, 1870. We started early in the morning and stopped at noon on the banks of the Gila. We travelled 200 miles along this stream, and took supper at a ranch, where we remained during the night.

*Thursday, May* 19, 1870. When we were about to resume our journey, Mother started in advance of us for a walk. On coming to a place where the roads crossed she took the wrong direction. After a short interval, not perceiving any trace of her, we became alarmed for her safety. Father and Sister Ambrosia immediately started in pursuit. When the driver descried her in the distance, he ran as fast as possible in order to overtake her; and she, on perceiving a man running after her, ran, too, with all her might. After her return, Father put her in penance by making her ride in his carriage. Sister Martha accompanied her. We rested from 12 M. till 3 P. M., and then continued our journey until 8 P. M.

*May* 20, 1870. At 6 A. M. we resumed our journey and came to a ranch about noon. The proprietor treated us very kindly and presented us with some canned fruit, and a new towel for our journey, which we resumed until 7 o'clock P. M., when we camped for the night, suffering much from the cold.

*Saturday, May* 21, 1870. We started on our way at 4 P. M. and passed many recently made graves of persons who had been killed by the Indians. One of these, we were informed, contained the remains of a father, mother and five children. These burial places looked so sadly neglected. The wolves had even made holes in them. The desolate, lonely places in which these poor creatures were laid to rest, and still more their melancholy and frightful death cast a damper over our spirits, as we had no certainty of not meeting the same fate. And yet, why should we be sad? Did we not risk our lives for the love of Jesus, and would it not be glorious to have the happiness of dying for Him? But poor nature is weak; and though in spirit we coveted the privilege of so glorious an end, yet our frail, earthly bodies shrank from so trying an ordeal. We passed at night the Indians' place of worship. It is a natural construction of huge, immovable rocks, on which they have cut the figures of their gods. They were various planets, different animals of the forest, and even reptiles. The figures appear to be well

made and are quite interesting to look at. Oh, how my heart burned
to make them know the true and only God! We camped about 8 o'clock
and took our supper by brush light, as usual.

*Sunday, May 22, 1870.* We had a lamb this morning for breakfast. We called it our Passover. After offering up our prayers and
placing ourselves with confidence under the protection of Heaven we
resumed our journey at rather an advanced hour of the day under the
rays of a scorching sun, the average heat in the shade being 125 de-
grees. We reached a ranch at noon, and were accommodated with a
room, where we enjoyed the luxury of a good wash and change of
clothing.. We dined at 3 o'clock, and after getting a supply of fresh
water for the journey we started at 6 P. M. We entered the Arizona
Desert, travelled all night, and were so much fatigued that almost everyone fell asleep, the driver permitting the horses to go at will. Father
and his driver slept so soundly that Sister Martha was obliged to drive
nearly all night. At 8 A. M. we refreshed ourselves with a cup of
coffee, and journeyed on until 2:30 P. M., when we were out of the
desert.

*May 23, 1870.* We took dinner at 5 P. M. and lodged at the house
of a generous-hearted Irishman, Mr. Cosgrove. Whenever we had the
good fortune to come across Irish or Mexicans we were sure of meeting
with a cordial reception and of finding in them all the characteristics of
true friends.

*Tuesday, May 24, 1870.* We started early, entering upon the
most dangerous portion of our journey, as we were in danger of being
attacked and massacred by the savages at any moment; but placing
ourselves in the hands of Providence, to whom we had consecrated our
lives, we courageously advanced, feeling assured that His all-seeing
eye would protect His chosen ones from danger—at all events, that
whatever would befall us would be in accordance with His most holy
will. When we stopped at noon, there was no room for us in the inn,
so that we had not even a tree to shelter us from the burning rays of a
tropical sun. The ruins of some old buildings were near. Mother and
Sister Martha went there to rest and fell asleep. A troop of nude
Indians, who are peaceable, came in the meantime. They had the consideration to be quiet and let them sleep. Sister Martha was resting
on an old cowhide. A warrior, perceiving her, stole softly up and sat
down beside her. The rest of the Sisters were in the wagon, while I
employed myself in washing some handkerchiefs and amused myself
by taking notes for my *Journal*. Father and the boy prepared dinner,
after which we resumed our journey. About 4 P. M. we passed the
Valley of the Pima Indians. Their dwellings are constructed of straw
and are shaped like a bird's nest, in an inverted position. They vary
from four to five feet in height, and have a small hole as a place of
entrance. Their costume consists of two pieces of calico or flannel
extending to the knees, one piece hanging in front, the other behind.

The young squaws are clothed with the inner bark of trees in the same manner. The old ladies are not so modestly attired. They dress their hair with a mixture of mud and water, which has the double effect of destroying the vermin and keeping the hair in its place. They are a brave-looking tribe, very unlike the poor, timid Indians of the frontier. We camped at 9 o'clock. Whilst partaking of our evening refection sixteen soldiers rode up and informed us that they had been sent to escort some travellers, they knew not whom, and supposed we were the persons, as they saw no others. We conjectured that our good Father, St. Joseph, had sent them to our assistance, though at the time we were not aware of how much we stood in need of their escort. We might in all probability have been massacred by the savages had they not been our safeguard. The Indians are afraid to appear when they hear the soldiers, unless they are sufficiently strong in number to fight them. They continued with us for the remaining seventy-five miles of our journey.

*May* 25, 1870. While we were at breakfast this morning three of the citizens of Tucson who were a portion of the number appointed to meet us (the others having remained at the next station), rode up. We resumed our journey at 5 P. M. Some miners joined us in order to share our protection. The soldiers followed close in the rear. They had two mules to carry their baggage—one carried the blankets, the other the cooking utensils. We titled them respectively the "chambermaid" and the "cook." The latter looked quite amusing with pots and pans hanging from each side. At noon we reached the station, where the remainder of the escort from Tucson was awaiting us—sixty-five miles from the city; but as they could speak neither French nor English we did not understand them. At 5 P. M. we set out again. Everyone was in fine spirits, especially the citizens. All passed off pleasantly until midnight, when a serious turn of mind and manner seemed to take possession of each and every one. We were then approaching Picacho Peak, where the Apaches are accustomed to attack travellers. A fearful massacre had been perpetrated there only a week previous. The road winds through a narrow pass in the mountain where the Indians conceal themselves and throw out their poisoned arrows at the passersby. The place is literally filled with graves, sorrowful monuments of savage barbarity. Each one prepared his firearms, even good Father Francisco. The citizens pressed around our carriage. The soldiers rode about like bloodhounds in search of prey. In passing through the peak the horses began to neigh, which is a sure indication of the proximity of the savages. "The Indians! the Indians!" was echoed from every mouth. Whip and spurs were given to the horses. We went like lightning, the men yelling all the while like so many fiends in order to frighten the savages. The novelty of the scene kept us from being afraid. We travelled in this manner until 4 A. M.

*Ascension Thursday, May* 26, 1870. When we had passed unharmed through the most dangerous portion of our route, we returned fervent, heartfelt thanks to our good God for our preservation. After refreshing ourselves with a cup of coffee, we continued our journey until within fifteen miles of Tucson, where we stopped for a short rest. The citizens wished us to remain there all night, as they wished us to enter Tucson in daylight, where a grand reception was in preparation. You see they were quite proud of us. After considerable reasoning they became very enthusiastic over the matter; but Father finally succeeded in obtaining their consent for us to enter that night. Four men went in advance with the joyful tidings of our arrival. We were expected at about 6 o'clock P. M., and were afterwards informed that the ladies and children had stationed themselves on the housetops, being too modest to mix in the crowd with men. At about three miles from the town we were met by the procession, which was headed by four priests on horseback; but as we came in sight they dismounted and ran rather than walked to meet us, the crowd in the meantime discharging firearms. Before we reached the city their number had increased to about 3000, some discharging firearms, others bearing lighted torches in their hands, all walking in order with heads uncovered. The city was illuminated, fireworks in full play. Balls of combustible matter were thrown in the streets through which we passed. At each explosion Sister Euphrasia made the sign of the cross. All the bells in the city were pealing forth their merriest strains. On reaching the convent we found our good Bishop in company with several ladies and gentlemen, awaiting our arrival. The crowd then fired a farewell salute and dispersed. We feel truly grateful to these good people for their kind reception, as it is a convincing testimony of their reverence for our holy Faith. After we had arranged our toilet the ladies ushered us into the refectory, where a nice supper had been prepared for us. They waited on us at supper, and endeavored to make everything as pleasant as possible. When we had finished our repast they departed, leaving us in quiet possession of our new home—"St. Joseph's Convent, Tucson, Arizona." Our first act was to return thanks to our glorious Patriarch, St. Joseph, for preserving us from the many and great dangers to which we had been exposed for love of Jesus and the salvation of souls. Our house is built of adobe or brick dried in the sun—simply mud—and consists of but one story. It adjoins the Cathedral, and one of the chapels thereof serves as our chapel.

Now that we are settled in our new home we trust our good Sisters will continue to pray for us, recommending the success of our mission, our schools and our own spiritual welfare to our dear Lord, to the end that we may labor earnestly to promote His greater glory, and have this alone in view in all our undertakings.

Dear Reverend Mother and Sisters in Christ,

SISTER MONICA OF THE SACRED HEART.[2]

September 17, 1870.

---

[2] Our readers may be interested to know that Sister Monica, the author of this *Diary*, is still alive and active; she now lives at the Nazareth House of the Community, Jefferson Barracks, St. Louis Co., Mo.

N. B.—The Bishop was never able to find out who had given the order for the soldiers to meet the Sisters. All that the Commandant of the fort could tell was that a very respectable, hasty messenger arrived at the fort, with a request that a detachment be sent immediately to escort some travellers through the dangerous passes.

Three years later, in 1873, Bishop Salpointe stopped at Carondelet on his way to Rome, and made arrangements for three more Sisters for the Arizona Mission. He returned from Rome in the fall, and met the Sisters who were to accompany him, in Kansas City. They left Kansas City December 1st, 1873, reached Denver where they remained until December 9. The Sisters were hospitably entertained by the Sisters of Loretto and the Bishop remained at the home of Bishop Machebeuf. From Denver they went by rail to Kit Carson, Colorado, where they were furnished with a covered wagon and horses for the remainder of the journey. They started for Trinidad by way of Raton Pass, got lost in a snowstorm, but had the good fortune to find a sheep ranch, where two shepherds gave up their hut to the travellers. On December 14 they resumed their journey, reached Trinidad in safety and spent several days with the Sisters of Charity. They arrived at Las Vegas in time to spend the Christmas holidays with the Sisters of Loretto. At Las Vegas the Bishop secured another team of horses, the Sisters of Loretto gave him an old coach for his own use, and, according to the written account, the travellers left Las Vegas "in style." They reached Tucson January 27, 1874.

# ORIGIN OF THE CREOLES OF GERMAN DESCENT

J. Hanno Deiler in his book on *"The Settlement of the German Coast of Louisiana"* (Americana Germanica Press, Philadelphia, 1909) defines the term "Creole":

Creoles are the descendants of the white people who emigrated from Europe to Louisiana during the colonial period, i. e. before 1803; and are properly only those born within the limits of the original territory of Louisiana.

In matters of descent not the language, but the blood is the vital matter, and the blood alone. We must therefore classify the Louisiana Creoles according to the blood of their progenitors and say: There are Creoles of French descent, Creoles of German descent, Creoles of Spanish descent, and still others, for instance, Creoles of Irish descent and Creoles of Scotch descent (H. Deiler ib. p. 116). The descendants of the founders of the "German Coast" and the descendants of all other Germans who came to Louisiana before the year 1803 are the "Creoles of German descent". The first Louisiana Creole was born in Mobile in 1704, the child of a French father, nationality of the mother unknown.

In 1717, under the leadership of the notorious Scottish speculator John Law and in connection with his bank in Paris, the Western Company was formed, called after 1719, "La Compagnie des Indes". This company had grants of land and was expected to realize immense sums by planting and commerce. It received the trade monopoly for twenty-five years, with the right to issue an unlimited number of shares of stock and the privilege not only of giving away land on conditions, but also of selling it outright. For these and other considerations the company obligated itself to bring into the colony during the life of its franchise at least 6,000 white people and 3,000 negroes.

In order to develop the supposedly inexhaustible mineral treasures of Louisiana and the fabulous wealth of its soil, large tracts of land, concessions, were given to such rich men in France as would obligate themselves to bring the necessary number of people from Europe to till the soil, and to work in the mines. One of the largest concessioners was John Law, the president of the company, who caused two concessions to be given to himself. The largest one was on the lower Arkansas River, on the peninsula formed by the Mississippi, White and Arkansas Rivers. His second concession was seven leagues below New Orleans, on the Mississippi River, below English Turn. As a shrewd business man, which he no doubt was, John Law knew that, to make his venture a success, he needed not only money but also

114

people able and willing to toil for him; and, as he knew from the reports of the former governors how little adapted to agriculture the French colonists had proven themselves, he resolved to engage for his own concessions Germans from the country on both sides of the Rhine, and from Switzerland.

A great agitation was now inaugurated, partly to induce rich people to take shares in the general enterprise and buy land for their own account and partly to entice poor people to become *engagés* (hired field hands). After a while, land was to be given to the poor field hands to enable them also to get rich. About this time, pamphlets in several languages were printed, containing extracts from letters of people who had already settled in Louisiana, and giving glowing descriptions of the country. Such a pamphlet, in German, which, perhaps, came to Louisiana with one of the pioneer families, was found by Hanno Deiler, the historian of the German Coast, about 1884, in a little book shop at New Orleans and was bought by the Fisk Library (v. Deiler p. 12). It was printed at Leipsic in 1720.

German historians state that, as a result of this agitation, 10,000 Germans emigrated to Louisiana. This seems a rather large number of people to be enticed by the promoter's promises to leave their fatherland and emigrate to a distant country; but we must consider the pitiable condition under which these people lived at home. No part of Germany had suffered more through the terrible "Thirty Years' War" (1618-1648), than the country on the Rhine and especially the Palatinate. After the Thirty Years' War came the dreadful period of Louis XIV; the Palatinate, cn both sides of the Rhine, was devastated in a most frightful manner. Never before were such barbarous deeds perpetrated as by Turenne, Melac and other French generals in the Palatinate. Whether French troops invaded Germany or Germans marched against the French, it was always the Palatinate and the other countries on the Rhine that suffered most through war and its fearful consequences: pestilence, famine and, often also, religious persecution.

The people on the Rhine had at last lost courage, and, as in 1709 and 1710, at the time of the great famine, 15,000 inhabitants of the Palatine had listened to the English agents and had gone down the Rhine to England to seek passage for the English colonies in America: so they were again only too eager to listen to the Louisiana promoter, promising them peace, political and religious freedom and wealth in the New World. So they went forth, not only from the Palatinate, but also from Alsace Lorraine, Baden, Wuertemberg, the electorates of Mayence and Treves and even from Switzerland, some of whose sons were already serving in the Swiss regiments of Halwyl and Karer, sent to Louisiana by France.

Only a small portion of these 10,000 Germans ever reached the shores of Louisiana. We read that the roads leading to the French ports of embarkation were covered with Germans, but that many broke down on their journey from hardships and privations. In the French ports, moreover, where no preparations had been made for the care of so many strangers, and where, while waiting for the departure of the vessels, the emigrants lay crowded together for months, and were insufficiently fed, diseases broke out among them and carried off many. Then came the great loss of human life on the voyage across the sea. Such a voyage often lasted several months, long stops being made at San Domingo, where the people were exposed to infection from tropical diseases. When even strong and healthy people succumbed to diseases brought on by the privations and hardships of such a voyage, by the miserable fare, by the lack of drinking water and disinfectants, and by the terrible odors in the ship's hold,—how must these emigrants have fared, weakened as they were from their journey through France and from sickness in the French ports? At one time only forty Germans landed in Louisiana of 200 who had gone on board; one author speaks of 200 Germans who landed out of 1,200 (H. Deiler ib. p. 16).

Sickness and starvation, however, were not the only dangers of the emigrant of those days. At that time the buccaneers, who had been driven from Yucatan by the Spaniards, in 1717, were yet in the Gulf of Mexico and pursued European vessels because these, in addition to emigrants, usually carried large quantities of provisions, arms, ammunition and money. Many a vessel that plied between France and Louisiana was never heard of again. In 1721 a French ship with "300 very sick Germans" on board was captured by bucaneers near the bay of Samana in San Domingo.

Following Hanno Deiler's careful inquiries, we must come to the conclusion that of the many thousands (6,000 to 10,000) who left Europe for Louisiana, only 2,000 actually reached the shores of the colony and were disembarked at Biloxi and upon Dauphine Island, in the harbor of Mobile.

In the fall of 1719 the French ship *Les Deux Frères* brought the first German colonists to Louisiana (Deiler p. 19). The ship was laden with all sorts of merchandise and effects "which belonged to them." These people could not have been intended for John Law; for judging from what they brought along with them, they must have been people of some means, who intended to become independent settlers. We may assume that they were the founders of the first German village (le premier ancien village allemand), on what is now called "The German Coast," [1] one and a half miles inland from the Mississippi River, on the right bank, about 30 miles above New Orleans (founded by Bienville only one year previously). In September 1721 (according to census of 1724), however, these people were drowned out by the stormwater of the "great hurricane," and the waters of the "Lac des Allemands". This storm lasted five days. Some of the inundated families of the German villages died, others moved to the river front, where the land was higher, and only three were

---

[1] The district which is now called the "German Coast" (Côte des Allemands) begins about 25 miles (by river) above New Orleans and extends about forty miles up the Mississippi on both banks. The land is perfectly level; at the banks of the river, however, it is a little higher, because of the deposit the Mississippi had left there at every overflow. At a distance from one to two miles from the river it becomes lower and gradually turns into cypress swamps. Since 1802 the lower part has been called "St. Charles Parish" and the upper "St. John the Baptist Parish."

found in the first German village by the census enumerator of 1724.

In the beginning of the year 1720, says Pénicaut[2], seven ships came with more than 4,000 persons, "French as well as German and Jews". They were the ships *La Gironde, L'Elephant, La Loire, La Seine, Le Dromadaire, Le Traversier and La Venus.* As *Le Droma-daire* brought the whole outfit for John Law's concession, the staff of Mr. Elias (Stultheus), the Jewish business manager of Law, may have been on board this vessel. For the same reason we may assume that the German people on board, or at least a large part of them, were so-called "Law People" and were mostly sent to the concession on the Arkansas River.

On the 16th of September, the ship *Le Profond* brought more than 240 Germans "for the concession of Mr. Law," and on November 9, 1720, the ship *La Marie* brought Mr. Levens, the second director of Law's concessions, and Mr. Maynard, "conducteur d'ouvriers." The Germans who came on the seven ships mentioned by Pénicaut and those who arrived on board *Le Profond* seem to have been the only ones of the thousands recruited for Law in Germany who actually reached the howling wilderness of the Arkansas River, traveling from Biloxi by way of the inland route: Lake Borgne, Lake Pontchartrain, Lake Maurepas, Amite River, Bayou Manchac and the Mississippi River. All later arrivals were detained at Biloxi and New Orleans and sent to the villages on the German Coast.

A rapid increase of the population would at all times, even in a well regulated community, be a source of embarrassment. It would need the most careful preparations and the purchasing and storing of a great quantity of provisions in order to solve the problem of subsistence in a satisfactory manner. On Dauphine Island and on Biloxi Bay, nevertheless, where the officials of the *Compagnie des Indes* ruled, nothing was done for the reception of so many newcomers. Everybody there seems to have lived like unto the lilies of the field: "They toiled not, neither did they spin." Nobody sowed, nobody harvested, and all waited for the provision ships from France and from San Domingo. Rather than work they would beg, steal or rob from the Indians. Thus the poor German immigrants were put on land where there was always more or less famine, sometimes even starvation. The provisions which the concessioners had brought with them to feed their own *engagés* were taken away from the ships by force to feed the soldiers and the immigrants were told to subsist on what they might be able to catch on the beach and on the corn which the Indians might let them have. Governor Bienville repeatedly demanded that these immigrants should not be landed on the gulf, but should be taken up the Mississippi River, but the question whether large vessels could enter and ascend the great river was not yet solved, although the colony had been in existence for about twenty years. As a very large number of smaller

---

[2] Pénicaut was a French carpenter who lived for twenty years (1699 to Oct. 1721) in the colony, and his "Relation" is an important source for the history of Louisiana. Mr. French, in his "Louisiana and Florida" has published a translation.

boats, by which the immigrants might easily have been taken to the concessions by the inland route through Lake Pontchartrain, had been allowed to go to wreck on the sands of Biloxi, the newcomers, especially those who arrived in 1721, had to stay for many months in Biloxi and on Dauphine Island, where they starved in masses or died of epidemic diseases.

On February 3, 1721, the ship *La Mutine* arrived at Ship Island with 147 (347?) Swiss "Ouvriers" of the *Compagnie des Indes.*" [3] Shortly before, on January 24, four ships had sailed from the French port of L'Orient for Louisiana with 875 Germans and 66 Swiss emigrants. The names of these four ships were *Les Deux Frères, La Garonne, La Sanone* and *La Charente.* But few of these 941 emigrants survived the horrors of the sea voyage and landed on the coast of Louisiana (v. Deiler, p. 28). On the ship *Lex Deux Frères* alone 173 lives out of 213 were lost on the sea. What suffering, what despair must have been endured on board these pest ships!

Towards the end of May 1721 two other ships with 270 Germans arrived in Louisiana; finally there came on June 4, the *Portefaix* with 330 immigrants, mostly Germans and originally intended for John Law's concessions. They were under the command of Karl Friedrich d'Arensburg, a former Swedish officer, then in the service of the *Compagnie des Indes.* [4] But in the meanwhile John Law's delusive scheme had failed. In the early spring of 1721 the news arrived in Louisiana, that Law had resigned his post of councillor of state and comptroller-general of the finances of France and for personal safety fled from Paris. [5] The news of Law's failure was a heavy blow to the *Compagnie des Indes.* It was decided to send no more Germans to the Law concessions, but to organize the immigrants under the leadership of d'Arensburg and to begin a new settlement with them. D'Arensburg, merging the survivors of the different troops into one body, departed with them from Biloxi for the banks of the Mississippi and transferred them to the two German villages on the German Coast, thirty miles

---

[3] Ever since 1719 the Swiss formed an integral part of the French troops in Louisiana. There were always at least four companies of fifty men each in the colony. At the expiration of their term of service, they usually remained in Louisiana, took up a trade or settled on some land contiguous to the German Coast. It was even a rule to give annually land, provisions and rations to two men from each Swiss company to facilitate their settling. The great majority of these Swiss soldiers, however, were not Swiss, but Germans from all parts of the fatherland.

[4] This remarkable man's name probably was Karl Friedrich, born at Arensburg on the isle of Oesel in the Baltic Sea (Bay of Riga). With other Swedish officers he left his home. because he preferred exile to Russification. The French officials of the *Compagnie des Indes,* mistaking "d'Arensburg" for his family name, issued his commission to "Charles Fréderic D'Arensbourg" With his Germans he took active part in the expulsion of Governor Ulloa from New Orleans in 1768. He died November 18, 1777, at the age of 84 years. (Deiler, p. 38, ss.)

[5] Law left Paris on December 10, 1720, for Brussels. Later on he lived in great obscurity, finally settling at Venice; there he died March 21, 1729, still occupied in vast schemes and fully convinced of the solidity of his system, the failure of which he attributed entirely to enmity and panic. (The Americana, Vol. XII, under Law John.)

from New Orleans, which in honor of Karl Friedrich d'Arensburg were called "Karlstein" (Deiler p. 54).

But the German *engagés* on the Arkansas River were in a precarious condition. Having arrived about the end of 1720, they had not been able to make a crop, as the preparatory work of clearing the ground and providing shelter for themselves had occupied most of their time; much sickness also prevailing amongst them, they were unable to begin farming operations on a larger scale before August 1721. These Germans therefore needed assistance until they could help themselves, for not another livre was to be expected from the bankrupt John Law. But when, in November 1721, the company had decided to manage Law's concessions in the future for their own account, the resolution to help the Germans was not carried out, as Law's agent on the Arkansas, Levens, refused to transfer the business to the company. So it happened that the forlorn Germans received help neither from the one side nor from the other to bridge them over to the harvesting time of their first crop. They were forced to ask help of their old friends, the Arkansas and the Sothui Indians. Finally, when help from this last source failed, and smallpox broke out amongst the Indians and the Germans, they were forced to give up all and abandon the concession.

They resolved to go down the Mississippi to New Orleans, end of January or in February 1722, to return to Europe. Only 47 persons remained behind, which Dudemaine Dufresne found there, when in March 1722 he was installed by La Harpe in the office of manager of the concession in place of Levens. When La Harpe returned from his other mission, the silly search for the imaginary "Smaragd Rock" in Arkansas, these too had departed.

The arrival of the flotilla of the Germans from the Arkansas River must have been a great surprise for the people of New Orleans. That the Teuton colonists who considerably outnumbered the population of the new town, could remain at New Orleans, was out of question. Nor would the ill treated people stay in the swampy and wild post. New Orleans was at that time in its very infancy and looked more like a miserable mining camp than a town. Indeed the Germans did not come to thank the Company for favors. Some very plain words were spoken by the desperate men to the officials of the Company; in fact, it is said that Governor Bienville interceded, and when they demanded passage back to Europe, tried his very best to induce them to remain. The results of the conferences were: first that the Germans from the Arkansas were given rich alluvial lands on the right bank of the Mississippi River, about 25 miles above New Orleans, on what is now known as the "German Coast," where the village of Karlstein already existed; secondly that the agent on the Arkansas, Levens, was deposed; and thirdly, that provisions were sent to the Germans who still remained there. (Deiler, p. 38).

But the grant of good land in the neighborhood of the infant city did not terminate the woes of the unfortunate colonists.

No pen can describe, says Deiler (p. 56), nor human fancy imagine the hardships which the German pioneers of Louisiana suffered even after they had survived the perils of the sea and epidemics and starvation on the sands of Biloxi. Had they been of a less hardy race, not one of these families would have survived. It should be remembered that the land assigned to them was virgin forest in the heavy alluvial bottoms of the Mississippi, with their tremendous germinating powers awakened by a semi-tropical sun. Giant oaks with wide-spreading arms and gray mossy beards stood there as if from eternity and defied the ax of man. Between them arose towering pines with thick undergrowth, bushes and shrubs and an impenetrable twist of running, spinning and climbing vines, under whose protection lurked a hell of hostile animals and savage men. Leopards, bears, panthers, wild cats, snakes and alligators, and their terrible allies, a scorching sun, the miasma rising from the disturbed virgin soil, and the floods of a mighty river,—all these combined to destroy the work of man and man himself. There were no levees then, no protecting dams, and only too often, when the spring floods came, the colonists were driven to climb upon the roofs of their houses and up into the trees; hundreds of miles of fertile land were inundated.

In spite of all the hardships which the pioneers had to endure and the difficulties to be encountered, the industry, energy and perseverance of these hardy colonists conquered all; and although hundreds perished, the survivors wrested from the soil not only a bare living, but in course of time a high degree of prosperity also. These German peasants more than once saved the city of New Orleans from famine. Karl Friedrich d'Arensburg served for more than forty years as commander and judge of the German Coast of Louisiana, sharing alike the joys and the hardships of his people.

In the Catholic Church in New Orleans, on the site of the present Cathedral, the Germans of the German Coast first attended divine service; here they also had their children christened, here their weddings were celebrated. The cathedral records from 1720 to 1730 contain many German names.

But in 1724, so the census of that year informs us, the Germans had a chapel of their own on the German Coast, which then may have stood already for one or two years, as the river settlement was made in the late fall of 1721. It is interesting to note this fact and to remember that this chapel was built about the same time when the Jesuit Charlevoix reported (1722) that the people of New Orleans "had lent the Lord half of a miserable store for divine service and that they want the Lord to move out again and accept shelter in a tent" (Deiler, p. 63). In the colonial budget for 1729 provision was made for a resident priest, the Capuchin Father Philip. The chapel was dedicated to St. Charles, to do honor to Karl Friedrich d'Arensburg. It was replaced in 1740 by the first "Red Church" on the other side of the river, twenty-five miles above New Orleans. The first Red Church was burnt in 1806 and in the same year replaced by the second, the present Red Church.[6]

---

[6] The church of St. Charles was called the "Red Church" from the traditional coat of red paint which both, the old and new church, had and which made them a landmark for boats on the Mississippi River.

In 1771 the Germans of the Upper German Coast built the church of St. John the Baptist, upon the right side of the river, a few miles from the place where the first chapel had been. The corner stone of the present church of St. John the Baptist was laid on June 4, 1820, and it was consecrated on March 17, 1822. The first parish priest of St. John the Baptist, the Capuchin P. Bernard de Limpach (1772-76) was also the first canonical pastor of the church of St. Louis, in Missouri (1776-1789).[7]

We now approach the question: What is the probable number of the Creoles of German descent? This question may be answered in the words of the promise given to Abraham: they are as numerous "as the sands on the sea shore."

The church registers of St. John the Baptist prove that the German pioneers were blessed with enormously large families.[8] It seems that heaven wanted to compensate them in this manner for the many dear ones they had lost in the ports of France, on the high seas, in Biloxi, and during the first period of their settling in Louisiana. Hanno Deiler found fourteen, sixteen, eighteen, and once even twenty-two children in a family.

Yet, in spite of this great number of children there was no difficulty in providing for the numerous daughters. There was a great scarcity of women in Louisiana in early times. Indeed prostitutes were gathered in Paris[9] and sent to Louisiana to provide wives for the colonists. Few of these lewd women ever had any children and their families became extinct in the second or third generations. No wonder that the young Frenchmen, especially those of the better class chose wives from among the German maidens, who were not only morally and physically strong, but had also been reared by their German mothers to be good house-wives. Even into the most exclusive circles into the families of the officials and of the richest merchants the German girls married; they became the wives of French and Spanish officers of ancient nobility in whose descendants German blood still flows.[10]

As a rule the German girls took German husbands and whole

---

[7] v. Pastoralblatt, St. Louis, Mo., August 1918. J. Rothensteiner.

[8] When, in 1877 a demented negro set fire to the priest's house of St. Charles' parish, all the records of the "Red Church" were burnt.

[9] The Chevalier Champigny in his memoir (La Haye, 1776) writes: They gathered up the poor, mendicants and prostitutes, and embarked them by force on the transports. On arriving in Louisiana they were married and had lands assigned to them to cultivate, but the idle life of three-fourths of these folks rendered them unfit for farming. You cannot find twenty of these vagabond families in Louisiana now. Most of them died in misery or returned to France, bringing back such ideas which their ill-success had inspired. The most frightful accounts of the country of the Mississippi soon began to spread among the public, at a time when German colonists were planting new and most successful establishments on the banks of the Mississippi. within five or seven leagues from New Orleans. This tract, still occupied by their descendants, is the best cultivated and most thickly settled part of the colony, and I regard the Germans and the Canadians as the founders of all our establishments in Louisiana.

[10] The proofs v. in Deiler's book, p. 116.

families married into one another. To give but one example, it may be mentioned here that out of ten children of one Jacob Troxler, not fewer than eight married into the Haydel family. In such families the German language survived longest. In consequence, however, of the many family ties between the Germans and the French, and in consequence of the custom of the Creoles to marry into related families, French gradually became the family language even in those German families which had preserved the German language during three generations.

The changes which the German family names underwent amongst the Creoles are most regrettable. Without exception, all names of the first German colonists were changed, and most of the Creoles of German descent at the present time no longer know how the names of their German ancestors looked. Sometimes they were changed beyond recognition (e. g. Zweig into La Branche). Various circumstances contributed to the changing of these names. The principal one was, no doubt, the fact, that some of the old German colonists were not able to write their names. Their youth had fallen into the period of the first fifty years after the Thirty Years' War, and into the last years of the war when the armies of Louis XIV of France devastated the Palatinate. In consequence of the general destruction and the widespread misery of that period, schools could hardly exist in their home towns. It was, therefore, not the fault of these people if they could neither read nor write. As the parents could not tell their children in Louisiana how to write their names, these children had to accept what French and Spanish teachers and priests told them, and what they found in official documents. But French and Spanish officials and priests heard the German names through French and Spanish ears and wrote them down as they thought these sounds should be written in French or Spanish.

The Creoles of German descent constitute even now a large, if not the largest, part of the white population of the German Coast, the parishes of St. Charles and St. John the Baptist. But they spread at an early time also over neighboring districts, where their many children took up new lands for cultivation.

There are still amongst the descendants of the early Germans many of the ancient stalwart German type, who betray the French blood received in the course of time only by their more lively disposition; there are still blue eyes and blond hair among them. But their economical condition has been changed considerably. Through the Civil War many of these families lost not only their slaves, but also their plantations, the source of their once very considerable wealth. They have shared the lot of the French Creoles. But, thanks to their inherited energy, they wrung an existence from the adverse conditions, and now that a new era of prosperity has dawned upon Lousiana, their prospects have become brighter. The great majority of the Creoles of German descent may be said to be again on the road to prosperity.

F. G. HOLWECK.

# NOTES

✠

Catholic Historical Society of St. Louis.

*Secretary's Report for* 1919-1920.

The Secretary's report for the twelve months just elapsed need be but very brief, as the main topics will be treated by the chairmen of the various committees.

At the last general meeting of the Society all the old officers were elected for another term, although that method did not seem altogether satisfactory to some. The officers, however, very faithfully attended to their duties. The attendance of our membership was not what could be expected, especially when the importance of our proposed work is taken into consideration. Yet we have to chronicle some progress. The membership grew in numbers, and our collections were enriched by some very important gifts, as the old Church Records of Old Mines Parish and the Letters of Archbishop Kain. His Grace of St. Louis was the donor of the Records, and Msgr. J. J. Tannrath of Archbishop Kain's Letters. At the September meeting Fathers Holweck and Van Tourenhout gave informal talks on the Old Parishes of Louisiana, which they had recently visited and partly explored. At the November meeting Mr. Edward Brown read an important paper on Governor McNair. At the January meeting Father Martin Brennan gave a highly interesting talk on the theory of the planets being inhabited, inclining to the negative side. At the March meeting the Secretary treated of the circumstances connected with the visit of an Indian delegation from beyond the Rocky Mountains to St. Louis for the purpose of obtaining a "Black Gown" for their people.

The publication of the Society's organ, the St. Louis Catholic Historical Review was delayed several times, owing, in part, to the disturbed condition of the times. The Society has a strong claim on the patriotic and Christian interest of the cultured classes of St. Louis and Missouri, and, we may add, of the entire Mississippi Valley. It is the Society's purpose to elucidate the religious and social influences that went out from St. Louis, far and wide, from the days of the earliest discoveries to our living present, which will soon be history, too. With greater interest aroused and with better financial support, the Catholic Historical Society of St. Louis could do imperishable work.

John Rothensteiner, Secretary.

## REPORT OF EXECUTIVE COMMITTEE CATHOLIC HISTORICAL SOCIETY OF ST. LOUIS FOR THE YEAR ENDING MAY, 1920.

The Committee met regularly each month next preceding the general meeting of the Society during the year.

The meetings of the Committee were generally well attended, current expenditures were authorized and arrangements made from time to time for the reading of a paper at each meeting of the Society during the year.

The urgent appeal made by the Committee a year ago for an increased membership and a more active interest in the work of the Society, on the part of the members enrolled, has not been heeded—six new members were enrolled during the year—two members died and one resigned, leaving the present membership 57—a net gain of only three members since our last Annual Meeting. The general meetings of the Society were poorly attended; sixty-four per cent of the total membership were not present at any meeting, and less than twelve members have taken any active interest in the work of the Society. The principal work of the Society has been in the publication of its Quarterly, the ST. LOUIS CATHOLIC HISTORICAL REVIEW, the first volume of which was completed with the publication of the July-October, 1919, number. One hundred copies of this volume will be bound in cloth as soon as the index to the volume has been received from the printer, and offered for sale at $4.00 per copy. The cost of publishing the REVIEW is about $600 per annum, while the entire membership dues and subscriptions for the REVIEW is about $460. While the Society, up to this time, has been able to meet its current obligations, it is obvious that the work cannot be continued very long without a deficit, unless there is a marked increase in the Society's membership, or a large number of new subscribers secured for the REVIEW.

Apart from the question of expense, there has been much delay and irregularity in issuing the REVIEW—each number being several months late. Although the July and October numbers were issued as a double number, it was not ready for distribution until after the first of the year. The January number is still in press, but will be issued shortly.

It is suggested that the Publication Committee reorganize or arrange its editorial work in some way to have the REVIEW appear each quarter with regularity. The very life of the Society, in the opinion of this Committee, depends upon the success of this publication.

The membership at large is again urged to lend the interest and co-operation necessary to maintain the Society and enable it to continue its work successfully.

The Treasurer's report showing the receipts and expenditures for the year and the amount of cash on hand, is submitted herewith:

FINANCIAL REPORT

*For the year ending April 30, 1920.*

| RECEIPTS. | | EXPENDITURES. | |
|---|---|---|---|
| Balance on hand May 1, 1919... | $ 11.34 | Postage and printing.......... | $ 6.20 |
| Dues paid by members........ | 268.13 | Printing Hist. Review........ | 389.62 |
| Subscriptions, etc., Historical | | M. V. Review................ | 4.00 |
| Review .................... | 220.25 | Exchange ................... | 1.15 |
| | | Balance .................... | 98.75 |
| | $499.72 | | |
| | | Total .....................| $499.72 |

J. J. TANNRATH, *Treasurer.*

Balance on hand May 1, 1920.$ 98.75

Respectfully Submitted,

EXECUTIVE COMMITTEE,

J. A. CONNOLLY, V. G., Chairman.

## ‑CATHOLIC BEGINNINGS IN KANSAS CITY,

*By Reverend Gilbert J. Garraghan, S.J.*

12mo., 137 pages, illustrated.   Price $1.25, postpaid.

The city and diocese of Kansas City may well be proud of the dainty booklet concerning its "Catholic Beginnings," which Father Gilbert J. Garraghan, S.J., of the St. Louis University has written, and the Loyola University Press of Chicago has published this year. It is a monograph of 137 pages, beautifully printed on fine paper, and tastefully bound. Father Garraghan is a writer who combines patient, laborious research with excellent judgment and fine literary ability; and this latest product of his genius proves once more that accuracy and historical truth are not incompatible with the graces of style. Father Garraghan's book reads like a romance, and yet it is exact and trustworthy history. The book is full of most interesting facts, gathered from numerous sources, mostly manuscripts not accessible heretofore, but hidden away in archives and libraries, yet facts touched to life once more by the glowing pen of a true historian, a lover of the ancient days. In fact, we have here the only authentic account of the early days of the second metropolis of Missouri, "the only complete first chapter of the general history of Kansas City," as it has been justly styled. Any future historian of that wonderful city must, of necessity, give this book the place of honor among his printed sources, for it is a source-book of the most important kind, embodying the very words of the actors in that early drama. The Roux letters form only one, though the most interesting, source of information: *The Westport Register, the Kickapoo Mission Record,* the Baptismal Records of Father De la Croix, the numerous illustrations, the old map of early Kansas City, with all the houses marked upon it, all are historical sources as rare and priceless as any in our state. If it be surprising what a mass of interesting information is compressed in such small compass, it is still more surprising how eminently readable the book proves to be. The secret of its attraction lies in the orderly arrangement of all the manifold detail, and the clear, concise, limpid style of writing. The beginnings of Kansas City were Catholic. Catholic traders from St. Louis were the pioneers in all the region, and the presence of the Catholic Church made itself felt as the earliest and most important religious influence in Westport and the surrounding country. Now that the mustard seed has grown up into the mighty tree of Catholic Kansas City, it is pleasant to read of the spirit of faith and charity and self-sacrifice that animated the first planters and cultivators of the spiritual soil in that one-time Western wilderness. We would recommend to all Missourians first, and to all lovers of heroic lives in general, the perusal of Father Garraghan's *Catholic Beginnings in Kansas City, Missouri.* We of the St. Louis Catholic Historical Review are specially proud of Father Garraghan's success, as we number him among the members of our editorial staff, and as one of the most valued contributors to our columns. Father Garraghan has erected a *monumentum aere perennius* to the greatness of Kansas

,City, and to the honor of our State. May this beautiful success encourage others to raise similar monuments to commemorate the labors and sacrifices and successes and triumphs of our fathers in the Faith.

Father G. J. Garraghan's book illustrates the fact that, from the time of its erection into an independent Episcopal See, the Church of St. Louis has taken to heart to prove herself pre-eminently apostolic. The leading article opening the present number of the REVIEW gives another evidence of that apostolic zeal. But not only the Church of St. Louis as an Ecclesiastical unit, but more restricted organizations in its bosom were looked up to as centers from which Catholic life and activity must radiate abroad. It was, no doubt, because he was convinced of this truth, that Bishop Salpointe applied to the Sisters of St. Joseph to send a colony in far-away Arizona. Fifty years have rolled by since the first Sisters set out from Carondelet on the long, tedious and perilous journey. Tucson, Arizona, is now within the distance of a three days' journey from St. Louis; no longer do the Indians lie in wait to slaughter the traveller through their jealously kept wilderness; we are tempted at times to judge the conditions of fifty years ago by those of to-day; from the Pullman window or the observation car one finds hard to believe traveling meant then well-nigh incredible hardships; the parlor-car philosopher smiles at the harrowing tales which are the history of but yesterday, and fails to recognize that nothing short of heroism was needed to launch on such journeys as the Sisters of St. Joseph undertook in 1870. But the parlor-car philosopher lacks the power to visualize past conditions; nor is it to him we look up for appreciation of devotedness prompted by no human interest and discernment of heroism. Neither does history look to him for judgment; and more and more, we are sure, will history extol the true worth of those zealous souls that set out from our midst to blaze the way of the Gospel. Honor to them, and particularly on this happy golden Jubilee year, honor to those apostolic Sisters of Carondelet who fearlessly started to the unknown West to do the work of Him who missioned His Church to teach all nations.

The missions to the Indians of Missouri and the great Northwest have been recounted; in the above-mentioned *Journal* we have a narrative of the commencement of Catholic education in the West; one field of the missionary activity kindled in St. Louis has so far been the object of little attention: we mean the Texas Missions. Let us hope that, no less than the others, these, too, will soon find in these pages an appreciative narrator.

\*　　\*　　\*　　\*

The nationality of P. Kino, S.J.—Since Mr. Herb. E. Bolton of the State University of California discovered the long-lost diary of P. Kino, called "Favores Celestiales," several Reviews have taken interest in the person of this great American Missionary. To settle the question of his nationality, Rev. F. G. Holweck asked one of the parish priests of the Val di Non, Trentino, the home of P. Kino, for information. Whereupon a well-known priest from Trent, Rev. Simone Weber, June 21, 1920, answered that P. Kino's real name was "Chini"; he was born August 10, 1645, at Segno, a village belonging to the Parish of Torra, Val di Non. His parents were Francisco Chini and Marg. Luchi. If P. Chini called himself "German," it was not to indicate his nationality, but solely because the ecclesiastic principality of Trent was a dependency of the Germano-Roman Empire. The "Germanus" of P. Chini must not be taken in the same sense that he was a Teuton; himself, his family, his country, his valley, were and are distinctly Italian. His education, however, was absolutely German; he studied at Hall near Innsbruck, at Freiburg, i. B. and at Ingolstadt. At Segno, the home village of P. Chini, there exist, at the present time, many families by the name of Chini.

*    *    *    *

*Why the Buffalo Vanished from the Plains.*

The Indian, once the proud possessor of all America, has almost vanished from the land. Pushed westward by the advancing tide of European immigration, the various tribes seemed destined, for a short time to become a great people of hunters and trappers on the Western plains from Nebraska to Texas. The land was full of game, especially of the so-called bison or Buffalo, which supplied a frugal people with food, clothing and fuel. But in a few years the buffalo had vanished, and the poor Indian was reduced to direst poverty.

How the wild game, particularly the bison, were swept from the Western plains, is told by a railroad poster resurrected from America's early days, says the *New York Sun.*

These posters, according to the California Fish and Game Commission, were posted throughout England. American hunters not coming in sufficient numbers, a bid was made oversees for more gunners, women being included.

The poster is headed "Grand Buffalo Hunt," and reads as follows:

"A grand buffalo hunt will be held in September next on the prairies of Nebraska and Colorado, U. S. A., and through the magnificent valley of the Republican River, the rich alluvial feeding grounds of the buffalo.

"The Burlington & Missouri River Railroad Company owns millions of acres, is one of the most wealthy corporations in the Western States of America, and will assist this hunting party in every way, in order that the sportsmen of England may see the Western country, and on their return be able to corroborate the statements as to climate, resources and the gigantic advancement made in so new a country.

"There are no hostile Indians in Nebraska whatever; friendly chiefs of the Otoes, Pawnees and other tribes will accompany the party.

"Sportsmen will be provided with army tents and beds during the hunt. There will be servants to take care of the horses, and, in fact, all arrangements have been made to give the hunting party the greatest amount of pleasure with the least possible trouble.

"Wagons will be provided for the conveyance of any trophies of the chase, such as buffalo skins, elk horns and antlers in limited quantity.

"The sportsman has there a field of nature's own planting on which to roam in pursuit of his healthy and invigorating pleasures, and where can the lover of scenery find greater, grander, lovelier views than are to be found on the continent of America?

"Fare for the round trip of about seven weeks, including every expense, except wines, liquors, cigars, guns, rifles and ammunition, 90 guineas.

"The arrangements will be such as to admit of ladies joining the party; but the charge for ladies will be 100 guineas each."

\*　　\*　　\*　　\*

We, of St. Louis, who, schooled in the spirit of grateful remembrance so strongly inculcated by St. Paul, (Heb. 13, 7), did not deem any celebration too grand for the worthy remembrance of the prelate who came here a century ago to speak the word of God on our shores. We are bending all our efforts upon the pleasant task of letting no particle of information escape our search, in order that to "the men of renown, and our fathers in their generation" may be in due time erected an historical monument worthy of their labors and of our appreciation. For we have long since made our own the earnest appeal of the learned Editor of the *Catholic Historical Review* (Washington, D. C.) that of every Bishop of the United States, the history should be written. No more ingratiating news, therefore, could reach us than that a life of Bishop Louis William Valentine Du Bourg is contemplated and in course of composition. We may add, without fear of betraying any secrets, that the writer is admirably well equipped for the task he has undertaken. Of the "Bishop of Louisiana" what most of us know best is his public life as Administrator and Bishop; the prelate's prospective historian is privileged to have access to an imposing mass of family papers which will reveal also the man. Most heartily do we wish godspeed to the zealous historian and do we pray for the happy completion of his labor of love and devotion.

\*　　\*　　\*　　\*

To some of our Ecclesiastical readers it may appear that the periodical conferences of the clergy are a relatively new-fangled institution, without precedent or even analogy in the past. Without going back to the pages of Europe's Church history, we may trace the wholesome practice *in this country*, and in the Diocese of Louisiana, of which St. Louis was then a part, for now more than a century back. For this purpose we need but quote here the following passage of a letter of Bishop Du Bourg to Father Bigeschi, Pastor of the Church of the Assumption, Bayou La Fourche, La. This letter was written from the Barrens, on August 15th, 1819:

> With regard to the Ecclesiastical Conferences, if Father Valezano is willing to gather the priests at his place, I believe that that would be most convenient, I appoint him President, and Father Tichitoli, Secretary.

I desire that Fathers Mina and Mariani should go there. Let the members begin with going to confession and assisting at High Mass. At the time appointed for the conference proper, one of the members shall have a little speech on some matter of ecclesiastical life or duties; after that, each one may submit his doubts, or some case of conscience. The Secretary shall take down the names of the members in attendance, and the minutes of the proceedings, with the questions propounded and the solutions given thereto; and he shall send me his minutes, either by mail, postpaid, to spare my exchequer, or by some occasion. It would be well for the Chairman to prepare the subjects beforehaand, and assign them for the next conference. These subjects may be on questions of Moral Theology. the Sacraments, the Decalogue, Justice, etc.—on Ecclesiastical duties, the means to reform abuses, to spread instruction, etc., etc., or finally difficult cases of conscience with their circumstances.

# DOCUMENTS FROM OUR ARCHIVES

## Correspondence of Bishop Du Bourg with Propaganda

### XXI.
### BISHOP DU BOURG TO THE CARDINAL PREFECT OF PROPAGANDA.[1]

Eminenitissime Praefecte.

. . . Quod vero attinet ad erectionem Novae Metropoleos, de qua unum solummodo verbum in praefato supplici libello factum est, inter Praesules praevalet opinio, *Civitatem S. Ludovici* inter omnes praeferendam, tum propter ipsius geographicam positionem, tum ob nascentem in dies circumvicinarum Regionum populationem et famam. Nullum profecto dubium est quin Religionis molumento valde profutura sit secunda Metropoleos creatio. Una tamen est difficultas, quae nos moratur. Nondum in Episcopalem Sedem erecta est *Civitas S. Ludovici,* nec ullatenus expedit ut dividatur, saltem ante longum tempus, Dioecesis Louisianensis. Inferior enim et Superior Louisiana sibi mutuo ita necessaria sunt, ut neque ista corporalem nec illa spiritualem pastum, a se invicem avulsae comparare valeret. Episcopali mensae, et Seminarii sustentationi utcumque providet inferior Louisiana; Superior sola est, unde altera Sacerdotes expectat. Utraque igitur societatis suae emolumentum habet, quo, si dividetur, in deterius utraque abeat necesse est. Dies forsan olim elucescet, cum alioqui expetenda divisio sine tam gravi detrimento effici poterit; at maturius semper in re tanti momenti erit procedendum, ne, sub specie majoris utilitatis, pessumdetur partis utriusque vigor. Impraesentiarum vero prorsus constat hujusmodi divisionem exitiosissimam fore, et summopere necessarium esse ut sub unius Episcopi auctoritate ambae remaneant, adjuncto tamen ipsi Coadjutore, qui in partem ipsius solicitudinis veniat. Haec cum ita sint, duobus dumtaxat modis erigi posset praefata Metropolis, videlicet, vel sub generico nomine *Louisianae,* vel erigendo Civititatem *San Ludovicensem* in titulum Archiepiscopalem *annexa ipsi Sede Neo-Aurelian-*

---

[1] Archives of Propaganda. *Acta S. Congregationis de Propaganda Fide,* 1822. These Documents, from the Roman Archives were copied in Rome (1882) by the Very Rev. Henry Van der Sanden, Chancellor of the Archdiocese. The dots indicate passages not copied, probably because they were deemed irrelevant to the History of the Diocese which the late Chancellor was compiling.

130

*ensi.* Quod si neutrum Sacrae Congregationi arriserit, nihil de nova Metropoli erit statuendum. Si vero posterius expedire videatur, propria San Ludovicensis Dioecesis circumscriptio esse potest *totus Status Missouriensis,* cum tota illa *Illinensis Status* parte quae inter flumen Mississippi et duodecimum longitudinis gradum jacet. Quod superest supremi hujus Status, cum Statu *Indianae,* nunc a Revmo Bardensi Antistite administratum, novam Dioecesim olim constituere poterit; sed nondum matura res est. Nova vero Metropolis, si erigere ipsam placuerit, omnes Sedes Episcopales citra juga Alleganensia, sibi subjectas habere convenit.

Ad sacrae purp . . . etc.

+Lud. Guil. Episc. Neo-Aurel

S. Ludovici, in Statu Missouriano,
 Aprilis 25, 1820.

## TRANSLATION.

Your Eminence :—

. . . [2]

Now touching the erection of a new Metropolitan See, about which only a word was said in the afore-mentioned petition,[3] the Bishops' prevailing opinion is that the *City of St. Louis* should have the preference above all others, on account of its geographical position, as well as of the increasing population and appreciation of the surrounding country. There can be no doubt that the creation of another Archbishopric is destined to serve greatly the interests of Religion. However, there is a difficulty which stops us: St. Louis has not yet been erected into an Episcopal See, and a division of Louisiana is in no wise advisable, at least for yet a good while. For Lower and Upper Louisiana are so necessary to each other, that if they be separated, the latter could not get temporal, and the other spiritual help. The Episcopal *mensa,* and the support of the seminary are somehow supplied by Lower Louisiana; from Upper Louisiana alone can priests be supplied. Each one, therefore, needs the society of the other; hence, if a division is made, both must of necessity suffer. At some future day, perhaps, it will be possible to make this division, otherwise desirable, without such great detriment; yet it will always be profitable to proceed slowly in a matter of such importance, lest, under the specious appearance of greater utility, the strength of both parts be impaired. For the present, at any rate, it is evident that the division would be a calamity; and it is of the utmost importance that both sections remain under the authority of only one Bishop, to whom, however, a Coadjutor should be given, to take a portion of his solicitude. In these conditions, only in two ways could

---

[2] The passage here omitted introduced the Rev. Angelo Inglesi (See Review, Vol. II, p. 46, n. 4) and asked he be appointed Coadjutor. Document XXIII deals at great length with this request.

[3] This was. no doubt. a petition by the "western" Bishops, Flaget and David. (See Spalding, *Life of Bishop Flaget,* p. 216 and foll.

the Metropolitan See of which we are speaking be erected: namely, by
designating it under the generic name of Louisiana, or by the creation
in St. Louis of an Archiepiscopal title to which would be joined the See
of New Orleans, and if neither way meets the approval of the S. Congregation, then nothing should be done in regard to a new Archbishopric. If, however, the latter of the above-indicated means should be
found expedient, then the Diocese of St. Louis proper might include
all the State of Missouri, with all the part of the State of Illinois
stretching between the Mississippi River and the 12th degree of longi-
tude. The rest of the State, together with the State of Indiana, now
under the jurisdiction of the Bishop of Bardstown, may, in the course
of time, constitute a new Diocese; but the matter is not yet ripe for consideration. The new Metropolis, if it is the good pleasure of the Congregation to erect it, might have properly as Suffragan all the Episcopal
Sees this side of the Alleghanies.

+L. Wm., Bp. of New Orl.

St. Louis, State of Missouri, April 25, 1820.

## XXII.

### BISHOP DU BOURG TO CARDINAL FONTANA, PREFECT OF PROPAGANDA.[1]

Deo favente, ad me nuper venerunt amplissimae litterae, quibus
me docet Eminentia Vestra, etsi Sacra illa Congregatio Coadjutorem
mihi dare sit parata, Domino tamen Ludovico Sibourd, Vicario meo
Generali. quem ad hoc onus proposueram, tum propter provectam ipsius
aetatem, sexaginta nempe et quatutor annorum, tum quia de ejus prudentia, virtute et doctrina satis ipsi non constat, nullo modo favere. Fateor
aetatem grandaevam non modicum difficultatis facessere, quippe quae
parum juvet ad immensas Episcopalis muneris, in tam dilatata Dioecesi,
molestias perferendas.—De caeteris dotibus putabam me abunde satis-
fecisse. Sufficit vero quod sub uno respectu Sacrae Congregationi
minus quam oportet idoneus videatur, ut ipsius sapientissimo oraculo
me penitus subjiciam. Declaraveram sane me Domino Sibourd hac de
causa adhaerere, quod praeter eum, vix alius praesto foret sacerdos in
mea Dioecesi, qui eam experientiam, et cognitionem rerum et hominum
in Episcopo summe necessarias, adquisivisset. In aliud igitur tempus
necesse erit differre Coadjutoris electionem. Forsan intra unum aut
alterum annum poterimus de alio cogitare, qui Sacrae Congregationis
vota, aeque ac mea valeat explere. Interim dum vires mihi suppetunt,
solus oneri humeros applicabo; et ad id juvabit quod infinita Dei miseri-
cordia mihi tandem omnium corda subjecit.

Puto Eminentiam Vestram non latere quanta odia in me prius in
ista inferiori Louisiana, efferbuissent, ita ut ipsam adire absque evidenti

---

[1] Archives of Propaganda, *Scritture referite nei Congressi*. Cod. 7. America Centrale. Dal Canada all Istmo di Panama. Dal 1821 a tto il 1822.
Eminentissime Praefecte.

periculo non valerem. Non modicam igitur ipsi admirationem faciet audire me in hac Dioceseos meae lustratione, ad Novam usque Aureliam inter unanimes ferme cleri et populorum congratulationes advenisse.

A Domino factum est istud, et ita mirabilis apparuit animorum conversio, ut vix oculis suis credant, qui priorum angustiarum conscii, nunc consolationes videntes, quibus misericors Deus animam meam laetificat. Inter omnes qui ad adventum meum majora dedere et gaudi et reverentiae signa conspicuum quam maxime se praebuit Rev. Pater Antonius de Sedella, ille ipse, qui antea, nescio cur, infensissimus mihi extiterat Verba non sufficiant si narrare velim, quot et quantis honoribus me exceperit, et prope dicere ausim: "Nullum nunc habeo tam unanimem qui sincera dictione sollicitus sit pro me." Hujus ad exemplum tota se composuit Civitas, ita ut publice Synodum in ea ipsa urbe celebrare non pertimuerim, in qua uno abhinc anno faciem meam monstrare summi fuisset periculi.—

Ad Synodum hanc convenerunt viginti circiter sacerdotes ex inferiori Louisiana; qui omnes unanimes se exhibuerunt, tum in sua erga me observantia, tum in zelo Ecclesiasticae disciplinae tuendae. Multum quoque solatii attulit videre morum reformationem et pietatis incrementum quae in universis prope parochiis intra tam breve spatium, fratrum meorum laboribus, obtinuerunt.

De caeteris Sacram hanc Congregationem fusius docebit Reverendus Dnus. Angelus Inglesi, Romanus patria . . . . de quo in praecedentibus. Hunc jam in Coadjutorem mihi rogare praesumerem, nisi meo judicio, satius esset aliquot annos expectare, ut sibi inter fratres suos majorem existimationem conciliaret.

Liceat mihi tamen, Eminentissime Praefecte, haec Tibi vota insinuare, ut si forte de vivis me auferri contigerit, antequam expleantur, sciat Eminentia Vestra nullum eo acceptiorem mihi fore in successorem. Gaudeo quod praesens occasio ipsum Eminentiae Vestrae caeterisque Eminentissimis S. Congregationis Patribus notum facere et desiderium meum promovere possit.

Ad Sylvicolarum, qui in superioribus Dioeceseos meae partibus abundant, conversionem, vix animum usquedum adjicere licuit; et si potuissem, deerant operarii. Dudum de Patribus Societatis Jesu ad hoc praecellentissimum opus charitatis cogitaveram, nullumque, ad obtinendos aliquot ex eis, non moveram lapidem. In hac re plurimum mihi favit Sanctissimus Dominus Noster, datis ad Superiorem Generalem etiam epistolis, ut meis votis obsecundaret. Nihil tamen hactenus profeceramus. Sed nunc audio Superiores in hoc opus se propensiores exhibere Dnum. Inglesi igitur monui, ut quod sibi ingenii et sollicitudinis inest, totum in maturando hoc consilo impendat. Et Eminentiam Vestram ferventissime precor ut ipsi adjutricem manum admoveat. Unus praecipue est inter Patres dictae Societatis, nomine *De Barat*, Burdigalae in inferiori Seminario degens, quem scio ardentissimo huc veniendi desiderio flagrare, vir pietate, doctrina, zeloque animarum nemini secundus; hunc suppliciter rogo mihi a Vicario Generali concedi, et Eminentiae Vestrae ad eum finem potentissimam mediationem mihi flagito. Huic se libenter comites adjicient aliqui ex junioribus inter

Gallos, aliique provectioris aetatis inter eos quos e Moscovitarum finibus Gallia nuper excepit. Quinque vel ad summum sex sufficerent, si
duo vel tres ex Marylandia ipsis se adjungerent, quod summopere est
peroptandum, tum propter linguae Anglicae peritiam, tum quia cum isti
fortuna abundant, possent inopiae fratrum supplere. Cum extra sub-
sidio, facile sibi iter pandet Evangelium ad gentes innumeras Mississippii
et Missourii oris undequaque circumjacentes. Ad Eminentiam Vestram spectat, Eminentissime Praefecte, tantum opus inchoare. Ad illud
viriliter se accingat. Ni faciat, vereor heterodoxos missionarios tam
optabilis victoriae palmam a nobis ablaturos.

Parcat Eminentia Vestra epistolae hujus incoherentiae, et obtuso
stylo. Iter agens scribo, in una ex his navibus, quae fervidae aquae
vapore propelluntur.

+LUD. GUIL. Ep. Neo-Aurel.
Ex Superiori Louisiana, die Sti. Mathiae Ap. 1821.

## TRANSLATION

Your Eminence :—

I thank God for the consolation afforded me recently by the reception of your long letter,[2] wherein Your Eminence advises me that, although the S. Congregation is disposed to give me a Coadjutor, yet it
does not at all favor the appointment of Father Louis Sibourd, my
Vicar General, whom I had proposed for this office. The objection is
taken from his advanced age—sixty-four—also from the lack of information as to his prudence, virtue and knowledge. I readily confess
that his age causes a certain amount of difficulty, as it does not permit
to undergo the considerable fatigues of the Episcopal charge in such an
immense Diocese. With regard to the other qualifications, I thought
I had explained myself quite sufficiently. But the fact that from one
point of view he does not come up to the mark of the S. Congregation
is enough for me to abide entirely by its most wise decision. I had
plainly stated, though, that my reason for holding so much for Father
Sibourd, was that, outside of him, I had scarcely any priest in my
Diocese in possession of that experience, and knowledge of men and
things, which are of prime necessity in a Bishop. We will have, therefore, to postpone to some other time the election of the Coadjutor.
Perhaps within one or two years will we be able to think of someone
else capable of meeting the requirements of the S. Congregation, and
my own. Meanwhile, as long as my strength permits, I will bear the
burden alone; and I will find no mean help in the fact that, by God's
infinite mercy, all hearts are now obedient to me.

Your Eminence is aware, I believe, of the amount of hatred first
aroused against me in this Lower Louisiana; it went so far that I could
go there only at considerable risk. It will be to you, therefore, a source

---

[2] This seems to refer to Propaganda Letter No. 14 (REVIEW, Vol. II, p. 51-
52), although the length of this document is not such as to justify the *"amplissi-
mas"* wherewith Bishop Du Bourg qualifies it. But the subject matter fits in
every point.

of great wonder to hear that, in this visitation of my Diocese, I have met, all the way to New Orleans, a practically unanimous welcome from the clergy and the people.[3]

This is truly the work of the Lord, and so wonderful has this change of spirit appeared, that the persons who knew the distress I was in, can scarcely believe their eyes when they behold the consolations with which the all-merciful God gladdens my soul. Among those who exhibited the greatest signs of joy and reverence at my coming, one of the most conspicuous was the Rev. Father Anthony de Sedella, the very same man who, in former times, I know not why, was most hostile to me. Words are unavailing to describe the honors with which he welcomed me, and I would dare say that there is no one more in harmony with me, no one to whom genuine affection prompts to more solicitude in my behalf. This example has given the tone to the whole city, so that I was not afraid to celebrate publicly a synod in that same city where, a year ago, merely to show myself would have meant extreme danger.

This Synod was made up of some twenty priests from Lower Louisiana. All manifested in unison both their obedience to me and their zeal for the maintenance of Ecclesiastical discipline. It afforded me likewise much consolation to see the change in morals and the increase of piety which, thanks to the labors of my brother-priests, has been effected in almost every parish within so short a space of time.[4]

As to the rest, the S. Congregation will be made fully cognizant of it by the Rev. Angelo Inglesi, a native of . . .[5] whom I mentioned in my preceding letter. I would not hesitate to ask him for my Coadjutor were it not proper, according to my judgment, to wait a few years, until he is more fully appreciated by his brother-priests.[6]

However, permit me, My Lord, to give you this hint of my wish, so that in case I should depart this life before this wish is fulfilled, Your Eminence may know that I deem no one to be more acceptable as my successor. I am glad that the present occasion is offered Your Eminence and the other Cardinals of the Sacred Congregation to know him and bring about the fulfilment of my desires.

---

[3] In several letters of this period, Bishop Du Bourg attributes this wonderful change to the exertions of Father Martial, whom he cannot praise too highly. Later events reversed considerably this feeling and this esteem.

[4] This glowing report appears too optimistic; or, if there was a change, it was not lasting: for, in a letter—perhaps somewhat pessimistic, although it mentions facts—of July 13, 1822, Father Martial wrote from New Orleans: "We had not, during this whole year, one single communion, not even at Easter, despite our instructions and pressing solicitations. Carelessness in regard to religion is rampant to a frightful degree." (Archives of Propaganda. *Scritture Referite*, Cod. 7). It should be noted, however, that religion fared quite differently in the city and in country districts.

[5] Word illegible.

[6] Bishop Du Bourg seems here to forget what he had already written in the beginning of his letter of April 25, 1820 (Document XXI, above). At any rate, he was not to wait "a few years" before making a strong plea for Inglesi's promotion, as may be seen from his very next letter, of May 3. The "few years" were reduced to a little more than two months.

So far I have scarcely been able to turn my attention to the conversion of the savages, who are in great numbers in the upper part of my Diocese. But even if I had been able to do so, there were no laborers. For some time past I have been thinking, for this paramount work of charity, of the Fathers of the Society of Jesus, and have left no stone unturned in order to secure some of them. In this regard I was greatly aided by His Holiness, who went so far as to write to the Superior General with a view to indorse my wishes. But hitherto our efforts have proved unsuccessful. However, I understand that the Superiors of the Society are now showing more willingness to undertake the work I have accordingly recommended to Father Inglesi to make use of every resource his intelligence and zeal could prompt in order to bring this project to maturity. I likewise beg most earnestly Your Eminence to second his efforts. There is, in particular, one of the Fathers of the Society, *De Barat* by name, now in the Little Seminary of Bordeaux, whom I know to be most anxious to come here; his piety, knowledge and zeal are beyond par. I most earnestly pray the Vicar General to give him to me; and beseech to this end the aid of Your Eminence's most powerful influence. With him some of the younger French Jesuits will be glad to come, as also others, of riper years, among those who came lately from Russia to France. Five, or six at most, would be sufficient, if to them were added two or three from Maryland—a thing most desirable on account of their knowledge of English, and also because, as these are well off financially, they could supply the want of their brothers. With this help the Gospel cannot fail to make headway among the numberless nations on both sides of the Mississippi and of the Missouri. Your Eminence should make it his business to undertake such a great work. Do manfully gird your loins to do it! If you do not, I am afraid the Protestant missionaries will wrest from us this so desirable palm of victory.

Please, Your Eminence, to pardon me the incoherence of this letter and its uncouth style. I am writing while on a journey on one of those boats propelled by steam.

+L. Wm., Bp. of New Orl.

Upper Louisiana, St. Mathias' Day, 1821.

## XXIII.

### BISHOP DU BOURG TO CARDINAL FONTANA, PREFECT OF PROPAGANDA.[1]

Eminentissime Praefecte.

Etsi per duos continuos annos Sacram hanc Congregationem impensius rogare non destiterim, ut Coadjutorem mihi, in partem Episcopalis meae solicitudinis, adciscere dignaretur, numquam tamen, animum

---

[1] Archives of Propaganda. *Scritture referite nei Congressi.* Cod. 7. This is really the "darkest page" in the history of Bishop Du Bourg's administration.

vehementius affecerat urgens auxilii hujusmodi necessitas, quam cum in immensum succrescentes curae, decrescentesque eadem ratione vires, monent me solum tanto oneri sustentando parem diu non futurum. E memoria quippe Eminentiae Vestrae excidere nolim Diocesim hanc sexcentis et amplius leucis in longitudinem extendi, cujus utraque extremitas Episcopi praesentiam prorsus exigit. Sex fere menses nuper absumpsi in cursoria perlustratione solius inferioris Louisianae, quae licet populationem praecipuam, vix tamen sextam extensione partem Dioecesis constituit. Ducentis supra mille millibus a Nova Aurelia distat oppidum Sti. Ludovici, alterum crescentis in dies populationis centrum. Interjacentes regiones disjectis hac illac, magnoque tractu, ut plurimum, a se invicem sejunctis habitationibus componuntur. Unde facile videre potest Eminentia Vestra Episcopum unum, etsi herculeo robore, vitamque integram in arduis visitationis laboribus agat, vix ac ne vix quidem, satis muneri suo facere usquam posse. Ad haec, timor ne, me intempestive inter tot curas et continua pericula sublato, longa viduitate afflicta Dioecesis in statum recidat pejorem priore, quiescere animum non sinit, donec per Coadjutoris institutionem, ipsius et praesenti necessitati et futurae firmitati provisum fuerit.

Non diffitebor equidem virum aetate provectum parum tantis solicitudinibus aptum esse. Hujusmodi tamen non levis auxilii fuisset, Sedem suam in alterutro Dioecesis fine constituens vigilantiae saltem et continuarum peregrinationum onere me partim levasset, praeterquam quod successionis quasi quoddam extitisset vinculum. Ideo nullum praesto habens mediae aetatis sacerdotem, quem ad hoc onus proporerem, veritusque ne longe majores adversus juniorem exceptiones assurgerent, senes duos successive designaveram, Revdos. scilicet *Antonium de Sedella et Ludovicum Sibourd*. His objecit Sacra Congregatio, nec conqueror. Restat igitur ut inter juniores unum seligam, qui maturitate judicii, sincera devotione, aliisque praeclaris dotibus aetatis defectui abundantius suppleat.

Hunc, ni me fallit affectus, inveni in dilectissimo filio meo Revdo. Angelo Inglesi, quem Divina Providentia mihi consolatorem in angustiis, et baculum ingruentis jam senectutis, mirabiliter deputavit. Dicam quod res est. Neminem unquam habui tam unanimem, qui sincera dilectione pro me et ovibus meis solicitiorem se praebuerit. Haec ipsa fuit solicitudo, quae, cum viderit me subsidiis quasi omnibus, sive ad vitam sustentandam, sive ad promovendam Missionum nostrarum utilitatem indigere, ad Europam illum abduxit, ut et aere proprio, utique non modico, et mendicatis fidelibus largitionibus, inopiae nostrae suppleret, novasque, quibus plurimum deficimus, operariorum copias colligeret. Adeo vere ipsum, praecipuum Dioecesis Fundatorem, a longe salutare non dubitem. Eminentiam Vestram latere non arbitror quot jam peregrinationes hac de causa susceperit, quanta dignitate legatione sua functus, quantoque honore ubicumque a maximis etiam principibus variarumque gentium proceribus fuerit cumulatus. Haec sane prudentiam arguunt supra aetatem, nec dubitare sinunt quin novus hic Timotheus ita se in Episcopali munere sit gesturus ut nemo adolescentiam ejus contemnat. Quidni igitur non jam votis meis, sed universi

cleri et plebis Louisianensis annuatur, qui cum consona voce in Coadjutorem et successorem meum advocant?

Forsan obstant Ecclesiae leges, quae quadragesimum annum ad
Episcopatum requirunt. Sed quoties cum ipsis dispensatum jam fuit!
Multum profecto a quadragesimo distabant Titus et Timotheus, quin et
dilectus Apostolus. Et ut ad tempus nostrum veniamus, caeteris pluri-
bus omissis, vix arbitror trigesimo excessisse Illmum. Dnum. De
Quelen, cum ad Archipiscopatum Nazianzenum et Sedis Parisiensis
Coadjutorium nuper est promotus. Parcat Eminentia Vestra. Dicam
quod sentio. Ubi concurrunt in praecellenti gradu, fides, prudentia,
docilitas et Religionis studium, nedum hujuscemodi promotioni obstare
debeat juvenilis aetas, plurimum e contrario juvare videtur. Hic enim
nondum agitur de potestatis Episcopalis exercitio, sed de ejusdem,
ut ita dicam, tyrocinio, quod, quanto citius incoeptum, quanto longius
protractum, tanto utiliorem experientiam ad futuram administrationem
comparabit. Successorem habere cupio, qui prius quam habenas susci-
piat longo usu jam sacris functionibus et gubernio assuefactus fuerit;
non quod ea sim praesumptione ut putem me capacem esse aliquem
ad tam formidandum opus docere, sed quod, divina afflante et auxiliante
gratia, ita praeter spem sucessit methodus quam diuturna et hominum
et locorum notitia mihi suggessit, ut jure verear ne, alia et jam inten-
tata ratione, tam fausta initia pessum itura sint.

Caeterum Eminentiae Vestrae et Sacrae huic Congregationi jam
notum esse puto Revm. Dnum. Inglesi; Literis enim datis Lutetiae
Parisiorum 23 Februarii decurrentis anni doceor eum tunc proxime in
Germaniam, inde Romam profecturum; unde colligo eum Romae fore,
cum istae ad manus Eminentiae Vestrae pertinent.

Judicio igitur Sacrae Congregationis omnia, ut aequum est, submitto, vehementer quidem cupiens, ut si ita Eminentissimis PP. videbitur, dictus Revus. Dnus. Romae episcopalis consecrationis ritum
subeat, id enim perfecto legationis ipsius successui non modicum inser-
viret; sin minus, Eminentiam Vestram persuasam esse volens de mea
ad nutum S. Congregationis integra resignatione. Sperans tamen me
tertia vice repulsam non passurum, unum adjiciam, ut, si contigerit eum
jam Roma discessum ipsius ei institutio per manus Burdigalensis Archiepiscopi quamprimum dirigatur ut episcopalem unctionem, ubicumque
fuerit, recipere valeat. Sane praevidere debeo eum, pro ingenita mo-
destia, tanto honori repugnaturum; confido tamen, cum Episcopi et
fratrum suorum votis, tum praesertim consiliis Eminentiae Vestrae et
Mandatis Summi Pontificis humiliter obtemperaturum.

✝Lud. Guil. Du Bourg, Ep. Neo.-Aurel.

Novae Aureliae, die Maii 3a, 1821.

## TRANSLATION.

My Lord Cardinal:—

Although for the space of two years I have never ceased to beseech
the S. Congregation to deign to give me a Coajutor who could take part

of my Episcopal charge, yet never was ever my mind so strongly affected by the urgent necessity of such a help, as when I hear, from the cares which increase almost to the infinite, and from my strength waning in proportion, the warning that 1 shall not be long able to bear alone such an immense burden. Your Eminence must not forget, indeed, that this Diocese extends to more than six hundred leagues in length, and that both ends require equally the presence of the Bishop. It has just taken me almost six months to make a rapid visitation of Lower Louisiana alone, which though it is the principal portion of the Diocese in regard to population,' is scarcely one-sixth of it in point of area. More than twelve hundred miles separate from New Orleans the town of St. Louis,[2] the second center of a population which grows every day. The territory between is made up of settlements scattered here and there, and usually at considerable distances from one another. From this Your Eminence may easily realize that one Bishop, were he even endowed with herculean strength and devoting his whole time to the arduous labor of the visitations, can hardly—nay, cannot—discharge all the duties of his charge. Besides, the fear that, should it happen that, amidst so many cares and dangers, I were suddenly taken away, the Diocese afflicted by a long vacancy might fall into a condition worse than before, will not leave any rest to my mind until the appointment of a Coadjutor provides for the present necessity of the said Diocese and its future maintenance.

I readily agree that a man advanced in years is little suited for such a great solicitude. Yet such a man would neverthless be of great help, as by fixing his residence in one portion of the Diocese, he would relieve me of the burden of watchfulness and incessant travel, besides establishing a kind of bond of succession. Because I have here no priest of middle age, whom I could propose for this office, and was afraid that stronger objections would be made against the appointment of a younger man, I had designated successively two old men, namely, the Revs. *Anthony de Sedella* and *Louis Sibourd*. That the S. Congregation objected to their appointment, I do not complain. But then it remains to me to choose from among the younger clergy one who, by the maturity of his judgment, his sincere devotion and his other remarkable qualifications may make up what he lacks in years.

Such a one, unless affection misleads me, I have found in the person of my most beloved son, the Rev. Angelo Inglesi, whom Divine Providence has placed by my side to be to me a comforter in my sorrows and the staff of my coming old age. To tell plainly the truth, never did I have anyone so congenial to me, and who ever showed greater affection for me and greater solicitude for my flock. This solicitude it was which, when he saw me destitute of almost every means either of supporting myself, or of promoting the interests of our missions, led him to Europe, in order that both with his own fortune, which is not small, and with the offerings that he would beg from the faithful,

---

[2] Distances were reckoned by the course of the Mississippi River, the only "highway" then available.

he might supply our want, and recruit a new band of laborers that we are so much in need of. For this reason I do not hesitate to salute him from afar as the chief founder of the Diocese. I believe that Your Eminence is aware of the journeys he has already undertaken for that purpose, of how worthily he has acquitted himself of his mission, and of the honors bestowed upon him everywhere, even by the greatest princes and the potentates of various countries. All this evinces certainly a prudence beyond his age and leaves no doubt that this new Timothy will so conduct himself in the Episcopate that no one shall despise his youth. Why should not, therefore, this satisfaction be given not only to my own wishes, but also to those of the whole clergy and people of Louisiana, who unanimously desire him for my Coajutor and successor.[3]

Perhaps this is contrary to the Church's law, requiring forty years of age for the Episcopal order.[4] But how often has not dispensation been given! No doubt, Titus and Timothy were far from their fortieth year; farther still the Beloved Apostle. And to speak of our own time, and without mentioning other cases, I am pretty sure that the Most Rev. De Quélen was scarcely over thirty years old when he was promoted to the Archbishopric of Nazianza and the Coadjutorship of Paris. I beg Your Eminence to pardon me; but I must tell all that is in my mind. Where are united in a superior degree faith, prudence, docility and zeal, far from being an obstacle, youth ought to be, on the contrary, a recommendation. For here there is not yet question of the exercise of the Episcopal power, but, if I may so say, of the apprenticeship thereof; and the sooner this is commenced, and the longer it lasts, the more useful the experience which it will impart for administration later on. The kind of successor I wish is one who, before taking in hand the reins, should be fully trained by a long practice of ecclesiastical functions and government. Not that I am so presumptuous as to think I am able to train anyone to so tremendous a work, but such unexpected happy results have, with the help of God's grace, been obtained by the method which a long acquaintance with men and places

---

[3] How much "the whole clergy of Louisiana" were desiring the appointment of Inglesi as Du Bourg's Coadjutor and successor, we may gather from the letter of Father Martial already quoted above: "A letter which I wrote to him last winter in reply to his, concerning his asking Fr. Inglesi as Coadjutor, came very near estranging us. . . . The opposition which manifested itself when it became known that he wished to have Father Inglesi for his Coadjutor so rent his soul asunder that he issued forth a circular letter to the priests to strike fear into them. True, he was sorry for it afterwards, when he beheld the effect it had produced: well, clever men make sometimes frightful mistakes!" It should be borne in mind, however, that this was written after the disclosures concerning Inglesi's reported misbehavior in Rome had reached Louisiana. and may be somewhat colored by these revelations. There is perhaps a little, in Father Martial's tone, of the "I told-you-so."

[4] Pishop Du Bourg is here apparently mistaken. The old ecclesiastical law required, like the new one (Can. 331), thirty years of age, in the candidates for the Episcopal Order. But this mistake in Canon Law affords to the Bishop the occasion for a display of eloquent pleading which, in view of later events, is truly pitiful.

dictated to me, that I have every reason to be afraid that, if another and untried means be adopted, these happy beginnings may turn into a failure.

At all events, I believe that by this time the Rev. Father Inglesi is known to Your Eminence and to the S. Congregation. A letter written to me from Paris on February 23 of the present year advises me that he was to leave shortly, first for Germany, then for Rome; hence I surmise he will be in Rome when this letter reaches Your Eminence.

Of course, I leave ultimately everything to the judgment of the S. Congregation; still I most earnestly desire that, if so please the Eminent Cardinals, the said Rev. Father may be consecrated over there, as this would contribute immensely to the complete success of his mission abroad; if, however, such is not your good pleasure, I want Your Eminence to be fully convinced of my unreserved resignation to the will of the Sacred Congregation. Hoping, however, that this time—it is the third time—I shall not meet with a refusal, I beg that, if he happened to have already left Rome, his brief of institution be sent him as soon as possible through the Archbishop of Bordeaux, so that he may receive Episcopal consecration at any place where he may happen to be. Of course, I must foresee that, in his modesty, he will be reluctant to accept the honor; I trust, nevertheless, that, in view of the wishes of his Bishop and of his brother-priests,[5] and still more, of the advice of Your Eminence and the command of the Sovereign Pontiff, he will humbly acquiesce.[6]

+L. WM. DU BOURG, Bp. of New Orl.

New Orleans, May 3, 1821.

## XXIV.

### CARDINAL FONTANA TO BISHOP DU BOURG.[1]

### NO. 15.

Maxima perfusus sum laetitia ex Ampls. Tuae litteris datis die 24 Februarii proxime elapsi, ex quibus non sine admiratione percepi magnam, ac salutarem Novae Aureliae factam esse spiritualium rerum

---

[5] See above, Note 3.

[6] Martial's letter adds to that story, already sad enough in itself, a statement as disparaging to Bishop Du Bourg as it is distasteful. There seems to have been a report circulating in Rome that Inglesi himself had asked to be appointed Du Bourg's Coadjutor. This is scarcely credible. How much truth there is in what follows is hard to discern: "Bishop Du Bourg." wrote Martial, "attested that the proposal that Inglesi be made Coadjutor was made to him by Propaganda itself through the Prefect, Card. Fontana; that Father Inglesi refused, and that the Sovereign Pontiff forced him to accept the Bulls, so that he might be consecrated later on in St. Louis. This last bit of information was communicated to us by the young men from Lyons and Turin which *the Count* sent us as missionaries." Bishop Du Bourg's statement must, of course, have been materially true: only he guarded carefully, in view of the prevailing opposition, from saying that Cardinal Fontana and Propaganda acted in compliance with his own (D. B.'s) earnest plea.

[1] Original in Archives of St. Louis Diocesan Chancery.

commutationem; visitationem Tuam non modo benevole, sed etiam lactanter exceptam tum a Parocho Antonio de Sedella, qui prius adeo Tibi infestus erat, tum a reliqua Catholicorum multitudine, eorum mores tuorum operariorum studio, ac labore aliquantum reformatos, Synodum celebration, et Ecclesiasticam Disciplinam jam pene collapsam in pristinum restitutam, Benedictus Deus Pater misericordiarum, qui gratia sua aberrantes ad bonam frugem revocare dignatus est; atque ex faustis hisce principiis sperare licet futurum, ut omnia in posterum feliciter componantur. Ad Coadjutorem vero tuum, quod attinet, non satis quidem nobis probatum erat, ut ad hoc munus deligeretur D. Ludovicus Sibourd, qui Te provectior aetate est; neque Amplo Tua vel senectute, vel valetudinis incommodis adeo confecta est, ut Coadjutore nunc egeat. Potius quam Coadjutore, majori quidem Pastorum numero vastissima ista Diocesis indigere videtur; non enim in tanta Regionum amplitudine unus tantum Episcopus tot dissitorum Fidelium Curam exercere facile potest; ideoque maxime profuturum putarem, si Dioecesis ista in Tres saltem Ecclesias divideretur, quarum una inferiorem Luisianam, altera Superiorem, tertia Floridas complecti posset; et cum ita se res haberent, Dnus Sibourd, cujus merita tantopere effers, ad unam posset ex novis ejusmodi Ecclesiis promoveri. R. D. Angelus Inglesi, qui nunc Romae versatur, ac de istius Ecclesiae statu apprime certiores nos fecit, pietate, studio, ac ceteris dotibus satis cumulatus esse videtur; sed viridi adhuc aetate, ac missione recens est, ideoque expectandum, ut adhuc majora praebeat suarum argumenta virtutum, nec non experientiam, ac Populorum fiduciam, et gratiam comparare Sibi possit. Voti tamen Tui suo loco, et tempore habebitur ratio. Illud interea, de quo non minus Ampl.o Tua quam S. Congreg.o, valde sollicita est, conversionem respicit Sylvicolarum, qui in Superioribus praesertim Luisianae Partibus affluunt, quique ex errorum tenebris ad Lumen veritatis facile perduci possunt, si operariorum copia suppeteret. Equidem sentio, nullos magis ad hoc opus idoneos fore, quam Patres Societatis Jesu; omnemque propterea navabo operam, ut P. Praepositus generalis faveat sententiae tuae, nec solum permittat Patri de Barat Burdigalae moranti, ut se cum aliis, qui e Russia migrarunt, isthuc se conferat, sed etiam curet, ut duo vel tres ex Marylandia mittantur. Ampl.m Tuam de rei exitu faciam quamprimum certiorem. Sed necesse est, ut Loca designes, ac circumscribas, quae PP. Jesuitarum Missioni sint tribuenda, ne dissidia, et collisiones postea exoriantur. De his omnibus rogo Ampl.m Tuam, ut mihi sententiam Tuam aperiat; atque interim Deum precor, ut eamdem diutissime servet, ac sospitet.

Ampl.s Tuae.

Romae ex aedibus S. Congñis de Propaganda Fide 2 Junii, 1821.

Uti Frater Studiosissimus,

F. Card. Fontana, Praefectus.

Illmo, ac Rmo D. Ludovico Guillelmo Du Bourg Epo Novae Aureliae in foederatis Americae Provinciis S. Ludovicum.

C. M. Pedicini, Sec.rius.

## TRANSLATION.

Right Reverend Sir:—

An immense pleasure was afforded me by your Lordship's letter in date of February 24 of this year, in which I have learned, with no small wonderment, the great and salutary change which has taken place in the spiritual life of New Orleans[2]: Your visitation was received not only with decency, but with gladness, both by the Rector, Father Anthony de Sedella, who formerly was so stubbornly opposed to you, and by the Catholics at large; the morals of the people, thanks to the zeal and work of your co-laborers, have undergone a change for the better; a synod was convened, and ecclesiastical discipline, which was almost ruined, has gained a new vigor. Blessed be God, the Father of mercies, whose grace has turned the refractory to better sentiments; from this happy beginning there is every reason to hope that everything henceforth will be arranged to satisfaction.

In regard to your Coajutator, I must say we could not see our way to select for this office Father Louis Sibourd, who is older than you; moreover, your Lordship is not so broken down either by age or by ill-health, as to be in need of a Coajutor just now. Rather than a Coadjutor, it seems that a greater number of Bishops is what that immense Diocese seems to want[3]; for in such a vast territory one Bishop alone can hardly care for the number of the faithful, scattered as they are. I should think, therefore, that it would be of the utmost interest of the Diocese if it were divided into three: one could comprise Lower Louisiana, another Upper Louisiana, and the third the Floridas. In this hypothesis, Father Sibourd, whose merit you extol so much, might well be promoted to one of these new churches. As to Rev. Angelo Inglesi, who is presently in Rome, and has given us at first hand a report of the state of your church, he seems to be possessed of enough piety, zeal and the other qualifications; but he is still quite young, and recently arrived in your Mission; we must wait, therefore, until he has a chance of giving yet better proofs of his virtue, acquiring experience and ingratiating himself into the confidence and good will of the people. Your wish, though, will be taken into account in the proper place and at the proper time.

Meanwhile what Your Lordship has no less at hand than the S. Congregation, concerns the conversion of the savages, who are in great numbers through Upper Louisiana, and may be easily brought from the darkness of error to the Light of truth, provided there are laborers. I indeed feel like yourself that no workers are better fitted for this task than the Fathers of the Society of Jesus; accordingly I will do my utmost to bring the Superior general to consent to your proposal, and not only permit to Father de Barat, now residing at Bordeaux, to go

---

[2] See above. Document XXII, Note 4.

[3] This seems to have been something like a deadlock: Bishop Du Bourg insisting all along on having a Coadjutor and opposing the division of the Diocese; at least, the separation of Upper from Lower Louisiana; Propaganda, on the other hand, far from keen about the Coadjutorship, but intent on dividing the Diocese.

over there with others who came recently from Russia, but also to see to it that two or three from Maryland be sent. I shall without delay notify Your Lordship of the result of this negotiation. But you ought to mention and specify exactly the places to be attributed to the Mission of the Jesuit Fathers, in order to preclude all misunderstandings and conflicts for the future.

Concerning all these matters I beg Your Lordship to give me your opinion. Meantime I pray God to give you yet long years and good health. Your Lordship's Most Devoted Brother,

F. CARD. FONTANA, Prefect.

Rome, Palace of the S. Congreg. of Propaganda, June 23, 1821.
The Right Rev. Louis William Du Bourg, Bp. of New Orleans.
St. Louis, U. S. A.

C. M. PEDICINI, Secretary.

## XXV.
### CARDINAL FONTANA TO BISHOP DU BOURG.[1]

Illme, ac Rme Dne.

Quae Ampl.o Tua de Missione erigenda in amplissima ista Diocesi sub directione, et Cura Patrum Societatis Jesu ad procurandam Sylvicolarum conversionem mihi proposuit, ea Praeposito Gen.li ejusdem Societatis enixe commendare non defui; sed ex responso, quod ille reddidit, cujusque exemplum his litteris adjungo, facile intelliges, illum pro nunc ob Operariorum paucitatem tam praeclarum opus aggredi nullo modo posse. Tuum itaque erit, alias persequi vias, quibus laudabile hoc tuum propositum perficiatur; nihil enim est tam sanctum, ac vere Apostolicum, quam barbaras gentes in errorum tenebris delitescentes ad lumen veritatis, ac aeternae salutis semitam perducere. Quod cum pro Tua satis mihi perspecta sollicitudine, ac studio Te minime neglecturum confido, D. O. M. precor, ut Ampl.m Tuam diutissime servet, ac sospitet.

Ampl.s Tuae,

Romae ex aedibus S. Congñis de Propaganda Fide 23. Junii, 1821.

Uti Frater Studiosissimus

F. CARD. FONTANA, Praefectus.

Illm, ac Rmo D. Ludovico Guillelmo Du Bourg, Epo. Novae Aureliae Luisiana.

S. Ludovicum.

C. M. PEDICINI, Secr.ius.

## TRANSLATION.

Right Reverend Sir:—

Your Lordship's proposal concerning the erection of a mission in your immense Diocese, for the evangelization of the savages, under the

---

[1] Original in Archives of St. Louis Diocesan Chancery.

direction, and in care of the Fathers of the Society of Jesus, I did not fail to recommend warmly to the Superior General of said society. But from the answer returned by him, a copy of which I enclose herein, you may easily understand that, by reason of the scarcity of laborers, he is for the present unable to undertake this noble work. It accordingly devolves upon you to adopt other means to bring about the realization of your praiseworthy design: no work, indeed, is holier and more apostolic than that of turning barbarous nations, plunged in the darkness of error, to the light of truth and the path of eternal salvation. What I know of your solicitude and zeal assures me that you will not neglect these means.

I pray Almighty God to give Your Lordship long years and perfect health. Your Lordship's Most Devoted Brother,

F. Card. *Fontana*, Prefect.·

Rome, Palace of the S. Cong. of Propaganda, June 23, 1821.

To the Right Rev. Louis William Du Bourg, Bishop of New Orleans, St. Louis, La.

C. M. Pedicini, Secretary.

## XXVI.

### CARDINAL FONTANA TO BISHOP DU BOURG.[1]

### NO. 17.

Illmo, ac Rme Dñe.

Cum ad examen revocata fuerint ea, quae Ampl.o Tua per literas 20. Aprilis elapsi anni exposuit circa liberatatem, quam sibi arrogare posse arbitrantur plerique istarum Provinciarum Episcopi, Promovendi nimirum ad Sacros Ordines eos, qui cum alienae sint Dioecesis in Americam proficiscuntur sacro ministerio operam daturi; non tanti quidem ponderis visa sunt Emis Patribus allata rationum momenta, ut id· licitum censendum sit. Patenter quippe obstat peroulgata Innocentii XII. Constitutio *Speculatores domus Israel* edita die 4. Novembris anni 1694, quae universam afficit Ecclesiam, et in qua ad evellendos abusus, et fraudes circa Sacras Ordinationes alienorum subditorum, nec non ad veteris Disciplinae instaurationem, totiusque Christiani Populi aedificationem edicitur, nulli Episcopo licere externum quempiam sibi non subditum ad Sacros Ordines promovere, nisi ille domicilium per decennium saltem ibi contraxerit, suumque revera esse animum ibi permanendi jurejurando spoponderit, exhibitis etiam Testimonialibus litteris Ordinarii, sub quo originem duxit, prout fusius in eadem Constitutione decernitur. Ex quo quidem satis patet, Apl.m Tuam in promovendo non subditos, non servatis iisdem conditionibus in eam incidisse poenam, quae per eamdem Constitutionem infertur, ut nempe Ordinarii ab Ordinum Collatione per annum, ordinati vera a susceptorum Ordinum exequutione, quamdiu proprio Ordinario expedire videbitur, eo ipso suspensi remaneant. Cum vero Emis Patribus satis persuasum

sit, Ampl.m Tuam non in spretum Aplicaé Constitutionis sed bona fide
illam violasse, censuerunt, supplicandum SSmo, ut tam Ampl.m Tuam,
quam eos, qui a Te sic ordinati fuerunt, Aplica sua auctoritate, qua-
tenus opus sit, a praedictis poenis absolvere dignaretur; cui S. Congñis
consilio Bmus Pater in audientia habita per infraptum Secretarium die
15. hujus mensis benigne annuit. Monitam tamen tum Ampl.m Tuam,
tum ceteros istarum Provinciarum Antistites esse velim, ut in posterum
eidem Constitutioni se plane conforment; atqué interim Deum precor,
ut Te diutissime servet, ac sospitet.

Ampl.s Tuae

Romae ex aedibus S. Congñis de Propaganda Fide 21 Julii 1821.

F. CARD. FONTANA, Praefectus.

Illmo, ac Rmo D. Ludovico Gúillelmo Du Bourg.

Epo Novae Aureliae in Luisiana.

S. Ludovicum in agro Illinensi.

C. M. PEDICINI, Secr.ius.


## TRANSLATION.

Right Reverend Sir:—

On examining the matter submitted by Your Lordship in your
letter of April 20 of last year, namely, the liberty which most of the
Bishops of the United States think they can arrogate to themselves, of
promoting to Sacred Orders those who, belonging to another Diocese,
go to America to exercise there the sacred ministry, their Eminences
did not deem the arguments alleged weighty enough to render the
practice lawful. It evidently indeed runs counter to the well-known
Constitution *Speculatores,* of Innocent XII, in date of November 4,
1694, which binds the whole Church, and in which, in view to uproot
abuses and prevent frauds in the matter of the ordinations of alien subjects to Sacred Orders, as well as to restore the old discipline and promote the edification of the Christian people, it is enacted that no Bishop
can lawfully raise anyone not his own subject to Sacred Orders, unless
the candidate has established there his domicile for at least ten years,
and affirmed under oath that he has truly the intention of remaining
there; he should, moreover, bring testimonial letters from the Ordinary
of the place of his birth, as is decreed quite at length in the aforesaid
Constitution.

From the foregoing it is quite clear that Your Lordship, in ordain-
ing men who were not your own subjects, without complying with the
above-mentioned conditions, incurred the penalty enacted by said Constitution, namely, that the Ordinaries are suspended *ipso facto* for one
year from conferring Orders, and those whom they ordained, from
the exercise of the Orders received, for as long as shall be deemed expedient by their Ordinary. As Their Eminences, however, are fully
convinced that Your Lordship broke the Apostolic Constitution in good
faith, and not out of contempt, they were of opinion that the Holy
Father should be beseeched to deign absolve from the afore-mentioned
penalties, by his Apostolic authority, insofar as needs be, both Your

Lordship and those who were thus ordained by you. The Holy Father, in the audience granted to the undersigned Secretary on the 15th inst., kindly acceded to the request of the S. Congregation. I wish, however, to warn Your Lordship and all the other Prelates of the United States, that they should henceforth conform in every point with the above-mentioned Constitution. Meanwhile I pray God to keep you yet many years, and in good health. Your Lordship's Most Devoted Brother,

F. CARD. FONTANA, Prefect.

Rome, Palace of the S. Congr. of Propaganda, July 21, 1821.

To the Right Rev. Louis William Du Bourg, Bp. of New Orleans, Louisiana.

St. Louis of the Illinois.

C. M. PEDICINI, Secretary.


## XXVII.

### CARDINAL FONTANA TO BISHOP DU BOURG.[1]

### NO. 20.[2]

Illmo ac Rme Dne.

Semel, atque iterum scripsi Ampl.ni Tuae, ut quoniam Ecclesia ista tam ampla est, ut Episcopus unus plenam ipsius curam exercere vix possait, nimis expedire visum fuerit, eam in tres saltem partes dividere, quarum una inferiorem Luisianae partem, altera superiorem, tertia denique Floridas complecteretur. Quoties ad hanc divisionem devenire, ut spero, consenseris, unus ex novis duobus Episcopis maxime idoneus esse posse videtur Rmus D. Patritius Kelly Richmondiensis Episcopus, vir sane pietate, prudentia, atque doctrina maxime commendatus. Cum enim S. Congo justis, gravibusque de causis illum ad aliam Ecclesiam transferre decreverit, nulla opportunior offerre se posset ad hanc translationem occasio, quam in aliqua ex duabus novis erigendis Ecclesiis. Dum igitur hac de re consilium tuum sollicite expecto, D. O. M. precor ut A. T. diutissime servet, ac sospitet.

Amp.dnis Tuae.

Romae ex Ædibus S. Connis de Prop.da Fide die 3. Octobris, 1821.

Uti Frater Studiosissimus

F. CARD. FONTANA, Praefectus.

R. P. D. Ludovico Guillelmo Du Bourg,
Epo Novae Aureliae.
S. Ludovicum.

C. M. PEDICINI, Secr. ius.

---

[1] Original in Archives of St. Louis Diocesan Chancery.

[2] It may be seen from the number affixed to this Document that Letters of Propaganda Nos. 18 and 19 are missing.

## TRANSLATION.

Twice did I write to Your Lordship that, as your Diocese is so extensive that one Bishop can hardly take full care of it, it seemed most expedient that it should be divided into at least three parts, the first to include Lower Louisiana, the second Upper Louisiana, and the third the Floridas. Whenever you consent, as I hope, to come to this dismemberment, the Right Rev. Patrick Kelly,[3] Bishop of Richmond, would, it seems, be most suitable as one of the two new Bishops: he is a man highly esteemed for his piety, his prudence and his knowledge. As the S. Congregation has, for grave reasons, decided to transfer him to another See, no better opportunity could be found for this transfer than to put him in one of the new Bishoprics to be established.

While anxiously waiting for your opinion in this matter, I pray Almighty God to keep Your Lordship yet many years and in good health. Your Lordship's Most Devoted Brother,           •

F. CARD. FONTANA, Prefect.

Rome, Palace of the S. Congr. of Propaganda, October 3, 1821.

To Right Rev. Louis William Du Bourg, Bishop of New Orleans. St. Louis.

C. M. PEDICINI, Secretary.


## BISHOP DU BOURG TO CARDINAL FONTANA.[1]

Eminentissime Praefecte.

Plurima laetitia me affecerunt literae Em.ae V.ae mensis Octobris proxime elapsi, ea potissimum ratione quod mihi spem certam afferant breve consummandam fore, quam saepius ab Emo antecessore Vestro, flebilis mem. Card. Litta, imo et a SS.DD. N. enixe postulaveram, *Floridarum* a mea jurisdictione separationem. Non solum igitur earum erectioni in Sedem Episcopalem, quantum ex me pendet, assentio, sed iterum atque iterum precor ut quanto citius executioni mandetur. . . Hujus Dioeceseos limites eum qui nunc vocatur *Ager Floridarum* et Alabamae Statum complecti possent. Titulus et Sedes, ut opinor, esse debet *Oppidum Mobilense,* utpote utrique parti confine et convenientissime, juxta os praecipui fluminis, Tom-big-bee non longe a mari situm.

Quod attinet ad erectionem alterius Sedis in Civitate S. Ludovici

---

[3] Born in Ireland, April 16, 1779; ordained at Lisbon, Portugal, July 18, 1802; consecrated August 24, 1820, as first Bishop of Richmond, erected in spite of the opposition of Archbishop Maréchal; the Holy See soon realized that the judgment of the Archbishop was correct, and placed the Diocese under the administration of the Archbishop of Baltimore, Bishop Kelly being transferred to the See of Lismore and Waterford (Ireland), in 1822. It will be seen that at the time of the writing of this letter, Propaganda had come to realize the impossibility of having a See at Richmond. The *"graves causae"* making the transfer of Bishop Kelly to another See are now transparent enough; but they may not have been for the Bishop of New Orleans.

[1] Archives of Propaganda. *Scritture referite nei Congressi.* Cod. 7.

in Statu Missouriano, nulli certe magis quam mihi ipsi arridere et in votis esse debet, quippe quae immensis laboribus et curis me liberaret; unum tamen me ab ea statim postulanda adhuc remoratur, nempe desiderium quo vehementer urgeor, possessiones satis amplas, quas in dotationem illius Sedis comparavi omni prorsus debito et onere prius solvendi; quod ante unum annum, Deo juvante, me effecturum confido. Libentissime tunc partem illam meae solicitudinis in manus Summi Pontificis resignabo, nulli sacrificio parcens, ut novus Antistes in ea collocatus, temporalibus curis et summa rerum omnium egestate, quae me per plures annos afflixerant, immunis esse possit. Consummato hoc opere, me accingam ad praeparandam viam formationi mediae Dioecesis inter S. Ludovicum et Novam Aureliam, quae *Statum Mississippi et Agrum Arcansas* complectatur. Sic ex una quatuor, intra paucos annos, conflabuntur, et si S.tae Sedi placuerit, novam ecclesiasticam provinciam constituere poterunt. Et quidem necesse duco de hoc prius cogitare quam ad divisionem quamcumque procedatur. Nam immensa distantia quae nos a Baltimoro separat, insuperque morum, indolum et linguarum diversitas quae vastissimam hanc regionem a caeteris Americae partibus distinguit, non patiuntur ut fractio aliqua meae Dioecesis Metropoli illi subjiciatur. Aliunde Novae Aureliae erigendarum Sedium stipiti, tum propter Episcopalem antiquitatem, tum ob ipsius opulentiam, immensamque populationem longe majore ex parte Catholicam, tum demum quia caeteris partibus facilis ad eam per commune flumen patet accessus, Metropolitana dignitas jure competere videtur.

Rev.mis et Dil.mis Fatribus et Collegis meis Bardensi, Mauricastrensi et Cincinnatensi me supplex adjungo ad postulandam denuo erectionem novae Sedis in oppido *San-Clarensi* vulgo *Detroit* in *Agro Michigan* cum annexa administratione *Agri Northwestensis* et ad proponendos ad eam occupandam, 1° loco, Rev.dum Bened.um Fenwick, S.J., qui nunc Charlestoniae Vicar Gen. . . . 2° loco *Principem Ruthenum Rev. D. Demetrium Augustinum* Galitzin . . .

✝Lud. Guil, Du Bourg, Ep. Neo-Aurel.

Novae Aureliae die 8 Februarii 1822.

TRANSLATION.

My Lord Cardinal:—

Much joy was afforded me by Your Eminence's letter of last October,[2] because, above all, it gave me certain hope that before long the Floridas will be withdrawn from my jurisdiction, as I had often earnestly requested your regretted predecessor, His Eminence, Card. Litta, and even the Holy Father himself. Not only, therefore, insofar as I am concrned, do I give my consent to their erection into an Episcopal See, but I repeat my prayer that this be done as soon as possible. . . . The limits of this new Diocese might include the present *Territory of the Floridas* and the State of Alabama. The title and the See, I think,

---

[2] The letter referred to is the above Document XXVII, of October 3, 1821.

ought to be the town of *Mobile,* as it is on the borders of both territories, and situated very conveniently near the mouth of the main river of that region, the Tom-big-bee, at a short distance from the sea.

As to the erection of another See in the City of St. Louis, Missouri, no one certainly can be pleased with it and desire it more than myself, as it means for me relief from immense labors and cares. Still, there is one reason why I delay asking at once for it, namely, the most earnest desire I have to free from all debts and obligations certain quite extensive properties which I have bought as an endowment for that See: I trust that, God helping, I may within a year reach this happy goal.[3] When this is accomplished I shall most gladly resign this part of my solicitude into the hands of the Sovereign Pontiff, hesitating at no sacrifice, in order that the Prelate who is appointed to this new See may be spared the temporal cares and the utmost destitution which were my lot for several years. When this is achieved I will set to work to pave the way for the formation of a new Diocese midway between St. Louis and New Orleans, which may include the *State of Mississippi* and the *Territory of Arkansas.* Thus from one Diocese four shall be made out within a few years, and if it please the Holy See these may constitute a new Ecclsesiastical province. As a matter of fact, I think that this ought to be considered before any division be decided upon. For the immense distance which separates us from Baltimore, and, besides, the differences of customs, characters and languages distinguishing this wide expanse of country from every other part of America, preclude the putting of any portion of my Diocese under the jurisdiction of that Metropolitan See. Moreover, New Orleans, the mother Church from which the Sees to be erected are springing forth, ought naturally to be given the Metropolitan dignity, on account of the antiquity of this Church, also of its wealth, and of its immense population, which is mostly Catholic, and lastly because, owing to the river flowing through all the other parts, it is easy to reach from every one of them.

I join my request to those of my Right Rev. and beloved Brothers and Colleagues of Bardstown, Mauricastrum and Cincinnati, to ask once more for the creation of a new See in the town of *St. Clair* (Detroit) in the Territory of Michigan, to which should be annexed the administration of the Northwestern Territory. As its incumbent I would propose, in the first place, the Rev. Benedict Fenwick, S.J., now Vicar General of Charleston . . . .; and as second choice, the Rev. Demetrius Augustine Prince Gallitzin. . . .

+L. Wm. Du Bourg, Bp. of N. Orl.

New Orleans, February 8, 1822.

---

[3] Bishop Du Bourg was always optimistic, he now asks for a year's respite; next year he will ask for more delay, and will at last try to have the division indefinitely postponed. Meantime he almost outdoes Propaganda's intention by proposing now a fourfold division.

# AN APPEAL

## HISTORICAL MATTER DESIRED

### by the Catholic Historical Society of St. Louis

✠

Books and pamphlets on American History and Biography, particularly those relating to Church institutions, ecclesiastical persons and Catholic lay people within the limits of the Louisiana Purchase;

Old newspapers; Catholic modern papers; Parish papers, whether old or recent :

*We will highly appreciate the courtesy of the Reverend Pastors who send us regularly their Parish publications;*

Manuscripts; narratives of early Catholic settlers or relating to early Catholic settlements; letters:

*In the case of family papers which the actual owners wish to keep in their possession, we shall be grateful for the privilege of taking copies of these papers;*

Engravings, portraits, Medals. etc;

In a word, every object whatsoever which, by the most liberal construction, may be regarded as an aid to, or illustration of the history of the Catholic Church in the Middle West.

Contributions will be credited to the donors and preserved in the Library or Archives of the Society, for the use and benefit of the members and other duly authorized persons.

Communications may be addressed either to the Secretary, or to the Librarians of the

*Catholic Historical Society of St. Louis,*

209 Walnut Street, St. Louis, Mo.

# ST. LOUIS

# CATHOLIC HISTORICAL

# REVIEW

Issued Quarterly

EDITOR-IN-CHIEF

REV. CHARLES L. SOUVAY, C. M., D. D.

ASSOCIATE EDITORS

REV. F. G. HOLWECK

REV. GILBERT J. GARRAGHAN, S. J.

REV. JOHN ROTHENSTEINER

EDWARD BROWN

*Volume II*     *OCTOBER 1920*     *Number 4*

PUBLISHED BY THE CATHOLIC HISTORICAL SOCIETY OF SAINT LOUIS

209 WALNUT STREET, ST. LOUIS, MO.

# CONTENTS

(155)

# Catholic Historical Society of St. Louis

## Established February 7th, 1917

## OFFICERS AND STANDING COMMITTEES
### 1920-1921

*President*—MOST REV. JOHN J. GLENNON, D. D.
*First Vice-President*—RT. REV. MGR. J. A. CONNOLLY, V. G.
*Second Vice-President and Treasurer*—EDWARD BROWN
*Third Vice-President*—LOUISE M. GARESCHE
*Secretary*—REV. EDWARD H. AMSINGER

*Librarians and Archivists*
{ REV. F. G. HOLWECK
REV. CHARLES L. SOUVAY, C. M., D. D.
REV. GILBERT J. GARRAGHAN, S. J.

*Executive Committee*
{ RT. REV. MGR. J. A. CONNOLLY, V. G., President
RT. REV. MGR. J. J. TANNRATH, Chancellor
REV. CHARLES L. SOUVAY, C. M., D. D.
REV. F. G. HOLWECK
REV. MARTIN L. BRENNAN, Sc D.
REV. JOHN ROTHENSTEINER
REV. EDWARD H. AMSINGER
EDWARD BROWN, Secretary

*Committee on Library and Publications*
{ REV. CHARLES L. SOUVAY, C. M., D. D.
REV. F. G. HOLWECK
REV. GILBERT J. GARRAGHAN, S. J.
REV. JOHN ROTHENSTEINER
EDWARD BROWN

## COMMUNICATIONS

General Correspondence should be addressed to Rev. Edward H. Amsinger, Secretary, 744 S. Third St., St. Louis, Mo.

Exchange publications and matter submitted for publication in the ST. LOUIS CATHOLIC HISTORICAL REVIEW should be sent to the Editor-in-chief, Rev. Charles L. Souvay, C.M., DD., Kenrick Seminary, Webster Groves, Mo.

Remittances should be made to Edward Brown, Treasurer, 511 Locust St., St. Louis, Mo.

# THE MISSION OF CENTRAL MISSOURI

## 1837—1861

### I.  St. Joseph's Residence, New Westphalia

In the autumn of 1837 Father Verhaegen, Superior of the Jesuit Mission of Missouri, while returning to St. Louis from the Kickapoo Mission near Fort Leavenworth, visited a colony of German emigrants, most of the mfrom Westphalia, who had settled not far from Jefferson City on the Maries River about four miles above its confluence with the Osage.[1] Here he found residing with the emigrants a Catholic priest, the Rev. Henry Meinkmann, who had accompanied some of them from Germany, but without having obtained the customary letters of dismissal from the bishop of his diocese.  Moreover, having failed to apply for jurisdiction to the Bishop of St. Louis, in whose territory he was now residing, he was disqualified from exercising the sacred ministry and, as a matter of fact, made no attempt to do so, but confined himself to the simple duties of school-teacher to the children of the emigrants.  Some time after his return to St. Louis, Father Verhaegen presented Father Meinkmann's case to Bishop Rosati, who in November 1837 granted the priest permission to exercise the ministry as resident pastor of New Westphalia Settlement, the latter having previously written to his former bishop, Mgr. Droste of Munster, for the canonical exeat customary in the case of priests withdrawing from one diocese into another.  Father Meinkmann thereupon assumed spiritual charge of the Westphalia Catholics who built

---

1 According to a manuscript note in the Archdiocesan Archives of St. Louis, the first priest to visit New Westphalia settlement was Father Christian Hoecken, S.J., who celebrated Mass there probably as early as 1835.  However, the baptismal records for his Central Missouri excursions of 1835 and 1836, though revealing his presence at Jefferson City and Cotesans-dessein in June, 1835, show no baptisms among the German settlers on Maries Creek (*Registre des Baptêmes pour la Mission du Missouri, 1832*).  Father Cornelius Walters, S.J., one of the "travelling missionaries" of St. Charles, Mo., is also mentioned as having followed Father C. Hoecken in ministering to the settlers in question.  Apart from Father Meinkmann, the first priest whose presence among them is vouched for by contemporary record is Father Verhaegen, whose visit in the autumn of 1837 is referred to in the text. "The Germans are most numerous in the neighborhood of Jefferson City.  People have assured us there are almost fifty Catholic families there.  They are pious and in better circumstances than those of Washington." Verhaegen à Rosati, November 17, 1837. It may be noted here that the first priest known to have visited the Catholics up the Missouri River was Father Charles De La Croix, who officiated at Franklin, Howard County, in 1819.
     The first recorded death in the *Liber Defunctorum* of St. Joseph's Parish, Westphalia, is that of Gaspar Anthony Linneman, December 4, 1836.  The burial was in St. Louis on December 6.  Mary Josephine Linneman died February 3, 1837, and in default of a Catholic cemetery was buried in unconsecrated ground.

157

him a small wooden chapel, named for St. John the Baptist, on the north side of the Maries River.[2]

In 1835, two years earlier than the incidents recorded in the preceding paragraph, a party of Catholics from Westphalia in Germany, many of them of considerable education, had come up the Osage river and settled on the Big Maries, an affluent of the Osage river. Dr. Bruns, a physician, together with a brother of his, located at the bend of the Maries, where the town of Westphalia was later laid out, while Messrs. Nacke, Hesse, Schroeder, Gramatica, Kolks and Kaiser took up land in the immediate vicinity. They were followed in a few months by the families Zellerhoff, Fennewald, Schwarze, Westermann, Bartmann and Geisberg. Some of the emigrants, it would appear, had hoped to establish or associate themselves in some way with an institution of learning in Central Missouri, but the primitive conditions they encountered soon disillusioned them and some of their number returned to Germany. Among these was a Mr. Hesse, who in 1838 sketched a valuable map of the Maries river region indicating the respective places of settlement of the German emigrant families. In the course of 1836 Dr. Bruns and Mr. Bartmann opened the first store in the locality, a picture of which appears on the Hesse map.[3]

The project of a Jesuit residence in the interior of Missouri had been under consideration for some time previous to the visit of Father Verhaegen to the Westphalia emigrants in the autumn of 1837. The eighteen or more Catholic stations scattered along both sides of the Missouri River as far as Booneville above Jefferson City were, during the period 1828-1838, visited four or five times a year by the Jesuits of St. Charles in missionary circuits averaging from four to six weeks' duration. But such arrangement was not by any means calculated to meet effectively the spiritual needs of the territory in question; it

---

2 Father Henry Meinkmann of the diocese of Münster in Germany was ordained in 1829 at Lucerne in Switzerland. For three years prior to his coming to America in 1836, he exercised the ministry at Hinsbeck in Münster. On relinquishing this post he obtained commendatory letters from the curé of Hinsbeck; but, on soliciting a document of like tenor from the Vicar-General of the diocese of Münster, was assured by that official, apparently in good faith, that no credentials other than those furnished by the curé of Hinsbeck would be found necessary in America. Father Meinkmann applied to Bishop Rosati for faculties in April 1837. Father Helias who became acquainted with the peculiar circumstances in which Father Meinkmann was placed and who speaks of him as "that Israelite in whom there is no guile," induced Father Verhaegen in November, 1837, to lay the case before Bishop Rosati: "The Germans of Westphalia, such is the name they give to their colony, said many fine things about the good priest of whom Father Helias speaks: but those of more influence among them observed to me that he would not suit, as he could not wield over them the authority and influence which the Sacred Ministry requires and this for the reason that he has resided so long among them without the usual powers of a priest, merely as a schoolteacher etc." Verhaegen à Rosati, November 17, 1837. Cf. also Meinkmann ad Rosati, April 13, 1837 (*Archdiocesan Archives of* St. Louis); Helias à Verhaegen, November 15, 1837; *Litterae Annuae,* 1838.

3 *History of Cole, Moniteau, Morgan, Benton, Miller, Maries and Osage Counties,* p. 679, Chicago, 1889. "From the mouth of the Maries up the following names appear: Dohmen, Messerschmidt, Scheulen, Hoecyway, Colson, Kunermann, Zellerhoff, H. Huber, Höcker, Hesse (jetzt Bössen), Geisberg, Gramatica, Dr. Bruns (at site of Westphalia); on the west fork, David Bruns, Herman Bruns, Fellups and Hilt; on the east fork, Abrez, Huber, Linnemann, Cons, Hesler and Schwarz; on the west uplands, Abrez, Clarenbach, Zurmegede, Chipley (Shipley), Carl Huber, Nacke and Fennewald; on the northeast uplands, F. Schwarze, Wilson, Lee (Smith's Postoffice) and the McDaniels. It will be seen that those to the northeast on the map are Americans. On the map, too, is a cut of the first loghouse at Westphalia, built by Dr. Bruns. . . . . There had been a few of these stations as early as 1825." Id. p. 635. A copy of Hesse's book, *Das westliche Nordamerika in besonderer Beziehung auf die deutschen Einwanderer in ihren landwirthschaftlichen, Handels- und Gewerbeverhaltnissen,* Paderborn, 1838, is in the library of the Jesuit residence of St. Joseph's, St. Louis.

was, perforce, provisional only, pending the establishment of a centrally located headquarters for the missionaries. Already in 1836 the author of the Annual Letters of the Missouri Mission pointed to the Catholic settlement of eighy souls on "St. Mary's Creek," the Westphalia settlement above referred to, as a likely place for a Jesuit residence. Partly, therefore, to supply the spiritual wants of the growing Catholic emigrant population of Osage and Gasconade Counties, and partly to secure a missionary center for the Fathers from which they could conveniently attend the various Catholic stations of Central Missouri, Father Verhaegen, with the consent of Bishop Rosati, decided to open a residence on Maries Creek. April 23, 1838, at a meeting of the Superior with his official advisers, it was determined that "Father Helias and Brother Morris be sent to the station generally known as Westphalia settlement near Jefferson City."

Father Helias, who was thus commissioned to take in hand the projected residence, is a figure of more than usual interest in the pioneer history of Missouri. Ferdinand Benoit Marie Guislain Helias d'Huddeghem came of a noble Flemish family, having been born August 3, 1796, at Ghent in Belgium in the Prinzen Hof, the same house in which the Emperor Charles the Fifth first saw the light of day.[4] As a student at the Jesuit College of Roulers in Belgium, he counted Father Van Quickenborne among his professors. He entered the Society of Jesus in his native town, Ghent, finished his novitiate at Montrouge in France, and was transferred thence to the college of Brieg in Switzerland. Fram there he came to the United States in 1833, where he spent the two following years in the newly erected Maryland Province, being employed in various charges, among others that of Assistent-Master of Novices. Transferred to the Missouri Mission in 1835 by order of the General, Father Roothaan, he arrived at St. Louis University August 22 of that year. Here in the course of the three following years, he taught French, German, and on occasion Canon Law and Moral Theology, and was, besides, employed as pastor of the German Catholics of North St. Louis, whom he began to organize into the future St. Joseph's parish.

Father Helias left St. Louis for his new destination May 3, 1838. An entry in the house-diary of St. Louis University chronicles the event:

> "May 3. Father Helias set out from this house to take in hand a mission in a place called Liel-town, a German settlement.[5] In that man burns a truly divine zeal, for courageously has he accepted the task imposed on him, an arduous one withal, as there are heartburnings and dissensions to be healed before any good can be accomplished among the people. A church and presbytery, both of logs, have been erected in the place."[6]

---

[4] Lebrocquy, *Vie du R. P. Helias D'Huddeghem de la Compagnie de Jesus.* Gand, 1878, pp.

[5] "In 1831 Benjamin Lisle started a settlement named after him, Lisle-town, at the head of the Maries Creek. The first post-office in Osage County was here. Owing to the growth of the neighboring Westphalia, Lisletown proved a failure." Conard, *Encyclopedia of the History of Missouri,* (?) The post-office was transferred about 1838 from Lisletown to Westphalia, Dr. Bernard Bruns, the Catholic doctor of the place, being appointed postmaster.

Father Helias was accompanied on his journey up the Missouri River by Fathers De Smet, Eysvogels and Verhaegen and Brother Claessens. Father De Smet was on his way to Council Bluffs, Father Eysvogels and Brother Claessens were destined for the Kickapoo Mission, while Father Verhaegen was to make an official visitation of the Kickapoo Mission. A fellow-passenger of the Jesuits was Captain Sutter, noted Santa Fe trader and the future discoverer of the California gold-fields. The steamer coming to a dead stop at least twice, owing to the complete collapse of her machinery, Father Helias at length took to land and made the last stgaes of his journey on horseback. He arrived on May 11, at Côte-sans-dessein, a Creole settlement on the left bank of the Missouri in Calloway County, near the mouth of the Osage River and said Mass there in a private house. The Sunday following, (May 12), the Fourth after Easter and Feast of the Patronage of St. Joseph, he celebrated Mass in Westphalia and was duly installed as pastor of the German Catholic congregation.[7] To the log-church, which his parishioners had begun to build the year before, he gave the name of St. Joseph. Several considerations determined this choice as his biographer informs us. First, there was the circumstance that his dear friend, Bishop Rosati of St. Louis, bore the name Joseph. Moreover, Father Helias had always cherished a particular devotion to the foster-father of the Savior, as the patron of his own Belgium and of the German Empire of the Middle Ages. Finally, even under the Spanish regime, the district laid out as Gasconade County had been organized into an administrative unit known as the Parish of St. Joseph, with headquarters at Côte-san-dessein.[8]

Father Helias at once took in hand the cultivation of the extensive spiritual field entrusted to his care, Father Meinkmann at fisrt assisting him in his labors. The latter appears to have been a man of excellent intentions, but without tact in dealing with the numerous parties of German emigrants that made up his congregation. Among the things charged against him was that he confined his ministrations to the group of Rhinelanders whom he had accompanied from Germany and neglected the other portions of his flock, the Westphalians in particular taking umbrage at the line of action followed by their pastor. As there seemed little prospect of healing the differences between Father Meinkmann and the Catholics of New Westphalia, Bishop Rosati transferred him in 1839 to the newly established parish

---

6 Helias, *Mémoires du Rd. P. Ferdinand Helias D'Huddeghem prêtre missionaire de la Compagnie de Jésus en Amérique* (Ms.). Contains prefatory letter addressed to Father De Smet from Taos, Cole County, Mo., St. Francis Xavier, 1867. According to the article in *Missouri Historical Review*, 5:87 (July 1915) Fathers Helias and De Smet left St. Louis for Westphalia on a trip of investigation April 4, 1838. On April 30, Father Helias blessed the marriage of Gerhard Aufderheide and Anna Mary Schlauermann, the first recorded in the Westphalia marriage register. Only three days after, May 3, occurred Father Helias's second departure from St. Louis for Westphalia.

7 Lebrocquy, *op. cit.*, p. 185. "13a Maii Dominica IVa Post Pascham, Festum Patrocinii Sti Joseph titular. Westphaliae instalavi me primum huius Paroeciae Pastorem primumque Sacrum dixi." Memorandum of Father Helias indorsed *"Dies Memorabiles F. Mae Helias S.J."*

8 Lebrocquy, *op. cit.*, p. 206. The statement that a civil district or parish named for St. Joseph was laid out in Central Missouri under the Spanish regime is not supported by any known historical evidence.

of St. Francis Borgia, in Washington, Franklin County.[9]
Although the colony of Westphalia emigrants settled on Maries
Creek went by the name of New Westphalia Settlement prior even to
the advent of Father Helias, the foundation proper of the town, known
first as New Westphalia and later simply as Westphalia, appears to
have been laid in 1838 under the immediate direction of Father Helias
himself.[10]  In the year named Fathers Verhaegen, DeTheux and
Smedts acquired from Francis Geisberg for a nominal consideration of
five dollars, forty acres of land on the left bank of the Maries River.
Shortly after his arrival Father Helias, with his Superior's approval,
after reserving fourteen acres to himself as a means of support, divided
the remaining twenty-six into lots which he offered to the mechanics
and laborers of the German colony, farmers being excluded from the
offer. They were to be given a ninety-nine year lease to their respective lots, which they were to hold rent free the first five years, and
afterwards on an annual payment of two or five dollars, according
to the value of the lot. The money derived from this source was to
go to the maintenance of the church. Subsequently, to remove all
ground of invidious gossip, the lots were deeded over to the tenants
in fee-simple.  Such was the beginning of the town of New Westphalia.[11]

The log-church which served the needs of the Catholics of New
Westphalia until the construction of a fine stone church in 1848 belonging to that type of architectural makeshift which includes both
church and presbytery under a single roof. Bishop Rosati blessed it
on the occasion of his first visit to New Westphalia October 14, 1838,
on which occasion he administered Confirmation to thirty-eight mem-

---

9 *Residentiae Sti Francisci Xaverii Centralis Exordium et Progressus,* 1838-1848
(Helias Mss), p. 3. Father Helias refers to Father Meinkmann as *vir ceteroquin simplex
et cordatus.*

10 Father Meinkmann's letter of April 13, 1837, to Bishop Rosati is dated from "New
Westphalia Settlement."

11 *Litterae Annuae,* 1838. The deed of transfer of the Westphalian property from Francis Geisberg to P. J. Verhaegen, Theodore De Theux and J. B. Smedts under date of
June 25, 1838, was recorded at Mount Sterling, Gasconade County, on July 5 of the same
year. According to the account in Goodspeed's *History of Moniteau etc.* Geisberg entered
200 acres of public land on the Maries, 40 of which he subsequently donated for the erection
of a Catholic church. Cf. in this connection Father Helias's Latin verse,
     *Atque novae fundamina fiximus Urbis*
     *Westphaliae.*
The forty acres conveyed by Francis Geisberg is described in the deed of transfer as
the N.E. ¼ of S.W. ¼ of Section 26, Tp. 43, Range 10 W. A forty foot street (Main
Street) cut it diagonally from Southeast to Northeast. The lots appear to have been
originally leased to the settlers for a ninety-nine year term (1839-1938). The conditions of
the lease were recorded by Father Helias in a Baptismal Register now preserved among the
records of St. Francis Xavier Church, Taos, Cole County, Mo. According to this document,
the town of Westphalia was laid out in two divisions, the second division being the property of a Mr. Gramatica. Father Helias's forty acres did not therefore comprise the entire
town-site of Westphalia. The tenant of Father Helias's lots promised "to keep his house
in good condition, to build a post-fence in a straight direction along the street and to hold
in his house or on his messuage no people of bad morality reputed as a nuisance and a
public disturber of the people."
All of the forty acres appears to have been sold by Father Helias with the exception
of the one acre on which the old church, subsequently used as a school-house, was standing in
1861. The property on which stand the present church, convent and school was purchased
from various parties. The present stone church was built on a lot acquired September 18,
1847, from Mrs. Gertrude Evans. a widow, whose skilful nursing saved Father Helias's
life when the doctors had given him up.

bers of the parish.[12]    The prelate preached on this day in English, while Father Verhaegen, his companion in the visitation of the diocese which he was then performing, also addressed the congregation in English.[13]  A school-building, also of logs, was put up within a year or two of Father Helias's arrival.   The duties of school-teacher were discharged for a while by Father James Buschotts, who joined Father Helias July 27, 1838.  Father Buschotts remained in New Westphalia to September 23 of the following year, when he was transferred to the new Jesuit residence of St. Francis Borgia in Washington, Missouri.   Father Helias was then left without an assistant priest until the arrival in 1846 of Father James Cotting.[14]

Ecconomic conditions among the German settlers of Osage County in its pioneer period were extremely crude.[15]  The journey to America had depleted the purse of most of the emigrants; as a consequence, they often were without capital in money or tools with which to begin the struggle for existence in the New World.  They were thus forced to borrow; but they found the American settlers who had preceded them into the wilderness, ready to lend.  "I have often heard," a Westphalia pastor, Father Nicolas Schlechter, S.J., wrote in 1884, "several German families saying that when they came to the county they were in great poverty and obliged to beg, and that for entire weeks and months; but they invariably added: 'The Americans were good; they never grew tired of our asking, but simply said: 'take it.' '"[16]

Good, strong wagons were the thing the farmers needed most of all.   Though these could be obtained in St. Louis, money was scarce and the cost of shipping the wagons all the way to Westphalia and other settlements in Osage County was prohibitive.  Necessity, however, suggested to the farmers the invention of a type of home-made wagon which for years answered all their needs of transportation.

---

12 "From Jefferson City we went to New Westphalia, 15 miles, in Gasconade County, a German Congr. F. Helias with F. Buschotts reside there and take care of the Congns. of Jefferson City and others. I blessed the church last Sunday, gave confirmation to 26 persons, blessed the Graveyard and gave confirmation the next day to 9 persons more." Rosati to Timon, Oct. 20, 1838. Cf. Lebrocquy, *op. cit.*, pp. 204-207 for some interesting details in connection with the blessing of the church. "Le souvenir de cette grande journée ne s'effaça jamais de la mémoire du P. Hélias."

13 *Litterae Annuae, 1838.*
We subjoin here Bishop Rosati's own account of the event as he described it in his *Diary:*
"October 14. XIXth Sunday after Pent. At 8 a. m. said Mass in the church and gave communion to the people. At 10, we assembled in the church, which I solemnly blessed according to the rite described in the Roman Ritual. Then Father Buschotts celebrated Mass solemnly; after the Gospel I preached in English, for most of the Germans know this language, and there were present a number of American protestants. After Mass and the singing of the Hymn *Veni Creator Spiritus,* I gave the sacrament of Confirmation to twenty-six persons of both sexes, whom I exhorted to perseverance. Finally Father Verhaegen preac'ed in English on Catholic Religicn.
At 3 p.m. we assembled at the church, whence we came to the adjacent cemetery, which I blessed solemnly according to the Roman Pontifical. Returned to the church, I talked to the people about the blessing just performed, the pious thoughts which the sight of the cemetery must rouse in the mind of the Catholics, to the persons to whom ecclesiastical burial is denied; and I requested Father Helias to repeat in German what I had said in English. At length, in order to return thanks to God for the benefit conferred upon this parish, we sang the *Te Deum.*"

14 *Residentiae Sti Francisci Xaverii* etc. p. 8.

15 Osage county was organized out of Gasconade county, January 29, 1841.

16 Father Schlechter was pastor in Westphalia, 1882-83 and in Loose Creek 1883-84.

Not a nail or bit of iron was used in the construction; wooden bolts held togetther beam, cross-beam, shaft and axle-tree. But the wheels were the most characteristic feature of this singular conveyance. These were of one piece, being circular-shaped slices from the trunks of huge sycamore trees. We may well believe that these curious wagons, as they were drawn along by plodding oxen, made a hideous clatter, proverbial throughout the county long after the pioneer stage of its history had come to an end.

## II. Missionary Excursions 1838-1842

Father Helias had scarcely arrived at New Westphalia when he began from there, as base of operation, the series of periodic missionary excursions which were to accomplish so much for the upbuilding of Catholicity in Central Missouri. Eleven counties, Franklin, Gasconade, Osage, Cole, Moniteau and Cooper on the south side of the Missouri and Warren, Montgomery, Callaway, Boone and Howard on the north side, were included in the area traversed.[17]

He said his first Mass at New Westphalia May 13, 1838. On May 24, Feast of the Ascension, he officiated at French Village and the day after at Côte-sans-dessein, where a number of adults made their First Holy Communion. Saturday he was at Hibernia or Hibe-

---

17 A manuscript account compiled by Father Helias in 1838 (*Excursiones Missionis Centralis*) contains a census of the Catholic stations along the Missouri with the names in many cases of the persons in whose houses divine services were held. The figures indicate the number of families. *South Side of the Missouri:* Manchester, St. Louis Co., 10; Washington, Franklin Co., (Uhlenbrouck's house near the town) 118; Burbus, Franklin Co., 11; Henry Reed's Settlement, Franklin Co. 5; Bailey's Creek, Gasconade Co., (Jh. Logsden), 22; French Village, (Louis Leblanc's house near the Osage River), 24; Loose Creek, (Aug. Pequinot), ; Cadet [Cade?] Creek (J. B. Bennot), 25 (services in these two places generally held in the district school-house); across the Osage at Herman Nieters, Liberty Township, 20; Jefferson City, (Henry Haar's tavern [*publica taberna*], the missionary lodging with Mr. Withnell, Architect of the Capitol); Barry's Settlement, Cole Co., (P. Barry), 10; Moniteau River (F. Joseph Weber), 40; Booneville (Anthony Fuchs [Fox] and Peter Joseph), 15; Pilot's Grove (on the prairie at Romersbergers [Anthony, Remsberger]), 15; near Georgetown, Pettis Co., (Dr. Bruhl). *North Side of the Missouri:* Fayette and Chariton, (Mr. Post) 5; Columbia, Boone Co., (Mr. Lynch, Jr., and outside the town, Mr. Lynch, Sr.), 13; Portland, (Priestly Gill), 8; Hancock Prairie, (John Shannon, 10; Cote-sans-dessein (Widow Roy), 20; Rocheport, 26 [families?]; Lay Creek, 34; Mount Pleasant, 30; Martinsville [Marthasville] opposite Washington, 3.

In another list mention is made of a congregation of Irish, perhaps Barry Settlement, near Marion, Cole Co., not to be identified, it would seem, with St. Patrick's congregation in Hibernia. Pisgah, Cooper Co., (house of John Fay) also occurs as one of the stations visited by Father Helias.

Father Helias's census of Catholic families in Central Missouri for April 1, 1839, is an historical document of value; it does not, however, include all the stations in the missionary's circuit. We reproduce it from the *Missouri Historical Review, July, 1915*, p. 85:

*Westphalia:* Bernard Bruns, Doctor of Medicine; Geisberg, Brockmann, Ottens, Gramatica, Walters, Schmitz, Otto, Debeis, Eppen of, Oldenlehre, Haler, Nacke, Bartmann, Eck, Knueve, Zellerhoff, Juchmann, Bose, Eckmeier, Kolks, Vennewald, Lueckenhoff, Meierpeter, Schuelen, Krekel, Dohmen, Stiefemann, Hagenbreck, Boessen, Linnemann, Goetzen, Arzt, Brockerhoff, Kern, Wilhaupt, Schwartze, Hasslag, Holtermann, Sudhoff, Borgmann, Kuess, J. Schater, Kolkmeyer, Richters, Hart.

*Jefferson City:* Withnell, Hannan, Buz, Kramer, Tellmann, Monaghan, Ryan, Gilman, Corker, Bauerdick, Brand, Doherty.

*Loose Creek:* Monnier, Valentin, Cordonier, Brichaud, Besson, Saulnier, Stoffen, Farrell, Reed, Burbus.

*French Village:* Peter Goujon, Louis Goujon, Angelica Mercer, widow; Gleizer, Picqueur, Vincennes, Denoyer, Luison, Leblanc.

*Cote-sans-dessein:* Roye, Faye, Arnould, Nicholas, Renaud

*Bailey's Creek:* Logsden, Simon, Welch, Howard, Folgs, Serpentin, Miller, Heth.

*Portland:* Priestly Gill.

*Hancock Prairie:* Joseph Shannon, Thomas Flood, Anna Catharina, widow of John Preis.

*Columbia:* Lynch and Kitt.

*Booneville:* Fuchs, Weler, Fis, Pecht, Fay, Morey, Dr. Heart, Rockwie, Briel.

*New Franklin:* Matthias Simon.

nium, some five miles·to the northeast of Jefferson City.[18]   The next·
day, Sunday, May 27, he celebrated Mass for the first time in Jefferson
City, in a private house, which is apparently still standing, being
No. 325 High Street.

Nowhere was he given a heartier welcome than in Jefferson City.[19]
The Catholic population of the town consisted of about one hundred
and fifty souls, chiefly German and Irish emigrants, most of whom
were employed as laborers on the new Capitol building then in process
of construction.[20]  Father Helias spent a few days among these good
people and afterwards revisited them regularly once a month.  Before
the close of 1838, sixteen hundred dollars had been collected among
the Catholics for a church and school to be placed under the invocation
of St. Ignatius of Loyola.  Mr. John Withnell, architect of the Capitol
and personally known to Father Helias, offered his professional services for the new edifice at a nominal charge.  The Irish and German
workmen employed on the Capitol also volunteered their help.  The
only difficulty that beset the venture was the lack of a suitable site.
Mr. Charles Dwyer of St. Louis offered Father Helias one of the
twelve lots which he owned in Jefferson City; but the property was
too remote from the heart of the town to serve the purpose of a suitable church-site.  However, a happy solution of the difficulty presented
itself from a rather unexpected quarter. The·old Capitol building,
rendered unnecessary for public business by the construction of the
new one, might perhaps be turned over to the Catholics for a church.

18 *Dies memorabiles* etc., Wetmore's *Gazetteer of Missouri* (St. Louis, 1837) lists
Hibernia as a post-office of Callaway County. ("Holt's Settlement [Summit], Hibernia, on
the C. and A. R. R. 20 miles south of Holton," Campbell, *Gazetteer of Missouri*, p. 97).
According to a *status animarum* for the Mission of Central Missouri compiled by Father
Helias, "St. Patrick's Congregation in Hibernium" counted only ten souls in 1838-39, a
number which has dwindled to five in 1849. On August 12. 1827, Father Van Quicken-
borne administered four baptisms at "Hibernia near Jefferson", among the recipients being
Francis Pomponius Atticus Dillon, son of Patrick M. and Anna C. Nash, born June 1, 1824.
*Baptismal Register*, St. Ferdinand's Church, Florissant, Mo.

19 The first Catholic priest mentioned in contemporary records as having visited Jefferson City was Father Verhaegen, S.J., who preached a mission there in 1828. Supra, p. 157.
A manuscript memorandum in the *Archdiocesan Archives*, St. Louis, states that he said
Mass in Jefferson City in 1836. According to a sketch of Catholicity in Jefferson City in
the *Missouri Volksfreund*, October 7, 1896, the first Mass in the place was celebrated by
Father Felix Verreydt, S.J., in 1831. It is certain that Mass was said there at least as early
as this date, though Father Helias in his *Dies Memorabiles* appears to lay claim to the honor
of celebrating the first Mass in Jefferson City, May 27, 1838. Services on this occasion
were held "in the large hall of the German Boarding House of Mr. Henry Haar," (Memorandum, *Archdiocesan Archives*, St. Louis), probably the house 325 High Street, still standing in 1896. Cf. *Missouri Volksfreund*, Oct. 7, 1896. The house of Gebhard Anthony Kramer
"near the Capitol" is also mentioned by Father Helias as a place where he held services in
his early visits to Jefferson City. Supra, p. 163, Note 17
    The earliest recorded baptisms in Jefferson City appear to be two performed by Father
Christian Hoecken on June 18, 1835, when he baptized George Ward, son of Patrick Ward
and Mary Dillon Ward, and Charles Julius Haebert, son of Caspar and Julia Haebert.
*Registre des Baptêmes pour la Mission du Missouri*, 1832). Father Helias's first baptism in
the town was that of Edmund Dougherty, son of Andrew and Helen Dougherty, May 26,
1838. The earliest Catholic burials in Jefferson City, as entered in the Westphalia *Liber
Defunctorum*, are those of Richard O'Connor, September 11, 1838, and John O'Brien, September 15, same year; Father Helias being the officiating priest on both occasions.

20 *Annuae Litterae*, 1838.   *Residentiae S. Francisci Xaverii Centralis Exordium* etc.·
(Helias Mss.)
    Bishop Rosati, assisted by Father Verhaegen, administered Confirmation in Jefferson
City in October, 1838. "I gave confirmation in the Hall of an Hotel in Jefferson City to
11 persons on a week day: there are now two hundred Catholics, not yet a church, but we have
begun to make arrangements to have a decent one in stone. Mr. Withnell, who is building
there the Capitol very kindly received us in his house: he will be of great service in the
building of the church." Rosati to Timon, October 20, 1838 (*Archdiocesan Archives*, St.
Louis).

The idea was taken up by some of the Catholic residents of Jefferson City, who secured a large number of signatures to a petition to this effect, even among the non-Catholic citizens. The petition was presented in due course of time to the Legislature. Here a resolution in its favor was carried in the Senate by a unanimous vote, but the same resolution going before the Lower House, was defeated by a majority of four. It was necessary, therefore, to look for another site. During all this time, hope was entertained by the Catholics of Jefferson City of having a Jesuit College or Academy in their midst. Father Verhaegen, Superior of the Missouri Mission, declined, however, to take any step in this direction, being too much pressed by the difficulties of the existing institutions of the Mission, to engage in any such perilous educational venture. But a church was a distinct need of the Catholics of the town and ground for a site having been purchased, a frame structure under the invocation of St. Ignatius Loyola was erected in 1841 and dedicated Easter Sunday, 1843. It continued to be served by Father Helias until the arrival in July, 1846, of Father P. Murphy, the first resident priest of Jefferson City.[21]

Father Helias was the first Catholic priest to minister to the inmates of the State penitentiary in Jefferson City.[22] One instance, occurring in 1839, of his success in dealing with the prisoners may be cited here. A young Englishman, Henry Lane by name, of aristocratic connections and a one-time college student, at least so report had it, was under sentence of death. His desperate antecedents promised small hope of any spiritual impression being made upon him. Father Helias, however, undertook to prepare him for death with the result that the young man underwent a complete change of heart and went to his fate with the most edifying sentiments of faith and repentance. The crowd who gathered to twitness the execution looked for a desperate struggle from the criminal when brought to the gallows. To their surprise, nothing of the kind occurred. On the contrary, he walked to the scaffold without handcuffs and with a crucifix in his hand, and the words of warning which he addressed to the spectators on the vice of drunkenness brought tears to the eyes of many. The breaking at the last moment of the hangman's rope when it was already around the neck of the condemned man failed to unnerve him. He persevered to the end in his pious sentiments, the sacred names of Jesus and Mary rising to his lips in the brief spell of agony that preceded death.[23]

In the Creole settlements of Côte-sans-dessein and French Village Father Helias found the fruits of his ministry somewhat meagre, owing to the habitual religious indifference of the people.[24] He notes in

---

21 The *Status Animarum* etc., 1848-49 (Helias Mss.) gives the date 1841 for the building, at least in its initial stages, *(fundatio templi)*, of the Jefferson City church. Father Helias's *Mémoires*, p. 54, fixes the date as 1842. The *Status Animarum*, compiled not later than 1850, is probably a safer guide on this point than the much later *Mémoires*. The church was dedicated Easter Sunday, 1843. "On Easter Sunday the neat frame church erected by Father Helias S.J. in the city of Jefferson was dedicated to Divine Worship under the invocation of St. Ignatius of Loyola." *Catholic Cabinet*, Vol. I, May 1843, p. 60.

22 *Status Animarum* etc. (Helias Mss.)

23 *Litterae Annuae*, 1840.

24 For notices of Cote-sans-dessein and French Village, cf. supra p. 163. Dauphine, later Bonnot's Mill, was a sort of second growth of French Village. St. Francis Regis was patron of the Cote-sans-dessein congregation.

his record for 1838 certain sudden and unhappy deaths among the more obdurate of the Creoles. One of their number felling an oak on Christmas Day, was crushed to pieces under the falling tree in the presence of his wife and mother. The Sunday following, a bitterly cold day, two men returning home from a tavern late at night in a drunken condition lost their way and were obliged to crawl along the ground on all fours in an effort to find the road. One of the men was frozen to death, the other nearly so, so that it was necessary to amputate his fingers and toes to save his life. Again, a woman of disedifying life who had listened to Father Helias preaching on the certainty of death, but without being moved to any attempt to amend her ways, was, on the very day after the sermon, suddenly stricken down. The lesson taught by these and other examples of what looked like summary divine punishment was not altogether lost on the inhabitants of French Village and Côte-sans-dessein. In pleasing contrast to the frivolous, irreligious ways of the latter was the strong faith and practical piety of a group of recently arrived French-Canadians of whom Father Helias makes mention, and who proposed to start a settlement of their own to be known as New Besançon. There is no record of such intention having been carried out. [25]

A much higher level of Catholic faith and practice prevailed in the other stations, near and far, which Father Helias was accustomed to attend in his missionary circuit. The stations nearest to Westphalia he visited monthly, the more remote ones, twice and three times a year. Typical of the eagerness of the pioneer Catholic settlers of Central Missouri to welcome a priest in their midst was an incident that occurred at Portland, Callaway County, a town on the north bank of the Missouri some miles below Jefferson City. Here one day the Catholics of the vicinity began to assemble in a private house to listen to a sermon which Father Helias was announced to preach. So many, however, had gathered for the occasion that there was no possibility of accommodating them within the four walls of the house. The entire congregation thereupon withdrew to an adjoining field and here under a scorching August sun the missionary conducted divine service. It is recorded that just as Father Helias began to read the Gospel of the Sunday, a great cloud hid the sun from view and that at the very moment the services came to an end the sun reappeared and glared again with great intensity. The people of Portland were so impressed by Father Helias's visit to them on this occasion that one of their number was dispatched to St. Louis to offer Father Verhaegen, in the name of the rest, a purse of $2000.00, together with five acres of land, as an inducement to the Superior to establish a Jesuit college in their town. [26]

25 *Historia Westphaliae*, p. 8. *Residentia Sti Francisci Xaverii Centralis Exordium et Progressus*, 1838-48 (Helias Mss.).

26 *Litterae Annuae*, 1839. Father Christian Hoecken S.J. baptized at Portland June 30, 1835, Mary Ann Gill, daughter of Priestly Gill and Mary Norris. *Registre des Baptêmes pour la Mission du Missouri*, 1832. Portland is in Callaway County on the Missouri River, twenty-four miles southeast of Fulton. At Hancock Prairie, also in Callaway County, a few miles from Portland, there was a small Catholic congregation.

Something of a clan-system developed among the German settlers as a consequence of their having arrived in Missouri in successive parties and from different districts of Germany. The emigrants from Westphalia and Hannover clustered together in and around New Westwhalia in the western part of Osage county. Those from the Lower Rhine settled in the northern parts of the county around Loose Creek as a centre. Finally, the Bavarians took up land in the southern part of the county near the Gasconade river, their principal settlement being named Richfontain by Father Helias on account of the abundance of clear spring water found in the neighborhood. Besides the settlements named, all of which were within the limits of Osage county, there was a colony of Belgian and Hanoverian emigrants, numbering in all about two hundred souls, west of the Osage river in Cole county. It was here that Father Helias, in 1840, built his second church, that of St. Francis Xavier.

The first visit of Father Helias to this locality, where he was destined to make his home for the greater part of his career in Central Missouri, occurred on May 28, 1838, when he celebrated Mass in the house of one of the settlers, Mr. L. Nieters, there being no church at the time in the place. [27] Having secured ten acres of land centrally situated with reference to the German farmers of the neighborhood, he began to lay plans for the erection of a wooden church. The site, however, did not commend itself to a certain group among the parishioners, who advocated the purchase of a tract of government land forty acres in extent. But Father Helias insisted on the choice already made. The property he had secured lay within easy reach of both Westphalia and Jefferson City, was near a public highway and had the advantage of an agreeable position on rising ground, with a fine spring of the coolest water at hand. Moreover, there was land enough for a presbytery and cemetery, both of which would have to be provided soon. Against the counter-proposition to build the church elsewhere, was the further objection that the site suggested besides being undesirable as a location, would have to be bought and that the money for this purpose would have to be borrowed: and, as Father Helias observes, "borrowed money and a foolish purchase make a sorry combination." The advocates, however, of a new site were insistent and even carried the case to St. Louis to Father Verhaegen, at that time Administrator of the diocese in the absence of Bishop Rosati in Europe. Happily, the controversy was adjusted and Father Helias was enabled to build the church in 1840 on the site he had chosen. [28]

The village which grew up in the course of time around the church of St. Francis Xavier owed its origin, in a sense, to Father

---

27 *Dies Memorabiles* (Helias Mss.)

28 *Litterae Annuae,* 1840. The church property, a tract of ten acres, was conveyed by Henry and Gertrude Haar, June 5, 1840, the consideration being five dollars, to Fathers Verhaegen, De Theux and Smedts. It was in N.E. ¼ of N.W. ¼ of Section 6, Range 10, Township 43. The church and residence stood close to the south side of the Versailles state-road. The graveyard, one and a half acres, was purchased October 19, 1849, from John Anthony Eck.

Helias. As the ground on which the church stood had been acquired by Father Helias from Mr. Henry Haar, a contractor and builder, the village went for some time by the name of Haarville. [29] Later, it took the name of the post-office of the district, Taos, the post-office quarters being in close proximity to the church. Taos was three miles from Lisletown at the junction of the Osage and Maries rivers, six from the Missouri river and five from Jefferson City.[30] Father Helias thus describes the place in his *Memoires*. "There are no bilious fevers here as elsewhere, the parish buildings are more pretentious than in the other residences established by this missionary; in a word, the place makes a much better appearance. Moreover, the settlers succeed better here owing to the nearness of the State capital and of the railroad, by which they are enabled to ship their produce to all points in the state. The land has all been taken up and old farms sell at a high price, while the soil is less broken up and much more productive than on the other side of the Osage River." [31]

The same year, 1840, that saw the church of St. Francis Xavier built in Taos in Cole County, saw also the building of the church of the Sacred Heart at Richfountain, the picturesque name which Father Helias gave the Bavarian colony near the Gasconade River.[32] Mass was said by Father Helias in the new church for the first time December 3, 1840.[33] In 1842 or earlier two hundred and fifty families who had emigrated from Bavaria to escape the unjust Bavarian laws concerning marriage settled in Richfountain.[34] Many couples among them had never been validly married at the time of their arrival in America, the government restrictions at home having made it impracticable for them to conform to the marriage laws of the Church. Father Helias, on learning this state of affairs, promptly corrected the defective unions of these poor emigrants. The parish of the Sacred Heart at Richfountain was destined to attain an excellence in piety and regularity of Christian practice which made it, in Father Helias's own words, "a model for all others." [35]

The first years of Father Helias's life as a missionary priest in Central Missouri were crowded with adventure and thrilling incidents.

---

29 "Haarville, Cole Co., St. Francis Xavier—Rev. Ferdinand Helias. He visits also once a month St. Ignatius, Jefferson City; St. Joseph's Westphalia; Sacred Heart, Richfountain; Conception of the Blessed Virgin, Cade's Creek; and occasionally the Assumption of the B. V. Manitou Creek; Booneville, Pilot-Grove, Columbia, Hybernium, Cote-sans-dessein, French Village etc." *Metropolitan Catholic Almanac*, 1843.

30 "Taos, a post-office 5 miles south [east] of Jefferson City." Campbell, *Gazetteer of Missouri*, p. 168.

31 *Mémoires*, p. 53. Family-names of children confirmed at Taos by Bishop Rosati in the early forties include those of Schneider, Thessen, Kolb, Wolken, Hoffmeyer, Laux, Schwaller, Hoecken, Schell, Roecker, Ihler, Schulte, Neumeyer, Prenger, Rakers, Kerperin, Nieters, Bekel, Motschman, Sannning, Rohling, Hermann, Schnieders. *Missouri Historical Review*, July, 1915, p. 85.

32 "Un endoit d'eaux, Riche Fontaine." *Mémoires*, p. 53. The land on which the church was built near his farm and opposite the "riche fontaine," was conveyed by John Stumpf and Elizabeth. his wife, February 2, 1843, for a consideration of five dollars to the authorities of the Missouri Vice-Province. The land was originally entered by a John Burns during the 'thirties. Cf. *History of Moniteau etc. Counties*, p. 682.

33 *Dics. Memorabiles* (Helias Mss.) *Mémoires*, p. 53.

34 Thus the *Mémoires*, p. 54. Two hundred and fifty for the number of emigrant families is probably an overstatement.

35 *Mémoires*, p. 54.

The country he moved about in was just emerging from a state of primitive nature. It was thinly settled and poorly provided with roads. To reach the stations yawning ravines and swollen streams had frequently to be crossed. It was no uncommon thing for the missionary to lose his way in the woods and spend the night under the open. Once, while riding in the dark, he and his horse fell headlong into a ditch, both, however, coming out of the accident without the slightest injury. Another time, crossing a stream together with his horse in a leaking boat, he had perforce to work desperately with the boatman to bale out the water and only the heroic efforts of the two kept the wretched craft from being swamped. A kindly Providence seemed ever on the alert to save the man of God from bodily harm.[36].

A fellow Jesuit who entered into Father Helias's labors in Osage County has sketched the tradition of tireless missionary which he found current in the 'eighties among the German Catholics of Osage County.[37]

> "Father Helias was a remarkable man. I have often heard old people speak of him with enthusiasm. In their feelings towards him there is the reverence for the priest blended with the warmth of the friend. He, the man of noble birth, must have been possessed of great kindness so that his aristocratic manners became winning in the eyes of the simple peasantry; and his severe virtue must have been blended with great cordiality, so that people remote from asceticism, were cheered by his conversation, while they were instructed."

Father Helias's actual residence in New Westphalia lasted only four years from his arrival there in May, 1838. In the Spring of 1842 he closed the church and presbytery and returned to St. Louis. The year 1841 had been a particularly trying one. There was considerable sickness in the settlement, an epidemic of some or other contagious disease having lasted four months, and left behind it numerous victims. Then there was a severe and protracted drought which entailed loss of crops and reduced the settlers to dire want. During these calamities Father Helias did his best to bring his stricken parishioners all the spiritual and temporal aid he could command, travelling sometimes one hundred and twenty miles to bring the dying the consolations of religion. Added to these trials was the opposition to his ministry which the good priest had to endure from some of his Westphalian parishioners. What the grounds of this opposition were is not clear from contemporary records. At all events, certain malicious persons sought to come between the Westphalian congregation and its pastor.[38] Their efforts were not unavailing. Father Helias notes sadly

---

36 *Litterae Annuae*, 1840.

37 Father Nicholas Schlechter in *Woodstock Letters*, 13:360.

38 A sort of anti-clerical party or faction appears to have existed for a number of years among the German settlers, even Catholic, of Missouri. They were sometimes dubbed the Latinians from the circumstance that they had, so it was alleged, studied Latin in the German gymnasia before coming to America. It was seemingly a group of Latinians who fomented trouble against Father Helias. (*Woostock Letters*, 13:23). "The epithet 'Latin farmers' has commonly been applied to the scholarly German settlers, who became quite numerous about the revolutionary periods of 1830 and 1848, a class of cultivated men, yet frequently unpractical, for whom manual labor proved a hard school of experience." Faust, *The German Element in the United States*, 1:442.

in his *Historia Westphaliae* that some of his most devoted parishioners who had formerly stood by him in his difficulties were at length won over to the opposition, intimidated or bribed, he knew not which. He now took a distinctly pessimistic view of the future, declaring that the only hope of saving the Faith in Central Missouri lay in the two parishes of the Sacred Heart at Richfountain and of St. Francis Xavier in Cole County. The trouble culminated in Father Helias's giving up his post at Westphalia and retiring to St. Louis, after affixing to the church door a Latin distich of his own composition:

*Ardua qui quaerit, rubros cur currit ad Indos*
*Westphaliam veniat, ardua cuncta dabunt.*[39]

"Meanwhile," says Father Helias's narrative, "the church of St. Joseph stands deserted and closed against the wolves, a reproach to those who, though of the number of the sheep, have by contentions, subtlety of speech and ambition for things beyond them forced the pastor to retire, reluctantly withal and for only a brief spell—but Westphalia has ceased forever to be a residence." And after these words follows the colophon, "Here ends the sad history of the colony of Westphalia founded by me. May 11, 1842." [40]

### III. FATHER HELIAS AT HAARVILLE

The pessimistic forecast of the future of Catholicity in Central Missouri which Father Helias was led to make in consequence of his difficulties in New Westphalia failed to be justified by the event. The years were to smooth away the frictions and scandals of the moment and bring to a golden maturity the harvest which he had sown in much travail and bitterness of soul. As we saw, Father Helias withdrew in the spring of 1842 from Westphalia to St. Louis, without, however, abandoning altogether the spiritual care of the district that had been consigned to him: From St. Louis he made occasional visits to the parishes he had started in and around Jefferson City and finally in the beginning of September, 1842, again took up his residence in Central Missouri. This time, however, with the approval of his Superiors, he made his headquarters not in Westphalia, where the opposition to him was still active, but in Haarville, subsequently Taos, Cole County, where in 1840 he had built the church of St. Francis Xavier. Here the missionary was destined to remain until his death in 1874. [41]

The years immediately following Father Helias's return to his beloved Mission were marked by the erection at his hand of several new churches. Though some obscurity veils the beginnings of the

---

39 "Why should the man who covets hardships hie to the dusky Indies? Let him come to Westphalia and he wil lfind hardships aplenty."

40 *Historia Westphaliae*, p. 27.

41 The transfer in 1842 of the headquarters of the Mission of Central Missouri from Westphalia to Haarville (Taos) is emphasized by Father Helias in the Latin title prefixed by him to the Westphalia *Burial Register*, "*Liber Defunctorum Residentiae Sti Iosephi Societatis Jesu in Nova Westphalia Comitatus Gasconade Status Missouriani Americae Confoederatae borealis ab anno Domini 1837. Moderatorum consensu atque expressa voluntate Residentia Centralis ad Sti Francisci Xaxerii translata est in Cole County, Mo., A. 1842.*"

church of St. Ignatius Loyola in Jefferson City, we may accept 1841 as the year in which its construction was begun. Certainly, the church was in use for divine service in 1843.[42] As only the churches of St. Joseph in Westphalia, St. Francis Xavier in Cole County and the Sacred Heart at Richfountain had been built prior to Father Helias's retirement from Westphalia in the spring of 1842, we may designate the Jefferson City edifice as the fourth of the seven churches built by the zealous missionary up to the end of 1845.[43] A fifth church, that of the Assumption, at the present Cedron in Moniteau County, was built before March, 1843.[44] April 6, 1844, the corner-stone was laid of the new church of St. Francis Xavier in Haarville. The edifice, 60 by 38 feet, could claim the distinction of being the first Catholic stone church to be built in the interior of Missouri. It was occupied for the first time on May 11, 1845, Father Helias on this occasion addressing the congregation in English, German and French.[45] Towards the end of 1844, the church of St. Thomas the Apostle was built at Indian Bottom, Cole County, near a bend in the Osage River.[46] Finally, on Ascension Day, May 1, 1845, the church of the Immaculate Conception at Loose Creek, in Osage County, on the main public road between Jefferson City and St. Louis, was opened for divine service.[47] Thus by the middle of 1845, Catholic churches had been built at Westphalia, Haarville, Richfountain, Jefferson City, Moniteau, Indian Bottom and Loose Creek. These seven churches, attesting the progress

42 Supra, p.

43 Cf. Father Helias's Latin epigram (Mémoires), p. 58:
nos Gallia, Roma,
"Flandria nos genuit, docuit nos Gallia, Roma,
Teutoniae Helvetiaeque sinus peragravimus omnes;
Post varios casus, terraeque marisque labores,
Sistimus; atque novae fundamina fiximus urbis
Westphaliae, septemque dicatas Numinis aedes.

44 Historia Westphaliae, p. 28. However, the Mémoires, p 55, (as also a Helias's Ms. dated about 1870), assigns the building of this church to 1845, while the Status Animarum etc. places it as early as 1841. The dates given in the Mémoires do not always tally with those in the Historia Westphaliae. The writer has followed generally the latter source as being more or less contemporary with the events recorded. The church of the Assumption referred to here is in the present Cedron, Moniteau Co., Mo. A second church of the Assumption appears to have been built by Father Helias in 1857 for a German congregation in Cole County, not far from Taos, but its location cannot be identified. The property of the Assumption church (Cedron) was acquired March 1, 1843, for a consideration of four dollars, from Ignace and Barbara Backer. It consisted of two acres in N.E. ¼ of Section 4, Tnp. 46, Range 15 of Cole County, (Moniteau County not yet organized). The church had been built at the time the property was transferred.

45 Litterae Annuae, 1845. A tract of four acres, including the site of St. Thomas's church, was conveyed, September 8, 1848, to the church authorities by Henry Stumpf and Christina, his wife. The consideration was five dollars. The tract was in S.W. corner of N.E. ¼ of S.E. ¼ of Section 22, Township 42, Range 12 W., Cole County.

46 Historia Westphaliae, p. 28. The dates 1843 and 1846 for the erection of the Indian Bottom church are also to be found in the Helias papers. Father Helias was led to choose St. Thomas the patron of this church in deference to the tradition, admittedly of slender historical value, which credits the apostle with having preached the gospel in America. Lebrocquy, Vie du P. Hélias, p. 228. Indian Bottom, now known as St. Thomas, is eight miles south of Jefferson City. "The first pastor, Father Helias came to the place when there were but three or four families." History of Osage, p. 302.

47 Dies Memorabiles (Helias Mss.); Mémoires, p. 54. The deed of conveyance of the Loose Creek church property, September 28, 1843, for a consideration of five dollars, from Louis Auguste Pequignot and his wife Joséphine to Fathers Verhaegen, De Theux, Smedts, describes it as the "certain tract of land on which the Roman Catholic Church of the Conception and Graveyard is situated." The tract was of six acres and began "at the north of the State Road of St. Louis to Jefferson City by Bolden's ferry to the North-east corner of the N.E. quarter of N.W. quarter, Section 5, Township 43, Range 9, West."

of Catholicity had made in Central Missouri, were abong the results
of Father Helias's first seven years of labor in that part of the St.
Louis diocese. [48]

The extent of the ministerial activities of Father Helias at this
period is revealed in his routine itinerary for the year 1843. On the
first Sunday of the month he officiated at St. Francis Xavier's in
Haarville; on the second Sunday at St. Ignatius Loyola's in Jefferson
City; on the third Sunday in Loose Creek, where, as the church building was not yet ready for use, services were held in the public school;
on the fourth Sunday at the Sacred Heart in Richfountain; on the
fifth Sunday, or, in default of that day, on some festival occurring
during the month, at St. Joseph's in Westphalia. Besides this monthly
round of visits, services were held three or four times a year at the
Assumption on Moniteau Creek, at St. Thomas the Apostle, Indian
Bottom, Cole County, and at Holy Cross in Pilot Grove, Cooper
County. Moreover, visits were paid once or twice a year to Booneville, Columbia, Hibernia, Côte-sans-dessein and other stations. [49]

As there was little money among the settlers, Father Helias had
to rely largely on the charitable donations of friends in Europe for
the means necessary to build and equip his numerous churches. Thus
the church of St. Francis Xavier at Taos, where he spent the last
thirty years of his life, was built and furnished largely through the
munificence of his mother, Marie Helias d'Huddeghem, née the
Countess of Lens. A remittance of $875.00 made to her son in 1844
and another one of $225.00 in 1845, are recorded as some of the fre-
quent contributions she was wont to make for this purpose. The
Countess died December 4, 1848, enjoining in her will that her heirs
were to provide out of her estate whatever should be necessary for the
complete furnishing of the church, of which, according to her son,
she deserved to be called the foundress. As such, she was entitled to
the special gratitude of the parish and Father Helias accordingly announced in 1845 that the Litany of Loretto should be recited every
Sunday before services in her behalf and a Mass said annually for the
same intention. After her death, the obligation of an annual *Requiem*
Mass for the dead benefactress was placed upon the church. [50]

---

48 The log-church at Westphalia, though begun in 1837, was finished under Father
Helias's direction. He always enumerated it among the seven churches he had built in
Central Missouri. *Septem extantes ecclesias ipse aedificandas curavi.*

49 *Historia Westphaliae*, p. 35. The congregation of the Holy Cross, Pilot Grove,
Cooper County (12 miles southeast of Booneville) was at this period (1843) still without
a church. Father Helias in his letter of Jan. 6, 1845, contributed to the *Berichte der Leopoldinen Stiftung*, XIX, gives a summary of his ministry in the various parishes and stations
of his Mission for the period 1838-1844.

| | 1838 | 1839 | 1840 | 1841 | 1842 | 1843 | 1844 |
|---|---|---|---|---|---|---|---|
| Number of souls | 620 | 700 | 950 | 1500 | 2000 | 2000 | 2500 |
| Infant Baptisms | 23 | 36 | 37 | 125 | 150 | 149 | 175 |
| Easter Communions | 423 | 560 | 700 | 1094 | 1090 | 1100 | 1300 |
| First Communions | 9 | 15 | 16 | 20 | 60 | 90 | 100 |
| Conversions | 3 | 4 | 5 | 4 | 4 | 3 | 4 |
| Marriages | 3 | 3 | 14 | 26 | 23 | 27 | 36 |
| Burials | 12 | 9 | 17 | 24 | 19 | 50 | 155 |

50 *Historia Westphaliae*, pp. 38, 45, 46. *Maria Carolina Guislena Comes de Lens et
Rom. Imperii Helias d'Huddeghem Fundatrix domus et ecclesiae jus habet quotannis ad
Anniversarium.* Others who helped Father Helias to build and furnish the church at Taos
were the Ladies of the Beguinage of Ghent, his cousin Mlle. Rodriguez d'Evora y Vega and
the Canon De La Croix of Ghent. Lebrocquy, *Vie du P. Hélias*, p. 256.

From the Leopoldine Association of Vienna, the object of which was the support of German Catholic missions in America, the Vice-Province of Missouri received in 1844 the sum of $1875.00. Of this sum $375.00 went to Father Helias for the churches he had built or was about to build. The Father was particularly anxious to receive aid from outside sources as he was thereby relieved of the necessity of relying on his parishioners for support. "Thanks to help of this kind, we can more effectively and with greater liberty announce the Gospel freely, and what we have freely received, freely give. Indeed, among the substantials of the [Jesuit] Institute, a gratuitous ministry is not by any means the last, and nothing is more detrimental to the good of souls than Iscariot-like avarice. Moreover, having what to eat, for Christ Himself has commanded us to eat what is placed before us, to what purpose are superfluities? Ought the Lord's work to be given over on this account? Many indeed are most ungrateful. But let us remember that chief among the concerns of Ignatius was Germany. He founded a college in Rome for German students. He was ready to recall St. Francis Xavier from distant India to send relief to the North. Of his first nine companions he gave five to Germany. Nay, he ordered his children, wheresoever scattered over the face of the earth, to say a Mass every month for the Northern countries. Let us not accordingly, fall below the lofty thoughts of so great a Father." [51]

An incident occurring in 1845 is recorded by Father Helias in terms that reveal the disappointment of which it was the occasion. Father Van de Velde, on his return from Europe in that year, brought with him a great quantity of altar furniture for the needy missions of the Vice-Province. Father Helias was counting on his share of the treasure and already in anticipation saw his poor mission chapels decently provided with all the accessories of divine service. But the steamer bearing the precious cargo, when almost in sight of St. Louis, unhappily caught fire and sank, a complete wreck. Nothing of Father Van de Velde's shipment appears to have been saved. To Father Helias the accident proved a real blow, retarding seriously as it did the progress of his parishes by depriving them of sorely needed equipment for the proper celebration of Mass and other sacred functions.[52]

51 *Historia Westphaliae.* p. 37. A letter from Father Helias, dated Jefferson City, Mo., Jan. 6, 1845, to the Leopoldine Association of Vienna gives an interesting account of the progress of Catholicity in Central Missouri, (*Berichte der Leopoldinen Stiftung*, 19:66-76, 1846). Considerable light is thrown on Father Helias's early struggles by his account-books, which he kept with painstaking accuracy and neatness. For the first eight years the honoraria in the shape of baptismal and marriage offerings, mass-stipends etc. which he received from the congregations under his care, amounted to the munificent sum of $184. In 1844 he received from his parishioners $90, the first money which they contributed directly to his support. "From the beginning the Congregation promised to pay $200.00 as annuities, but could never give it." In his first year at New Westphalia, 1838, his income amounted to $725.12½, of which sum $10.00 came from Mother Duchesne, Superioress of the Religious of the Sacred Heart, and the rest from the estate of Bishop Barrett of Liege who had remembered the Jesuit Missions of Missouri in his will. Beginning with 1839 he received almost annually generous donations from his family in Belgium, while occasional appropriations from the Lyons Association for the Propagation of the Faith as also from the Austrian or Leopoldine Association helped towards the financing of his numerous parishes and stations. Sometimes money would be received for some specific purpose as this under date Feb. 16, 1841, "Thro P. J. Verhaegen for an expedition to Lexington, where I lost my horse. $20."

52 *Historia Westphaliae,* p. 37.

The year 1844 was a calamitous one for Father Helias. The
Missouri river flood of that year, the greatest in the history of the
river, followed by a protracted drought, brought widespread sickness
in its wake.[53] There was no house without its patient, and in most
houses all the inmates were down with disease at the same time. In
one dwelling which he visited, Father Helias found no fewer than
twenty persons in the last stages of disease. The one compensating
circumstance was that it was a season of divine grace for many of the
victims, who found their way back to God's friendship as the shadows
of death crept upon them. Father Helias himself was not to escape
the consequence of the great physical strain and constant exposure to
infection put upon him by the exercise of his ministry at this critical
time. His health broke down and he began to waste away, his skin,
as he expressed it in Scriptural phrase, cleaving to his bone. The
doctors could do nothing for him and despaired of his recovery. And
yet, he passed through the crisis, regained his strength and was able
in time to take up again his burden of parochial missionary duties.
The next year, 1845, he was repeating his experience of the past year,
wearing himself out with attendance on the sick and running every
risk of infection. A second collapse followed and the Father lay on
what seemed from every human outlook his bed of death. The most
skillful physicians in the county pronounced him beyond reach of
medical aid. For some days he lay in a coma, a cold sweat bathing
his forehead and the extremities of his body stiff with the icy rigors
of approaching dissolution. Funeral arrangements began to be made
and the parishes were notified to send their quota of pall-bearers. But
at the last moment the skill of a worthy widow, Gertrude Evens by
name, saved the priest's life. She succeeded in forcing a long reed
tube between his firmly clenched teeth, with the result that some needed
medicine was successfully administered. He rallied, grew steadily
stronger and in a short while was again performing his customary
round of labors.

But the health of Father Helias was at best a precarious thing,
liable to break utterly at any time under the severe physical and mental
strain he was put to in the exercise of his ministry. And still he kept
at his post, declining the offer made by his Superior to allow him to
return to Belgium. The minutes of the meeting on April 16, 1846,
of the consultorial board of the Vice?Province of Missouri, contain
this item: "Father Helias declines to return to Belgium, desiring to
consummate the sacrifice of his health and life. Let him then remain
where he is." However, Father Helias's Superiors determined now to
send him an assistant-priest, a step that would have been taken earlier,
had the very meagre personnel of the Vice-Province permitted.
Accordingly on December 8, 1846, Father Helias was joined at the
little Jesuit residence in Haarville, Cole County, by Father James
Cotting, a Swiss, who had been employed in the Vice-Province in
various parochial charges since his arrival in Missouri in 1840. He

---

53 Barns, *Commonwealth of Missouri*, St. Louis, 1877, has an account of the Missouri-
river rise of 1844.

was a man of robust health, wth energy and zeal to match, in Father Helias's own words, "an exceeding zealous and active young missionary." Father Helias found him an admirable companion and, as he records, was cheered up more than words can tell by his kind and sympathetic charity and the efficient service he rendered in the ministry. From June up to the arrival of Father Cotting in December, Father Helias had been subject to a chonic and troublesome fever, but on the arrival of his companion, the fever disappeared and thence-forth he enjoyed the best of health. [54]

Even prior to the arrival of Father Cotting, Father Helias had begun to enjoy some measure of relief, when, in 1848, the parishes of Jefferson City and Moniteau were taken over by a secular priest, the Reverend James Murphy, according to an agreement entered into between Bishop Kenrick of St. Louis and Father Van de Velde, the Jesuit Vice-Provincial. With Father Cotting now at hand to share his labors, the position of the pioneer missionary was vastly improved. *Semper et perpetuus in equo mobilis*, "forever moving about on horse-back," is the descriptive detail with which Father Helias seeeks to picture the kind of man he had for assistant. Father Cotting on his arrival immediately won the favor of the parishioners of St. Joseph in Westphalia by at once pushing forward the building of the new stone church which they had already begun at the instance of Father Helias. The corner-stone of the church was laid on March 19, 1848, with considerable ceremony. The weather was superb and a great throng of people, Catholic and non-Catholic, gathered for the occasion. Some Mexican cannon, trophies fresh from the siege of Sacramento in the Mexican war, broke the slumbers of the townsfolk at early dawn with their jubilant booming. Services were held in the old church from which there was a procession to the site of the new edifice, where Father Helias blessed the corner-stone with appropriate ceremony. [55]

A sort of anti-clerical faction, dubbed the Latinians from the alleged circumstance of their having studied Latin in their native country, was found among the German Catholics of Westphalia. They were the same faction, it appears, who had fomented the opposition to Father Helias in 1842, which resulted in the temporary closing of the parish church. Now their efforts were directed against Father Cotting, whose authority they sought to undermine by calumny and abuse. Unfortunately, some unguarded statements of the priest, who was quick-tempered and frank of speech, were eagerly seized on by his enemies and turned to his disadvantage. A riotous disturbance which occurred in Westphalia on February 2, 1848, was laid to his charge. A law-suit followed at Jefferson City in which the Father appeared as defendant. The suit went against him and only the inter-vention of Father Helias with some of the public officials saved Father

. 54 *Historia Westphaliae*, p. 52.
55 *Historia Westphaliae*, p. 61. Father Cotting appears to have resided at Taos with Father Helias for the greater part of his stay in Central Missouri. It was not until the pastorate of Father Ehrensberger that Westphalia again assumed the status of an independent Residence.

Cotting from the payment of a heavy fine. Father Cotting was thereupon removed by his Superior from Westphalia, to which he bade farewell, January 18, 1849. His connection with the Missouri Vice-Province ceased at the same time and he spent the remainder of his days a member of the Maryland Province of his Order.[56]

. Father Cotting's place at Westphalia was filled by Father Andrew Ehrensberger, a Bavarian, one of the exiled German Jesuits who found a home in the Vice-Province of Missouri in 1848. Father Ehrensberger took up his residence at Westphalia on November 17 of that year. From this time forward there were two independent residences in Central Missouri, Westphalia and Taos. Father Ehrensberger gave much of his time and attention to the little Bavarian settlement at Richfountain.[57] Some little skill which he possessed as a painter he turned to good account by decorating the parish church. Father Helias's estimate of Father Ehrensberger's capabilities as a pastor of souls was high. He calls him a "capital preacher," *optimus concionator*, and sums up his record as a pastor of Westphalia in the words, "that redoubtable companion of Christ has so acquitted himself that no one can speak ill of him without untruth." Father Ehrensberger left Westphalia in 1851 to take up the duties of a professor in St. Xavier's College, Cincinnati. He was subsequently recalled to Germany where he achieved distinction as a missionary and preacher.[58]

Father Ehrenberger was succeeded as Superior of the Westphalia Residence by Father Kalcher of the Austrian Province. Father Helias syles him "an excellent *operarius*." Thenceforward the line of Superiors at Westphalia down to the period of the Civil War, includes the names of Father Joseph Brunner, Anthony Eysvogels and John Baptist Goeldlin. Other Fathers attached to the residence as assistants during the same years were James Busschots, Joseph Weber, James Bruhl, John Schulc, William Niederkorn and Henry Van Mierlo, while aiding the Fathers in the domestic concerns of the house were the lay-brothers Sebastian Schlienger, Caspar Wohler, Joseph Prasneg, Wenceslaus Kossnar, Daniel Kochendorfer and Michael Schmidt.

## IV. GROWTH OF THE PARISHES

During the ten or fifteen years that preceded the opening of the Civil War the Mission of Central Missouri prospered in every way. We shall touch briefly on the course of events in the more important of the parishes during that period.

The steeple of the new stone church of St. Joseph in Westphalia was not finished until some years later than the dedication of the church, a circumstance which seemed tot lend point, according to the author of the "Annual Letters," to the Latin inscription over the church door, placed there by the architect,

---

56 *Historia Westphaliae*, p. 58.

57 He "helped greatly to render the Mission of the Sacred Heart settled by his Bavarian countrymen a model mission by reason of the piety and fervor which distinguish it from all others."

58 Father Ehrensberger returned to Westphalia as Superior in 1852, remaining there, however, not more than a year.

*Concordia res crescunt discordia dilabuntur.*

Happily the mischief-making tendencies of a part of the congregation during the early period of its history had been corrected, so that Father Goeldlin, Superior of the Westphalia Residence, could write in 1862: "The spirit of the people is in general, good. They have learned that in annoying and contradicting their priests there is neither peace nor the blessing of God." [59]

Four miles to the north of Westphalia was the church of the Immaculate Conception at Loose Creek. The name Loose is usually explained as a corruption of the French *l'ours*, bear.[60] The parish was composed partly of German Rhinelanders and partly of Creoles, which latter element, however, appeared to display no very active interest in the affairs of the congregation. From 1851 on, Loose Creek had its Sunday Mass by one of the Fathers from Westphalia. 1853 and 1854 were cholera years, the epidemic finding its way into the interior of Missouri. Among the Irish laborers employed in the neighborhood of Loose Creek on the construction of the Missouri Pacific Railroad, there were numerous cases of the dreaded disease. These were attended to by the Westphalia pastors, not without difficulty, as the latter were hard pressed to care for the numerous cholera patients in Westphalia itself. In recognition of the charitable services of the Fathers, the Irish laborers on the Missouri Pacific contributed generously in 1855 to the interior decoration of the Loose Creek church, besides donating the two side altars of St. Joseph and our Blessed Lady.

At Richfountain, some five or six miles southeast of Westphalia, the little frame church of the Sacred Heart, built in 1840, was enlarged in 1854 to the dimensions 75 by 24 feet and topped off with a steeple. The village physician, a converted Lutheran, composed a "chronographus" for the church-bell, which was consecrated to the Immaculate Conception of the Virgin Mother in memory of the solemn promulgation of that doctrine by Pius IX in 1854.[61]

In 1849, when the cholera was at its height, the congregation of the Sacred Heart vowed an annual exposition and adoration of the Blessed Sacrament for ten hours. Everyone in the parish escaped unharmed from the scourge. Accordingly, every year on the Sunday within the Octave of the Feast of the Sacred Heart, the people were wont to fulfill their vow with great dveotion. Years after, when cholera again broke out in the state, no case was reported from Richfountain, an indication, as the author of the "Annual Letters" observes, of how

---

[59] *Missio Missouriensis centralis comprehendens Comitatus Osage, Cole, Miller, Maries 1852-1862.* (Mc.). The author is apparently Father John Goeldlin, Superior of the Westphalia Residence during the period 1857-1872. The present brief summary of the course of events in the central Missouri parishes during the decade or so of years immediately prior to the beginning of the Civil War is based largely on this source.

[60] See note 17, supra for list of families in Loose Creek, April 1, 1839, showing the Creole element in the majority at this period. The German settlers came in later. origin of the name cf. note 47, page 13.

[61] *Sacrati Domini Cordis quae nomine gaudet*
    *Ad ditis statio parvula fontis aquas*
*Campanam hancce, Maria tibi, quo consecrat anno*
    *Quod pia crediderat, credere jussa fuit:*
*Peccati exsortem solam Te protoparentem*
    *Conceptam patris Consilio esse Dei. ..*

pleasing to the Lord was the pious faith of the congregation. Another instance of the piety of the parishioners of Richfountain was the annual Solemn High Mass for a successful harvest. The Mass stipend was made up by small contributions from the farmers. It is related that one of their number ridiculed the idea of a collection taken up for this purpose and refused to contribute, saying jocosely that he would share in the blessings showered on his neighbors' crops. The harvest of this season surpassed expectation. The skeptic's wheat, cut and stacked to a great height in his field, made his heart rejoice. But one day, on a sudden, a storm came up and scattered his wheat far and wide, leaving nothing of the splendid crop except the straw. At the same time, the wheat in the adjoining fields lay untouched. The lesson was not lost on the light-minded farmer. Thereafter, he came forward every year unsolicited with a generous contribution for the Harvest Mass.

Though poorer in a material sense than were the other parishes of the Mission, Richfountain surpassed them in its zeal for Catholic education. The old school becoming too small for the needs of the parish, a new one of stone, 35 by 25 feet, was built in 1858 close to the church. Shortly after the erection of the school-house, the property on which it stood was claimed by a disaffected Catholic who proposed, however, to leave it in the hands of the parish on condition that the new building be used as a public school. Though the claimant found many to stand by him, most of the parishioners rejected the proposal indignantly and fought the case in court, with the result that both school building and property were saved to the parish. The litigation, however, caused a slight rift in the harmony that generally obtained among the Richfountain Catholics, while for years after the debt incurred by the erection of the new school-house lay as a heavy burden on the hundred families that made up the congregation.

Fifteen miles southwest of Westphalia, near a bend in the Osage river, was the church of St. Thomas the Apostle. Though situated in Cole County the limits of the parish extended for some miles into the neighboring Osage and Miller Counties. In 1844 when the first log-chapel was built, the families numbered only seven. This number had trebled in 1854, when a frame church, 30 by 26 feet, was put up, the old church being utilized as a presbytery. But the location of the church proved unsatisfactory, for the only approach tto it lay through the property of an ill-humored farmer, who threatened all the rigors of the law against the church-goers. Hence both church-building and presbytery were moved in 1856 to a more accessible site, where a settlement named St. Thomas was gradually formed. In 1860 the parish counted no more than thirty-five families, many of the former parishioners having moved down to Miller County where fertile land was in abundance.[62]

Ten miles south of Westphalia was a settlement originally known as St. Boniface, from the name of the parish-church, and later as Koeltztown, from the name of the chief property-owner of the locality.

---

62 Supra, note 46.

In 1856 the sale of public lands to the south of Westphalia at attractively low prices induced many of the parishioners of St. Joseph to move in that direction. A Protestant lady, Mrs. Koeltz, who had purchased several thousand acres of land in the locality in question, conceived the idea that the best means of attracting settlers would be the erection of a Catholic church. She accordingly offered ten acres of land for this purpose and, besides, promised to contribute generously to the building-fund. In 1857 Father Goeldlin, then Superior at Westphalia, was invited to come down to the new settlement to superintend the construction of the proposed church. However, the Father was under strict orders from the Vice-Provincial to open no more stations and wished, moreover, first to see the site offered for the church, as an imprudent choice of location had just made it necessary to move the church of St. Thomas to another place at a considerable outlay of money. But the promoters of the new church at Koelztown were impatient of delay and sent a delegation to Archbishop Kenrick of St. Louis to offer him the church property, which he accepted. Foundations for an elaborate stone edifice which was to eclipse St. Joseph's in Westphalia were immediately laid and in July 1858, Father Goeldlin, at Archbishop Kenrick's request, laid the corner-stone. However, a young carpenter, who had ventured to play the role of achitect of the new church, finding himself incompetent to prosecute his task, made off with a considerable part of the building fund. The original lan was thereuon discontinued and a modest frame church erected, more in keeping with the humble circumstances of the settlers.

The difficulty of securing a pastor for the new church had now to be met. The Archbishop of St. Louis had no one to send. The Jesuits were again petitioned to assume charge of the station, but had to decline. However, an arrangement was made between Archbishop Kenrick and Father Coosemans, the Jesuit Vice-Provincial, by which Koeltztown was to be attended from Westhalia until a diocesan priest could be found for the post. Accordingly, beginning with June 1861, the place began to be visited by one of the Westphalia Fathers every second Sunday of the month.[63]

Twenty-three miles south of Westphalia in Maries' County was the town of Vienna, which could boast its own Catholic church, St. Mary's. In the beginning of the fifties, Vienna was a wilderness. A widely advertised sale of public lands at a low figure attracted settlers to the locality, among them a number of Irish Catholic families from the cities. These were soon planning to secure to themselves the blessing of a church and pastor. As the settlers were scattered over a considerable strech of territory, two stations were formed for their accommodation. The settlers in the town and its immediate vicinity were the first of the two groups to build a church, which was named St. Mary's. The second station, eight miles distant from St. Mary's, was after 1862 visited every two months from Westphalia. The neat little St. Mary's church, a frame structure forty feet long, was attended by about thirty-five families. Father Goeldlin remarks in the "Annual

---

63 "Koeltztown was named after the first merchant, August Koeltz." *History of Moniteau etc. Counties*, p.  .

Letters" that when a new station is formed, all things have, so to speak, to be created anew. Not only does lack of money retard the work, but the parishioners, however devoutly they may have lived in the cities, are not easily brought to put up with the inconvenience of bad roads. The parishioners of Vienna, continues the Father, are chiefly Irish who give promise of becoming not less fervent than the rest of their countrymen, nor less generous, provided Heaven blesses their efforts and brings their good intentions to fruition. [64]

Towards the close of 1861, the Jesuit pastors assumed charge of another station, about sixteen miles east of Westphalia, known as St. Isidore's, where a group of French settlers had put up a little church. The site had been chosen and the building begun by the settlers on their own initiative and without consulting the Fathers of Westphalia. Unfortunately the location of the church was a poor one. Moreover, the church was destitute of proper furniture and vestments, while the *Annual Letters* note, "it will require great zeal and labor and a considerable measure of divine grace to realize any fruit." About the same time that St. Isidore's was taken in charge, two additional stations, one six and the other about twelve miles south of St. Isidore's, were started and attended from Loose Creek. [65]

At Taos, where Father Helias resided ever since his withdrawal from Westphalia in 1842, he had the satisfaction of seeing his parish of St. Francis Xavier grow steadily in loyalty to its pastor and regard for ecclesiastical authority. The old attempt at schism on the part of a small but agrressive faction which had provoked warning letters to the congregation from Bishop Rosati and his successor, Bishop Kenrick, were no longer renewed. The material condition of the colonists likewise went on improving. Many of them who had enlisted in the Mexican War shared in the bounty of the Government, which settled a quarter-section of land on each of the volunteers when they were discharged from service at the end of the war. The arrival in the autumn of 1847 of a party of fifty Belgian emigrants from the neighborhood of Ghent, who came highly recommended by M. Beaulieu, Belgian Minister in Washington, boded well for the future of the parish. They had probably been attracted to Central Missouri by a report published at Brussels by the Baron Van der Straten-Pantholz, Secretary of the Belgian Legation at Washington. The Baron made a trip through Osage and Cole Counties in 1845 to ascertain by per-

64 Conard, *Cyclopedia of the History of Missouri* and *History of Moniteau etc. Counties* have brief accounts of Vienna. Among the first Catholic settlers were Mr. Felkner, Thomas and Dennis Fennessy and Michael Owen. The first church was built as early as 1859.

65 The church property at St. Isidore, near Linn, a tract of three and a quarter acres, (S.W. ¼ of N.E. ¼ of Section 33, Tnp. 44, Range 8, W.)r was conveyed February 18, 1860, by Irene Curtit to the Jesuit Father for $25.00. The church erected by the French was of logs. The parish of Maria Hilf, Mary Help of the Christians, near Isbell station on the Missouri Pacific R. R. some fifteen miles north of Westphalia was organized in 1862 by Father Buschotts, S.J. The church property, two acres, (Sections 2 and 11, Tnp. 44, Range 9), was acquired May 26, 1873.

St. Ignatius's parish, Bailey's Creek, was established by Father Buschotts in 1858. Father Verhaegen, visiting the place the fall of 1837, found there some ten or twelve families, all Americans. (Verhaegen à Rosati, Nov. 17, 1837). Th church property, six acres, (N.W. ¼ of S.W. ½ of Section 22, Twp. 44, Range 7 W.), was acquired for a consideration of five dollars, June 23, 1859, from Peter and Catherine Jordan. A log church was built in 1859. Bailey's Creek is fifteen miles northeast of Westphalia

St. George's parish in Linn, the county-seat of Osage County, was organized by Father Goeldlin in 1867.

sonal observation the prospects it held out to Belgium emigrants. Clad in a heavy buffalo-robe, for it was the depth of winter, and accompanied by Father Helias who was similarly protected, he visited the various stations of the mission, entering the farm-houses and chatting pleasantly with the occupants on the success, or perhaps the lack of it, that had attended their efforts. Much useful information was in this way gleaned for the benefit of such of his countrymen as might care to try their fortune in the New World.[66] The actual arrival in Cole County in 1847 of the party of Belgian emigrants above referred to gladdened the heart of Father Helias.

"Mr. Pierre Dirckx, an energetic, intelligent and very religious young man, acts as agent for the emigrants and shows me great consideration. So far our countrymen have escaped the bilious fever of this country, a sort of Polders fever. but more acute and painful. The Belgian farmers make themselves favorably known in Missouri as everywhere else by their industry, methodical habits, perseverance, love of hard work and incomparable neatness. An air of prosperity hangs over their places which might serve as model farms for all the emigrants. When I ask our Flemings how they are satisfied here, they answer that "they are as happy as King Leopold on his throne".

I am delighted with the new parishioners; they are good Catholics and always ready to render me a service. Mr. Pierre Dirckx. my nearest neighbor, is a constant visitor at the presbytery and shows me every attention. Together with his partner, Mr. Charles Beckaert, he runs a successful farm of which he is the owner and which yields him a handsome income. Their hired men Edouard Van Voeren François Steippens, François Goessens, etc., are mostly Belgians. These young fellows are all equipped with trades, not only useful but highly lucrative in a country like this which has just been thrown open to civilization. For example, François Goessens is an excellent maker of wooden shoes. People come from twenty miles around to fit themselves out at his shop. I have known him to sell as many as five hundred sabots in a single day. It's a smooth business for wood here costs nothing or almost nothing. [67]

We may conclude our account of Father Helias and his ministry at Taos by citing the words in which he pictures the condition of the parish in the decade immediately preceding the Civil War.

"While in so many localities both of the Old and New World, corruption, the fruit of wicked doctrines, makes incessant headway, the moral condition of our settlement recalls the beautiful days of the primitive church. Here one may without the slightest risk, go away from his house, leaving the doors right open. You need have no fear of theft or trespassing of any kind. Irreligious or licentious publications fail to reach our excellent people. Libertinism is unknown: God's name is not, as elsewhere, the object of profanity. My priestly heart experiences a joy ever new in seeing our churches crowded on Sundays and feast-days, with throngs of faithful souls who emulate one another in singing the praises of the Lord." [68]

66 *Historia Westphaliae*, p. 47.

67 Lebrocquy, *Vie du P. Hélias*, p. 254.

68 The "Mission of Central Missouri," as described in the *Annual Letters*, (1853-1862), had an area of 2500 square miles lying between the Missouri, Osage and Gasconade Rivers and a line fifty miles south. It took in all of Osage County and part of Maries, Miller and Cole Counties. The Catholic population numbered three thousand. The Residence of St. Francis Xavier at Taos, with its dependent stations, lay outside the limits of the "Mission of Central Missouri" proper, the headquarters of which were at Westphalia. Here there were generally three Fathers attached to the Residence, a fourth being added in 1860. At a later period, Richfountain, Loose Creek and Linn had resident Jesuit pastors, who, however, remained under the authority of the Westphalia Superior, whom they were required to visit personally once a week.

Thus did the course of events in the Jesuit parishes of Central Missouri run on calmly down to the dark days of the Civil War, when they were made to face the invasion of political passion and strife. Father Helias's *Historia Westphaliae* ends about 1861 with the fervent apostrophe:

> "O Ferdinand, why so dumb? Everything proceeds A. M. D. G. and without change, as from the beginning. Why therefore should I repeat? Of one thing, however, I must make mention A. M. D. G., to wit, the singular favor wrought by St. Francis Xavier, who cured suddenly my friend and guest, Charles Louis Bekaert, a settler of sixty years of a cancer which had fairly eaten through his hand, and besides, freed me in an instant of acutely painful rheumatism. Moreover, I have experienced over and over again and hereby gratefully acknowledge A. M. D. G. the most visible assistance of my Guardian Angel. O God! Thou hast given thine Angels charge over me, that they may keep me in my ways."

The purpose of this article has been to sketch the beginnings of Catholicity in Osage and Cole Counties, Missouri, with the narrative brought down to the period of the Civil War as a convenient stopping-place. Subsequent to that period the pioneer Jesuit parishes of the counties named were resigned one by one by their founders into the hands of the diocesan clergy, the last of the group, Loose Creek, being ceded in 1886. The outstanding figure throughout this well-nigh half-century of Jesuit parochial activity in Central Missouri was, it need not be said, Father Ferdinand Helias, who, after witnessing the seeds of Catholicity which he had planted in much travail of soul and body take root and grow unto the ripened harvest, died at Taos, Cole County, August 11, 1874. He was indeed a veritable apostle of the Faith in these parts and the incidents of his strenuous missionray career will ever remain a chapter of fascinating interest in the story of the up-building of Catholicity in the great state of Missouri.

BIBLIOGRAPHICAL NOTE. Material for a history of the early Catholic missions of Osage and Cole counties, Missouri, is more abundant than is usually the case in ecclesiastical beginnings due largely to the fact that Father Helias, founder of these missions, wielded a facile and ready pen. Among manuscript sources may be mentioned, in addition to the usual parish registers of baptism, marriages and funerals, the annual reports (*Litterae Annuae*) forwarded by Father Helias to his Superiors in St. Louis, *Historia Westphaliae*, a Latin narrative of some seventy pages and a French autobiographical Memoir drawn up in 1867, *Mémoires du Rd. P. Ferdinand Hélias D'Huddeghem, pretre missionaire de la Compagnie de Jésus en Amérique.* Father Francis Braun S.J. left an exhaustive manuscript account in German especially valuable for its lists of early Catholic settlers in Central Missouri. Printed sources include Rev. F. Holweck sketch of Father Helias in the St. Louis *Pastoral-Blatt*, March, 1919, by far the best biographical account in print; Lebrocquy, *Vie du R. P. Hélias D'Huddeghem de la Compagnie de Jésus*, Gand, 1878, a work based largely on Father Helias's letters to his family in Belgium; *Berichte der Leopoldinen-Stiftung im Kaiserthume Oesterreich*, 1843-1850 (cf. *Catholic Historical Review*, July, 1915), *Missouri Historical Review*, 5:83 (1911), article, *Recollections of the First Catholic Mission Work in Central Missouri*, by Rev. Joseph B. Schmidt; *History of Cole, Moniteau, Morgan, Benton, Miller, Maries and Osage Counties, Missouri*, Chicago, Goodspeed Publishing Co., 1889.

GILBERT J. GARRAGHAN, S.J.

# THE FLAT-HEAD AND NEZ PERCE DELEGATION TO ST. LOUIS

## 1831--1839

Towards the close of the year 1831 a delegation of four Indians from beyond the Rocky Mountains reached the city of St. Louis. Their language[1] was different from all the Indian dialects with which the inhabitants had some acquaintance. Yet, as these visitors gradually made themselves understood, it was learnt that they had come to obtain religious teachers for their people, the Flat-Head and Nez Percé tribes[2] near the Pacific Ocean. They visited the Catholic Cathedral,[3] and attended-divine service with all possible reverence. Owing to the change of climate and the unwonted life in a city, these children of the wilderness grew ill; two of them were baptized on their death bed by Fathers Roux and Saulnier of the Cathedral, and were buried with all the rites of the Church. The other two started in the Spring of 1832 on their return voyage, but only one reached his home, as the other died on the way. These are the simple facts of the occurrences, similar in many ways to numerous other delegations sent to St. Louis by the Indian tribes round about for the purpose of obtaining a Black Robe as their guide and teacher. Yet this visit is specially remarkable in our early annals, not only on account of the vast distance these seekers after God had traveled, but even more so on account of the great and lasting results it eventually matured in the Catholic missions of Oregon. There is another point of interest connected with this embassy, namely the legendary embellishment it has found up to the present day, in the Protestant missionary story of the saving of Oregon

---

1 Most of the Indians that had come in contact with the people of St. Louis were of the Algonquin linguistic stock, so the various branches of the Illinois, the Sacs and Reynards of the North, Indians of New England, New York, Pennsylvania and Delaware. The Kansas and Osages were of Siouan linguistic stock. But these newcomers from beyond the Rocky Mountains belonged to the Salishan group, which had no affinity with any of the Eastern and Central linguistic groups. General Clark, indeed, had been in their country for an extended period, but had conversed with them by means of an interpreter. Cf. Palladino, Indian and White in the Northwest p. 6.

2 Flathead and Nez Percé (Pierced Noses) although these Indians did not indulge in the practices which their names might indicate. They called themselves Salish. "The country of the Flatheads," says Palladino, "was that part of Montana lying west at the base of the main range of the Rocky Mountains. It was called in their language Spetleman, which means 'place of the bitter root,' whence the name of the Bitter Root Valley." *Indian and White in the Northwest*. ch. I, p. 1.

3 The Catholic Cathedral of 1831 was Bishop Du Bourg's church of brick on Rue de l'Eglise (2nd Street) near Market, which was used for divine service until October 1834, when the new Cathedral, on Walnut Street was consecrated by Bishop Rosati. The old dilapidated structure was consumed by fire on the night of April 6, 1835.

183

for the Union, or as it is called by later historical writers, "the Marcus Whitman Legend."[4]

The legendary story takes account of the facts as we have related them, with one exception. Not for Black gowns, Catholic missionaries, did the Flat-Head and Nez Percé come from the far-away Pacific slope, but for the Book, the Book of Heaven, the Bible. And if they asked Governor Clark for a missionary, it was not a Catholic priest they desired but a Protestant preacher. After two had died, and been buried in the Cathedral Cemetery, the two remaining delegates were entertained at a banquet by General Clark; at which the Old Chief, a Nez Percé, is introduced as delivering the following lament:[5] "I came to You, the Great Father of the White Men, with but one eye partly opened. I am to return to my people beyond the mountains of snow, at the setting sun, with both eyes in darkness, and both arms broken. I came for teachers and am going back without them. I came to You for the Book of God. You have not led me to it. You have taken me to Your big house, where multitudes of Your children assemble, and where Your young women dance as we do not allow our women to dance, and You have taken me to many other big houses where the people bow down to each other and light torches to worship pictures. The Book of God was not there. And I am to return to my people to die in darkness." This parting speech of the Nez Percé chief, was first published by the Rev. H. H. Spalding in the *Walla-Walla Statesman*, February 16, 1866, about thirty-four years after the supposed event. The Reverend Mr. Spalding further stated, that the lament was overheard by a young man of the Methodist Church; but that he himself had "received it from the only surviving one of the delegation." In 1870 the Reverend Mr. Spalding wrote a slightly different version of the Lament for the *Chicago Advance*. In 1883 we find the Lament beautifully amplified and indianized in the Rev. William Barrow's "Oregon": "I came to You over the trail of many moons from the setting sun" . . . and so on in the vein of Brand and Logan, "My people sent me to get the white man's Book from Heaven." "You took me where they worship the Great Spirit with candles, and the Book was not there. . . . You made my feet heavy with burdens of gifts, and my moccasins will grow old in carrying them, but the Book is not among them." These are only a few samples of the Rev. William Barrows amplifications of the Rev. Mr. Spalding's account of the young Nez Percé's report of the old Nez Percé chief's lament to General Clark, concerning "the Book that was not there." This

---

4 A vast and tangled mass of literature has grown up around this remarkable visit of the Flat-Head Indian Mission. To separate truth from legend was not an easy task. Non-Catholic writers are in the ascendancy, as far as quantity is concerned, but the Catholic writers are far superior, in regard to quality. Father Palladino's book "Indian and White in the Northwest. Baltimore. 1894" outweighs all the Spaldings, Barrows, Nixons, Lees, Eels, Mowrys, Bashfords of the Protestant side. Bancroft, in his History of Oregon is reliable though not exhaustive. H. Addington Bruce is fair and judicial. The myth that Marcus Whitman saved Oregon for the Union is exploded long since. The *American Catholic Historical Researches* contain two articles of great importance on this question. Vol. XVI: "The Story of Marcus Whitman refuted," by H. N. Beadle, and Vol. XVIII: "The Legend of Marcus Whitman" by E. G. Bourne.

5 Cf. the interesting monograph, "The Evolution of a Lament" by C. T. Johnson (F. M. Elliott), reprinted from *Washington Historical Quarterly*, Vol. II, No. 3.

might do as a speech in a Leatherstocking Tale but is a blot on the page of history. Yet Mowry in his *Marcus Whitman and the Early Days of Oregon,* 1901, goes one step further, in his eagerness to secure this gem of oratory as the historic cornerstone of the Protestant Missions on the Pacific slope. In his introduction Mowry states: "This book is a history, not an embellished story . . . from first to last it has to do with facts." Here is one of the facts intended to bolster up the authenticity of the Indian chief's lament: "One of the clerks in General Clark's office took down at the moment the speech of the Indian as it was interpreted to General Clark, and it began to be circulated." Mowry offers not a single authority for this assertion; he seems to think that a fact does not need any proof, proof sufficient that it is a fact. He makes his statement in 1901, the fact is supposed to have occurred in 1832, that is about sixty-nine years ago, and in all these years no one, not even the Rev. Mr. Spalding ventured to assert that the lament had been circulated in writing immediately after the event. Yet in Mowry's book the romantic address is printed in full as an authentic fact of history, thus leading Edwin Eels to make the dramatic statement: "These were the words that saved Old Oregon and the Pacific Northwest to the government of the United States."[6]

I have dwelt at greater length on the so-called Indian Lament because it has been used by Protestant writers to clinch the argument in favor of the view that the purpose of the Flat-Head and Nez Percé delegation to St. Louis was to obtain teachers of the Protestant brand of Christianity, together with their book, the Bible, and not, what Bishop Rosati offered them, Catholic missionaries, and the holy Mass.

Now what are the real facts of the case? Or what are the historical grounds for the Catholic version of this interesting episode in our missionary annals? The supporters of the Protestant version, with one exception, were not eyewitnesses of the occurrences during the Indian delegation's stay in St. Louis, in fact had not met them at any time, but only spoke from hearsay. The young halfbreed Wyandot, indeed, a member of the Methodist Church, of whom we shall have more to say ere long, spoke with the Têtes Plattes and Nez Percés: but on the point at issue he appeals to the authority of General Clark, and Clark himself must be considered a witness for the Catholic side. All the other Protestant authorities can, at best, only say "*relata refero.*" But the witnesses for the Catholic side of the question, namely that this delegation from beyond the Rocky Mountains came to seek, not a Book, nor a Protestant missionary, but a living Black gown, a Priest of the Catholic Church, the witnesses for this version are well able to tell us true because they saw and heard what was going on at the time, and they will tell us true because they, both Protestants and Catholics, are men of highest character for veracity and honesty of purpose.

Joseph Rosati, Bishop of St. Louis, was a most exact and pains-

---

6 *Ibidem.* at the end.

taking recorder of contemporary events. In his Letter Book for 1831 he notes under date of December 31, that he had sent a letter to Mgr. Pélagaud, of Lyon, with information in regard to two savages, *Têtes Plattes*, baptized and subsequently buried in St. Louis.

This letter was published in the Annals of the Association of the Propagation of the Faith. Under date of December 31, 1831, Bishop Rosati wrote as follows:.

"Some three months ago four Indians who live across the Rocky Mountains near the Columbia river (Clark's Fork of the Columbia), arrived at St. Louis. After visiting General Clark, who, in his celebrated travels, has visited their nation and has been well treated by them, they came to see our church and appeared to be exceedingly well pleased with it. Unfortunately, there was not one who understood their language. Some time afterwards two of them fell dangerously ill. I was then absent from St. Louis.

"Two of our priests visited them and the poor Indians seemed to be delighted with the visit. They made signs of the cross and other signs which appeared to have some relation to baptism. The Sacrament was administered to them; they gave expressions of satisfaction. A little cross was presented to them. They took it with eagerness. kissed it repeatedly and it could be taken from them only after death. It was truly distressing that they could not be spoken to. Their remains were carried to the church, and their funeral was conducted with all the Catholic ceremonies. The other two attended and acted very becomingly. We have since learned from a Canadian, who has crossed the country which they inhabit, that they belong to the nation of Flat-Heads, who, as also another called Black Feet, had received some notions of the Catholic religion from two Indians who had been to Canada and who had related what they had seen, giving a striking description of the beautiful ceremonies of the Catholic worship and telling them that it was also the religion of the whites. They have retained what they could of it, and they have learned to make the Sign of the Cross and pray. These nations have not yet been corrupted by intercourse with others. Their manners and customs are simple and they are very numerous. Mr. Condamine (Rev. Matthew Condamine was one of Bishop Rosati's clergy attached to the Cathedral) has offered himself to go to them next spring with another. In the meantime we shall obtain some further information of what we have been told and of the means of travel." [7]

The Book of Sepultures 1781-1832 of the St. Louis Cathedral, contains the entries of Baptisms and Burial of the two members of the delegation, the one signed by Benedict Roux, the other by Edmond Saulnier.[8]

S. A. Clark,[9] in his *"Pioneer Days of Oregon History"* quotes another letter of Bishop Rosati sent to the General of the So-

---

[7] Cf. Palladino. *l. c.* p. p. 11 & 12.

[8] Book of Sepultures 1781-1832 of St. Louis Cathedral, kept at Chancery of Archdiocese of St. Louis, has these two entries:
Le trente et un d'Octobre mil huit cent trente et un, Je sousigné ai inhumané dans le Cemetière de cette Paroisse le corps de Keepeellele ou Pipe Bard du Nez Percé de la tribu de Chopoweck Nation appellée Têtes Plates agé d'environs quarante quatre ans, administré du St. Bapteme venant de la rivière Columbia au dela des Rocky Mountains.
EDM. SAULNIER, PR.
Le dix sept de Novembre mil huit cent trente et un, Je sousigné, ai inhumané dans le Cemetière de cette Paroisse le corps de Paul sauvage de la Nation des Têtes Plattes venant de la rivière Columbia au dela des Rock Mountains, administré du St. Bapteme et de l'extrême onction.
ROUX, PR.

[9] Clark, S. A. "Pioneer Days of Oregon History, Portland, 1905."

ciety of Jesus at Rome, saying that as early as 1816 some Catholic Iroquois from Canada had settled among the Flat-Heads and taught them religion, and that about 1830, again in 1832, and once more in 1839 Flat-Heads or Iroquois-Flatheads came to St. Louis for more light. It is to be regretted that our authority for this extract, James. W. Bashford, does not give the entire letter of Bishop Rosati, for then he might have been enabled to correct the dates given by Clark 1831-32, and 1835, leaving 1839 as it is.

We will insert the original letter, as we find it reprinted by C. B. Palladino, S.J. It is dated St. Louis, October 20, 1839, and addressed to the Father General of the Society of Jesus at Rome :[10]

*"Reverend Father:*

"Eight or nine years ago (1831) some of the Flat-Head nation came to St. Louis. The object of their journey was to ascertain if the religion spoken of with so much praise by the Iroquois warriors was in reality such as represented, and above all, if the nations that have white skins had adopted and practiced it. Soon after their arrival in St. Louis they fell sick (two of them), called for a priest and earnestly asked to be baptized. Their request was promptly granted and they received the holy baptism with great devotion. Then holding the crucifix they covered it with affectionate kisses and expired.

"Some years after (1835) the Flat-Head nation sent again one of the Iroquois nation to St. Louis (Old Ignace). There he came with two of his children. who were instructed and baptized by the Fathers of the College. He asked missionaries for his countrymen and started with the hope that one day the desire of the nation would be accomplished, but on his journey was killed by the infidel Indians of the Sioux nation."

"At last," continues Bishop Rosati, "a third expedition (Left-Handed Peter and Young Ignace) arrived at St. Louis, after a voyage of three months. It was composed of two Christian Iroquois. These Indians, who talk French, have edified us by their truly exemplary conduct and interested us by their discourses. The Fathers of the College have heard their confessions and today they approached the holy table at High Mass in the Cathedral church. Afterwards I administered to them the sacrament of Confirmation and in an address delivered after the ceremony I rejoiced with them at their happiness and gave them the hope to have soon a priest.

"They will depart tomorrow: one of them will carry the good news promptly to the Flat-Heads; the other will spend the winter at the mouth of the Bear river, and in the spring he will continue his journey with the missionary whom we will send them. Of the twenty-four Iroquois who formerly emigrated from Canada only four are still living. Not only have they planted the faith in those wild countries, but they have besides defended it against the encroachment of the Protestant ministers. When these pretended missionaries presented themselves among them, our good Catholics refused to accept them. 'These are not the priests about whom we have spoken to you,' they would say to the Flat-Heads, 'they are not the blackrobed priests who have no wives, who say Mass, who carry the crucifix with them!' For the love of God my Very Reverend Father, do not abandon these souls!' "

On the very date that this letter was written, Bishop Rosati made the following entry in his *Diary:*

1839 Oct. 20. Dominica XXII post Pentecosten. . . . Post Missam pontificalibus vestibus assumptis, et hymno *Veni Creator Spiritus* can-

---

10 For the full letter cf. Palladino, *l. c.* p. p. 31 & 22.

tato, sermonem habui ad Confirmandos. Confirmationis Sacramentum administravi duobus indigenis, Ignatio Ootstagleave, et Petro Okassaweita ex natione Iroquois. Hi in Canada ex Catholicis parentibus nati, et in Catholica Religione instructi, ante tres et viginti annos ad regiones quae intra oras pacifici Oceani et Montes petrosos continentur migrarunt, apud tribum quae *têtes plattes* (Flathead) dicuntur constiterunt, et ex illorum foeminis uxores duxerunt, Religioni addicti illam nedum obliti fuerunt sed et infideles apud quos degebant docuerunt, nunc post trium mensium iter huc advenerunt, et petunt Sacerdotem Missionarium, qui apud gentes illas Evangelium praedicet." [11]

These accounts written by Bishop Rosati in 1839, about eight years after the first Flathead and Nez Percé delegation, refer, for the most part, to the later developments of the event under discussion; yet they throw a bright light on the origin and the purpose of the delegation of 1831.

Twenty-four Iroquois braves, members of the fierce warrior-tribe, but now tamed by the Catholic religion under the leadership of Ignace La Mousse, or Old Ignace, had joined the Flatheads and intermarried with them as early as 1816. They had not only not forgotten their religion, but had instructed the heathens among whom they lived in its tenets, and caused the petition to be made for a missionary to teach them the Gospel.

These documents further state that the prime movers in this religious effort did not lose courage after the first failure, but had sent one of their own number, the Iroquois Old Ignace, with his two sons[12] as the second delegation to St. Louis. This second embassy certainly did not ask for the "Book" but for living missionaries, Jesuit Black gowns. It must be noted here that Old Ignace was killed by the Sioux, not on his homeward journey but on the third embassy, which set out from the Flathead country in the summer of 1837, but never having reached its destination is generally omitted from the count. Bishop Rosati's letter also gives promise of fulfilling the ardent wish of these men of good will. The reason that the Flatheads and Nez Percés had to wait some years longer for the advent of the desired Black gown is the scarcity of priests in the vast diocese, a circumstance which Bishop Rosati hopes will be relieved by the intervention of the General of the Society of Jesus. On the 7th of October 1832 Father Condamine was appointed Pastor of Kaskaskia, and on the 8th of August, 1836, he died in Cahokia.

But now we must return to the forlorn Flatheads and Nez Percés of 1832, awaiting the opening of the season for travel, mourning their dead comrades and being entertained at a banquet by General Clark.

General Clark, in company with Meriwether Lewis, was among the first white men that came to the country about the Columbia River

---

11 *Diary* of Bishop Rosati, Oct. 20, 1839.

12 Old Ignace was the leader of the third Flat-Head mission in the summer of 1837. His band, only five in number, was attacked by a war-party of 300 of the Sioux. Old Ignace was told to stand aside, being an Iroquois, with whom the Sioux had no quarrel, but the brave fellow chose the lot of his adopted brethren and fell fighting. "Thus perished he who may justly be called the apostle of the Flat-Heads, and through them also of many of the other Indian tribes of the Rocky Mountains." Palladino, *l. c.* p. 20 & 21.

Sept. 1805. At the time of which we are writing, 1831-1832, he was Superintendent of Indian Affairs in the West. He was a man of untarnished honor, and highly respected by all. His interest in the Indians was generous and unselfish. Our Flathead and Nez Percé delegation called on him, as a matter of course, and enjoyed his hospitality. The death of the two members occurred at his house. Let us hear what General Clark has to say on the purpose of the embassy. As we have not his direct testimony on the matter, we must elicit it from the testimony of others. William Walker Jr., a halfbreed of the Wyandotte nation, member of the Methodist Church, and government Indian agent, came to St. Louis in 1832 and called on his chief, General Clark. Being told of three Indians from the West lying ill, in another room, he visited them at General Clark's request, and learnt, as he himself states, that they had come 3000 miles on foot (should be 2000 miles on horse back) to consult their Great Father on very important matters.

What were these important matters? The Wyandot Christian Walker, the chief witness of the Protestant side, does not claim that the Indians themselves, but rather the Superintendent of Indian Affairs, told him about them. Walker in his letter to S. P. Disoway of Pittsburg, dated Upper Sandusky, Jan. 19, 1833, makes the following statement:

> General Clark related to me the object of their mission, . . . and I will here relate it briefly as well as I can: It appears that some white man had penetrated into their country and happened to be a spectator at one of their religious ceremonies, which they scrupulously performed at stated periods. He informed them that their mode of worshipping the Supreme Being was radically wrong, and instead of being acceptable and pleasing, it was displeasing to Him; he also informed them that the white people away toward the rising of the sun had been put in possession of the true mode of worshipping the Great Spirit. They had a book containing directions how to conduct themselves in order to enjoy His favor and hold converse with Him; and with this guide, no one need go astray; but everyone that would follow the directions laid down there could enjoy, in this life, His favor, and after death would be received into the country where the Great Spirit resides, and live forever with Him.
>
> Upon receiving this information, they called a national council to take this subject into consideration. Some said, if this be true, it is certainly high time we were put in possession of this mode, and if our mode of worshipping be wrong and displeasing to the Great Spirit, it is time we had laid it aside. We must know something about this— it is a matter that cannot be put off—the sooner we know it the better. They accordingly deputed four of the chiefs to proceed to St. Louis to see their great father, General Clark, to inquire of him, having no doubt but he would tell them the whole truth about it.
>
> They arrived at St. Louis and presented themselves to General Clark. The latter was somewhat puzzled, being sensible of the responsibility that rested on him; he, however, proceeded by informing them that what they had been told by the white man was true. Then he went into a succinct history of man, from his creation down to the advent of the Saviour; explained to them all the moral precepts contained in the Bible, expounded to them the decalogue; informed them of the advent of the Savior, his life. precepts, his death, resurrection, ascension, and the relation he now stands to man as mediator—that he will judge the world, etc."

The letter of Mr. Walker, published in the *Christian Advocate,* the leading Methodist publication, March 1, 1833, was the occasion of a sudden and widespread movement among the Protestants of the East in favor of a missionary establishment among the Flatheads.[13] Many a writer's enthusiasm improved the occasion by letting his imagination supplant laborious investigation; and so we have a vast bulk of so-called historical literature clustering around this Indian cry, that "the white people had a book containing directions how to conduct themselves." The inference drawn by later writers that the Indian delegation came to get this book and to carry it back to their people is certainly not warranted, much less is it indicated by Walker himself.

It will be noticed that the passage I have cited is given, not on the direct authority of the Indians, whose language the Wyandot very probably did not understand, but on the authority of General Clark Walker's testimony is, therefore, only a résumé of what Clark had told him. Now, did Walker give the true sense of General Clark's words? A gentleman of St. Louis, Mr. E. W. Sehon, as Bishop Bashford[14] informs us, submitted the *Christian Advocate* of March 1, 1833, containing Walker's letter, to the Superintendent of Indian Affairs, asking him whether the account of his conversation with Walker was correct. "General Clark informed me," says Mr. Sehon, "that the publication was correct, and that the cause of the visit of the Indians was: Two of their number had received an education at some Jesuitical School in Montreal, Canada, and had returned to the tribe, and endeavored, as far as possible, to instruct their brethren how the whites approached the Great Spirit. A spirit of enquiry was aroused, a deputation was appointed, and a tedious journey of three thousand miles was performed to learn for themselves of Jesus and Him crucified." Of course, "Jesuitical" for Jesuit, and "three thousand miles" for two thousand are not slips of the tongue of Governor Clark, but slips of the pen of Mr. Sehon. There are other slight discrepancies from the full and correct account of Bishop Rosati which may be or may not be due to General Clark. In any case, Mr Sehon's report of General Clark's explanation establishes the fact that the delegation was sent under Catholic auspices, and therefore could not have come for Protestant missionaries and their Book of Directions, but only for Catholic Priests, who would teach their nations the religion they had learnt to love and practice in Catholic Canada.

The Reverend Samuel Parker in his *Journal of an Exploring Tour Beyond the Rocky Mountains,* is quoted by James W. Bashford as attributing the first knowledge of Christianity among the Nez Percés to Pierre C. Pambrun, a Roman Catholic, but this testimony is not to the point, as it refers to a somewhat later date, when the Americans were already swarming through the wild, cold mountains.[15] Yet it is

---

13 Reprinted in full in C. T. Johnson's *The Evolution of a Lament,* p. p. 8-10.
14 Cf. Bashford, *The Oregon Missions,* p. 3.
15 There is a brief note on Pierre C. Pambrun in Bancroft's *History of Oregon,* Vol. I, p. 35, with a reference to Blanchet's *Catholic Church in Oregon.* Cf. W. Irving, *Captain Bonneville,* p. 301. Chapter 34.

not only possible, but more than probable that the Flat-Heads and Nez Percés received some early knowledge of the Christian religion from the trappers and traders of the Northwest and Pacific Fur Companies, the rank and file of whom were, as Chittenden says, "staunch Roman Catholics," who certainly would not help in promoting a scheme of introducing Protestant missionaries anywhere, least of all in their own wild haunts of the Rocky Mountains.

But whatever persons, White or Indian, were instrumental in bringing the earliest knowledge of the Christian religion to the tribes, on the Columbia River, it is plain that to them, teachers as well as disciples, Christianity meant Catholicity, and furthermore that their instructions had fallen on good ground. Bancroft in the *History of Oregon* has a long note[16] in further elucidation of the acknowledged fact, that the Flatheads were in the habit of placing a wooden cross at the head of the graves of their dead, giving a number of religious ideas and practices of the natives. "It will be remembered," says Bancroft, "that the Dalles people observed Sunday as a holiday, in the manner of the Catholic Church. . . . So well advanced in the Christian religion were they (the Flatheads, Nez Percés and their neighbors), according to Bonneville, that they would not raise their camps on Sunday, nor fish, hunt or trade on that day, except in case of severe necessity, but passed a portion of the day in religious ceremonies, the chiefs leading the devotions and afterwards giving a sort of sermon upon abstaining from lying, stealing, cheating and quarrelling, and the duty of being hospitable to strangers. Prayers and exhortations were also made in the morning on week days. . . . Besides Sundays they likewise observe the cardinal holidays of the Roman Catholic Church." Of the Flatheads John Wyeth, a companion of Captain Bonneville, says: "I have never known an instance of theft among them, neither have I known any quarrelling nor lying. . . . They have a mild, playful, laughing disposition, and this is portrayed in their countenances. They are polite and unobstrusive. With all their quietness of spirit, they are brave when put to the test, and are an over-match for an equal number of Black feet, their inveterate enemies." All these traits had been observed among the Flatheads and Nez Percés long before any missionary, Catholic or Protestant, had been seen among them, and find their best, I may say their only satisfactory explanation in the fact that as early as 1816 Catholic Iroquois had instructed them, as best they could, in the tenets and practices of the Catholic religion.

We have seen from the testimony so far adduced, that two of the St. Louis party of four Flatheads and Nez Percés received Baptism at the hand of the priests of the St. Louis Cathedral and, having died, were buried with the Catholic rites. What became of the two remaining members of the embassy? In 1841 there appeared the celebrated work of George Catlin, *Letters and Notes on the Manners, Customs and Conditions of the North American Indians,* written during the

---

16 Bancroft, *l. c.* vol. I. p. p. 116-118.

eight years of travel from 1832-1839. Letter No. 48 in Volume II.
refers to these Indians, who as Catlin states, "were a part of a delegation that came across the Rocky Mountains to St. Louis a few years
since to enquire for the truth of the representation which, they said,
some white men had made amongst them, that our religion was better
than theirs, and that they would all be lost if they did not embrace it.
Two old and venerable men[17] of this party died in St. Louis, and I
traveled 2000 miles (companion of these two young fellows) toward
their own country, and became much pleased with their manners and
dispositions. The last mentioned of the two died near the mouth of
the Yellowstone River on his way home, with disease he had contracted in the civilized district; and the other one, I have since learned,
arrived safely among his friends, conveying to them the melancholy
intelligence of the deaths of all the rest of the party; but with assur-
ances at the same time from General Clark and many Reverend gentlemen that the report which they had heard was well founded, and that
missionaries — good and religious men — would soon come amongst
them to teach this religion, so that they could all understand and have
the benefits of it. When I first heard the report of the object of this
extraordinary mission across the mountains I could scarcely believe
it, but on conversing with General Clark on a later occasion, I was
fully convinced of the fact."

It will be seen that George Catlin's report of what he heard from
the two surviving members of the Nez Percé and Flathead Indian
delegation, agrees substantially with that of Bishop Rosati, except
that the first bringers of Gospel tidings according to Rosati were "two
Indians"; according to Catlin, "some white men"; but this difference
is not necessarily contradictory, but rather complementary, in as far
as some of the Indians may have first heard of the Christian religion
from some Catholic woodranger or trader, whilst others depended for
their information on their Iroquois friends from Canada.

Another account, namely that of the trader with whom Catlin
and the two Indians made the homeward journey, is recorded by
Marcus Whitman himself in his Journal of 1835. It gives one new
fact which fits in perfectly with the accounts we have so far seen. But
we must give it entire

The following is the history of these Indians that came to St. Louis
to gain a knowledge of the Christian religion, as I received it from the
trader[18] under whose protection they came and returned. He says, their
object was to gain religious knowledge. For this purpose the Flat-Head
Tribe delegated one of their principal chiefs, and two of their principal
men, and the Nez Percé tribe a like delegation, it being a joint delegation of both tribes. In addition to this delegation a young Nez Percé
came along. When they came to Council Bluffs, two of the Flat-Heasd

---

17 It has been objected that the description "two old and venerable men" does not fit
the two Indians that died in St. Louis in 1831, as one of them is described by Edmond Saulnier
as being about forty-four years old. Yet, in the estimation of a mere boy, as the narrator
was at the time, forty-four years may have seemed to be sufficiently advanced to merit the
epithets old and venerable. And the Indian called Paul may have been much older for all
we know, his age not being mentioned in the Record.

18 Who the trader was we cannot say, but as the great majority of them were French
Catholics, we may assume that the one mentioned was of the Faith also.

and one of the Nez Percé returned home, and the other Flathead, the chief. and the Nez Percé chief, and the remaining one of the delegation, and the young Indian (Nez Percé) came to St. Louis, where they remained through the winter. At St. Louis two of them died, and the only remaining one of the delegation died on his return at the mouth of the Yellowstone, so that there was no one to return but the young man."

According to this there were originally six delegates, three from the Nez Percé, Choppunich, and three from the Flat-Heads (Salishan) together with the Nez Percé youth, seven all told. But as two Flat-Head and one Nez Percé delegate returned home from about halfway of the journey, there were only two Nez Percé and one Flat-Head left of the delegation, four in all, if we add the Indian companion. Of these one Nez Percé and the only Flat-Head left were baptized on their death bed and buried in St. Louis. The two remaining Nez Percés left St. Louis in the Spring of 1832, but the only remaining delegate dying on the way, the volunteer companion alone returned to the expectant tribes.

We have one more testimony to offer, one we have never seen quoted, by the Rev. P. J. Verhaegen, S.J., Provincial of the Western Province of the Society of Jesus, written on May 3, 1840:

We had it in contemplation to open a new mission among the Flathead Indians, on the other side of the Rocky Mountains. During the administration of the Rt. Rev. Bishop Du Bourg, (Rosati) a deputy from them arrived in St. Louis, for the purpose of procuring a priest. This deputy died shortly after his arrival at this place. In 1835 a second deputation of a father and his two sons, reached the University of St. Louis. We could not, at that time, entertain the project, on account of the paucity of our numbers and the limited means at the disposal of the Superior of Missions. We therefore beheld with the deepest regret, the deputies returning to their remote country, without having accomplished their object. In the month of October 1839 a third deputation of two Indians, arrived at the University, having the same object in view. Moved by the ardent desires of these distant and desolate children, who called so perseveringly for those who might break the bread of life to them, we resolved to gratify their wishes and to send two Fathers in the Spring. The two deputies left St. Louis, full of joy at the happy prospect—one of them remained at Westport, (now Kansas City) to await the arrival of the Fathers, the other returned to the nations beyond the Rocky Mountains, by whom he had been sent, to report to then the success of his mission and to prepare a band of warriors. with whom he was to return in the Spring to meet the missionaries and his companion at a designated point. At the opening of Spring, the time appointed for the fulfilment of our promise, when the Caravan of the Fur Company was about to start for the mountains, the want of the necessary funds rendered it impossible for us to send two Fathers. The scarcity of money was so great, that we could not obtain, on loan, the small amount of one thousand dollars, required for the outfit. In consequence of these difficulties we were enabled to send only one Father (De Smet). He left us on the fifth of April to accompany the caravan of the Fur Company.[19]

_____

[19] Father Verhaegen's Report To the Most Rev. Archbishop and Right Rev. Bishops in Provincial Council assembled, May 3, 1840. MS. in Archives of Catholic Historical Society of St. Louis.

It will be noticed that Father Verhaegen speaks of but one delegate of the Flatheads arriving and dying in St. Louis. According to Whitman's account there was but one Flathead, the other three being Nez Percés, and Father Verhaegen is speaking exclusively of the Flathead mission. The second deputation was on its way, when Whitman wrote, and the third and last brought permanent results in the mission established among the tribe by Father De Smet, S.J.

It is hardly necessary, in the face of this testimony corroborating Bishop Rosati's account as contained in his letter of Dec. 31, 1831, to advert to the legendary story with a slight foundation in fact, that these Indians really came to secure a Book, the Protestant Bible, and departed with the wild lament, that they had come for the "Book of Heaven," the "Book of God," but that the Book was not there where General Clark had brought them; that they had been loaded with gifts, but that the Book was not among them, that no white man would go with them, and no white man's Book would make the way plain. This Protestant embellishment of the historical facts, originating as we have seen, with the Wyandot half-breed William Walker Jr., who stated that the Flatheads and Nez Percés on the far away Columbia River had been told, that the white men far to the rising sun had a book containing directions "as to the way of pleasing the Great Spirit." Here was a call for Protestant enlightenment; for, of course, the Catholics of St. Louis, had not the Book, or at least would not give it.[20] The Protestants of St. Louis, at that time, must also have been short of Bibles: for living at St. Louis about half a year, and being led here and there, the white man's book, alas, was not among the gifts they had been loaded with, and the "Book of Heaven" would not make their way plain. The whole story has such an unnatural tone, and is so plainly gotten up for a special purpose, that the author of *The Evolution of a Lament*[21] comes to the conclusion that, "in the historical garden of the Pacific Northwest, in the course of years, these rootless flowers will die out, and there will yet remain strength and beauty in abundance." Mr. Elliott's words seem but an echo of the prediction made by one of the early Fathers in these missions, the Rev. F. X. Kuppens, S.J.: "These rocky hills will bloom like a garden of roses."

The real flowering and fruitage of these remarkable embassies are to be found in the celebrated Catholic Oregon Missions founded by Father Peter De Smet, S.J., in 1840, and continued to the present day by the Fathers of the Society of Jesus of the California Province.[22]

It would be a most pleasant task to sketch the origin and the early triumphs and vicissitudes of the Oregon missions: yet that subject is a very wide one, and has been ably treated by such historians,

---

20 Of course, there was no shortage of Bibles in St. Louis at the time, at least not among the Catholic priests and people. But what good would a Bible in any of the languages of the world, except, perhaps the Salishan tongue, have done the poor Indians, who could very probably neither read nor write? The talk about the Book which the Indians came to get and carry with them is mere camouflage, *i. e.* an untruth with a sinister purpose.

21 C. T. Johnson, or rather J. M. Elliott.

22 Cf. L. B. Palladino, S.J., *Indian and White in the Northwest*, Baltimore, 1894, of which noble monument of a noble work, we understand, a new edition is in preparation.

as Father Palladino,[23] Bishop Blanchet,[24] Father Van Rensselaer,[25] Ronan,[26] Chittenden and Richardson,[27] and by the Founder, Father De Smet[28] himself. These authors give us a comprehensive view of the grandest missionary work of the nineteenth century in its religious, social, economical and political aspect. In regard to its civilizing influence I would quote• the generous words of a man, who for many years held the highest position of honor and trust our State could confer, and whose name is enrolled among the truly great men of the nation, Senator George G. Vest. It was in the summer of 1884, shortly after my ordination, that I had the honor of making the acquaintance of Senator Vest. Impressed as I was by the historical importance of a former member of the Cabinet of President Jefferson Davis and the present United States Senator, I was, of course, delighted when a few weeks later, in my quiet country mission of Portage des Sioux, I received a copy of a speech delivered by him in the Senate on the burning question of the appropriations for the Catholic Indian Schools. From this speech I would quote a few passages of praise and just acknowledgment of what the Jesuit Fathers of the Oregon Mission have accomplished in civilizing and christianizing the Indians in the Oregon country, and what they would have accomplished in the Indian Territory as well, if they had been given a free hand and a little more generous support. Senator Vest had been apointed a member of a Special Committee sent out to investigate the Indian Reservations in the West. On May 12. 1884, the question as to the appropriation for the schools came up in the United States Senate, and the Senator from Missouri made his report in an impressive speech, from which I quote:

> "In all my wanderings in Montana last summer I saw but one ray of light on the subject of Indian education . . . the system adopted by the Jesuits is the only practical system for the education of the Indian, and the only one that has resulted in anything at all."

Realizing that there was an anti-Catholic feeling at the bottom of the opposition to the Jesuit Schools, Senator Vest thought proper to state his own position in regard to the Catholic religion:

> I was reared in the old Scotch Presbyterian church; my father was an elder in it, and my earliest impressions were that the Jesuits had horns and hoofs and tails and that there was a faint tinge of sulphur in the circumambient air whenever one crossed your path Some years ago, I was assigned by the Senate to duty upon the Commitee of Indian

---

23 *Indian and White in the Northwest.* L. B. Palladino, Baltimore, John Murphy, 1894.

24 Blanchet, *Notes on the Oregon Mission*, Portland, Oregon, 1883.

25 Van Rensselaer, S.J., *Sketch of the Catholic Church in Montana.* American Catholic Quarterly Review, Phil. 1887.

26 Ronan, P., *History of the Flathead Indians.* Helena, Montana, 1876.

27 Chittenden and Richardson, *Life, Letters and Travels of Father Pierre-Jean De Smet, S.J.* 1801-1873. (Four Volumes). New York, Francis Harper, 1905.

28 Of De Smet's works, the most important in this connection are the *Letters and Sketches*, Philadelphia, 1843, *The Origin, Progress, and Prospects of the Catholic Missions of the Rocky Mountains*, Philadelphia, 1843, *Oregon Missions and Travels over the Rocky Mountains* 1845 and 1846, New York, Edward Dunnigan, 1847, and lastly, *New Indian Sketches*, New York, Sadlier (1885).

Affairs, and I was assigned by the committee, of which Mr. Dawes was then the very zealous chairman, to examine the Indian schools in Wyoming and Montana. I did so under great difficulties and with labor which I could not now physically perform. I visited every one of them. I crossed the great buffalo expanses of country,. where you can now see only the wallows and trails of those extinct animals, and I went to all these schools. I wish to say now what I have said before in the Senate, and it is not the popular side of the question by any means, that I did not see in all my journey, which lasted for several weeks, a single school that was doing any educational work worthy the name of educational work unless it was under the control of the Jesuits. I did not see a single government school. especially these day schools, where there was any work done at all.

Something has been said here about the difference between enrollment and attendance. I .found day schools with 1500 Indian children enrolled, and not ten in attendance, except on meat days. as they call it, when beeves were killed by the agent and distributed to the tribe. Then there was a full attendance. I found schools where there were old, broken-down preachers and politicians receiving $1,200 a year and a house to live in for the purpose of conducting these Indian day schools, and when I cross-examined them, as I did in every instance, I found that the actual attendance was about three to five in the hundred of the enrollment. I do not care what reports were made, for they generally come from interested parties. You cannot educate the children with the day school.

The Jesuits have elevated the Indian wherever they have been allowed to do so. without interference by bigotry and fanaticism, and the cowardice of insectivorous politicians, who are afraid of the A. P. A., and the votes that can be cast against them in their districts and their states. They have made him a Christian, and, above even that, they have made him a workman able to support himself and those dependent upon him. Go to the Flathead Reservation in Montana and look from the cars of the Northern Pacific Railroad, and you will see the result of what Father De Smet and his associates began and what was carried on successfully until the A. P. A. and the cowards who are afraid of it struck down the appropriation.

Go through this reservation and look at the work of the Jesuits, and what is seen? You find comfortable dwellings, herds of cattle and horses, intelligent, self-respecting Indians. I have been to their houses. and found under the system adopted by the Jesuits that after they have educated these boys and girls, and they had intermarried, the Jesuits would go out and break up a piece of land and build them a house, and that couple became the nucleus of civilization in the neighborhood. They had been educated under the system which prevented them from going back to the tepee after a day's tuition. The Jesuits found that in order to .accomplish their purpose of teaching them how to work and depend upon themselves, it was necessary to keep them in school, a boarding school, by day and night, and to allow their parents to see them only in presence of the brothers or the nuns.

These Jesuits are not there, as one of them told me. for the love of the Indian. Old Father Ravalli told me, lying upon his back in that narrow cell, with the crucifix above him: "I am here not for the love of the Indian, but for the love of Christ." He was there without any pay except the approval of his own conscience. If you send one of our people, a clergyman, a politician even, to perform this work among the Indians, he looks back to the fleshpots of Egypt. He has a family, perchance, that he cannot take with him on the salary he receives. He is divided between the habits and customs and luxuries of civilized life, and the self-sacrificing duties that devolve upon him in this work of teaching the Indians.

The Jesuit has no family. He has no ambition. He has no idea except to do his duty as God has given him to see it; and I am not afraid to say this, because I speak from personal observation, and no man ever went among these Indians with more intense prejudice against the Jesuits than I did, when I left the city of Washington to perform this duty.

These brave words of Senator Vest, whilst placing the seal of condemnation on our narrow-minded national policy in regard to the Catholic Indian schools, open, at the same time, a bright vista into a most interesting historical field. We, however, must stop here, with the conclusion, from well established facts, that the purpose of the first as well as of the second and third Indian delegation to St. Louis from the Pacific slope, was not to get "the Book," but rather to get a Black gown, in other words, was not a Protestant but a Catholic venture, leading to great results for the Country as well as for the Church.

JOHN ROTHENSTEINER

# AN APPEAL

## HISTORICAL MATTER DESIRED

## by the Catholic Historical Society of St. Louis

✠

Books and pamphlets on American History and Biography, particularly those relating to Church institutions, ecclesiastical persons and Catholic lay people within the limits of the Louisiana Purchase;

Old newspapers; Catholic modern papers; Parish papers, whether old or recent:

> *We will highly appreciate the courtesy of the Reverend Pastors who send us regularly their Parish publications;*

Manuscripts; narratives of early Catholic settlers or relating to early Catholic settlements; letters:

> *In the case of family papers which the actual owners wish to keep in their possession, we shall be grateful for the privilege of taking copies of these papers;*

Engravings, portraits, Medals. etc;

In a word, every object whatsoever which, by the most liberal construction, may be regarded as an aid to, or illustration of the history of the Catholic Church in the Middle West.

Contributions will be credited to the donors and preserved in the Library or Archives of the Society, for the use and benefit of the members and other duly authorized persons.

Communications may be addressed either to the Secretary, or to the Librarians of the

*Catholic Historical Society of St. Louis,*

209 Walnut Street, St. Louis, Mo.

# NOTES

## HISTORICAL

The question as to the exact spot within the present city limits of St. Louis, where the sacrifice of the Mass was first offered, may not seem so easy of solution.

Edwards, in his *Great West,* seems to imply that it was the "Church block" between Market, Walnut, Second and Third streets, probably on account of the fact that it really did contain the first church edifice ever erected in St. Louis. Father L. Kenny, S.J., in establishing the claims of the long-forgotten village of "La Rivière des Pères" as the earliest white settlement in Missouri, and incidentally placing it on the north bank of the river of that name, must, of necessity, claim that the first Mass in St. Louis was celebrated by some Jesuit Father at the mouth of the River des Peres about December 3, 1700.

But there was an earlier encampment of priests, though only a temporary one, on the site of St. Louis, when the Priests of the Foreign Missions, Montigny, Saint-Cosme, Davion and Thaumer de la Source voyaged down the Mississippi in 1699. We quote from Saint-Cosme's letter to the Bishop of Quebec: "The next day (i. e., December 7, 1699), about noon we reached the Tamarois. . . . As they had given trouble to some of Mr. de Tonty's men, a year before, they were afraid, and all the women and children fled from the village (Cahokia) ; but we did not go to it; as we wished to prepare for the Feast of the Conception, we cabined on the other side of the river. Mr. de Tonty went to the village and, having reassured them a little, he brought us the chief, who begged us to go and see him in his village (Cahokia). We promised to do so, and next day, Feast of the Conception, *after saying our Masses,* we went with Mr. de Tonty and seven of our men armed. . . . The Tamarois were cabined on an island lower down than their village." (Shea, *Early Voyages up and down the Mississippi,* p. 66).

Now, the village of the Tamarois was in the neighborhood of the present Cahokia, opposite about the foot of Arsenal street; the island on which they cabined at the time was our Arsenal Island. The place where the first Mass was said in St. Louis is the river bank somewhat north of Arsenal Street, and the day was December 8, 1699, Feast of the Immaculate Conception. Four priests were in the company: Montigny, Saint-Cosme, Da,vion and Thaumer de la Source; and most probably, all four celebrated the holy sacrifice on that day, two hundred and twenty-one years ago next December.

---

Various references are made to Father Angelo Inglesi in the correspondence exchanged between Bishop Du Bourg and Propaganda during the years 1821 and 1822, published in the pages of the REVIEW. Little is found there, however, touching the activity of the Bishop's envoy on behalf of the Louisiana Mission. To his credit must be ascribed in part the organization of the Lyons Association for the Propagation of the Faith, and the sending to America of several bands of zealous laborers, one of whom was to occupy a place of prominence in the American hierarchy as first Bishop of Galveston and Archbishop of New Orleans—John Mary Odin. Inglesi secured money, too: donations and loans. Of the latter one, the "Montmorenci loan," indirectly at least, was to play a part in the financing of the Cathedral on Walnut Street. The story of this loan is a curious aftermath of Inglesi's embassy.

While in France, Bishop Du Bourg's envoy who, thanks to his family connections, obtained entrance into the most exclusive circles and rubbed elbows with the nobility, contracted with Duke Matthew of Montmorenci and his consort for a loan of 30,000 francs ($6,000) in the name of his Bishop. There was, it appears, an understanding between the prelate and his agent that the latter would eventually, after his return to America, pay off the debt out of his own patrimony. For reasons sufficiently explained in the Notes accompanying the Correspondence, Inglesi did not come back west; he remained some time in Philadelphia, where he became involved in the Harold controversy, and left shortly afterwards for Haiti, where he died June 13, 1825, of yellow fever contracted in attending the patients stricken with the epidemic.

His estrangement from Bishop Du Bourg in 1823, and still more his death, put the prelate in a rather delicate position. The Montmorenci loan had been negotiated in his name; and, indeed, as soon as he had received the money, he had invested it in the purchase of a piece of property on the River des Peres, which he intended as an endowment for the See of St. Louis. After his return to France in 1826, in one of his first letters he promised to Bishop Rosati to make over to him all that he had acquired for the Mission. Months passed, however, before he spoke again of this settlement. The reason was that he considered himself in honor bound personally for the Montmorenci debt; and, though no mortgage had been given, he regarded it as a matter of equity that the land in St. Louis County should be kept by him as a guarantee of the loan. From Montauban he confided his scruples on this score to Bishop Rosati on April 22 and November 29, 1827:

> I carry in France a heavy debt, contracted in my name by Father Inglesi, the amount of which (it was to be paid back by him) was used for the purchase of the St. Louis land. It is a matter of 30,000 francs ($6,000). I have devoted to its payment all that I hope to get from my patrimony in San Domingo. But how much will this bring. I know not; still, on the other hand, I must not neglect a transaction wherein my honor is involved. Now, this will eat up all my savings for years. . . . Fortunately. the deal was made with people of high rank, very rich and very pious, who do not want me *to bother myself about* it, and ask for no interests, although they do not renounce the principal. . . .

> I consider the land on the River des Peres as mortgaged *de jure* (although it is not *de facto*) to the Montmorenci family, which furnished the money for it—until I am able to pay it back.

As time rolled on Bishop Du Bourg saw that savings he could realise none, as, despite the strictest economy (he even lived some time in his seminary to save expenses), the paltry salary which the French royal government doled out to its Bishops was but a miserable pittance, scarcely enabling them to live. Moreover, it became every day more evident that nothing was to be expected from San Domingo. He had not as yet made conveyance to Bishop Rosati of *any* of his American holdings, and the St. Louis prelate felt all the more uneasy that he was then planning his Cathedral. On January 28, 1829, Du Bourg wrote to him:

> I have qualms of conscience on the matter of leaving the Montmorenci family without any other security to cover the 30,000 francs which I mentioned tot you, but the land on the River des Peres. It would be a sorry return for their zeal and generosity · Hitherto I had reckoned on my savings to gradually pay off that debt. But I am not yet out of the debts I had to make for settling here. . . . The indemnity which I had been hoping to receive in compensation for our losses in San Domingo will, it seems, dwindle down to nothing. For these reasons have I hesitated to make a pure donation of the various holdings I still have in America.

He accordingly proposed that Rosati buy from him the property on the Des Peres, "Henry's family" (of negroes), his library[1] and whatever articles of furniture he had left behind—the whole for 20,000 francs, payable in four yearly notes of 5,000 francs each, in favor of the Montmorenci family. There would thus remain to him (Du Bourg) only 10,000 francs to pay, for which he deemed the furniture of his episcopal residence to be sufficient security. This was, he added, for the Bishop of St. Louis an excellent bargain, as the whole was practically worth twice as much as the price asked for.

The offer looked good to Rosati; he accepted it, and early in the summer, 1829, sent the four notes payable March 1, 1830, 1831, 1832 and 1833 (the date of maturity of the last three notes was, the following year, on Du Bourg's advice and for reasons of convenience, changed to July 1st). Still Bishop Du Bourg in return did not release the property on the Des Peres, as we learn from his letter of September 25, 1829:

> I am forwarding your four notes to the Duchess Matthew of Montmorenci, together with two from myself, to complete the 30,000 francs due her and thus put an end to a matter of honor which has caused me much trouble. . . . Life's uncertainty, however, compels me to maintain the mortgage on the property until the last cent is paid.

Rosati's first note was honored at maturity by the treasurer of the Association for the Propagation of the Faith, out of the allowance to the Diocese of St. Louis. The arrangement was that the other three notes would be paid in the same way. During the first months of 1831, however, Bishop Rosati found himself in sore need of money for push-

---

[1] Thus did Bishop Du Bourg's library become the possession of the Bishops and Archbishops of St. Louis. It forms the bulk of the "St. Louis Diocesan Library," the home of which was formerly at St. John's Rectory, and is now at the Kenrick Seminary.

ing on the work of the Cathedral. In such circumstances, $1,000 yearly meant a great deal. On March 12, 1831, he proposed to Bishop Du Bourg a new arrangement in regard to the remaining two notes.

"I see," replied the latter on June 13, "your great difficulty to get ready money for the construction of your Cathedral, and I realize how critical your position is. . . . I shall neglect nothing in order to help you. According to your wishes, I will assume your obligation for your two notes (July 1, 1832 and 1833) yet due to Mrs. de Montmorenci, that is, 10,000 francs. I am going to try to sell some government bonds left me by my poor brother, Louis [2] to the amount of 20 to 22,000 francs, in order to put the proceeds at your disposal. I trust I may be able to sell them without difficulty. . . . The whole means a loan to you of the sum of 30 to 32,000 francs (about 6 to 7,000 dollars), for which I am willing to take as payment a bonded interest of 6 per cent, covered by a mortgage on the interest of the Church property you have just sold to Morton, of St. Louis. In other words, you will be selling me for 30,000 francs, for instance, 1800 francs of the interest owed you by Morton on said property, and so on in proportion to the funds I may procure you; for it is possible that there are still some large outstanding notes due to my brother Louis, in which case I shall be happy to put eventually the returns at your disposal. But as, on the other hand, the inheritance of this dear brother was given me only in trust on behalf of some of our nephews who are in poverty; and, on the other hand, French government bonds yield now at least 6 per cent, I should be guilty of injustice in their regard, did I not stipulate for this interest.

Three months later Bishop Du Bourg announced to Father Saulnier, who was his proxy in this business, that, instead of 30,000, it was 35,000 francs which he put at the disposal of Bishop Rosati; for this sum Saulnier could draw at once on Mr. Huguenin, of Bordeaux; for the remainder of the Morton loan on half of the Church property (the whole loan represented a principal of 44,000 francs), he (Saulnier) would sign two notes of 4,500 francs each, payable, the one after one year, and the other after two years. In the beginning of August, 1832, all these transactions were concluded, and Bishop Du Bourg sent the following statement to St. Louis:

| Dr. L. W. Du Bourg, Bishop of Montauban, to Rt. Cr. Rev. Rosati, Bishop of St. Louis, Mo. | |
| --- | --- |
| To sale of a land interest at 6 % of 2640 francs.....44,000 | By interest at 6 % on 35,000 from April 1, 1831, to April 1, 1833 (two years) 4,200 |
| To yearly interest payable April 1, 1833........... 2,640 | By dº on 6,000 francs since April 1, 1833 (1 year and 9 months)......... 450 |
| | By dº on 2,000 francs from July 1, 1832 to April 1, 1833 .................... 80 |
| Balance due to L. W. Du Bourg ................ 1,095 | By principal paid at above-mentioned dates .......43,000 |
| 47,735 | 47,735 |

2 Louis Joseph Du Bourg, "le Beau Du Bourg," as he was surnamed in New Orleans, was, after his return to Bordeaux, the unofficial, but most active agent in France for the Louisiana Mission. He died at the old family mansion, 7 Rue St. Seurin, at Bordeaux, on November 4, 1830. As he was a bachelor, his estate went to the Bishop, his sole surviving brother.

Agreed on the amount of the present account, amounting to *forty-seven thousand seven hundred and thirty-five francs,* whereby, beside the interest of 2640 francs, maturing on April 1, 1833, there remains due to L. W. Du Bourg a balance of *one thousand and ninety-five francs,* which he begs Bishop Rosati kindly to accept as an humble offering for his Cathedral. Montauban, August 13, 1832.

✝L. Wm. Du Bourg, Bp. of Montauban.

But what of the Montmorenci notes? It will be recalled that Du Bourg, besides the two which he took in 1831 from Bishop Rosati, had subscribed two in his own name. The two turned over from St. Louis matured on July 1, 1832 and 1833, respectively; his own were payable in 1834 and 1835. He paid at maturity the Rosati notes; but when he died at Besançon, on December 12, 1833, his own notes were still due. We must, therefore, turn to his last will, dictated to Canon Querry, his secretary, from his death-bed, just a week before his demise, to find out his dispositions in regard to this debt:

I owe two notes of 5,000 francs each, which I, out of an excessive tenderness of conscience, which I have much regretted, consented to the widowed Duchess of Montmorenci, maturing, the one about next May or June, and the other a year after. Believing I am about to appear before God, I do not hesitate to declare solemnly to said Lady, that, in conscience, she has no right to that money. A few reflections on the origin of this pretended debt will suffice, if needs be, to convince her of that. My executor shall make for her a copy of the present article of this, my last will; if My Lady insists on the payment of these notes, my signature must be honored; at all events, he should not neglect to take back the notes.

Whether "My Lady" insisted or not on the payment of these notes, we know not. At any rate, the issue, one way or the other, was not to benefit any either Bishop Rosati or the Diocese of St. Louis: a codicil to Archbishop Du Bourg's will stipulated that, in case the Montmorenci notes were canceled, Father Leclerc and Canon Querry were to receive one thousand francs each out of that money, the remainder going, according to the tenor of the will, to the Archbishop's niece, Caroline Du Bourg de Sainte-Marie, who was a widow and in very moderate circumstances.

From Cardinal Gibbons' book, *A Retrospect of Fifty Years,* we will quote the following words in just appreciation of our great Archbishop Kenrick, with whom he was on intimate terms: In describing the proceedings of the Vatican Council, he says:

Archbishop Kenrick of St. Louis was among the most noteworthy prelates from the United States. Archbishop Kenrick spoke Latin with most admirable ease and elegance. I observed him, day after day, reclining in his seat with half-closed eyes, listening attentively to the debates without taking any notes. And yet so tenacious was his memory that, when his turn came to ascend the rostrum, he reviewed the speeches of his colleagues with remarkable fidelity and precision without the aid of manuscript or memoranda.

In regard to the question that the Vatican Council had to settle as to where the true seat of infallibility lies, he again refers to Archbishop Kenrick, who was opposed to the definition of papal infallibility, but when the council decided in favor of it, "then he most nobly accepted it and published it in his diocese. Years afterward somebody spoke of the Archbishop to Pope Leo XIII, and criticised his attitude during the Vatican Council to the Holy Father, upon which the Holy Father replied, indignantly, "The metropolitan of St. Louis was a noble man and a true Christian Bishop. When he sat in council as a judge of the faith, he did according to his conscience and the moment the decision was taken, although it was against him, submitted with filial piety of a Catholic and a Christian." And from this Cardinal Gibbons comments upon the theory of some that the Catholic Church has no freedom of thought. He quotes Archbishop Kenrick again as saying that "the Pope's power was given for edification, not for destruction; if he used it for love of domination scarcely will he meet with obedient populations."

In this connection it is proper to refer to the fact that Cardinal Gibbons is the last "living Father of the Vatican Council." "Now alone upon this earth," he says, "I can report what happened within these sacred walls." It will prove interesting to compare the Cardinal's opinion with that rendered by Father Granderath in his great *History of the Vatican Council*.

---

To Mr. Scannell O'Neill, who kindly contributed the interesting *Notes on Sister Mary Theonella Hite and her Family*, published in our last number (pp. 97—100), we are once more indebted for the following, dealing with a member of one our old St. Louis families—the Garesché famliy, so well represented to this day among the Catholics of our city. This genealogico-biographical note was first printed in *The Catholic Columbian* (Columbus, O.), of July 30, 1920:

### THE CATHOLIC DAUGHTERS OF LOUIS McLANE

In the year 1811, James Peale, the famous American painter, placed on enduring canvas the "Rencontre Between Colonel Allen McLane and Two British Horsemen." Colonel McLane (1746-1829) was a valiant patriot of the Revolutionary era who took an active part in many of its principal battles. In personal combat with three British dragoons near Frankford, Penna., he killed one, wounded another, and compelled the third to flee. Two of Col. McLane's granddaughters, Juliette and Mary, have peculiar interest for us, for the reason that both of them became Catholics. Juliette McLane Garesché and Mary McLane Hobbins (let their names be held in reverent affection) were the daughters of Louis McLane (1786-1857) and Catherine Mary Milligan. Their father, whose handsome features adorn our old Treasury Notes, was successfully member of Congress, United States Senator twice Minister to England, on the last occasioin of which he had as his Secretary of Legation no less a personage than Washington. Irving; Secretary of the U. S. Treasury, 1831-1833; Secretary of State, 1833-34, and president of the Baltimore & Ohio Railroad. They were the sisters of Robert M. McLane (1815-1898), member of Congress, envoy to Japan, China, Korea, etc., Minister to Mexico, Governor of Maryland and Unitetd States Minister to France; of Rebecca, wife of Philip Hamilton, son of the great Alexander Hamilton; and of Lydia, wife of General Joseph E. Johnston, the noted commander of Confederate forces during the Civil War.

Juliette McLane was born at Wilmington, Delaware, in 1826, and died at St. Michael, La., in 1885. The prospect of marriage with a Catholic gentleman of St. Louis, Mr. Bauduy P. Garesché, brought her into intimate relations with her future sisters-in-law, who endeavored to enlighten her concerning the saving truths of the Catholic religion. Finding that she was unable 'to reply to their criticisms of Protestantism, Miss McLane procured books and began a long and systematic study of the controversy between Protestantism and Catholicity. The result was that she lost faith in her own creed and absented herself from the services of her denomination. Her parents, noting her change of views, suggested to their parish clergyman that he do something to bring her to a knowledge of the "error of her ways." To this end he one Sunday preached a virulently anti-Catholic sermon. To show her disapproval, Miss McLane arose right in the middle of the sermon and walked out of the church. Her family spent the following winter in New York City, where Juliette followed with closest attention and profit to herself the eloquent sermons then being preached in the Cathedral by Archbishop Hughes. Her doubts now having been entirely set at rest, she was, with the reluctant consent of her parents. received into the Church by the Archbishop in the following spring. Her father was shortly afterward appointed United States Minister to England, and while resident in London. Miss McLane came to know and to reverence the Religious of the Sacred Heart. Her marriage to Mr. Garesché occurred on September 25, 1849, after which she left Baltimore, to which city her family had returned, to live in St. Louis. Two of her daughters—Lily and Catherine—having become Religious of the Sacred Heart, and Mrs. Garesché now being a widow and her other two children in the bosom of God, she entered the Convent of the Sacred Heart at Grand Coteau, La., on May 5, 1876, pronounced her vows in St. Louis in 1878, and made her solemn profession at the Mother House of her Order in Paris in 1881. After having served God faithfully in this country and New Zealand, Madame Garesché closed her eyes on the world at St. Michael, La., in 1885.

Madame Garesché's sister, Mary, married Dr. Joseph Hobbins (1816-1894), founder of the Medical Department of the University of Wisconsin, and eminent as a horticulturist, to whose efforts Madison, Wisconsin, owes the possession of so many fine trees. Dr. Hobbins was a native of England and became a Catholic through the influence of his future wife. Indeed from the day she was received into the Church Mary McLane Hobbins was ever a most zealous apostle of Jesus Christ, and to her edifying life and example many owed their grace of conversion. She often recounted her recollections of the great men and women she met in her father's house in London, including Tom Moore, and of having as a child sat entranced on the lap of Washington Irving as he spun his fascinating stories of the Alhambra and Sleepy Hollow. Mrs. Hobbins died at Madison, Wis., in 1897.

The above note supplements excellently those given on the Garesché family by Joseph Willcox in elucidation of the *Extracts from the Diary of Rev. Patrick Kenny,* published by him in the Records of the American Catholic Historical Society (Vol. IX, No. 3, pp. 338 and foll.).

From the *Registre des Mariages* of the parish of St. Landry of
Opelousas, La., was culled the following entry:

> 1812. September 16.
>     CHARTRAN, Louis, a native of St. Louis, of the Illinois, legitimate
> son of . . . (*paper water-worn*) . . . Chartran and Marie
> Gerardin, was united in matrimony to Zoe Courtableau, daughter
> of James Courtableau and . . . widow of Mr. Luke Collins.
>                        Michael Bernard BARRIÈRE, Rector.

We are in receipt of *The Catholic Citizen's* Golden Jubilee Souvenir. This is, in size, a tiny booklet, but its few pages, as a short inscription on an historic landmark, brim over with the nervous energy
which has inspired the valiant Catholic editors from the now long-
distant day when the *Star of Bethlehem* arose over the green waters of
the Bay of Milwaukee (October 1, 1869), and the *Catholic Vindicator*
came forth, armed cap and pie, from the Rectory of Rev. John Casey, at
Monroe, Wis. (November 3), 1870). Fifty years is a long span of life
for any newspaper; and for a militant Catholic organ to attain this ma-
ture age is in itself evidence of a powerful vital principle animating the
whole being. Humphrey J. Desmond has been, for well-nigh thirty
years, *The Catholic Citizen's* life-principle. To the able, valiant and
staunchly Catholic Editor and to the newspaper to which he has consecrated the best of his life, we offer our sincere congratulations and our
earnest wishes.

Perhaps of all the charitable organizations of to-day none is so
well known and so widespread as that of the St. Vincent de Paul Society. Founded upon prinicples of charity laid down by the illustrious
Saint whose name it bears, as a kind messenger, it has brought and is
still bringing help and succor to the needy of every color and creed
throughout the world. Far back in the sixteenth century there was born
in Pouy, Gascony, France, Vincent de Paul, whose charity and love of
the poor has confounded the world. Led on by a true love of God,
which is best evinced in the love of neighbor, he devoted his best endeavors to the service of the needy and the afflicted. Calling about him
bands of noble men and women, he formed them into conference and
through them collected and distributetd the necessaries of life to the
starving thousands of Paris and its surrounding regions. It is his spirit
and principles that have guided the Catholic charities since his time.
It was not, however, until May, 1833, that the organization that bears
the name of St. Vincent de Paul was founded and elevated to its present
high standard and efficiency. Frederick Ozanam, a brilliant young law-
yer and author in Paris gathered about him seven of his youthful companions and formulated plans for the organization of a society whose
object should be to administer to the wants of the poor and thereby
answer the taunts of an irreligious world which was proclaiming the
death of the Christian spirit of charity. The rules then formulated
upon the principles of St. Vincent are those by which our conferences

are governed to-day. The society quickly gained in membership; new conferences were erected, so that to-day it can claim over two hundred thousand members, and there is no country on the globe whose poor do not feel its kind and benevolent influence.

Just twelve years after the inauguration of this noble work, Dr. Timothy Papin, returning from his studies in Paris, enthused by the achievements of the society in France and aided by Mr. Bryan Mullanphy, called together the prominent Catholic laymen of St. Louis, and in the same room in which the present Conference of the Old Cathedral meets, was organized the first Conference of the St. Vincent de Paul Society in America, Thursday evening, November 20, 1845. In the minutes of this meeting, still extant, we read that Bryan Mullanphy presided; an election of officers took place. Dr. M. L. Linton was elected president; Bryan Mullanphy, first vice-president; Dennis Galvin, second vice-president; James Maguire Jr., secretary, and Patrick Ryder, treasurer. Glancing over the roster of members we find there many names pominent in the history of our city.

---

Missouri, though a *de facto* State since 1820, was admitted as such into the Union in 1821 by the proclamation of President Monroe. Admission into the Union was the necessary seal set upon the people's action by the national authorities. In 1820 Missouri had elected, as Walter B. Stevens remarks, "State officers who entered upon their duties. It had a Legislature which passed statutes. It chose, in due form, senators and representatives in Congress. It created a code which was interpreted by a Supreme Court. Congress, however, delayed the final recognition while statesmen wrangled over the technicalities of a compromise on the slavery question." The coming year, 1921, is, therefore, the Centennial year of our Statehood. A great civic celebration is contemplated to mark the auspicious event. The Church, that has proved itself the greatest civilizing influence in the State during its long and varied course will, no doubt, have a leading part in the proposed festivities.

---

The following account of the finding of the petrified body of a priest on the banks of the Arkansas River cannot claim any degree of historical certitude, as neither the correspondent's name, nor the precise locality of the incident are given; yet as a possible clue to further investigations it may prove of interest and value. We copy from the *Sunday Visitor*:

#### PETRIFIED BODY OF MISSIONARY

Acorrespondent of an Eastern paper gives this account of the finding of the petrified body of a Catholic Missionary on the bank of the Arkansas (in 1890):

"The laborers on a farm near this place exhumed yesterday the petrified body of a man clothed in the habit of a Roman Catholic priest. The dress and shoes and hose had also become stone, and the figure might have passed for the cunning handiwork of some great master of sculpture. The two hands were clasped about an ivory crucifix, which hung from a rosary suspended about the neck, while the head of an arrow still protruding from the breast told the story of how the worthy Father met his death; and the fact, so plain to be seen. that the body was hastily buried without coffin, and the grave, unmarked by the smallest token, showed that he and his brethren, or some faithful friend, were fleeing from the Indians when he was killed. The petrified body was removed to the church, where it is now visited by crowds, and when it will shortly be given burial in consecrated ground: The face is that of a young man of refined and intellectual features, and the hands and feet are of elegant proportions. Those who profess to know declare that his shoes are of a fashion worn in the latter part of the seventeenth century."

Now the fact of the finding and its circumstances being admitted for argument's sake, further enquiry would undoubtedly lead to the *Poste of Arkansas,* the earliest settlement of whites within the territory of Arkansas, situated at the confluence of the Arkansas and Mississippi Rivers. There was a Jesuit Mission established here among the Quapaw Indians on July 7, 1727, by Father Poisson, though the beginnings of the Arkansas Mission date back as far as November 26, 1689, when Tonty gave to Father Dablon, the Superior of the Canada Missions, a strip of land on Arkansas River, a little east of his fort, about eight acres, for a chapel and mission house. The Mission was to begin in November, 1690 (Cf. SHEA, *Catholic Missions,* p. 439).

---

The Librarians of the *Catholic Historical Society of St. Louis* are happy to report the following additions to the Library of the Society, and to express their thanks to the generous donors:

Gilbert Garraghan, S.J., Catholic Beginnings of Kansas City, Missouri. An Historical Sketch. Loyola University Press, Chicago, Ill. 1920. Donated by the Author.

Hepner, Adolf, America's Aid to Germany in 1870-71. St. Louis, Mo., 1905. Gift of Rev. F. G. Holweck.

Wm. Cullen Bryant and Sydney Howard Gay, A Popular History of the United States. Four Volumes. New York, Chas. Scribner's Sons, 1878.

John R. Spears and A. H. Clark, A History of the Mississippi Valley, from Its Discovery to the End of Foreign Dominion. New York, A. S. Clark, 1903.

The Future of Foreign-Born Catholics. St. Louis, Mo. B. Herder, 1884.

P. Oswald Moosmueller, O.S.B. Bonifaz Wimmer, Erzabt von St. Vinzenz in Pennsylvania. New York, Benziger Brothers, 1891. Donated by Rev. J. Waeltermann.

Pastoral Instruction of the Bishop of Alton. Issued April 12th, 1875. Alton, Ill., 1875. Donated by Rev. P. Kaenders, Venice, Ill.

Pastoral Instruction of the Bishop of Alton. Issued February, the 23d, 1880. Alton, Ill., 1880. Donated by Rev. P. Kaenders.

SS. Patriarchae Benedicti Familiae Confoederatae. Romae, Typis Vaticanis, 1905. Gift of Conception Abbey, Mo.

Annuario Pontificio. Roma, Tipografia Poliglotta Vaticana. Seven Volumes, 1913-1919. Donated by Rev. F. G. Holweck.

Progress of the Catholic Church in America and the Great Columbian Catholic Congress of 1913. Fourth Edition. Chicago. J. S. Hyland & Company. 1893.

The United States. A Catalogue of Books relating to the History of its various States, Counties and Cities. Cleveland, O. The Arthur H. Clark Company, 1920.

The Catholic Advance. Christmas, 1919. Commemorating the Golden Jubilee of the Rt. Rev. John J. Hennessy, D.D., Bishop of Wichita.

Canon Glancey. Orbis Catholicus, A Year Book of the Catholic World. First Year of issue, 1916. London, the Courier Press.

J. B. Mueller, Schematismus der deutschen und deutsch-sprechenden Priester in den Ver. Staaten Nord-Amerika's. St. Louis, B. Herder, 1882. Donated by Rev. Dr. J. Molitor, Columbus, O.

Geo. F. Houck, The Church in Northern Ohio and in the diocese of Cleveland. Cleveland, Short and Forman. 1888. Donated by Dr. Jos. Molitor, Columbus, O.

Anuario Ecclesiastico, 1917. Año III. E. Subirana, Barcelona. Gift of Rev. F. G. Holweck.

Deed of Transfer of some property at Gravois (Kirkwood), St. Louis Co., from the United States to Rev. Peter R. Donnelly. St. Louis, Mo. Gift of Rt. Rev. Msgr. Tannrath.

Souvenir Book, Jasper, Indiana. 1916. Donated by Rev. Basil Heusler, O.S.B.

St. Michael's Church, Brookville, In. Official Year Book, 1920.

Louis De Cailly. Memoirs of Bishop Loras, First Bishop of Dubuque, Iowa. New York, 1897. Donated by Rev. F. A. Marks, Collinsville, Ill.

# DOCUMENTS FROM OUR ARCHIVES

## Correspondence of Bishop Du Bourg with Propaganda

### XXVIII.
### CARDINAL CONSALVI TO BISHOP DU BOURG.[1]

No. 28.

Illme ac Rme Domine

Quae nobis A. T. de florente statu, in quo res Catholica Loysia-nae[2] superioris versatur, ac non exiguis tam infidelium, quam hetero-doxorum conversionibus novissime significavit, ea Emos Patres lae-titia, ac solatio maximo affecerunt. Quare dum Deo Patri miseri-cordiarum debitas pro tanto beneficio gratias ago, tuam etiam sol-licitudinem, ac sedulitatem plurimum in Domino commendo; ac licet Ampdo Tua stimulis non egeat, eam tamen etiam atque etiam ex-citare non desum, ut quod tanta laude coepisti, id pari semper alacri-tate, ac studio perficere velis, diligenter curans, ut et sylvicolae, apud quos Missionem instituisti, in sinum S. Matris Ecclesiae, opitulante Domino, perducantur, et incolae Novae Aureliae, ubi intemperantia, et multa vitiorum seges invaluit, ad rectam semitam revocentur. Quod S. Sedes peragere potuit in auxilium indigae istius Dioecesis, id quidem praestare non defuit munifica quatuor millium scutatorum Romanorum largitione, quorum mille jam accepisse te arbitror per Rmum D. Guillelmum Poynter Vicarium Aplicum Londinensem, cui tutius visum est hanc pecuniae summam mittere; reliqua vero su-binde per camdem viam ad te perferri curabo. Accepi autem epis-tolae exemplum, quae scripta fertur a muliere Perret Dno Inglesi: sed quamvis etiam ipse justificari vellet a crimine, quod illi (nescio an vere, vel perperam) imputatum est, alia tamen is praebuit levita-tis, ac paucae modestiae specimina tum in choreis agendis, tum usu vestium, quae Ecclesiastico viro minime congruunt. Quamobrem licet ipse dexteritate, ac rebus agendis magnopere praestet, non eum tamen tanti facias velim, ut vigilare non debeas, ejusque spiritum

---

[1] Original in the Archives of the St. Louis Archdioc. Chancery.

[2] The uncommon spelling Loysiana, as well as the handwriting of this docu-ment stamp it as the work of a new *minutante*.

diligenter probare. Quod autem attinet ad amplissimae istius Dioecesis divisionem, ea, quae proposita sunt, non satis adhuc matura
videntur. Unum est, cui sine mora prospiciatur oportet, nempe neg-
lecta Floridarum cura, quam Ampdo Tua, ut declaravit, ob magnam
illius Provinciae distantiam gerere nullo modo potest. Quid autem
consilii circa Floridas S. Cong. susceperit, de hoc quamprimum te
faciam certiorem. Interim Deum precor ut Ampdm Tuam diutissime servet, ac sospitet.

Ampdnis Tuae

Romae ex Ædibus S. Congnis de Propda Fide Die 11. Januarii,
1822.

Uti Frater studiosissimus,
H. Card. CONSALVI, Pro-Prf.

R. P. D. Ludovico Guillelmo
Du Bourg Epo Novae Aureliae
in Loysiana / S. Ludovicum in Statu Missouri /
C. M. Pedicini Secrius.

## TRANSLATION.

Right Reverend Dear Sir:—

Your Lordship's latest report[3] of the flourishing condition of
Catholicity in Upper Louisiana ,and of the numerous conversions
of both infidels and heretics, has greatly rejoiced and consoled Their
Eminences. Wherefore to God, the Father of mercies, I return due
thanks for these benefits, whilst your solicitude and activity I most
highly commend in the Lord; and although Your Lordship stands
in no need of the spur, yet again and again I must urge that what
you have so laudably begun, you should determine to achieve with
the same eagerness and zeal, working diligently in order to bring,
with the help of God, the savages among whom you have established missions[4] into the bosom of Holy Mother Church; and also
in order that the people of New Orleans, among whom intemperance
and a plentiful crop of vices are prevalent, may be turned back to
the right path.

What the Holy See found itself able to do in order to help that
destitute Diocese, it has not failed to accomplish by a magnificent
donation of four thousand Roman *scudi;* I reckon you have received
already one thousand through the Right Rev. William Poynter, Vicar
Apostolic of London, through whom it seemed a surer way to send this
money; I will attend shortly to the forwarding of the balance through
the same channel.

---

[3] We are not in possession of this report.

[4] Clearly an allusion to the mission of Father De la Croix among the Osage
Indians. See J. ROTHENSTEINER, *Early Missionary Efforts among the Indians in
the Diocese of St. Louis,* St. Louis Catholic Hist. Review, 1920, p. 66 foll.

I have received copy of a letter supposed to be written by the
Perret woman to Father Inglesi[5]; but even if the latter would try to

---

[5] This is undoubtedly the letter of which Bishop Du Bourg gave the gist to
Father Martial: "You will be glad to learn that these infamous machinations are
the result of the most abominable intrigue; but God has permitted that the
woman who played therein the leading role entered into herself, and made in
writing to Father Inglesi, after the latter's departure from Rome, full confession
of the whole matter. I have that letter in my possession. The main point of the
intrigue is as follows: Father Inglesi had received $10,000 from the Torlonia
Bank in settlement of some family business, which sum of money was destined
for the payment for his brother's inheritance. One of the clerks of the bank
concocted a plan on the basis of this. He insinuated himself into the familiarity
of Inglesi, showed him many courtesies and repeatedly offered his services; and
as Fr. Inglesi expressed to him his desire of finding lodgings in a healthy and
quiet part of the city, the fellow offered him board and lodging in his own home.
Fr. Inglesi accepted, and had his belongings and his money carried there. A few
days later the clerk in question absentetd himself on purpose one evening, after
arranging with his wife that the latter was to go about 9 p. m. to Fr. Inglesi's
apartment, do what she could to seduce him, and manage some way or other to
remain with him until about 11 o'clock, when he himself would come as to catch
them by surprise, and would frighten Inglesi into buying him off with all the
money he had. Divine Providence permitted that, on that very evening Fr. Inglesi
returned from town only a short while before 11. At once the woman went to his
quarters, and whether on purpose or because she was horror-struck by her crime
she fell upon a trunk, saying she was fainting. Just as Fr. Inglesi was rushing to
his wardrobe for a bottle of cologne water, her husband came in in a great fury.
However, he was somewhat disconcerted by what he saw, and hence manifested
some embarrassment. Fr. Inglesi profited by this hesitation to skip out of the
room and leave the house. Early in the morning he sent for his trunk, which
the clerk refused to give; then, without delay, he (Inglesi), went to Card. Consalvi, who ordered the trunk to be given back to its owner. The scoundrel, whose
plan was foiled, lost no time in spreading the slander, which was eagerly taken up,
aand received admittance even with many good people—for good people are often
as credulous as others in regard to such stories. Such are the details confessed
by that woman, whom remorse has prompted to trust in the generosity of Father
Inglesi to give, if he wishes, publicity to tthis letter." (Archives of Propaganda.
*Scritture refenite nei Congressi.* Codice 7. In letter of Martial to Billard, October 20, 1822). It should be noted that, whilst the Cardinal's judgment remained
in suspense in regard to the truth or untruth of this affair, Bishop Du Bourg had
no such hesitation: "I am confident," he wrote to Father Martial, "that he
(Inglesi) is fully justified."

Bishop Du Bourg, by the time he received this letter (probably some time
in April, 1822) was long since acquainted with the misdemeanor of Fr. Inglesi in
Rome, for Propaganda has reported it to him in a letter in date of September 22,
1821 (see next letter, XXIX). He evidently disbelieved entirely the report. At
any rate, writing to Father Rosati on Easter Sunday (April 7), 1822, he spoke
of Inglesi in the following terms: "Father Inglesi will bring us recruits. He is
not a Bishop, neither does he wish to hear of it. He was sorry to have written to
me a certain letter which I communicated to you. He announces he will be here
about the beginning of the year (1823). I cannot tire of admiring his devotedness
and zeal. But as you may imagine, this disappointment (clearly that Inglesi was
not made a Bishop) causes me some uneasiness. But it matters not! God
knows what is best. We ought not to lose courage." Four months later, and
certainly after he had received this letter, speaking of the unecclesiastical behavior
of Inglesi ,and recommending watchfulness, his enthusiasm had not yet abated.
On August 7 he wrote to Father Rosati: "Good news! Five or six subjects have
just arrived from France for the Seminary. One of them is Subdeacon; the
others have Minor Orders. There is, moreover, a Deacon, who, I believe, is ready

justify himself of the grave misdemeanor which is imputed to him (right or wrong, I know not), still, he exhibited other signs of levity and impropriety, both by taking part in dances and by a mode of dress in no way befitting an Ecclesiastic. For this cause, clever and most skillful in business though he be, yet I do not wish that your high estimate of him should dispense you from watching and from carefully investigating his character.

In regard to the division of your vast Diocese, the proposals made do not appear to have as yet attained maturity. One thing, however, should be attended to without delay, namely the fact that the Floridas are not taken care of, as Your Lordship has declared that, owing to the great distance of that territory, you are totally unable to look after it. Whatever course of action the S. Congr. resolves to take about the Floridas, I shall let you know at the first opportunity. Meanwhile I pray to God to keep Your Lordship yet many years, and in good health.

Your Lordship's Most Devoted Brother,

H. Card. CONSALVI, Pro Prefect.

Rome, Palace of the S. Congr. of Propaganda, January 11, 1822 To the Right Rev. William Du Bourg, Bishop of New Orleans, Louisiana.

St. Louis, Missouri. C. M. Pedicini, Secretary.

## XXIX.

## CARDINAL CONSALVI TO BISHOP DU BOURG.[1]

No. 21.

Ill.me, ac R.me D. ne.

Jamdudum est, ex quo proposita fuit Amplit.i Tuae vastissimae istius Dioecesis divisio; non enim in tanta dissitarum regionum amplitudine unus tantum Episcopus adauctorum Fidelium curam exercere facile potest; ideoque maxime profuturum visum est, si Dioecesis ista in tres saltem Ecclesias divideretur, quarum una inferiorem Luisianam, altera superiorem, tertia Floridas complecti posset. Cum vero nullum adhuc habitum fuerit abs te responsum, vereor, ne Sac.ae Cong.nis Litterae ad te pervenerint. Quare Ampl.m Tuam rogo, ut quid de hujusmodi divisione sentias, mihi quantocius indicare velis; et quoties in ea, ut spero, convenias, mens esset Sacrae Cong.nis, ut, una ex iis a te

---

for Ordination. . . . This reinforcement which has just come to us from Europe is but the forerunner of another including four or five, perhaps even ten, priests. You understand that it is the indefatigable Father Inglesi who is sending them to me. I expect him towards the end of this year." The following month (September 6), very much the same note is sounded. "I am in a quandary in regard to St. Genevieve" (it was only a few days after the death of Father Pratte). "The thought came to my mind to keep that place for Father Inglesi. I have strong reasons for so doing."

[1] Original in Archives of St. Louis Archdioc. Chancery.

retenta, duabus aliis praeficeretur vel D. Ludovicus Sibourd Vicarius tuus Gn.lis, cujus merita tantopere extulisti, et quem primo in tuum Coadjutorem postulasti, vel etiam D.nus Rosati, aut Dnus Rossetti, qui ita probati sunt, ut nulla in eos cadere videatur exceptio. Quoad D. Angelum Inglesi, accepisse te arbitror Sacrae Congnis litteras datas die 22. 7mbris elapsi anni, quibus certiorem te fecimus, quanto dedecore idem Romae se gesserit, ideoque non est, cur de illo promovendo jam cogites. Quod vero valde me angit, illud est, quod nobis ex Nova Aurelia nunciatum est, nimirum diffusa ibi voce, quod Amplitudo Tua illum sibi Coadjutorem adscire vellet, magnam in tota Luisiana perturbationem obortam, omnesque operarios ita animo cecidisse, ut aliqui ex ista provincia migraverint, alii vero, pristino posthabito studio, ac sollicitudine, remisse atque incurie se gerant. Quamobrem Ampl.m Tuam hortor in Dno, ut perniciosam hanc vocem dissipare cures, clerumque ad officium revocare, ne quod tanto labore, et cura aedificasti hac de causa ruat. Quod dum sedulo te praestiturum esse confido, Deum O. M. precor, ut Ampl.m Tuam diutissime servet, ac sospitet.

Amplitudinis Tuae.

Romae ex aedibus Sacrae Congnis de Propaganda Fide die 27. Aprilis 1822.

Uti Frater studiosissimus,

H. Card. Consalvi Pro Praef.

R. P. D. Ludovico Guillelmo Dubourg
Neo-Aurelianensi Episcopo in
America Septli.

S. Ludovicum in Territorio, Illinensi

C. M. Pedicini, Secrius.

## TRANSLATION

Right Reverend Dear Sir :—

Some time ago was proposed to Your Lordship the division of your most extensive Diocese,[2] for the reason that in such a large territory with places far apart it is difficult for one Bishop to take care of the increasing number of the faithful; wherefore it was deemed that it would be for the interest of that Diocese if it were divided into at least three Churches, the one including Lower Louisiana, the second Upper Louisiana, and the third the two Floridas. As, however, no answer of yours has been as yet received, I am afraid that the letter of the Sacred Congregation failed to reach you. For this reason I beg Your Lordship to let me know as soon as possible your opinion about this division; and in case it is agreeable to you, as I hope, it is the intention of the S. Congregation that, while you shall keep one of these Churches, to the other two should be appointed either Fr. Louis Sibourd, your Vicar General, whose merit you have so much commended and whom you first asked

---

[2] Reference is here made obviously to Letter No. 15 of Propaganda in date of June 2, 1821 (St. Louis Catholic Historical Review, Vol. II, Nos. 2-3, pp. 141, foll.).

for your Coadjutor, or even Father Rosati, or Father Rossetti,[3] who have given such proofs of their sterling qualities that no objection can be raised against them.  In regard to the Rev. Angelo Inglesi, I reckon you are now in possession of the letter of this S. Congregation in date of September 22 last,[4] in which we informed you of his improper demeanor in Rome; hence you must no longer be thinking of his promotion.  One thing in this connection vexes me very sorely, namely that we heard from New Orleans[5] that, as the rumor was spread there that Your Lordship wanted him as Coadjutor, a great deal of trouble arose throughout Louisiana, and all the missionaries were so downhearted that some left the Diocese, while others, forgetful of their former zeal and solicitude, became slack and careless in the discharge of their duties. Wherefore I earnestly beg you in the Lord to do everything in your power to suppress that evil rumor, and to recall the clergy to their duty, in order that what you have built up with so much pain and care may not, on this account, fall in ruins.  Trusting that you will spare no efforts to this end, I pray Almighty God to keep Your Lordship yet many years, and in good health.

Your Lordship's Most Devoted Brother,

H. Card. CONSALVI, Pro-Prefect.

Rome, Palace of the S. Congr. of Propaganda, April 27, 1822.
To the Right Rev. Louis William Du Bourg, Bishop of New Orleans, North America.  St. Louis of the Illinois.

C. M. Pedicini, Secretary.

---

[3] On Father John Mary Rossetti, see above, Vol. II, No. 1, p. 50, note 4; also below, the end of Letter XXXI.

[4] This letter is not extant.  It must have been the Propaganda Letter No. 18 or 19, which, as was noticed above (p. 147), are missing from the collection.  The fact is that none of the documents dealing *ex professo* with the Inglesi affair have been preserved.  Bishop Du Bourg either destroyed them, or else kept them in a secret place with other personal papers.  Why he should have done so is easy enough to understand.

[5] There can scarcely be any doubt that the information referred to here was furnished by Father Martial, who was in correspondence with one Billard, a friend of his at the French Embassy.  Several letters of Martial to Billard, written with ultimate purpose that their contents should be made known to the ecclesiastical authorities, are preserved in the Archives of Propaganda.  In one of them, dated July 13, 1822, Martial alludes to a former letter written some months before to Billard "for himself alone," for, as he adds: "I did not think you cared to communicate it, lest the friendship between Bishop Du Bourg and myself should be altered."  This letter apparently had nevertheless been handed to Propaganda.  At any rate, Martial adds: "The opposition which manifested itself at the time when it became known he (Bishop Du Bourg) wished to have Father Inglesi for coadjutor rent his soul asunder to such an extent that he fulminated a Circular Letter to frighten the priests; but he was very sorry for it when he saw the effect it had produced; clever men may sometimes make great mistakes.  There remains in the heart of some missionaries a wound which will be hard to heal.  I tried, but in vain, to stotp some from going away; they replied to me: 'One's first duty is to save one's self.  Assure us that in exercising the ministry as we do here, we can save ourselves. . . .'".  There can be no doubt that the infatuation of the Bishop for the clever young priest, and his well-known desires in regard to his promotion caused a great deal of dissatisfaction among the clergy of Lower Louisiana.

## XXX.
## CARDINAL CONSALVI TO BISHOP DU BOURG.[1]
No. 24.[2]

Illme ac Rme Domine.

Perjucundae mihi fuerunt Litterae Tuae, ex quibus intellexi Ampdm Tuam ultro assentiri, ut tam Floridarum provinciae, quam Louisiana superior a Neo-Aurelianensi Dioecesi distractae, in novas erigantur Ecclesias. Tua enim accepi consilia, nimirum ut nova pariter Episcopalis Ecclesia instituatur in Oppido Sanclarensi, vulgo Detroit in Agro Michigan; et altera etiam in media Louisiana, quae Missisipi statum complectitur, et Arcansas, postquam A. T. ea omnia paraverit, quae ad constituendum ibi antistitem necessaria sunt; demum ut Nova Aurelia in Metropolim erigatur. Haec omnia Emorum PP. judicio quamprimum subjicienda curabo, et inde Ampdm Tuam de illorum sententia certiorem facere non praetermittam. Petitam interim tibi adjungo renovationem facultatis, dispensandi scilicet in secundo cognationis gradu ad sexaginta casus extensam, nec non dispensationem in primo affinitatis gradu, quae ex Summi Pontificis indulgentia benigne concessa est pro Laurentio Millaudon et Maria Francisca Stella, ac te monens, ut conditionibus, quae in utroque documento appositae sunt, te accurate conformes, D. O. M. precor ut Ampdm T. diutissime servet, ac sospitet.

Ampdnis Tuae

Romae ex Aedibus S. Congnis de Prpa Fide Die 28. Septembris, 1822.

Uti Frater studiosissimus

H. Card. Consalvi, Pro-Prf.

R. P. D. Guillelmo Du Bourg,
Epo Neo-Aurelianensi in
Louisiana. | Novam Aureliam |

C. M. Pedicini, Secrius.

## TRANSLATION

Right Reverend Dear Sir:—

The greatest pleasure was afforded me by your letter[3] from which I understand it to tbe perfectly agreeable to your Lordship that the State of Florida and Upper Louisiana[4] be dismembered from the Diocese of

---

[1] Original in Archives of St. Louis Archdioc. Chancery.

[2] Again two letters from Propaganda are missing. It may well be that one at least contained no more than the renewal of certain Episcopal faculties.

[3] Card. Consalvi has unquestionably in view Du Bourg's letter dated February 8 of that same year, 1822, given in our last issue, pp. 148 foll.

[4] With regard to the erection of a new Episcopal See in Upper Louisiana Bishop Du Bourg had, however, requested a delay—one year at the outside. The next letter informs us that shortly after advising Propaganda on February 8, of his consent to the dismemberment, he had retracted it. Evidently this subsequent communication had not yet reached Rome. Another was sent from St. Louis during the first days of September. Of this new letter the Bishop wrote to Rosati, on September 12: "I have written again to forestall the division of the

New Orleans and erected into new churches. I have taken good note of your recommendations, to wit: that a new Episcopal See should be likewise instituted in the town of St. Clair (Detroit) in the Territory of Michigan; and another in Central Louisiana, comprising the State of Mississippi and that of Arkansas, when Your Lordship has prepared in that district everything required for the establishment of a Bishop; also, that New Orleans be erected into an Archbishopric. I shall see to it that all these recommendations are submitted at the first opportunity to the judgment of Their Eminences, of whose opinion I will not fail to advise Your Lordship. Meanwhile I herewith enclose the renewal you asked of your faculty to grant dispensation of the second degree of relationship—this faculty extends to sixty cases—; I add also the dispensation of the first degree of affinity, kindly granted by the Sovereign Pontiff in favor of Lawrence Millaudon and Mary Frances Stella; and enjoining you to conform most exactly with the conditions marked in these two documents, I pray Almighty God to keep Your Lordship yet many years, and in good health.

Your Lordship's Most Devoted Brother,

H. Card. Coñsalvi, Pro-Prefect.

Rome, Palace of the S. Congr. of Propaganda, September 28, 1822.
To the Right Rev. William Du Bourg, Bishop of New Orleans, Louisiana. New Orleans.

C. M. Pedicini, Secretary.

XXXI.

## BISHOP DU BOURG TO THE CARDINAL PREFECT OF PROPAGANDA.[1]

Eminentissime Cardinalis:

Baltimorum urgentissimis meae Dioeceseos negotiis vocatus, ab Arch. nuper reduce, summo cordis dolore, audivi Rev.um Rosati ad administrationem Statuum Alabamae et Mississippi, cum titulo Episcopali a Sac. Cong. nominatum. Longius ab eo distans, nescio quae fuerit mentis ejus conditio, cum ad eum hujusmodi nuntius pervenerit; sed probe novi quis futurus sit hujus acceptationis effectus. Ruet in tota Louisiana Missionis Cong. quae jam ejus cura multum florescere coeperat, et cui nullus alius praeter eum adhuc praeesse potest. Ruet seminarium clericorum, unica spes immensae illius regionis; ad illam ruinam perculti undequaque dispergentur Sacerdotes et alumni, quos ego tot sumptibus comparavi. Quod ad me spectat, videns conatus meos frustratos, sin dolore conficiar, certe desperatione tabescam. Oh!

---

Diocese, as premature. My letter is very strong. It is the fruit of the most serious reflections; and my soul is much quieter since I wrote it. A Coadjutor is all that we will need for a long time. Fortunately, even in case the division should already be made, I am sure that Fr. B. (who is this Fr. B.?) would not accept the appointment."

[1] Copy by Bishop Du Bourg's own hand (sent to Rosati in a letter to the same), in Archives of St. Louis Archdioc. Chancery.

Eminentiss. Patres! quid fecistis? Quis vobis suasit hujus modi consilium, ut a pauperrimo Episc.o adimeretis ultimam et unicam suae spei
anchoram? Episcopatum una hac lege susceperam, quod mihi Congregationis Miss. Sacerdotes in auxilium darentur. Duos solum qui eam
in Dioecesi mea efformari possent accepi DD. de Andreis et Rosati.
Unus morte ablatus est, et nunc alterum a me surripitis, postquam ego
immensos labores et sumptus maximos in ipsorum Societatis fundationem absumpsi. Una die pereunt sudores et conatus septem annorum.
Jam satis est; si ad effectum perducatur illa nominatio, nihil mihi amplius sperandum, nihil ultra moliendum. Sedens sedebo, lugens ruinam
aedificii quod jam, Deo juvante, tanto labore meo assurgere coeperat.
Sed quidni potius sperarem humillimis meis supplicationibus profusisque lacrimis movendas esse Eminentias Vestras? Certe cum agebatur
Romae de subtrahendo a R.mo Ep.o Bardensi ipsius unico et praecipuo
coadjutore Rev.o D.o David, quem ad Sedem Philadelphiensem promovere volebant, venerandi Praesulis exauditae sunt querelae. Mutata
est mens Sac. Cong. et quem ab eo auferre cogitaverant, ipsi in Coadjutorem dederunt. Ita unione duorum illorum virorum in dies floret Bardensis Dioecesis. Eminent.imi Patres, meis precibus similiter annuetis.
Ecce me prostratum habetis pedibus vestris, ejulatus edentem super
contritione filiae populi mei; non surgam donec nominationem illam
retractaveritis. Coadjutorem mihi date eumdem Rev.um Rosati; et
alio, quo placuerit, modo, providete Statibus Mississippi et Alabamae.
Cur destruetur Louisiana ad fovendam alibi Ecclesiam, quae forsan
cum formari coeperit, similiter in foetu praefocabitur?

Sed attendant Eminent.ae Vestrae sequentibus observationibus.

Florida Episcopali Sede procul dubio indiget, sed huic, propter
propinquitatem annecti convenit Statum *Alabamae,* in quo nunc perpauci sunt Catholici, ferme omnes in oppido *Mobiliensi.* In Statu Mississippi, unica est cathol. cong., scilicet in civitate *Natchez,* triginta ad
summum familiis constans, quae cum duorum solummodo dierum spatio
a Nov. Aurelia distet, facillime potest ab Ep.o istius urbis, vel ab ipsius
Vic.o gen. administrari. Praedictis duabus congregationibus, sive in
*Natchez,* sive in *Mobili* jam provideram, optimo in utraque sacerdote
constituto. Quid amplius faciet Administrator Episcopali caractere
insignitus? Sed undenam ipse, non dicam dignitatis subsidium, sed
communem victum comparabit, cum hi duo sacerdotes aegre ab illis
catholicis sustentari possint?

Jam de erigenda Sede Floridiensi mecum pluries egit Sac. Cong.
Huic propositioni non solum annui, sed eam saepius ipse suggesseram,
ut testantur varia scripta mea, quae in scriniis Sac. Cong. forsan asservantur. Non ita pridem mentem meam aperui de variis ad hujus sedis
erectionem postulatis, et sacerdotem ad eam implendam proposui,
nempe R.um Enochum Fenwick Marylandiensem Soc. Jesu, alias Rev.
issimi Arch. D.ni Joan. Carroll Vic. gen., nunc praesidem Collegii Georgiopolitani. His omnibus peractis, putabam finem mox illi negotio datum
iri; sed mihi maximam admirationem fecit quod a Rev.mo Arch.o
Maréchal nunc audio, nempe dubium Romae exortum fuisse utrum
Florida meae an Havanensi Sedi pertineret, cum constet in Bulla erec

tionis *Sedis Neo Aurelian.* (data 27 ap. 1793) eam ipsi, postulante Hisp.ae Rege, *cum expresso Havanensis Episcopi consensu,* annexam fuisse. Equidem post deditam Foederatis Statibus Louisianam, et translatum ab ea Episcopum Hispanum D. de Peñalver, Jussu Regis Hispaniarum, Episcopus Havanensis utpote vicinior, jurisdictionem in Floridas resumpserat, virtute, ut opinor, concordatorum inter illam coronam et Sanctam Sedem, quibus sancitum est ne unquam Episcop.s alienigena in ullam Hispani Dominii partem jus dicere valeat. Sed tandem Floridis Americanae jam Foederationi unitis, renunciavit dictus praesul, et suos ab eis sacerdotes retraxit. Nihil igitur remanet quod vel levissimo dubio locum dare queat, nihil quod erectionem illius Sedit debeat remorari, cum ego, solus earum partium Ordinarius, ipsi toto corde assentiam.

Rebus ita constitutis, supererit peragenda ulterior divisio meae Dioecesis, in duas partes, Inferiorem scilicet et Superiorem Louisianam. Jam, importunitatibus victus, consensum huc dederam, quem paulo post retractavi. In hac ultima mentis dispositione, gravissimis fretus rationibus, persevero, nempe quia nondum consolidatis fundationibus quas in utraque jacere coepi, praematura mihi videtur divisio et Religionis utilitati summe adversa. Haec in posteriori Epistola fusius explicavi, supplicans ut mihi daretur Coadjutor in partem immensi mei laboris. Si his annuat Sac. Cong. spondeo ante quinque annos omnia parata fore ad propositam divisionem, sin minus, certo sciat Sac. Cong. omnia in confusionem casura.

Jam vos pro Coadjutore D. Bruté Sacerdotem S.ti Sulpicii bene·meritissimum postulaveram, verens ne D. Rosati, si ad illud munus eligeretur, a regimine suae Soc. arceretur. Nunc autem quoniam ad episcopatum iste jam nominatus est, peto ut posthabito D.o Bruté Ipse D. Rosati mihi Coadjutor assignetur, et simul Cong. suae praeesse pergat donec alius praesto sit, qui ipsi in hoc officio suffici valeat. Ita facili negotio, omnia conciliabuntur. In Superori Louisiana residens D. Rosati, quae suae Cong. et Seminarii sedes est, illam partem, Episcopali auctoritate, meo nomine administrabit, simulque nascentem Societatem suo sinu fovebit. Ego inferioris Louisianae praecipue curam gerens, simul exiguo gregi Mississipiensi providere pergam; demum Alabamae et Floridarum Catholici proprium Episcopum habebunt.

De D.nis Sibourd et Rossetti quorum mentionem pluries fecit Sac. Congr. unum dicam: prior jam aetate provectus, et viribus fractus, polypio insuper in naribus afflictus, Episcopatus laboribus penitus impar evasit. Posterior nulla neque corporis nec animi dote, huic dignitati unquam aptus fuit. Multo minus ex quo prorsus *amens* factus est, quod duobus retro annis summo omnium nostrum dolore et molestia evenit. Post annum itegrum in illo deplorabili statu transactum, ratione partim recuperata, non Religionis sensu, quem in amentia conspuerat, Mediolanum sua sponte regressus est ubi eum incolumem appulisse precor.

## TRANSLATION

My Lord Cardinal:—

Being now in Baltimore, where I was called by most urgent affairs concerning my Diocese,[2] from the Archbishop just returned from abroad, I have heard, to my heart's most grievous sorrow, that the S. Congregation has appointed the Rev. Rosati to the administratorship, with the title of Bishop, of the State of Alabama and Mississippi.[3] As I am far away from him, I know not what he will think when he receives this news[4]; but I know full well what will surely be the conse-

[2] The object which induced Bishop Du Bourg to undertake this journey is explained by him in a letter to Propaganda March 29, 1823. But before he started even with his friends he was scarcely ever more explicit than he is here as to his purpose. Thus, for instance, writing to Father Bruté from St. Louis on July 6, he said: "We shall have the opportunity to converse *os ad os,* for affairs of the highest importance will oblige me to visit your quarters this coming fall." (Original in *Catholic Archives of America,* Notre Dame, Indiana, Case *Bishops of New Orleans).* In his letters to Rosati we find no allusion to this intended journey; but, no doubt, the subject was discussed during the two visits made by the Bishop to the Barrens during the summer. The trip commenced rather ominously. From Bardstown, where he stopped a few days, Du Bourg wrote to Rosati on October 30: "So far I have had a most unpleasant trip; the roads were in a wretched condition, and the weather was abominable for several days, a circumstance which detained us three days in an inn. But it's an ill wind that blows no one good: this rain gave the Ohio water enough for the steamboats to run. I am sailing tonight for Wheeling, and, barring any mishaps, we expect to be in Baltimore sometime between the 10th and the 15th of November" (Archives of St. Louis Archdioc. Chancery). It was, by the way, during this stay of Bishop Du Bourg in Kentucky that for the first time was broached the subject of bringing to Missouri a colony of Sisters of Loretto. Here is what the Bishop says of this project, which was to come to realization the following year, on his trip back to tSt. Louis: "I noticed the great use which the Bishop (Bishop Flaget) is making of the Sisters, especially those of Father Nerinckx. And the thought came to my mind to ask some of these Sisters for the Barrens. These nuns would be a treasure of edification: they would teach the young girls and, moreover, they would supply the seminary with clothes, and all this practically at no cost, for they also do some farming. I did not wish to do anything without consulting you; if you wish to have them, talk it over with your parishioners, and write to Father Nerincks. A few buildings would have to be put up for them, but I think that the parish would be glad to help you. The matter is worth thinking over.—Another great advantage which would accrue from these holy women is that, as they would multiply, we could find among them some for the domestic department of our colleges. The Bishop has seven of them in his establishment of Bardstown."

[3] The Brief appointing Father Rosati was issued August 13, 1822. It was confided to the care of Archbishop Maréchal, then in Rome, who was to forward it, together with a number of other papers, to the Vicar Apostolic elect. It reached the Barrens on November 20, almost two weeks before Bishop Du Bourg heard of the appointment. Archbishop Maréchal seems to have had a great deal tot do, if not with Rosati's appointment. at least with the creation of the new Vicariate Apostolic (See Manuscript *Life of Rosati,* quoted in *Catholic Historical Review,* Vol. III, No. 1, p. 13).

[4] We know Rosati's feelings from a letter written by him to Father Baccari, V. G. of the C. M. at Rome. the very next day after he received the Brief of his appointment: "Yesterday evening I received your letters sent me through the Archbishop ot Baltimore. The joy and delight first experienced on reading them have given place to the greatest affliction, which assailed me on unfolding a document from the S. Cong. of Propaganda despatched to me through the same channel, notifying me that I have been appointed Bishop *in partibus* and Vicar

quence, if he accepts. It is the downfall, in all Louisiana, of the Congregation of the Mission, which, under his care was beginning to flourish nicely, and at the head of which no one, besides him, can be put for the time being. It is the downfall of our Ecclesiastical Seminary, our only hope for this immense country; and this downfall will bring about the dispersion of excellently trained priests and of the pupils, whom I had secured at so great a price. As to me, seeing my endeavors frustrated, if I do not die of sorrow, I will at least languish in despondency.[5] Oh! Your Eminences! What have you done? Who ever prompted you this advice to take from the poorest of Bishops the last and only anchor of his hope? I had accepted the Episcopate only on the condition that priests of the Congregation of the Mission would be given me to help me. I got only two capable to build up that Congregation in my Diocese, Father De Andreis and Father Rosati. One was taken away by death, and now you are depriving me of the other, when I have consumed immense labors and a great deal of money for the foundation of their Society. In one day are annihilated the fatigues and efforts of seven years. It is all over: if that appointment takes effect, there is nothing more for me to hope, nothing to attempt. Dejected I shall sit, bemoaning the ruin of the edifice which, with the help of God, my labors had begun to erect. But why should I not rather hope that my most humble supplications and my abundant tears shall move Your Eminences? It gives me courage to think that, when there was question in Rome of taking away from the Right Rev. Bishop of Bardstown his only and main co-laborer, Father David, then destined for the See of Philadelphia, the complaints of the venerable Prelate were graciously heard: the S. Congregation changed their minds, and the very man whom they had thought of taking from the Bishop was

---

Apostolic of the Territories of Mississippi and Alabama. That was "truly for me a thunderbolt. I did not hesitate for a moment to resolve to refuse a burden which is beyond my strength in every regard. To this end I warmly recommend myself to you, in order that you may obtain that the Holy Father and His Eminence Card. Consalvi grant me the favor of accepting my refusal." (*Archives of the Procurator General C. M., Rome.* America, p. ii, Monsig. Rosati, pp. 31-32; quoted in *Catholic Historical Review*, Vol. III, No .1, p. 14). The letters sent through Archbishop Maréchal, reached the Barrens before Du Bourg's letter of December 3, which was mailed only after Dec. 6.

5 To Father Rosati Bishop Du Bourg wrote (December 3): "I pray God to direct you in your answer; but in my opinion all is lost in the whole of Louisiana if the thing comes to effect. And, besides the damage caused to Religion, what an injustice to me! and what motive of despondency for all the Bishops! God preserve me from ever believing that this affair may be consummated! Did I believe it I would not go back to my Diocese, but I would go and tender my resignation at the feet of the Pope" (*Archives of St. Louis Archdioc., Chancery*). The thing, in so far as Rosati was concerned, was already settled: On November 26 the Bishop-elect had written to Card. Consalvi: "Knowing my strength, and feeling it to be absolutely unequal to bear the burden of the Episcopate, I cannot persuade myself that it is safe for me to assume it. Therefore, most instantly do I pray and beseech Your Eminence to spare my infirmity and to have somebody else appointetd to the government of the churches of Mississippi and Alabama."

given him as Coadjutor. And thus, thanks to the union of these two men, the Diocese of Bardstown is flourishing more and more. Your Eminences, you shall likewise, I trust, accede to my prayers. Behold me prostrate at your feet, loudly moaning for the destruction of the daughter of my people: I shall not arise until you revoke this appointment. Give me for Coadjutor that same Father Rosati, and provide any other way you wish for the States of Mississippi and Alabama. Why should Louisiana be sacrificed in favor of another Church which shall perhaps, when it begins to take shape, be likewise ruthlessly strangled?

At any rate, may it please Your Eminences to take into consideration the following observations:

Florida, no doubt, needs an Episcopal See; but to that State it will be good to add, because of the nearness, the State of *Alabama*, in which there are now very few Catholics, practically all in the town of *Mobile*. In the State of Mississippi there is only one Catholic Congregation, namely in the city of *Natchez*; it consists of at most thirty families, and as it is only two days from New Orleans, it may be very easily looked after by the Bishop of this place, or by his Vicar General. As a matter of fact, I had provided for the two aforementioned parishes, namely of *Natchez* and of *Mobile*, by establishing in each of them an excellent priest. What more may do an Administrator with Episcopal character? Nay, wherefrom will he get, I shall not say wherewith to uphold his dignity, but simple maintenance, when these two priests can scarcely be supported by those Catholics?[6]

Several times already has the S. Congregation mentioned to me the erection of a See in Florida. This proposal, not only did I consent to, but in fact I had repeatedly suggested myself, as may be seen from various letters of mine possibly preserved in the Archives of the S. Congregation. Not long since I spoke quite plainly concerning several things demanded for the erection of that See, and even proposed a candidate for it, namely the Rev. Enoch Fenwick, S.J., from Maryland, former Vicar General of the Most Rev. Archbishop John Carroll, and now President of the College of Georgetown. After having done all this, I thought that this affair was to be finished shortly; but I am immensely surprised to hear from Archbishop Maréchal that doubts have been raised at Rome as to whether Florida belonged to my Diocese or to that of Havana. It is clear from the Bull of erection of the *See of New Orleans,* in date of April 27, 1793, that Florida was annexed to this See, at the request of the King of Spain, and *with the express consent of the Bishop of Havana.* True, after the sale of Louisiana to the United States, and the transfer from New Orleans of the Spanish Bishop, the Right Rev. De Peñalver, the Bishop of Havana, being the

---

[6] On December 8, writing again to Father Rosati, the Bishop expressed himself somewhat more sharply on the same subject: "Truth to tell, I do not understand anything in the decisions of Propaganda. It seems to them they need only to appoint Bishops and to send them, without inquiring whether there are parishes to receive and support them, and without providing them with any means, even to work. What, pray, would you do as a Bishop in Mississippi and Alabama, and what would become of you there?"

nearest Bishop, resumed, by order of the King of Spain, jurisdiction over Florida, by virtue, I suppose, of the Concordats between the Spanish Crown and the Holy See, whereby it is enactetd that no foreign Bishop can ever have jurisdiction over any part of the Spanish Dominion. But when finally Florida was added to the United States, the Bishop of Havana renounced his jurisdiction over it, and recalled his priests who were there. There remains, therefore, no room for the slightest doubt, no impediment capable of delaying the erection of that See, inasmuch as I, the sole Ordniary of that territory, am giving my hearty consent.

When this is settled, there will remain to effect the further division of my Diocese into two parts, to wit: Lower and Upper Louisiana. Already I had, yielding to imortunities,[7] given my consent to this division; shortly afterwards I retractetd it.[8] Very grave reasons urge me to remain in the latter disposition of mind, and the reason is that, as the foundations I have startetd in both parts of the Diocese are not yet well grounded, the division appears to me premature and most prejudicial to the interests of Religion. These motives I explained at length in my last letter,[9] begging that a Coadjutor be given me to share in my immense labors. If this request is granted by the S. Congregation, I promise that within five years everything will be in shape for this intended division; but should my request be turned down, the Sacred Congregatior may consider it as certain that everything will be thrown into confusion. .

In a former letter I asked that Father Bruté, a Sulpician priest of the highest merit, be given me for Coadjutor,[10] as I was afraid that if Father Rosati were appointetd he would be taken away from the superiorship of his society. But now that he has already been designated for the Episcopate, I ask that he be given the preference over Father Bruté for the Coadjutorship,[11] and may continue at the same time to

---

[7] It must be confessed that Du Bourg's letter of February 8, 1822 (St. Louis Catholic Historical Heview, Vol. II, p. II, p. 148 foll.), does not leave the impression he was then "yielding to importunities." His words are worth recalling: "As to the erection of another See in the City of St. Louis, Missouri, no one certainly can be pleased with it and desire it more than myself (*nulli certe magis quam mihi ipsi arridere et in votis esse debet*), as it means for me relief from immense labors and cares. Still, there is one reason why I delay asking at once for it _namely, the most earnest desire I have to free from all debts and obligations certain quite extensive properties which I have bought as an endowment for that See: I trust that, God helping, I may within a year reach this happy goal. When this is accomplished, I shall most gladly resign this part of my solicitude into the hands of the Sovereign Pontiff (*libentissime tunc partem illam meae solicitudinis in manus Summi, Pontificis resignabo*), hesitating at no sacrifice in order. . . ."

[8] We do not know when this change of views was manifested the first time; it was pointed out above that the Prelate wrote again in that sense from St. Louis in the first days of September.

[9] The one just alluded to in the preceding Note (September, 1822).

[10] When this proposal was made to Rome, we do not know, but we do know from the Bishop's letters to Bruté, that he was anxious to have him come west.

[11] In view of this and of the many proposals made to Rome at different times in regard to the Coadjutorship since the question was first agitated, one

be Superior of his Congregation until someone else may take his place in this office. This is an easy way of reconciling every interest. Father Rosati, residing in Upper Louisiana, where are the headquarters of his Congregation and the Seminary, will administer, in my name, with Epis-. copal authority, that portion of the Diocese, while at the same time he will foster the progress of the infant society. I, on the other hand, shall principally take care of Lower Louisiana, and continue to provide for the little flock in Mississippi; finally, the Catholics of Alabama and Florida will have their own Bishop.

Touching Fathers Sibourd and Rosetti, who were repeatedly mentioned by the S. Congregation I have only this to say: The former, who is now advanced in years and infirm, is, moreover, afflicted by a polyp of the nose, so that he has become quite incapable to stand the work of the Episcopate. As to the latter,[12] he never had the bodily and mental qualifications fitting one for that dignity. Still less since he has become *insane,* a calamity which, to the extreme sorrow and annoyance of us all, occurred two years ago. After one full year of this deplorable condition, as he recevored partly his reason, but not the sense of Religion, which in his period of madness he had cursed, he determined to return to Milan, where, I trust, he arrived safely.

---

cannot help feeling the good Bishop was slighlty overstating the truth when he wrote to Rosati from Washington on February 6, 1823: "The ill-wind will blow us some good, if all these transactions bring you to the point whither I have been —unknown to you—working steadily to lead you. I then received a formal refusal; no motives were alleged. . . . Your actual promotion cannot but end as I desire." (Original in *Archives of St. Louis Archdioc. Chancery*).

[12] See St. Louis Catholic Historical Review, Vol. II, No. 1, p. 50, Note 4; also above, Letter XXIX; already from St. Louis, two months before, October 1, Bishop Du Bourg had written (we have only a short excerpt from this letter taken in 1882 by Father Van der Sanden: this is the reason why we have not assigned to these few lines a place and number apart in the correspondence): "To discharge this office (of Coadjutor) the Rev. L. Sibourd is now too old and broken down. As to Father Rossetti, from Milan, the fact that the Sacred Cngation has twice already proposed him to me as Coadjutor is clear enough evidence that this priest is very little known to it. Indeed, besides being disgraced by a deformity of body which would make the mere sight of him an object of ridicule to our Americans, he is woefully devoid of all culture, either profane or ecclesiastical, and incapable to speak either French or English. But, what is still worse, two years ago, to the extreme sorrow and annoyance of us all, he became completely insane believing he was the king of England, and forgetful of all rules of decency and Religion. Finally, after a whole year spent in this deplorable condition, as he partly recovered his reason, he wished to go back to his native country, where I hope he must, at the time of this writing, have arrived safely." In *Catholic Historical Review* (Vol. III, No. 1, p. 10), part of this letter was quoted and assigned the date October 1, 1821; this is a misprint, and should be read 1822.

# INDEX.

Lightning Source UK Ltd.
Milton Keynes UK
UKHW020328081118
331957UK00008B/587/P